Alien Theory

The Alien as Archetype in the Science Fiction Short Story

PATRICIA MONK

THE SCARECROW PRESS, INC.
Lanham, Maryland • Toronto • Oxford
2006

SCARECROW PRESS, INC.

Published in the United States of America
by Scarecrow Press, Inc.
A wholly owned subsidiary of
The Rowman & Littlefield Publishing Group, Inc.
4501 Forbes Boulevard, Suite 200, Lanham, Maryland 20706
www.scarecrowpress.com

PO Box 317
Oxford
OX2 9RU, UK

Copyright © 2006 by Patricia Monk

British Library Cataloguing in Publication Information Available

Library of Congress Cataloging-in-Publication Data

Monk, Patricia, 1938–
   Alien theory : the alien as archetype in the science fiction short story / Patricia Monk.
      p. cm.
   Includes bibliographical references and index.
   ISBN-13: 978-0-8108-5746-9 (alk. paper)
   ISBN-10: 0-8108-5746-4 (alk. paper)
   1. Science fiction, American—History and criticism. 2. Aliens in literature. 3.
American fiction—20th century—History and criticism. 4. Science fiction, English—
History and criticism. 5. Human-alien encounters in literature. 6. Life on other planets
in literature. 7. Monsters in literature. 8. Archetype (Psychology) in literature. I. Title.

PS374.S35M66 2006
813'.08762099208691—dc22

                                                                    2006001420

This book is dedicated with love

to

Kitty

my sister, my friend

to know can only wonder breede—
but not to know is wonders seede

—*Anon*

Contents

Abbreviations

Amazing	*Amazing Stories*
Analog	*Analog* continues *Astounding/Analog*, beginning with the issue for October 1960 (vol. 23, no. 3); the subtitle varies throughout
Astounding	*Astounding* title varies as *Astounding Stories of Super Science, Astounding Stories,* and *Astounding,* to become *Astounding Science Fiction* with the issue for May 1939 (vol. 23, no. 3); continued by *Astounding/ Analog (q.v.)*
Asimov's	*Asimov's Science Fiction* continues *Isaac Asimov's Science Fiction Magazine* starting with the October 1992 issue
Astounding/Analog	*Astounding/Analog* continues *Astounding* from January 1960 (vol. 64, no. 5) through September 1960 (vol. 66, no. 1), during which period the cover and title page had *Astounding* and *Analog* superimposed, subtitled during this transition period *Science Fact & Fiction;* continued by *Analog (q.v.)*
CETI	Contact with Extraterrestrial Intelligence
COED2	*Compact Oxford English Dictionary* (2nd edition on CD-ROM)

COD	*Concise Oxford Dictionary* (10th edition, 1999)
CW	*The Collected Works of C. G. Jung.* Individual items are identified in the format *CW* 14:*474*:336, where 14 is the volume number, *474* is the paragraph number, and 336 is the page number (since paging changes between different editions and printings)
ESF2	*Encyclopedia of Science Fiction* (2nd edition on CD-ROM)
F&SF	*Fantasy and Science Fiction*
Galaxy	*Galaxy Science Fiction*
IASFM	*Isaac Asimov's Science Fiction Magazine* from the beginning until 1992, when the title changed to *Asimov's Science Fiction* (*q.v.*)
If	*If—Worlds of Science Fiction* (March 1952–September 1961); as *Worlds of If* (November 1961–November/December 1974)
Letters	*C. G. Jung Letters*
SETI	Search for Extraterrestrial Intelligence
TSF	*Thrilling Science Fiction*
TWS	*Thrilling Wonder Stories*

Preface

Alien Theory: The Alien as Archetype in the Science Fiction Short Story is a study of the Alien in science fiction. It is designed to explain why the Alien is something that should not be ignored and why, when a science fiction writer writes about aliens, she or he is saying something relevant to readers and is saying it in a particular story-telling mode that deserves to be understood according to the recognized parameters of that modality. The discussion deals only with written science fiction, concentrating on the shorter texts (short stories, novellas, and novelettes), although some novels will be mentioned in passing. The period covered is roughly from 1900 to the present. Primary texts are drawn from professionally published work in a fairly wide range of magazines but with an emphasis on *Amazing Stories, Astounding,* and *Thrilling Science Fiction* for the early years; on *Analog, Galaxy, If, Fantasy & Science Fiction,* and *Isaac Asimov's Science Fiction Magazine* for the later ones; and from anthologies and single-author collections. There is a selected bibliography, and, where necessary, additional incidental information is provided in the endnotes to each chapter.

Acknowledgments

I would like to thank my colleague at Dalhousie, Dr. Marjorie Stone, for her considerable assistance on chapter 2, as well as for her support throughout the writing of this book. I should like to acknowledge the patient assistance of the librarians and staff of the Killam Library of Dalhousie University (especially of the members of the document delivery section) in the face of a very large number of really far-out requests. In addition, I would like to acknowledge help from James Gunn, Fiona Kelleghan, Duncan Lunan, Frederik Pohl, Mike Resnick, Tom Shippey, Jim Wallace, and the late Bob Shaw, all of whom provided help in response to queries.

Introduction:
Theorizing OtherSelfness

"The only universal message in science fiction reads as follows: There are minds that think as well as we do, or better, but differently," says Larry Niven in "The Alien in Our Minds" (640). As Niven claims, contact with aliens has always dominated science fiction: It is a topic that has been overwhelmingly popular among readers of science fiction and has attracted the attention of almost every major science fiction writer.[1] Indeed, in his recent controversial survey of the genre, *The Dreams Our Stuff Is Made Of* (1998), one of the leading critics of science fiction, Thomas Disch, speaks of "SF's most versatile metaphor, its signature trope, the Alien" (186). Extraterrestrial aliens appear as the most popular topic, by far, in science fiction, featuring in higher proportion than any other topic in the short stories, novellas, novelettes, and novels that constitute the body of science fiction.[2] Considered as a class, the aliens of science fiction constitute an exemplum of the Other at its most extreme, which has developed contemporaneously with the psychological and sociological theories of the individual self and of individual and collective alienation. Nevertheless, what science fiction has to say about aliens has not received the extended investigative treatment that it deserves. Specifically, therefore, my study is designed to provide such an extended investigation.

I begin with the contention that to account for this popularity, it is necessary to understand that the Alien is an archetype—in the strictly Jungian sense of the term—called into existence as an attempt by writers to constellate a figure which encompasses all that relates, as extraterrestrial OtherSelf, to the human Self, and that Jung's analytical psychology, properly understood, has a substantial advantage for the discussion of this particular science fiction "signature trope" (Disch 1998, 186), since Jung was above all the proponent of the Self. To be human in his terms means to be a Self in the process of individuation (the maturation and integration of all elements of personality within a single individual). It is as a Self, moreover, that each of us experiences the world around us, and it is only from an understanding of the human Self that we can truly engage in the proleptic activity of imagining the Self in the Other. Consequently, an examination of the multifarious examples of the Alien in the short stories, novellas, and novelettes of science fiction will produce not only an understanding of why this archetype of the OtherSelf is necessary in the development of humanity's understanding of its own intrinsic nature as a being characterized by sapience but also a concept of how that sapience might manifest in other beings. The key to this proleptic activity is the concept of *OtherSelfness*, or *alterity*. *OtherSelfness* is not to be confused with *otherness*.

Otherness is, broadly speaking, merely the not-Self. It is found widely in literature and characterizes, for example, the Monster, the theory of which has elsewhere been explored elegantly in a number of articles and essays. Two features emerge from the discussion to distinguish monster from alien: the Monster's essential humanity and its terrestrial origin. Janeen Webb writes in "The Monster as Hero" (1985), for example, that "[t]he Monster . . . appears to be an essential part of the human condition" (21), and in *Immortal Monster* (1999), Joseph Andriano concurs: "[O]ur monster tales reflect what we know in our hearts to be true—we evolved from Beasts" (xi). Andriano specifically distinguishes the monster from the alien in his introduction, when he points out that

> [b]eginning with *Moby Dick* (1851) as the Ur-text, the prototype of the modern beast-monster, this book explores the monomyth of the evolving monster from its modern to its postmodern manifestation. The myth does not include extraterrestrial creatures; Leviathan/Behemoth evolves *here*, in the ocean, on earth, and in our racial memory. (xiii)

By contrast, George E. Slusser and Eric Rabkin write in their introduction to *Aliens: The Anthropology of Science Fiction* (1987) that the Alien "is the creation of a need—man's need to designate something that is genuinely outside himself, something that is truly nonman, that has no initial relation to man except for the fact that it has no relation. Why man needs the alien is the subject of these essays" (vii). As I demonstrate in my stipulative definition of the term *alien* later in this introduction, the point of the science fiction Alien is precisely that it is *not* human in nature and *not* terrestrial in origin. It is as unhuman and extraterrestrial as the skill and determination of the writer allow.

Alterity begins in otherness, but it does not end there. It includes the concept of the existence of a Self, or selfness, in the extraterrestrial nonhuman other that I designate the science-fictional Alien. The recognition of alterity, moreover, is the result of a developmental process that begins with the newborn who is not even self-aware and concludes with the adult who is not only self-aware (aware of itself as a Self) but aware of other human Selfs around it. But these other Selfs are human, though not identical with that of the individual, and therefore essentially very like the Self and like each other. Full alterity requires the further awareness of the Self in the nonhuman other, and the process of this recognition is played out in the writing and reading of the science-fictional Alien. The Alien is therefore a special case of OtherSelf: It must be both idiomorphic (like us in being a Self) and allomorphic (unlike us in being a different kind of Self), manifesting itself in the gestalt of the existence and activity of its species—culture—as humans do in theirs. Consequently, an understanding of the nature of alterity in the Alien is only achieved through an understanding of both the unlikeness of the Alien and its likeness.

But although it is important not to confuse otherness and alterity, the issue is nevertheless one of distinction not disjunction. The key to the distinction is *potentiation.* I am starting from the premise (drawn from Jung's psychological theory of the archetype as a means by which psychic energy constitutes itself as a presence in the individual) that all humans share the archetypal impulse—writers more (or at least more accessibly) than other people. One of the psyche's functions is that of differentiation—recognition of the Other. The ubiquity of the figure of the Alien is a result of the attempt by writers to manifest the ubiquitous archetypal impulse. All aliens invented and described in science fiction are manifestations of a particular archetype that differentiates not merely the Other but the OtherSelf. In psychological terms, *alterity* occurs when the numinous archetype is potentiated—realized at its fullest, so that the reader is exposed to the numinosity transmitted through the medium of the writer's consciousness. *Otherness* occurs when the numinosity is mitigated (muted or flattened) rather than potentiated in the process of realization and transmission through the writer's consciousness.

The distinction between otherness and alterity as qualities of the archetypal manifestation also goes a long way to solving the most awkward problem that inspection of the large body of alien stories presents, namely, that whereas aliens manifesting otherness are ubiquitous, aliens manifesting alterity are rare. The rarity of the alien manifesting alterity (the potentiated alien) is the result of a number of factors attributable to the skills of the writer in any given case, one of which would seem to be his or her ability to recognize and respond to the numinosity of the archetype as well as to complete the full manifestation of the archetype as a particular alien without mitigation of that numinosity.

Manifestations of the archetype considered from the literary standpoint also benefit from the concept of potentiation as a distinguishing factor. Considered as a trope[3] with regard to characterization, the potentiated alien is explicable as a round character (in E. M. Forster's sense in *Aspects of the Novel* (1927), as I discuss in chapter 6) and capable of surprising us. The merely other alien, however, is flat—its flatness explicable by the mitigation of the archetypal numinosity.

In any given story an alien's otherness must be present on two levels. At the primary and most obvious level, it must be characterized by physical, psychological, and societal otherness. Skill in producing otherness in an alien is essential to success in producing its likeness: Paradoxically, only if the alien "works" as a sapient creature unlike the human in its bodily form, its behavior, and its membership in an appropriate social structure can it be appreciated as a creature like the human in being an appropriate vehicle for a Self (idiomorphic). Beyond this, however, it must be different again: It must not be simply a human Self masked by otherness, but a different kind of Self appropriate to the otherness of its vehicle (allomorphic). In any given story, the alien must be judged as to the success of the otherness of its vehicle and also as to the success of the otherness of the Self manifest in that vehicle. Obviously, some writers succeed better in this task than others, but the best of them will produce what I argue is full alterity in which the otherness of the alien or nonhuman Self is fully realized and fully potentiated. In my argument, alterity is valorized because it produces a more "telling" manifestation of the archetype.

Since I valorize full alterity, only hard science fiction, given the terms of its definition, permits a valid system of comparison between the fictional and the actual manifestation of sapience. To a considerable extent, therefore, I privilege hard science fiction, with varying degrees of flexibility and exclusivity or nonexclusivity, as it was envisaged in the early years by its writers. Science fiction is now, admittedly, as consistently marginalized and difficult to define as it has always been, but writers in the field have nevertheless repeatedly reflected on what characterizes not only science fiction in general but also the sapient alien. As early as 1939, L. Sprague de Camp in "Design for Life," his valuable two-part article that introduced the principles of the invention of sapient alien creatures to *Astounding*'s readers, suggested what he saw as the principle by which science fiction writers tried to operate: "In science-fiction we try not to go contrary to known fact, however thinly we may spread our speculations about the unknown" (1:107–8), and he specifically laid down the parameters for appropriate aliens in accordance with this principle. Much later, in his contribution to the 1964 symposium *Of Worlds Beyond*, Robert A. Heinlein, making the basic distinction between science fiction and other forms of speculative fiction (a recently popular catch-all term that seems to include not only science fiction but also fantasy, sword-and-sorcery, occult, and horror fiction), articulated a much stronger version of de Camp's distinguishing criterion of science fiction:

> [N]o established fact shall be violated, and, furthermore, when the story requires that a theory contrary to present accepted theory be used, the new theory should be rendered reasonably plausible and it must include and explain established facts as satisfactorily as the one the author saw fit to junk. . . . It may be far-fetched, it may seem fantastic, but it must *not* be at variance with observed facts. ("On the Writing of Speculative Fiction" 17; original emphasis)

Heinlein's longstanding authority among science fiction fans is probably responsible for the widespread acceptance of this principle as what might be called the primary constraint or prime criterion for what is to be considered hard science fiction. Stanley Schmidt (John W. Campbell Jr.'s most recent successor as editor of *Analog*) reiterates Heinlein's position even more rigorously, however, in his article "The Science in Science Fiction" (1977), expanding it to include the requirement that science fiction involve both extrapolation— "speculation based on extensions, developments, and applications of well established scientific knowledge"—and innovation—"new principles . . . introduced in such a way that they don't contradict any accepted principles *in any region of experience where the accepted ideas have been experimentally verified*" (31, original emphasis). This specification effectively reinforces Heinlein's exclusion of the other varieties of speculative fiction that permit the inclusion of the supernatural and/or magic, as well as the growing number of works in which the alleged science is actually nonsense.

The rule was perhaps promulgated more vigorously than it was enforced. Even Campbell himself, for whom Heinlein wrote much of the time, was prepared to be a little more flexible than Heinlein, for the sake of salable stories, when he says in "Science Fiction We Can Buy," an article for *The Writer* (1968), that "[m]inor goofs in science—provided they're not crucial to the theme of the story—can be forgiven" (28). In the context of British science fiction, the writer, editor, and critic Kingsley Amis offers a milder perspective on the principle as laid out by de Camp, Heinlein, and Schmidt when he asserts in *New Maps of Hell* (1960) that

> science fiction is that class of prose narrative treating of a situation that could not arise in the world we know, but which is hypothesized on the basis of some innovation in science or technology, or pseudo-science or pseudo-technology, whether human or extraterrestrial in origin [and] presents with verisimilitude the human effects of spectacular changes in our environment, changes either deliberately or involuntarily suffered. (497)[4]

In her *Galaxy* article "Escape Routes" (1974), Ursula K. Le Guin also alerts would-be writers of science fiction to the existence of this criterion:

> The first of these is the criterion of intellectual coherence and scientific plausibility. The basic canon of fantasy, of course, is: you get to make up the rules, but then you've got to follow them. Science fiction refines upon this: you get to make up the rules, but within limits. A science fiction story must not flout the evidence of science, must not, as Chip Delany puts it, deny what is known to be known. Or if it does the writer must know it, and defend the liberty taken, either with a genuine hypothesis or with a sound, convincing fake. (41)

Writer John Barnes, in response to a reader who took him to task on the subject of error in his story "The Limits of Vision," confessed that he had "screwed up in the worldbuilding for the planet Randall in a whole lot of ways" and that he had even included a deliberate error in the story: "the added atmospheric CO_2 I used as one of the gases to get the number I wanted was above the level where people would have needed respirators to sleep" (Letter, 10). Far from demanding a return of the payment for the story, Asimov himself commented that "stretching science while indicating that you know what you're talking about is permissible" (Response to John Barnes, 10). Asimov's proffered license to stretch the principle of scientific accuracy is, however, so articulated that it could not be construed by any reasonable writer or reader as permission to abandon the principle altogether, and it returns much more closely to de Camp's original formulation. Spider Robinson, too, offers a looser formulation without allowing departure from the principle. In the introduction to the collection of stories in *Melancholy Elephants* (1984), he explains that "Sf examines fictons [invented space-time continua] which are *imaginary but viable*, different from but plausibly related to this one" (xiii; original emphasis). Most recently, Frederik Pohl has said in a video interview clip that science fiction "should never violate known scientific laws *by accident*" ("What Science Fiction Should Do"; my emphasis). Although all these definitions in effect privilege so-called *hard science fiction* principle, only Heinlein and Schmidt appear to do so to the point of absolute exclusion.[5] Amis, de Camp, Le Guin, Barnes, Pohl, Asimov, and Robinson, on the other hand, seem to privilege the principle only *non*exclusively. In selecting the texts to discuss the science-fictional Alien, consequently, I follow the example of these six writers—I have selected texts by privileging the hard science fiction principle nonexclusively.

In addition, therefore, I am simultaneously also privileging a stipulative hard science fiction definition of the term *alien*. The *alien*, as the derivation of the word indicates, means essentially the *other*, for it derives, according to the second edition of the *Oxford English Dictionary*, from the Latin adjective *alienus*, meaning "of or belonging to another person or place," itself a derivative of *alius*, meaning "other, another" and used as a noun. In English, the older sense of the term *alien* ("a person belonging to another family, race, or nation; a stranger, a foreigner" [*OED2*]) has only relatively recently, following in the wake of previous use in science fiction for a number of years, been extended to include the concept of extraterrestrial origin. The newer sense seems to have been first recognized by the makers of dictionaries in the late 1970s, in such illustrative examples as "any being or thing foreign to the environment in which it now exists: an alien from another planet" in *Collins Dictionary of the English*

Language (1979), and it has since been recognized by the *Concise Oxford Dictionary*, where it is defined as "a being from another world" (10th ed. 1999).[6] Gardner Dozois, in his introduction to *Aliens!* (1980), an anthology of stories devoted to alien contact, points out that "as the twentieth century advances, the Other has increasingly become the alien, the creature from another world" (ix) and that this happens because, as the unknown parts of the world steadily shrink, the location of the unknown tends to move further out. Science fiction, with its huge volume of texts about extraterrestrial aliens impinging upon the sense among the general populace that the "known" is constantly expanding, may even be the reason why the extraterrestrial Alien is now effectively the popularly recognized sense for the term *alien* (for evidence of this popular recognition, there is no need to look further than the headlines of the various supermarket tabloids). Occasionally, deliberate attempts are made to eschew the term for other reasons. For instance, Maya Kaathryn Bonhoff, in a letter to *Analog* in the January 1992 issue, writes, "I have always been interested in where other writers get names for OROM characters (that's Other Race of Men— 'aliens' seems so arrogant)" (316),[7] and she subsequently uses this coined acronym in her own novel *Squatter's Rights*, serialized in *Analog* in 1993. Nevertheless, the term *alien* is generally understood as sufficiently neutral to remain the most widely accepted term, and for me, therefore, to use it as such in setting up parameters that define the extraterrestrial Other within the context of hard science fiction.

To begin with, the Alien must be a natural being. The science-fictional Alien who is truly comparable to humans is naturally evolved, as a human is naturally evolved, and distinct from both the supernatural and the "unnatural" (mechanical or electronic) Alien. In early literature, the other world was most often the supernatural world, and its strange inhabitants equally supernatural (ghosts, elves, demons), although the term *alien* seems not to have been used of them. The supernatural other, moreover, is by definition not possible in hard-science science fiction, which, as indicated above, deals only with what is or could be possible within the constraints of physical laws of the universe as known to science. It appears in all types of speculative fiction and in many forms, whether these are borrowed from the annals of folklore and superstition, or are adapted from the theological apparatus of various religions, or are simply invented from scratch. The supernatural other may be a god, a demon, a ghost, an elemental, or almost anything else that can be identified as supernatural or magic because its existence and powers are not subject to the laws of physical science as we understand them at present. Since science fiction sets itself to exclude magic and the supernatural, all forms of the *other* in those texts that include the supernatural (regardless of whether these forms are themselves supernatural creatures or not—as Barbara Hambly's *isueg* (in her fantasy Darwath Trilogy) are not—are therefore excluded from my discussion of the science-fictional Alien.

The natural Alien must, however, also be the product of a *different* although analogous biological evolutionary development from that of humans and, in fact, be *substantially* differentiated from the human—not merely a distorted or disguised version of it (a transmutation). Transmutations may be either naturally mutated or deliberately gengineered (i.e., genetically engineered) variants of human originals. Gengineering and mutation are together becoming increasingly popular thematically (as are *psi* and AI) with their own growing mass of texts. But these variants are simply human self-revisions in organic form, and are excluded.[8]

Requiring the science-fictional Alien to be a natural and evolved creature forces the exclusion of artificial intelligent (AI) forms. Robots, androids, self-aware computers, and so-called expert systems are in their conception unnatural or nonnatural beings, since they are essentially merely mechanical or electronic copies (just as mutants are organic derivatives), in whole or in part, of their human makers, often explicitly so. Although this mimicry inherent in AI (whether explicit, implicit, or, in many cases, apparently unnoticed by the writer) may provide some insight into the way humans think about what constitutes a human being from the point of view of what might be called loosely "mind," it does so by treating it as a separable element, removing the mind from its original organic matrix and placing it into an inorganic one. The point of android design, indeed, seems to be to produce something that is, as nearly as possible, indistinguishable from a human being. It could even be argued that it is impossible for humans to create an artificial intelligence that is not implicitly an extension of human nature. Indeed, in her novel *Hellspark* (1988), Janet Kagan explores the nature of alien sapience in tandem with the observation of an example of developing AI (the self-aware consciousness in a powerful computer), and the parallel is explicitly drawn by characterizing the emerging AI as a precocious child. Moreover, the number of texts dealing with AI has multiplied with increasing rapidity following the spread of the so-called computer revolution in the last thirty years, so that although the unnatural Alien is certainly a legitimate inhabitant of science fiction, science fiction focusing on artificial intelligences constitutes a separate major theme with its own set of parameters.

The biological evolution of the science-fictional Alien must be scientifically plausible—constructed, that is, in accordance with biological principles so far as these were understood at the time of writing. The design principles suggested in such texts as de Camp's previously cited "Design for Life" articles in the May and June 1939 issues of *Astounding*, for example, introduce ways of deciding on a scientific (bioengineering or biomechanical) basis how an alien might reasonably be expected to look. Aliens designed with these and similar "instructional" texts in mind would thus conform to de Camp's principle that science fiction does not contradict current scientific knowledge although it may bend it somewhat in the course of speculation. Because of this science-fictional rigor, the Alien appears only in science-fictional texts (the narratives of UFOlogy, whether presented as fiction or nonfiction, are not science fiction), although not all aliens in science-fictional texts measure up to de Camp's standard or contribute to the understanding of alterity.

The significantly differentiated science-fictional Alien, moreover, must be intrinsically differentiated—for reasons of a genuine need for otherness in its creation—and not serve as a distorting mirror for human beings. In many texts in which significant differentiation of the Alien seems evident, it nevertheless becomes clear on further examination that what is operating is pseudo-differentiation. Pseudo-differentiation is found where the intent of the text, overtly or covertly, is satiric. In most of the pre-twentieth-century texts usually claimed as part of the beginnings of science fiction, the Other, even where it is not supernatural, is almost inevitably a satiric reflection of the human being, whether for good (as the shining example) or bad (as the awful warning). The same tactic is, of course, often used with total legitimacy to produce great stories in twentieth-century science fiction. This framing of the Alien as a satiric reflection of the human, however, introduces external constraints and additional parameters that have nothing to do with otherness per se, and it does so in the same way as the other major science fiction themes. It does not, however, offer any contribution to the understanding of alterity.

Equally, the science-fictional Alien must be sufficiently "present" and developed in the text to give adequate ground for argument about the nature of alien sapience as exemplified in the particular alien described. This criterion excludes from my discussion texts in which aliens are present only incidentally. These are texts of which the principal theme is either one of the other major themes of science fiction (such as time travel, alternate universes, alternate history, *psi*, mutation, AI, etc.) or texts of which the principal focus is eccentric or indeterminable. This criterion does not, however, exclude texts where the alien, although apparently intended to be sufficiently present and developed, fails to be sufficiently developed.

The science-fictional Alien, finally, is a being possessed of a slippery and controversial quality that I shall call *sapience*. The most usual terms for this quality in science fiction are *intelligence* and *sentience*. Occasionally, the term *sophont*, referring to individuals possessing *sophos*, occurs, but *sophos* [Gk. *wisdom*] itself is not found in science fiction and is not, in any case, naturalized in English, so far as I can tell. *Sentience*, which is quite common in science fiction as an alternative to intelligence, possibly through some misplaced feeling of political correctness (as though it were not polite to talk about the intelligence of a species in case you appear to be by implication defining other species as stupid), is too broad; it is defined as "[the] condition or quality of being sentient, consciousness, susceptibility to feeling," and the noun *sentient* is defined as something "that feels or is capable of feeling; having the power or function of sensation or of perception by the senses" (*OED2*), with no reference to thought or affect, and hence could well include all living organisms. *Intelligence*, which is very common in science fiction, as in science, would be the obvious choice, on the grounds of familiarity and general acceptance. Awkwardly, however, in spite of its wide use, it lacks an agreed upon definition in reference to mental capacity: The *OED2* lists seven different senses among which general use and acceptance rarely discriminate. The adjective (*intelligent*) in particular, moreover, has come to be more or less synonymous with *clever* and is not restricted to humans. In my discussion, I shall use *intelligence* in the primary sense—"the faculty of understanding"—to refer to mental capacity in general at any (human, alien, animal) level, and *intellect* to refer to that part of mental capacity to which *intelligence* is usually applied when distinguishing it from emotional capacity or *affect*. *Sapience*, however, avoids these problems. Derived from the Latin *sapire*, to be wise, it directs attention to the taxonomical label that distinguishes human from animal (humans as a species are labeled taxonomically as *sapiens*, i.e., as *homo sapiens*

sapiens) and hence, by implication, will equally well distinguish extraterrestrial person from extraterrestrial animal. It also includes, without restricting itself to, what is suggested by the combination of *intelligence* and *sentience*—that is, that the combination is necessary to the concept of sapience but is not sufficient to produce it. *Sapience* may sound awkward and unfamiliar (*sapients are beings possessed of sapience*), but it at least has the virtue of being more accurate and precise than the alternatives, and it is possible to become accustomed to it.[9]

Sapience in my present usage, however, although a specific term, does not identify a specific referent. Humans, according to themselves, possess sapience—animals do not. Nevertheless, although it is assumed that humans will recognize sapience in other terrestrial or extraterrestrial beings when they encounter it and will then be able to acknowledge those beings to be not animals but nonhuman persons, precisely what it is that would be recognized in such beings remains substantially unspecific. Moreover, this assumption requires the belief that, because humans have not recognized them, there are therefore no other sapient beings on Earth.[10] John W. Campbell Jr., however, encapsulated the working principle of the term *sapience*, insofar as it applies to the construction of sapient aliens, in his famous instruction to writers for *Astounding* (later *Analog*), to "give me a creature that thinks like a man but is not a man," which is cited in Theodore Sturgeon's "Galaxy Bookshelf" column in the February 1974 issue of *Galaxy* (92).[11] This formulation, however succinct and (as I shall show) useful, nevertheless does not provide a definition. (How humans think and even what constitutes *thinking* are still under discussion in some quarters.) The same is true, moreover, of almost any other attempted definition of the quality. Sapience cannot be identified, in the current circumstances, except by demonstrating that animals lack certain properties or characteristics and considering the presence of these qualities to indicate a sapient creature and the aggregate of them to constitute a quality called sapience. Campbell's request, deliberately perhaps, is open to multiple interpretations. Consequently, in the absence of a scientific definition of sapience, science fiction writers have gone along with his preferences in the introduction of aliens into their work, taking advantage of the open-endedness to be as casual or as precise, as rigid or as liberal, as they choose, according to their individual temperaments and understanding. It is the resulting spectrum of understanding that I hope to chart in my discussion.

The science-fictional Alien of my stipulative definition, furthermore, is a creature of the twentieth century alone. Although a number of seventeenth-, eighteenth-, and nineteenth-century texts are claimed as science fiction (among them, for example, Kepler's *Somnium Seu Astronomia Lunari* [1634] and Mary Shelley's *Frankenstein or the Modern Prometheus* [1818]), some of which include extraterrestrial beings, it is not until the turn of the century that aliens begin to be introduced that fulfill all the criteria I have described above. The earliest properly science-fictional Alien, according to my criteria, is found in H. G. Wells's *The War of the Worlds*, published in 1898. Wells's Martians are possible within the limits of the scientific knowledge of their time, and from the little we see of them they appear to be significantly differentiated from the human and to be natural (biological) evolved beings. The Martians are, moreover, since they reach earth in advanced and well-armed spacecraft, sapient according to at least one of the rules of thumb (possession of technology or tools) that are subsequently developed as a test for the elusive quality of sapience. Importantly, too, although the behavior of most of the human characters during the interplanetary invasion reveals a satirical view of humanity, the satiric distortion does not include the Martians themselves: They and their activities are the undisputed thematic focus of the text.[12] It is this lack of distortion that most clearly distinguishes Wells's aliens as science-fictional aliens and as different from those of his predecessors and even his contemporaries. The point may be clarified, perhaps, by contrasting Wells's achievement with that of Robert William Cole in *The Struggle for Empire* (1900). This novel, which also introduces nonsupernatural aliens into an apparently scientifically grounded narrative, is not particularly helpful to any examination of the development of the Alien in science fiction. The author fails to describe any characteristics of his aliens that distinguish the two species (humans and Sirians), and the story is clearly designed as satire (the humans and their equally aggressive and rapacious counterparts from another star-system declare war over a particularly profitable planet that both are trying to claim for colonization). More or less the same can be said, without detracting from the attractiveness of the books as a whole, of the other-planetary creatures of Garrett Putnam Serviss's *A Columbus of Space* (1894), subsequently serialized in *Amazing* (August, September, and October 1926), and of the Martians in the very popular *Two Planets* [*Auf Zwei Planeten*] of Kurt Lasswitz (1897): They both reflect, in different ways, human nature for the purpose of social commentary, but they contribute nothing to the topic of alterity. Because Wells's Martians are so solid an example of aliens that fit the criteria for my stipulative definition of aliens, the publication of the novel of which they are the focus may be said to mark the beginnings of the alien invasion of modern science fiction.

This invasion initially happened almost entirely in the popular magazines of science fiction and only later migrated to the novel form, and in this initial stage it owes much, although not all, of its success to writer/publisher Hugo Gernsback. According to John Clute and Peter Nicholls's *Encyclopedia of Science Fiction* (1993), the "Aug[ust] 1923 issue of *SAI* [*Science and Invention*] . . . was effectively Gernsback's first sf magazine" (1060), being "a special issue devoted to 'science fiction'" (1067). The first issue of *Amazing Stories* (vol. 1, no. 1, April 1926) soon followed, and in the March 1927 issue Gernsback published T. S. Stribling's "The Green Splotches" about the predatory Jovian plantman ("Mr. Three") who came to Earth but was easily defeated by the protagonist and his friends. Although Stribling himself produced nothing of further interest in the study of aliens, this story was the first of many on the topic, written by many writers in the pages of *Amazing*.

Nevertheless, although the Alien of modern science fiction may begin to appear at the turn of the century and only become widespread almost twenty years later, it has multiple antecedents in other disciplines. The figure of the Other, from which it derives—although it manifests imaginatively for the most part as the supernatural stranger of folklore and fiction, pervading it extensively and globally—is also found recurrently as the hypothesized extraterrestrial Alien in the philosophical and scientific thought of earlier centuries. The "plurality of worlds" debate, from earliest times to 1900, finds the focus of its contention in the question of the existence of other inhabited worlds. The historical pervasiveness and persistence of the figure of the Other has profound psychological implications for its transfiguration into the extraterrestrial Alien in science fiction. Moreover, the nature and multiplying appearances of this new figure have implications for the parameters of the new kind of fiction in which it functions as an important literary trope. The presence of the science-fictional Alien in magazine fiction is characterized, consequently, by a multifariousness (multiplicity and variety), a strangeness, a fascination, and a persistence extremely similar to those which characterize its antecedents in philosophical and scientific discussion as well as in folklore and fantastic fiction.

The multifariousness of the appearances of the Alien is extraordinary by any standards. The stories in the magazines in particular—in *Astounding, Analog, Amazing, Galaxy, If,* and *Asimov's,* where hard science fiction has always been dominant—offer a very large assortment of aliens: In a rough count, stories about aliens far outnumber the stories on any other single topic. Short fiction involving aliens read for this study amounts to slightly more than two thousand titles and has been gathered from magazines, single-author collections, and anthologies, and should not be considered exhaustive. Moreover, although the number of aliens alone might be called no more than multiplicity, to the factor of numbers is added the factor of variety (hence multifariousness): Many of the stories introduce more than one kind of alien. In addition, aliens created by writers are not borrowed in the work of other writers: Some of them may be very similar, and they can certainly be categorized in broadly defined groups, but they are not—with only very rare exceptions—identical, so that additional multifariousness is introduced. One of the few exceptions to this rule about borrowing, however, is the recent use of Larry Niven's alien Kzin in "Galley Slave," a story by Jean Lamb, in the August 1996 issue of *Analog.* The accompanying editorial note says, "This story uses the background of Larry Niven's 'man/kzin wars' stories, with Mr. Niven's kind permission" (97). Intertextuality of this kind is common in science fiction, as I have demonstrated elsewhere (Monk, "The Shared Universe Thing"), although it does not always involve aliens. Although the phrasing of the note suggests that a legal point is involved—that the *idea* or design of a particular alien is copyright to the writer in the same way as the story in which it appears is copyright—it is not the only point. Copyright or not, the alien remains the personal image of the author's understanding of the nature of OtherSelfness and cannot be borrowed without compromising it by the borrower's own imaginative process. Consequently, there are at least as many forms of the Alien in science fiction as there are writers who can envision them, and as many more as each writer can devise.

The strangeness of the Alien is similarly complex. Although, at first glance, the strangeness of the Alien might be assumed to be simply a part of the "cognitive estrangement," which for Darko Suvin in *Metamorphoses of Science Fiction* is the defining characteristic of science fiction, the strangeness of the Alien is actually distinct from, although it may coexist with, estrangement in Suvin's sense. My divergence from Suvin, and from critics who follow him, begins with his remark that "[e]strangement differentiates SF from the 'realistic' literary mainstream extending from the eighteenth century into the twentieth. Cognition differentiates it not only from myth, but also from the folk (fairy) tale and the fantasy" (8). The strangeness of the science-fictional Alien with which I am concerned is, however, not merely a consequence of its appearance in a particular group of texts in a literary mode distinct from realism (i.e., as part of a genre characterized by general estrangement), although science fiction may be so differentiated from the literary mainstream. Nor is the strangeness I am investigating different from the strangeness of creatures of myth, folk tale, and fantasy—in fact, paradoxically, it can only be properly understood in terms of its links with the strangeness of such beings. To go back to the most basic dictionary definition, *strangeness* is "[t]he quality of being strange, foreign, unfamiliar, uncommon, unusual, extraordinary" (*OED2*). Even more pertinent, however, is one of the senses of the adjective *strange*: "Added or introduced from outside, not belonging to the place or person where it is found, adventitious, external" (*OED2*). In this sense, the qualities of "from outside" and "external" offer key suggestions about the nature of the science-fictional Alien. There are forms of strangeness in the world, but we are closer to them than is often imagined. In *Through a Window* (1990), for example, Jane Goodall reminds us that "genetically, in the structure of the DNA, chimps and humans differ by only just over one per cent" (13). At differing greater distances, moreover, we are related to every other animal species on our planet. Terrestrial beings, however strange, do not—indeed, cannot—prepare us for the strangeness of extraterrestrial beings. The Alien comes, in particular, not merely from "outside" the world (the planet), but from "outside" our experience of sapience, since we humans are the only sapient species we know of.

The strangeness of the Alien is further problematized by the mode of its conception in the mind of the writer. As we can infer from the phenomenological concept of Embodiment in its most basic formulation (in *The Harper Dictionary of Modern Thought* 1988), which asserts "that perception and understanding of the world are partly a function of the fact that consciousness is not 'pure', but exists within a membrane of flesh and blood" (Roger Poole, "Embodiment," 264), the mind of each writer is specific in its perception and understanding, since every such membrane of flesh and blood contains only one individual—and is therefore as specific in its response to strangeness as it is to anything else.[13] The strangeness of the Alien is, therefore, idiopathogenic (that is, in the extended sense of producing *idiopathy* or "an individual or personal state of feeling" [*OED2*]). Whether it occurs in a short story or novel, it cannot exemplify more than one mind's (the writer's) perception and understanding of strangeness—filtered/reflected through that mind's receptivity/creativity, however multiphasic (extending the sense of this term "[a]pplied to tests or investigations designed to reveal various phases or aspects of personality, health, etc. . . . more generally discriminatory process" [*OED2*]) that receptivity/creativity may be. Although different aliens produced by the same writer may be linked and similar, however, even they are not identical in their manifestation of strangeness, and the same is true of aliens produced by different writers: They may be similar but they are not identical. All the multiple apparent strangenesses of an alien, as imagined and reified in a text, are actually one—the strangeness of the OtherSelf, split by the attempt to articulate it (as light is split by a prism) and reassembled imperfectly by the writer's unifying imagination and skill with that problematic tool language. But even this one strangeness is a manifestation of OtherSelf strangeness different from that of any human Self.[14]

The fascination of the Alien is also complex and problematic. It is partly attributable to the pervasiveness of the human trait of curiosity, for just as the curious child automatically investigates everything from a new toy to an electrical outlet, the adult writer/reader of science fiction investigates unknowns. But few of these unknowns share the strength of the fascination exerted by aliens—nonhuman people. *Fascination* is the result of activity by someone or something that fascinates us, and *to fascinate* means to "attract and retain the attention of (a person) by an irresistible influence" (*OED2*). Although the fascination of the Alien cannot be universally irresistible, since many people, even some readers of science fiction, do not care for aliens, nevertheless the powerful attraction, as well as the uncanniness of the effect, are all present in the various senses of the word.

The persistence is evident in the fact that the number of short stories and novels dealing with aliens runs at a consistently high level from the beginning of the period examined in this book to the present day. The short stories in the bibliography are all dated between 1927 and 2006, and there is little variation between the numbers for the different years. Once the publication of science fiction in novel form takes off as part of the general development of mass market paperback publishing, novels about aliens achieve and maintain similarly high average numbers. A quick comparison of current numbers of works about aliens to numbers of works about other science-fictional topics suggests that in the last decade the fastest-growing topics for stories have been computers (including AI and Virtual Reality) and nanotechnology. Nevertheless, although such stories may be gaining ground on alien stories, they are a long way from overtaking them. The Alien maintains its topicality, and its persistence is important because it indicates that the Alien is a living concept, not fixed, and continues to change as human awareness changes.

The Alien, however, is in other respects like any other subject in fiction. It is pulled into fiction from the acculturated perceptions of the writer in the process of imaginative composition and undergoes the usual process of literary modeling. Specifically, however, in the short fiction of the science fiction magazines, several different types of alien portrayals (which I call *humanoids, bems, little green men,* and *potentiated aliens*) have come into existence, offering through these simpler versions a perspective of the complexity that underlies them. In science fiction, however, because the readers have come to expect that the physical and biological sciences be rigorously applied in the design of aliens, there also comes into play a form of scientific modeling (the way in which writers work with these design parameters and take into account what degree of biological difference is involved in any other kind of difference in order to produce possible and impossible aliens) that contributes further to the concept of the Alien. The increasingly important disciplines of psychology, social anthropology, and sociology introduce psychological modeling (the way in which the writer tries to determine, by heuristic experiments and the formulation of the rules of thumb for sapience, the parameters of the alien psyche), and social modeling (as she/he imagines how aliens interact either within their own species or in a multispecies context). Consequently, although what is often found in short science fiction texts is the merely notional Alien—a sketchy version of another kind of sapient being in an illustrative situation of some sort—it is nevertheless an important albeit often unconscious attempt to manifest accessibly an image of the power and nature of the OtherSelf.

The science fiction stories about alien contact that appear on magazine stands month after month are full of unconscious assumptions and conscious theories about sapience (changing as the state of knowledge about humanity and its origins and its circumstances changed) that have informed the idea of the alien. This idea is constantly created, articulated, revised, reconsidered, discussed, argued over, rearticulated, and re-created, both in the stories and around them. But it is never formally defined. Consequently, somewhat akin to the way in which the nature of cyberspace can be described, according to William Gibson's protagonist Case in *Neuromancer* (1984), as a "consensual hallucination" (5), the nature of the Alien in science fiction can be described as a *consensual hypothesis*. This consensual hypothesis of the Alien exists independently of the mind of any single writer/reader of science fiction—all writers/readers contribute to and participate in it but the fact of its existence in no way lessens the creativity of any individual writer.

Analysis of this consensual hypothesis allows the reading of alterity—in what might be called paradigmatic form—as a contribution to the understanding of sapience according to the writers of science fiction. I propose to conduct such a reading, therefore, in three stages. In part I, Conceiving the Alien, after sketching a historical overview of the Other in the nineteenth and early twentieth century (see chapter 1), I conduct an examination of the Alien in pre-postmodernist and postmodernist criticism and theory (see chapter 2). In part II, Writing the Alien, I present three chapters, examining in their many versions, first, the creation of the form of the science-fictional Alien (see chapter 3); second, the creation of the psyche of the Alien inhabiting those forms (see chapter 4); and third, the creation of the context in which aliens and humans interact (see chapter 5). These chapters are necessitated to a large extent by the peculiarities of the genre: Any serious approach to science fiction has to understand and account for what science fiction writers, editors, and readers themselves have articulated about the alien during the process of writing the stories. Science fiction is a modernist literature insofar as it tells readers how to read it, but unlike other forms of literature, modernist or postmodernist, it also expects readers to know how it is written—an expectation at least partially helped to fulfillment by the multitude of accompanying texts that explain how to write it. By studying the ways in which these documents tell readers how to read the Alien in particular—and how to write about it—the science-fictional concept can be contextually refined. In part III, Reading the Alien, chapter 6 considers the literary modeling of the Alien as a fictional character—how figuration (characterization) is deployed in the presentation of aliens as characters alongside humans in fictions in the form of the trope of OtherSelfness or alterity. My final chapter (see chapter 7) argues how our understanding of the psychological substrate of the trope of OtherSelfness—the psychological drive behind the creation of the forms, the minds, the commensality, and the characterization of the different aliens—reveals a continuing human need, which I term *necessary alterity*, to construct and to play with the concept of the Alien; in the process I offer a reading of the Alien as a unique and necessary instance of alterity—the archetype of alterity—in terms derived from the Jungian theory of the archetype. In my conclusion I identify the relevance of my theory of necessary alterity to two continuing issues—I argue that it contributes substantially to humanity's understanding of its present status and future potential in the universe by constituting a new mythology of humanity, and I also contend that it identifies the stories out of which it arises as an infrastructure for the continued vitality of the theme of alien contact and interaction in the novels of science fiction.

NOTES

1. I am concerned only with written science fiction, although I acknowledge that television and movie aliens are also very attractive and popular, and obviously offer considerable opportunities for investigation in terms of archetypal theory. But it would be difficult to make a case for including them here, even were I a media analyst as well as a literary analyst, for a prima facie case could be made that the parameters of *reader* response to a text are different in kind from those of *audience* response to media in the form of movies or television programs, particularly since the latter are subject to manipulation by a variety of factors to which texts are not. The movie *Alien* and its sequels, for example, are an important cultural phenomenon. But most television and movie aliens are, if not fantasy, at best "sci-fi" (that is, eschewing what I suggest in this introduction is the first rule of science fiction—to be scientifically rigorous) rather than science fiction, and their treatment of alien beings is incoherent, inconsistent, and for the most part unintelligent. I do not think that the alien portraits of these media constructs are particularly relevant in any way to what I am trying to discuss here.

2. Since exact statistics are not yet available, this count is reached by inspection (of magazine stories and of available published novels) and is not the result of rigorous statistical analysis.

3. I use the term *trope*, which is strictly defined as "a figure of speech which consists in the use of a word or phrase in a sense other than that which is proper to it" (*OED2*), in order to avoid having to repeatedly qualify the more common *device* as literary.

4. The influence of Campbell, Schmidt, and Heinlein was wide. Examples of "bad science" are frequently castigated by Lester del Rey in his book review column for *If* in the 1970s. In his review of George Bamber's *The Sea is Boiling Hot* in the January-February issue for 1972, he writes, "[T]his should be a timely story of struggle against pollution at a time when man can exist only in enclosed cities. . . . 'Science' is introduced when the author, who apparently never heard of oxidation and reduction, suggests that the opposite of 'combustion' must be given a new term, 'imbustion.' (Doesn't know much about language, either, it seems.)" (156). There are similar complaints about violations of the rule by other critics, and the criterion continues to be applied up to the present. When reviewing Susan Schwartz's novel *Hostile Takeover* in the May 2005 issue of *Analog*, Tom Easton demands, "Can an author who cannot be bothered to check basic facts be trusted to deliver a decent story?" (135), and he details two complaints, one about the treatment for radiation sickness and one about a confusion of cornea and retina in a procedure for recording identity. His judgment of the novel is firmly qualified by these errors: "[I]f you can get past the gaffes, you will find an interesting, exciting tale" (136).

5. Even this distinction between *hard* and *soft* science fiction in itself provokes further contentiousness, since for many readers *hard science fiction* refers only to what is more colloquially called "toys-for-boys science fiction" or "rockets-and-robots science fiction"—that is, science fiction that involves only the hard or physical sciences—whereas for many others it simply means science fiction in which all sciences, including the social sciences, are treated with sufficient rigor according to contemporary state-of-the-art standards. Moreover, in the interests of precise nomenclature, the term if used should properly be hard-science science fiction.

6. Nevertheless, in both dictionaries, the extraterrestrial sense takes second place to the original in referring to a foreigner. Increasingly, moreover, other than its use to describe extraterrestrial beings, *alien* may be becoming limited to its use as a legal term, "a foreigner, especially one who is not a naturalized citizen of the country where they are living" (*COD*), as in *resident alien* or *nonresident alien* (these seem, for example, to be the principal concern of the U.S. Immigration and Naturalization Service on various websites). In the colloquial dialogue of television dramas, at least, "illegals" expands to illegal immigrants, not illegal aliens (a completely nonscientific poll of Internet hits produced the following: alien + illegal = 153,000; alien + extraterrestrial = ca. 31,700; immigrant + illegal = 237,000). At first glance, therefore, the problem with the current waves of migrants sloshing backward and forward across national boundaries in North America and Europe would seem to be not that they are alien (other or different) but that they are unlicensed incomers, of whom some are more

visible than others. I return to this point in chapter 1, in the discussion of *alien* as *stranger.*

7. But the use of *men* for *human*, presumably, is not. The inaccurate use of man/men for human is characteristic of earlier science fiction; this is merely a late example.

8. They should be distinguished, however, from aliens in many stories in the science fiction magazines that are intended to be genuinely other but which in fact are simply variants of the human because of the author's misunderstanding of what constitutes otherness. Since such texts—at least as clearly as successful texts—often provide insight into some of the unconscious assumptions about aliens, they are included.

9. None of them sounds particularly idiomatic in use. Although *intelligence* names the abstract quality and an adjective deriving from it exists (*intelligent*), the adjective does not seem to be used as a noun for individual beings possessed of the quality, and both *intelligents are beings possessed of intelligence* and *intelligences are beings possessed of intelligence* sound extremely awkward. *Sentience* would produce a similar problem (*sentients are beings possessed of sentience* and *sentiences are beings possessed of sentience*), although to a lesser extent, since *sentience* and *sentient* are less familiar.

10. This assumption persists in spite of the strong advocacy on behalf of sapience in cetaceans and nonhuman primates. Many people believe that cetaceans and the other primates are nonsapient; many others believe that they are sapient but that we have simply failed to recognize their sapience because our concept of sapience is faulty. Scientists have failed to settle the issue finally one way or the other; science fiction writers appear to be continuing the debate, often explicitly.

11. Cited earlier, before Campbell's death in 1971, also by Sturgeon, in the pages of the *National Review* as "Give me a story about aliens . . . in which they think as well as a man but not like a man" (266). The change in phrasing suggests that Sturgeon himself may have been the writer to whom it was addressed. I have been unable to find any version of it in Campbell's editorials or published letters.

12. Although they can be read as encoding the human as a being reduced to pure intellect unmitigated by emotion or moral sense, this depiction is not in itself necessarily satiric but merely speculative—albeit speculation carried to the extreme. It is a theme found elsewhere in early science fiction stories without satiric motivation.

13. Obviously I am begging the question of the mechanisms of embodied consciousness. I am painfully aware of the controversies and complexities involved in the term beyond what appears to be its basic implication of one consciousness per body, however they may be related. In his contribution on "Consciousness" in *The Oxford Com-*

panion to the Mind (1987), for example, D. C. Dennett begins by saying, "Consciousness is both the most obvious and the most mysterious feature of our minds," and continues, "not only have we so far no good theory of consciousness, we lack even a clear and uncontroversial pre-theoretical description of the presumed phenomenon" (160). But even the *Companion* does not include a definition (consensus) about what *mind* is, although both Dennett and the editor R. L. Gregory in the preface imply that *mind* is distinct from *consciousness*. There is no entry for the word *mind* itself, although there are entries for "Mind and Body," for "Mind and Brain," for "The Mind-Body Problem: Luria's Philosophy," and for "The Mind-Body Problem: Philosophical Theories." Moreover, Gregory writes in his preface that "the concept of Mind accepted here is far broader than what may (at least at first) come to mind as one thinks of Mind: especially thinking and consciousness. We do not, however, limit 'Mind' to consciousness or awareness, for even long before Freud it was clear that a great deal goes on 'mentally' that is beyond (or beneath, or at least outside) our awareness" (v). I elect to go with this loose introductory definition since my observation suggests that in the short stories I am examining the consensus itself does not appear to go beyond this level (see chapter 3 for further discussion).

14. Because of the idiopathogenic nature of strangeness, no one fiction can offer a representative envisioning version—an exemplar text—of strangeness. This is entirely supportive of my basic argument—that the Alien in science fiction is the product of consensus—and effectively precludes the selection of exemplar texts. Although selected short texts are discussed at greater length than the majority, no one of these discussions is intended as a discussion of anything that might be supposed to be an exemplar text.

I

CONCEIVING THE ALIEN

1

Who Goes There?
The Concept of the
Extraterrestrial Alien
since Darwin

The extraterrestrial Alien of science fiction is a manifestation of something deeply embedded in human sensibility—the Other. The history of this embedded Other forms a background for the stipulative definition of the science-fictional Alien already set up in the introduction. In spite of this relationship, significant distinctions exist, on the one hand, between the various manifestations of the Other such as the human Other in the form of the stranger and the supernatural Other, and, on the other hand, between the science-fictional Alien and the extraterrestrial Other. These distinctions exist according to both scientific speculation and psychological and sociological theory. Consequently, it is necessary to go beyond existing theories of the Other to account for the fascination, persistence, strangeness, and increasing complexity of the science-fictional Alien and its multifarious specimens.

THE HISTORY OF THE OTHER
The evidence of history, folklore, and literature suggests that some version of the Other has always been part of human awareness. According to Gardner Dozois, in his introduction to *Aliens!*

> People have always been fascinated by the Alien: the Stranger, the remorseless and unknowable Other whose motivations, thoughts, and actions we can never fully understand. . . . For uncountable centuries, the Other was supernatural—gods, ghosts, demons, elves, vampires, night-gangers, the dark and inscrutable

face of the Other dimly visible behind whatever mask it wore. At best, the Other
was one of the people who lived around the curve of the river or across the sea.
. . . As the twentieth century advances, the Other has increasingly become the
Alien, the creature from another world. (ix)

Dozois's enumeration of the different varieties of the supernatural Other is
obviously incomplete, for a list of such terms could be continued almost indefinitely and yet not exhaust the possibilities. But in making the suggestion
that each of the separate manifestations is merely one mask of a single Other
that can never be named or seen for itself, Dozois points unerringly to one of
the critic's primary problems with the science-fictional Alien. Not only is the
Alien always a part of the indefinable Other, a partial vision, but each story or
novel about the Alien deals only with *an* alien, a partial realization of a partial
vision.

Nevertheless, the categorization of the manifestations of the Other is in itself necessary to our understanding of the concept of the Other. The shape
and location of what is common to them all, mapped out through the exclu-
sions and inclusions of the process, determines what is the essential Other,
and similarly, the shape of the essential Alien is mapped out through the ex-
clusions and inclusions revealed in the presentation of individual concepts of
aliens. In twentieth-century understanding of the Other, it is possible to distinguish three different kinds: the human Other, the supernatural Other, and
the extraterrestrial Other. The categories are not as mutually exclusive in their
separation as might be expected, but the division, without setting up an im-
passable boundary, offers several useful opportunities for comparison and
contrast.

Probably the first of these Others was the human Other—the human
whom you met for the first time and did not know, or even know about. The
human Other is the *stranger*. *Stranger* is a term frequently used in science fiction with reference to aliens. It is, for example, the term used by Robert Silverberg in his anthology of alien contact stories *Earthmen and Strangers*
(1971). In the introduction he makes the point that in the experience of the
child,

[s]trangers are those who do not fit into the family circle, people who cannot be
recognized, whose existence is an uncomfortable mystery. Until he has met his

first stranger, the child has known nothing but love. Now comes a challenge; for the stranger, being a stranger, does not necessarily love the child. . . . Growing up . . . is a process of collisions with strangers, and a test of maturity is the ability to handle such collisions. (7)

Even the process Silverberg outlines has always had its dangers. The stranger may not merely be someone who "does not necessarily love the child" (7); he or she may be someone one who is actively hostile and dangerous. Children today are therefore still warned against talking to strangers, for it is not until the stranger has been vetted by someone with more experience of strangers than the child that he or she can be allowed to meet the child and be admitted into its circle of the familiar and the known. Subsequently, the adult's continually expanding awareness of the world as a series of larger and larger environments merely increases the possible number of strangers. There is a form of progression: Strangers are those who are not of the same family or tribe (in the earliest times), not of the same village (later), not of the same country (more recently), not of the same ethnic group or race (also more recently). Because they do not belong to the same family, they might be dangerous.

Moreover, *stranger* is not such a simple term as Silverberg's definition and subsequent use of it would imply. In *The Stranger: A Study in Social Relationships* (1934), Margaret M. Wood set out to examine the concept of *stranger* in a complex synthetistic study in which she defines *stranger* as "one who has come into face-to-face contact with the group for the first time" (43), thus giving the term a sense of "one who is unknown" (8; Fr. *inconnu*) since at that encounter he or she will still be "outside the system of relationships which unite the group" (8), but "if he is to be included, these relationships must be extended to him" (8–9). Once assigned a position within the group, however, the individual is no longer the stranger (unknown) but, by becoming partially known, becomes something else—an *incomer* (a foreigner, "something introduced from the outside," fr. L. *foraneus* [*OED2*]). Wood's study, together with the easy availability of the relevant section of Georg Simmel's *Soziologie* (1908) in the Chicago sociological school's textbook—*Science of Sociology* (1924), edited by R. E. Park and E. W. Burgess—suggest the cultural ambience surrounding the concept of the stranger that was contemporary with the early science fiction short stories.[1] The Alien of science fiction, therefore, may function as either a stranger or a foreigner in respect to the human group in the encounter.

What distinguishes the human Other—stranger or foreigner—from the extraterrestrial Other is that, regardless of any differences in skin color, hair, eye shape, and so on, all human beings are—as is now known—members of a single biological species. Some strangers, when they are first encountered, are easily distinguishable from members of the group they encounter; some of them are not. But otherness within the species is, biologically speaking, minimal. Given the Gaia hypothesis of Lovelock, the biota of one planet must be astronomically (sorry about that!) different from and unrelated to the biota of another.

Admittedly, even minimal biological otherness may be accompanied by differences in culture that are profound and divisive. According to American anthropologist Edward Hall in *The Hidden Dimension* (1969), for example, the differences between groups of cultural strangers can run deep enough to create serious problems even with goodwill on both sides *and* even if no physical difference exists:

> Superficially, these groups may all look alike and sound somewhat alike, but beneath the surface are manifold unstated, unformulated differences in their structuring of time, space, materials, and relationships. It is these very differences that often result in the distortion of meaning, regardless of good intentions, when people of different cultures interact. (x)

On a larger scale, too, where fear and conflict exist, they are more likely to result from a difference of opinion over territory or beliefs with someone familiar (Northern Ireland, Kosovo, the Middle East) than to result from an encounter with someone totally unknown. Nevertheless, improved communications and increased ease of travel since primitive times have considerably lessened the impact of the human stranger as the Other. There is simply too much knowledge of other humans available for them to be the stranger as the *unknown*, although the stranger as the *incomer* still persists in some relatively closed cultures (among them most notably Japan).[2] Over the past century, and over the past decade especially, globalization has increased dramatically (as a result of exploration, easy international travel, web communication, television images, etc.) and so has familiarization among humans who previously might never have known about the Other except as names on a map but who now encounter each other either directly (in person) or indirectly (through the media).[3] From viewing surrounding national groups as foreigners (and for centuries, as enemies), for example, the countries of Europe are moving rapidly toward becoming an integrated collection of neighbors.[4] The "global village" of Marshall McLuhan is today's reality, even if some of the villagers are in conflict.

The second kind of Other is the supernatural Other. Roughly speaking, the supernatural Other belongs to either theology or folklore, sometimes to both, and is characterized by its freedom from physical laws. As late as the beginning of the twenty-first century, in the process of growing up and handling the necessary "collisions," as Silverberg calls them, with the human Other, a child would almost always become aware simultaneously, to a greater or lesser extent, of the supernatural Other—the magical entity. The awareness would come from oral tradition in earlier times, and from literature or visual media more recently. In *The Discoverie of Witchcraft* (1584), Reginald Scot not only provides a partial list of the entities of folklore but also indicates how they come into individual awareness:

> But in our childhood our mothers maids haue so terrified vs with an ouglie diuell hauing hornes on his head, fier in his mouth, and a taile in his breech . . . whereby we start and are afraid when we heare one crie Bough: and they haue so fraied us with bull beggers, spirits, witches, orchens, elues, hags, fairies, satyrs, pans, faunes, sylens, kit with the cansticke, tritons, centaurs, dwarfes, giants, imps, calcars, coniurors, nymphes, changelings, Incubus, Robin good-fellowe, the spoorne, the mare, the man in the oke, the hell waine, the fierdrake, the puckle, Tom thombe, hob gobblin, Tom tumbler, boneles, and such other bugs, that we are afraid of our owne shadowes. (VII.xv.153–54)

Within the various religious faiths, moreover, such folkloric beings had their theological counterparts. For example, by the end of the fifth century AD, the Christian church had already acquired celestial beings in the

> commonly used hierarchy of nine orders . . . popularized by the Pseudo-Areopagite or Pseudo-Dionysius . . . in his *De Hierarchia Celesti*, which arranges them in three triads . . . Seraphim, Cherubim, and Thrones in the first circle . . . Dominions, Virtues, and Powers in the second circle . . . Principalities, Archangels, and Angels in the third circle. (Pickering, Isaacs, and Martin 1992, 34)

In the Western hemisphere at least, knowledge of angels would be acquired by the child as part of church attendance, from scripture readings and sermons, and from his or her parents, and would include information about the fallen angels—Lucifer and his companions. In the history of human development, these supernatural Others were usually considered at least as dangerous as human strangers, if not unimaginably more so.

In the twentieth century, the importance of the earlier supernatural forms of the Other has been significantly reduced. Admittedly, the theological Other continues in modified form within the traditional faiths and modern religious groups, and a considerable market exists for fiction loosely classified in bookstores as "horror and occult," indicating a persistent interest in "ghoulies and ghosties and long-leggety beasties, / And things that go bump in the night" (Cornish Prayer). But, with a few exceptions (which I shall return to later), the folkloric supernatural Other (elf, wizard, elemental) is found between bookcovers clearly labeled *fantasy* or *sword-and-sorcery*. In horror and occult fiction, moreover, the unrelieved and monotonous hostility of the supernatural entities involved and the total lack of an underlying rationale for their existence distinguishes them unmistakably from the science-fictional Alien. The supernatural Other may still be present in the consciousness of the child—with (or without) the encouragement of adults. Francis Church's response "Yes, Virginia, there is a Santa Claus!"[5] to young Virginia O'Hanlon on the editorial page of the *New York Sun* for 21 September 1897 is a case in point. But in the consciousness of the adults themselves, who are acculturated not to believe seriously in ghosts, demons, or Santa Claus outside the covers of fiction or the walls of the movie theater or the screen of a television set, they linger only as vestiges of their former selves, and as often as not have slipped into the unconscious.[6]

THE ASTROPHYSICISTS AND THE OTHER

As a result of the advance of scientific rationalism and the discovery of the evolutionary principle (which excludes the possibility of the supernatural Other), the extraterrestrial Other—the Alien, a new, scientifically sanctioned version of the Other—eventually emerged, however, and has largely ousted the supernatural Other. Science fiction, which introduces the earliest rationalized forms of the extraterrestrial Alien is, however, itself the product of that scientific rationalism. In principle, therefore, the Alien is the product of science fiction, and it is found exclusively in science fiction.[7] In spite of this relationship, paradoxically, scientists themselves came late to the consideration of the possibility of the Alien, whom they usually refer to guardedly as *extraterrestrial intelligence* (ETI), in the actual world outside science fiction.

In its earliest forms, in fact, the ETI problem was as much the province of philosophy as of science, for it came into being very early as a minor subtopic of the larger ongoing cosmological debate among philosophers. In "A Historical Introduction" summarizing the history of the ETI debate at a 1984 conference on the subject, Michael Papagiannis traces the "Plurality of Worlds" topic back beyond Aristotle: "As early as around 400 B.C. . . . Metrodorus of Chios was writing: 'It is unnatural in a large field to have only one shaft of wheat and in the infinite Universe only one living world'" (5). In spite of this early emergence of the concept, the traditional cosmology tended overwhelmingly toward theocentrism and the single world. Implicit in the notion of a cosmos that came into being in ordered form was the notion of something beyond the cosmos by which, or by whom, the order had been determined: at the very least, an ordering principle, or multiple gods, or even a single divine creator. It was an orderly and safe way for individual humans and groups to perceive the larger cosmos from the viewpoint of an everyday life full of change and hazards. Gradually, the idea stabilized into the theory of "The Great Chain of Being," whose history is examined in some detail by Arthur O. Lovejoy in *The Great Chain of Being: A Study of the History of an Idea* (1936). Toward the end of his discussion, Lovejoy points out that in the eighteenth century, cosmology became increasingly temporalized—that is, less the province of theology and philosophy and more the province of natural history and science. Finally, Lovejoy suggests, in the nineteenth century the publication of Darwin's theory of evolution in *On the Origin of Species by Natural Selection* (1858) dealt the whole of the traditional cosmology, including the argument against the plurality of worlds, a shattering blow.

What accompanied the temporalization and final collapse into disorder of the traditional ordered cosmology was the extension into public view of the longstanding cosmological debate. Discussion of Darwin's ideas was not confined to learned periodicals but was also widely disseminated in newspapers and magazines, and brought with it an awareness of the idea of the plurality of worlds and its implications for the possibility of ETI—so that the debate was now being carried on not only by scientists, theologians, and natural philosophers, but also by any other parties who happened to be interested and had access to the popular press. Most of the contributions to the nineteenth-century debate on the plurality of worlds, the earliest of which in fact preceded Darwin's work (David Brewster's *More Worlds Than One* [1854], William Whewell's *Of the Plurality of Worlds: An Essay; Also, A Dialogue on the Same Subject* [1854], and Richard A. Proctor's many volumes on the subject including *Our Place Among the Infinities* [1886] and *Other Worlds Than Ours* [1896]), are of little interest as preparation for the development of the science-fictional Alien. But Percival Lowell's *Mars* (1895), *Mars as an Abode of Life* (1908), and *The Evolution of Worlds* (1909) are clearly exceptions, as is Garrett Putnam Serviss's *Other Worlds: Their Nature, Possibilities and Habitability in the Light of the Latest Discoveries* (1901). Serviss's earlier novel, *A Columbus of Space* (1894), which remains a classic of late-Victorian science fantasy, equal to the early Wells (although, as I have already pointed out, not contributing very much to the concept of alterity), may have recommended his nonfictional study to potential readers and writers of science fiction.

Simultaneously with the published debate, moreover, the spread of education among the general population provoked increasing interest in the sort of questions that the lost cosmology had attempted to answer, and, in the wake of Darwin's work and fame, it was to scientists in particular that the questioners turned for new answers. It is in this context that Alfred Russell Wallace's *Man's Place in the Universe: A Study of the Results of Scientific Research in Relation to the Unity or Plurality of Worlds* (1903) is worth noticing, as is his *Is Mars Habitable?* (1907). Wallace was, at the time of the publication of *Man's Place,* an elderly and distinguished member of the scientific community, his career having been given an early boost by the fact that he had been acknowledged by Darwin as the codiscoverer of the theory of natural selection. After several essays on the subject of cosmology and the plurality of worlds, Wallace published the larger study *Man's Place in the Universe* for reasons which he himself explains:

> Having long been acquainted with most of the works dealing with the question of the supposed *Plurality of Worlds*, I was quite aware of the very superficial treatment the subject had received, even in the hands of the most able writers, and this made me the more willing to set forth the whole of the available evidence—astronomical, physical, and biological—in such a way as to show both what was proved and what suggested by it. (vi)

Wallace concluded that not only did the evidence not support the hypothesis of other inhabited worlds, but that "any direct evidence which may be held to support the view is almost wholly wanting, and that the greater part of the arguments are weak and flimsy in the extreme" and that "the probabilities and the weight of direct evidence tend to an exactly opposite conclusion" (10). For a number of years after the publication of *Man's Place in the Universe*, the plurality-of-worlds topic seems to have received no serious attention in scientific thinking about the nature of the universe. This absence cannot have been entirely due to Wallace's influence on the scientists of the early years of the new century, but his opinion must certainly have had some weight.

When, in the early years of the twentieth century, the plurality of worlds and the possibility of ETI was touched upon by scientists, it was addressed gingerly and usually in highly theoretical contexts. Writing in the late 1920s, for example, the eminent biologist J. B. S. Haldane—whose suspicion that "the universe is not only queerer than we suppose, but queerer than we *can* suppose" ("Possible Worlds" 1927, 298) is often misquoted (and nearly as often misattributed) in science fiction circles—treats the question of "possible worlds" as no more than a topic for philosophical speculation: "Generally philosophers who construct a funny [i.e., possible] world come to believe that it is the real world. . . . But philosophers damage their minds by coming to believe in their own hypotheses. This is a more or less irreversible process like ankylosing in one position a joint which should be flexible" (273). Contrasting biologists with philosophers on the same point, he comments that

> our way of thinking has led some of us to a very shrewd idea of how an organism will behave in given circumstances. . . . But I do not feel that any of us know enough about the possible kinds of being and thought, to make it worth while taking any of our metaphysical systems very much more seriously than those at which a thinking barnacle might arrive. (293)

Although his remarks might well be taken to heart by some science fiction writers, they clearly do not represent any kind of concession to the actual existence of other possible worlds. Similarly, as late as 1960, the mathematician Hans Freudenthal arrived at the topic of communication with aliens as part of his two-part book, *Lincos: Design of a Language for Cosmic Intercourse,* which incorporated his study of the differences between "natural" and "mathematical" languages. In the course of his discussion, he says, "I arrived at the problem of designing a language for cosmic intercourse. Lincos, the name of this language, is an abbreviation of '*lingua cosmica*'" (14), but his accompanying reference to the existence of aliens with whom it might actually be used to communicate seems sufficiently offhand to indicate either a lack of any real interest in the notion or a desire not to be thought to be taking the possibility too seriously: "Of course I do not know whether there is any humanlike being on other celestial bodies, and even if there were millions of planets in the universe inhabited by humanlike beings, it is possible that our nearest neighbour lives at a distance of a million light-years" (14). Clearly, for Freudenthal, Lincos is merely a solution to an abstract problem in mathematics, distinct from any serious consideration of practical application in the world outside mathematics.

With the maturity of scientists who have grown up with science fiction, however, scientific speculation about aliens has noticeably become more realistic, practical, and immediate. The process of this speculation is known as the "contact debate." David Brin, in "Xenology: The New Science of Asking 'Who's Out There?'" (1983), an article on the scientific community and the contact debate, points out that "[t]he great debate seems to be a war among scientists all of whom grew up reading science fiction" (94).[8] Some of the debaters write science fiction as well as read it: Carl Sagan, one of the most prominent scientists among the contact debaters, was the author of a science fiction novel, *Contact* (1986). Brin himself is both writer and scientist—an astrophysicist— with published scientific papers on the debate, such as "The 'Great Silence': The Controversy Concerning Extraterrestrial Intelligent Life" in the *Quarterly Journal of the Royal Astronomical Society* (1983); "Neoteny and Two-Way Sexual Selection in Human Evolution: Paleo-Anthropological Speculation on the Origins of Secondary Sexual Traits, Male Nurturing, and the Child as Sexual Image" in the *Journal of Social and Evolutionary Systems* (1995); and (with T. H. Kuiper, also a scientist and contact debater) "Resource Letter ETC–1: Extraterrestrial Civilization" in the *American Journal of Physics* (1989), as well as science-fact articles for *Analog*. But even scientists who do not write science fiction may be reading it. F. H. Crick and L. E. Orgel, for example, demonstrate an awareness of science fiction in general and of the recurrence in science-fictional discussions of the topic they are presenting scientifically. In their paper on "Directed Panspermia" (1973), they write that "[t]he possibility that terrestrial life derives from the deliberate activity of an extraterrestrial society has often been considered in science fiction and more or less light-heartedly in a number of scientific papers" (342). Some references to science fiction by scientists, however, especially if they are expressing a liking for it, seem to require a certain distancing on the part of the scientist concerned. George Simpson, for example, is careful to produce this distancing in "The Nonprevalence of Humanoids" (1964), his contribution to the contact debate:

> Before proceeding, I should define "humanoid" for those not as addicted as I am to science fiction. A humanoid, in science-fiction terminology adaptable to the present also somewhat fanciful subject, is a natural, living organism with intelligence comparable to man's in quantity and quality, hence with the possibility of rational communication with us. Its anatomy and indeed its means of communication are not defined as identical with ours. (771)

His use of "addicted" (in referring to his interest in science fiction) and "somewhat fanciful" (in referring to the topic of ETI itself) is carefully dismissive of any attempt to attribute anything less than pure speculation to him. But in spite of such awareness of fictional speculation, even now that serious consideration of the possible existence of extraterrestrial beings has become respectable among many scientists, the alien has continued to be included in purely scientific theories, but generally as no more than a contributory datum to a general cosmological theory, and arguments about it tend to focus on the possibility and probability of its existence.

Nevertheless, serious speculation about the Alien does exist and is being carried on in some very respectable scientific forums. As Rood and Trefil point out in *Are We Alone? The Possibility of Extraterrestrial Civilizations* (1981), their evenhanded study of the origins, development, and issues of the contact debate on ETI,

> [T]he existence of nonhuman extraterrestrials is hardly a revolutionary idea these days. . . . It is possible to identify a short period (from 1959 to 1962) during which the scientific attitude toward extraterrestrial intelligence (ETI) changed from one of slightly amused neglect to one of open-minded enquiry. As so often happens in science, the transition occurred because someone pointed out that technological developments had brought within reach a goal previously thought to be unattainable. (1–2)

David Brin, calling it "the Second Xenological Revolution," also recognizes the importance of this period, although (unlike Rood and Trefil) he emphasizes that the change that took place then had its roots in science fiction. In the "early 60s" ("Xenology" 1983, 66), he notes that "[f]or the first time it was legitimate for leading scientists to publicly consider the possibility of contact with intelligent species off of the planet Earth. Of course a lot of thought had gone into the subject previously, on the pages of science fiction novels and magazines" (65). Rood and Trefil date real progress along the road to this goal of finding and contacting ETI as having begun at the Greenbank Conference organized by Frank Drake in 1961, and they maintain that all subsequent consideration of ETI has to take into account the conference and the equation that emerged from it (the Greenbank equation, sometimes also referred to as the Drake equation). Scientists who attended this conference are among the principals who continue to be concerned with the topic, and their names are repeatedly invoked in science fiction approaches to it. Subsequently, they have been joined by many others.

The Greenbank Conference led, in fact, to some serious steps toward searching for and attempting to contact extraterrestrial life. The most immediate response was indirect and unfortunately negative from the point of view of the Greenbank participants, although it was not apparent to anyone at the time. In a legislative initiative simultaneously paranoid, optimistic, and secretive, the U.S. Congress passed the "Extraterrestrial Exposure Law," which prohibited contact between U.S. citizens and extraterrestrials:[9]

> On October 5, 1982, Dr. Brian T. Clifford of the Pentagon announced at a press conference (*The Star*, New York, Oct. 5, 1982) that contact between US citizens and extraterrestrials or their vehicles is strictly illegal. According to a law already on the books (Title 14, Section 1211 of the Code of Federal Regulations, adopted on July 16, 1969, before the Apollo moon shots), anyone found to have had such contact can be jailed for one year and fined $5,000. The NASA administrator is empowered to determine with or without a hearing that a person or object has been "extraterrestrially exposed" and impose an indeterminate quarantine under armed guard, which could not be broken even by court order. There is no limit placed on the number of individuals who could thus be arbitrarily quarantined. (Lyster 1)

The law was repealed in 1991 (3–4). The scientific community, however, responded more positively to the conclusions of the Greenbank Conference. Radio searches of the sky were stepped up, and soft and hard-copy messages were sent out. A hard-copy message was sent in 1972, when Pioneer 10 carried in addition to its usual instruments "a cosmic greeting card" in the form of a plaque whose "radial pattern situates the sun within our galaxy; the sun and planets, with a satellite leaving earth, are depicted at the bottom" (Mason, *Life in Space* 1983, 267). A soft message followed in 1974, when the staff of the National Astronomy and Ionosphere Center at Arecibo launched the "Arecibo Message," which they describe, in a paper included in the proceedings of the Life in the Universe Conference held at NASA's Ames Research Center in 1979, as "a simple and brief [radio] signal to the fringes of the Galaxy telling of the existence and nature of human life" (293). Both Frank Drake and Carl Sagan took part in the construction of the Arecibo Message. Most elaborately, however, the Voyager probes launched in 1977 carried the famed "Murmurs of Earth" recording. By 1989 an official international document was in existence, produced by the International Academy of Astronautics and the International Institute of Space Law and adopted as "Resolution C16: Concerning Extraterrestrial Intelligence" by Commission 51 of the International Academy of Astronautics, under the title "Declaration of Principles Concerning Activities Following the Detection of Extraterrestrial Intelligence," which specifies what is to be done and who is to be notified if signals are detected that, in the opinion of the scientists concerned, appear to have an intelligent extraterrestrial source. Ben Bova's article in the June 1996 issue of *Analog*, "Extraterrestrial Life: A New Era Begins," outlines the history of the radio searches conducted in the recent past and gives indications of new patterns that may be followed by future searchers as a result of the detection of extrasolar planets in late 1995 and early 1996. The detection of these planets, reported in such articles as Jeffrey Winters's "The Planet at 51 Peg" in *Discover* (January 1996), moved the topic of extraterrestrial intelligent life from the front page of the *Weekly World News* (30 October 1990) to the cover of *Time* (5 February 1996). A further boost was given by the August 1996 announcement of the discovery of what appear to be organic traces on a meteorite from Mars identified as #84-001 ("On the Question of the Mars Meteorite"), and yet another by the discovery in 1999 by astronomers Marcy, Brown, Noyes, and Fischer that Upsilon Andromedae is a solar system with three planets (King and Hayden, "Dawn of a New Solar System"). Currently, moreover, many science fiction readers and others are participating in SETI@Home Project located at the University of

California at Berkeley, in which individuals can be provided on request with a data-crunching program in the form of a special screensaver that, when left running on individual personal computers, is used to process data (supplied by the project) from radio telescopes, searching through it for patterns which might be extraterrestrial signals and which can then be examined more closely by the astronomers in the project. In spite of setbacks, therefore, the process launched at Greenbank continues.

Even at the time of the original Greenbank Conference, however, a certain disunity among the scientists concerned was evident, and this has since deteriorated into a definite split into two camps in what is now known as the contact debate. In "The 'Great Silence'" (1983), David Brin describes the situation as follows:

> Philosophical battle lines have been drawn between those who might be called "Contact Optimists"—who contend that simple reasoning indicates a Universe in which life and intelligence must be relatively common—and proponents of the "Uniqueness Hypothesis," who suggest that Earth is probably the first and only abode of technical civilization in our Galaxy. (283)

Eminent members of the former group, on the basis of their contributions to the debate, include Sebastian Von Hoerner, Marvin Minsky, the late Carl Sagan, and John Ball. Equally eminent members of the latter group include Frank R. Tipler, Ben Zuckerman, Stephen Gillett, Michael Hart, and Ernst Mayr. Within each group there is a wide spectrum of varying degrees of commitment and interest. Some optimists are interested in pursuing the matter actively; others are not. Some supporters of the uniqueness hypothesis appear willing to go on listening for ETI, but others would prefer to abandon the idea altogether and spend the money on something else. In a 1996 debate with Carl Sagan, Ernest Mayr described the possibility of success in the search for extraterrestrial intelligence as "an improbability of astronomic dimensions" (Mayr and Sagan, "The Seach for Extraterrestrial Intelligence: Scientific Question or Hopeful Folly?" 1996, 7). Most recently, Peter D. Ward and Donald Brownlee have presented a strong contribution to the debate in *Rare Earth: Why Complex Life is Uncommon in the Universe* (2000), in which they clearly favor the uniqueness hypothesis without actually committing themselves to the term *unique*; they assert their position as follows: "What has been called the principle of mediocrity—the idea that the Earth is but one of a myriad of worlds harboring advanced life—deserves a counter point" (x). Throughout the debate, arguments for and against the possibility are drawn from an equally wide range of scientific specialties and include theories as diverse as the mathematical odds against the development of intelligence (Tipler) and the possibility that any workable space drive will destroy the earth as the spaceship departs (Kafatos). There are a few people who express minor interest in the debate but appear in the end to be uncommitted one way or the other, suggesting that to be involved at all is to be strongly committed one way or other.

In the years immediately following the Greenbank Conference, very strong feelings were evident between the two groups, even within the constraints of formal academic scientific publishing. The head-to-head clash between Carl Sagan and Frank Tipler in the pages of the *Quarterly Journal of the Royal Astronomical Society* (and elsewhere) is probably the most vigorous expression of this antagonism. Tipler's series of papers in the journal begins with the challenging assertion (in its title) that "Extraterrestrial Intelligent Beings Do Not Exist" (1980). Although the title is probably the most directly belligerent part of the paper, Tipler, in the course of arguing that "we are the only intelligent species now existing in this galaxy," manages nevertheless within a single paragraph both to concede that "the evidence is not utterly conclusive" and to insult the optimists by asserting that "a belief in the existence of extraterrestrial intelligent beings anywhere in the galaxy is not significantly different from the widespread belief that UFOs are extraterrestrial spaceships" (267, 268). In "The Solipsist Approach to Extraterrestrial Intelligence" (1983), his response to Tipler's articles, Sagan retorts equally sharply that "[d]espite the utter mediocrity of our position in space and time, it is occasionally asserted, with no sense of irony, that our intelligence and technology are unparalleled in the history of the cosmos. It seems to us more likely that this is merely the latest in the long series of anthropocentric and self-congratulatory pronouncements on scientific issues" (13). By way of conclusion, he characterizes the difficulties of the Fermi Paradox as merely "apparent" and deriving "partly from a conceptual model of interstellar colonization that is in poor accord with long-term human history . . . and partly from an inappropriate and self-contradictory application of recent human history to the circumstances which prevail after the invention of weapons of mass destruction" (Sagan and Newman 1983, 120). Sagan's optimism continued undiminished in the debate with Ernst Mayr; Sagan's contribution to the debate is subtitled "The Abundance of

Life-Bearing Planets" (8), in which his final comment is that "I draw the tentative conclusion that other Earth-like planets have millions of species of life on them from the same data set that leads Professor Mayr to conclude that there are no extraterrestrial technical civilizations" (13). It should perhaps be noted, however, that antagonism in the journals need not necessarily spill over beyond their pages. Rood and Trefil themselves, for example, in the course of their collaboration on *Are We Alone?* take pains to point out that their personal relationships remain amicable although they find themselves fiercely engaged on opposite sides of the debate.

What transformed the contact debate from the relatively cool, openminded inquiry that Rood and Trefil imply in their history of the debate to the kind of passionate free-for-all exemplified by the Sagan-Tipler argument and the Sagan-Mayr debate was the escalating urgency of dealing with Fermi's paradox. In essence, Fermi wanted an answer: "Where are they?" For, if sufficiently advanced extraterrestrial intelligences existed, they would have been able to make contact with us by now, and they have not. Much scientific ingenuity has been expended in responses to Fermi's paradox as part of the contact debate, but nothing is yet final.

The importance of the contact debate for the development of the concept of the Alien in science fiction is twofold. On the one hand, it provides, for conscientious science fiction writers, an accessible and consistent source of appropriate scientific background material for creating scientifically acceptable alien beings. On the other, it provides suggestions for the speculative solution of associated scientific problems in a way that accords with the writers' literary need for compelling and attractive narrative forms. Both have implications for the concepts of alterity and sapience.

In its presentation of strictly orthodox scientific theory, the contact debate is a tremendously handy information source for the creation of alien worlds and alien beings that do not violate by either their existence or their nature what I have described earlier as the prime constraint of science fiction. Some writers who introduce aliens into their science fiction undoubtedly read the scientists of the contact debate firsthand in the pages of the science journals. But there are other sources even more easily available than the expensive specialist journals. Scientific material is also transmitted in the pages of other periodicals (notably in the science fiction magazines *Analog* and *IASFM*), not only by scientists such as Stephen L. Gillett and Robert A. Freitas, who direct popular articles to science fiction readers, but also by writer-scientists such as David Brin and Robert Forward.

All the most important theories of the contact-debate scientists in the science journals seem at one point or another to have been discussed in mediated (popular) versions. Such mediated versions, for example, discuss the assumption of mediocrity (Von Hoerner), the Greenbank equation (Drake, Sagan), the anthropic principle (Carter, Tipler), and the zoo hypothesis (Ball). Much of the overall effort is concentrated on ways of dealing with Fermi's paradox, the pros and cons of which are presented, for example, in contrasting articles by Gillett and Freitas in *IASFM*. Gillett's contribution, "The Fermi Paradox" (1984), denying the existence of extraterrestrial intelligence, ends with an exhortation: "OK, you budding SF authors. Enough of cutesy aliens at every port of call. Get out there and tell it like it is!" (50). Replying in the following issue, under the title "Fermi's Paradox: A Real Howler" (1984), Freitas calls Fermi's paradox "a toothless tiger" dependent on the faulty logic of an argument that he lays out, by way of emphasis, in the baldest terms:

> (1) If the aliens exist, then They should be here. (2) If They are here, then we should observe Them. (3) We do not observe Them. (4) Hence They are not here. (5) Hence They do not exist. . . . The error is that the "should" in steps (1) and (2) is not a logical operator at all. "Should" is only a subjective judgement, tainted with assumptions, prejudices, unknowns, hidden agendas and chauvinism. "Should" is not "must." "Should" is barely maybe. Consequently, the arrow of logical implication cannot validly be reversed, given the fact of null evidence. (34–35)

Granting that both articles are presented as provocatively as possible to encourage reader interest, they nevertheless perform an important educational function with reference to the creation of credible science fiction with direct reference to the existence of aliens, in addition to suggesting the more basic point that differing opinions are always possible. Duncan Lunan returns to the topic in "Fermi Paradox—The Final Solution?" (1986). Elsewhere, Brin's previously cited article, "Xenology" (1983), represents a concentrated discussion of the problems and possible solutions involved in dealing with the Greenbank equation and Fermi's paradox, and it is significant that the discussion involves much prior reader participation.

In the presentation of theories that challenge orthodoxy, mediated articles lend support to science fiction writers in the preparation of credible aliens by offering the possibility of alternative solutions to problems created by the physical nature of the universe. Storytellers need to be able to present their credibly constituted aliens in contexts in which they can plausibly interact. Two of these problems, in particular, are of major importance to writers desiring to create a story line about a multispecies galaxy: interstellar travel and interspecies communication.

Science fiction requires plausibly possible methods of interstellar travel that will allow different species to reach each other in order to make contact. Ideally, such a method should make this contact possible in a conventional narrative of real-time action without violating the prohibition on faster than light (FTL) travel imposed by Einstein's theory of special relativity. As explained by Kingsley Amis, writer and critic of science fiction, in *New Maps of Hell* (1960), the problem for science fiction writers is that "to reach any but the nearest stars would take several hundred years even if one travelled at the speed of light, in the course of doing which one would, if I understand Einstein's popularizers correctly, become infinite in mass and zero in volume, and this is felt to be undesirable" (15). Abundant conventions (such as hyperspace, folded space, warp drives, and matter transmission, for example) for evasion exist, and Amis lists a number that had already done so for some years at the time he was writing. But to remain usefully convincing, such conventions require the periodic infusion of fresh, scientifically oriented hypotheses. For writers in need of such methods, therefore, the science fiction magazines often provided articles such as "Our Many Roads to the Stars" (*Galaxy*, September 1975), in which Poul Anderson reviews current scientific approaches to Einstein's relativity theory and to the problems of FTL, including Gerald Feinberg's tachyon theory, a theory of hyperspace, and wormhole theory: "Hyperspace turns out to be more than a hoary science fiction catchphrase. Geometrodynamics now allows a transit from point to point without crossing the space between, via a warp going 'outside' that space—often called a wormhole" (84). Similarly, Thomas Donaldson's "How to Go Faster Than Light" (1985) provides essential stimulus to the imagination of readers and writers alike: "This is an article about heterodox interpretations of relativity, that is, *absurdities*. It's almost all theory. Even worse, none of it coincides with the King James Version of Relativity" (77). The article does not suggest that Ein-

stein could or should be contradicted, but what it does suggest provides a scientifically plausible hypothesis that could serve as a basis for evading the effect of relativity theory on FTL travel. Like both Gillett and Freitas, Donaldson
writes provocatively:

> [T]he Special Theory of Relativity depends fundamentally upon Maxwell's equa-
> tions for an electromagnetic field. If STR is somehow wrong, Maxwell's equa-
> tions are also wrong. Discovery that Maxwell's equations were wrong would
> reduce virtually all of contemporary physics to rubble. Almost all physicists have
> a vested interest in Maxwell's equations; the Universe, however, has no vested in-
> terest in physicists. Let's consider some theoretical and experimental work raised
> against Maxwell's equations. (88–89)

Also, like Gillett and Freitas, he provides writers who need it with something
on which to base their speculations. More recently even than Donaldson,
John G. Cramer returns to the wormhole hypothesis in two articles for *Analog*, "Wormholes and Time Machines" (1989) and "More about Wormholes—To the Stars in No Time" (1990), and the appropriate references to
the scientific literature are provided. In the second of the two, Cramer
points out that "a sufficiently advanced civilization might construct a stable
wormhole (a curved-space shortcut between one region of space and another) and use it both for faster-than-light travel and for time travel, with
no laws of physics violated in the process except *causality* (the principle that
a cause must precede its effects" (99). He goes on to explore the practical applications. Wormhole theory bears a strong resemblance to the theory of
"folded space" used to evade the constraints of relativity theory; the "folded
space" theory was first suggested in science-fictional form by Robert Heinlein in *Starman Jones* (1953). Most recently of all, Cramer, in his article "The
Alcubierre Warp Drive" in the November 1996 issue of *Analog*, presented an
outline of "The Warp Drive: Hyper-Fast Travel within General Relativity" by
Miguel Alcubierre, published in 1994 as a letter to the editor in *Classical and
Quantum Gravity*. In his abstract, Alcubierre himself refers to the fact that
the space-time distortion involved "is reminiscent of the 'warp drive' of science fiction" (L73). That Alcubierre's mathematics has been, as many good
scientific hypotheses are, subsequently challenged does not, however, inval-
idate the article and the hypothesis as a suggestive stimulus for science fiction writers.

A second issue of major importance in the multispecies galaxy is communication. Getting there may be only half the problem of contact, for it has often been suggested that communication with a truly alien being would be as
near to impossible as makes no significant difference—a daunting prospect
for the science fiction writer. Assistance with this problem comes from outside
the immediate context of the contact debate in Marvin Minsky's article on
alien communication, "Communication with Alien Intelligence" (1985),
which appeared in the computer magazine *Byte*. This discussion, which does
not directly address itself either to the contact debate or to science fiction,
nevertheless offers a foundation for speculation in both:

> When we first meet those aliens in outer space, will we and they be able to con-
> verse? I believe that, yes, we will—provided they are motivated to cooperate—
> because we'll both think in similar ways. I propose two kinds of arguments . . .
> based on the idea that all intelligent problem solvers are subject to the same ul-
> timate constraints—limitations on space, time, and materials. For animals to
> evolve powerful ways to deal with such constraints, they must have ways to rep-
> resent the situations they face, and they must have processes for manipulating
> those representations. (127)

Such an assertion of problem solving as a universal activity in sapient life included in discussion of the mathematical constraints involved in communication and identified in the context of artificial intelligence theory by one of its
leading practitioners offers powerful support to writers needing to make the
achievement of interspecies communication not only possible but probable.

Similarly, articles and comments by scientists drawing attention to points
overlooked by writers in dealing with multispecies galaxies also lend support
to writers in achieving credibility and plausibility. It is possible that the widespread ignorance of biology that Dean R. Lambe, a biologist and writer, had
drawn attention to in an article several years previously ("Biological Ignorance," 1978) has much to do with the refusal by many science fiction writers
to deal with biological incompatibilities among different species. Lambe's article concentrates on public ignorance of biological theory in general and of
the facts of evolutionary principle in particular. Asserting that "we, as a society, are biologically ignorant," he goes on to include the writers, editors, and
readers of science fiction in this cloud of unknowing:

Even SF readers, who tend to be better educated in science than the general populace, are guilty of this ignorance. . . . Why . . . do we still have plots where the
word "clone" could be replaced by the word "robot" with no meaningful change
in the story? Why do writers religiously adhere to the laws of physics . . . but
wreak havoc with the laws of natural selection? . . . Because we are biologically
ignorant. (5–6)

Lambe himself, however, could not cover all the problems created by biological ignorance in a single article targeted specifically to the immediate problem
of the damage being done to scientific education by non-scientifically educated educators. But he made a start by drawing attention to a problem that
would require the attention of conscientious science fiction writers.

The contributions to the creation of the plausible alien by the orthodox scientific theory of the contact debate and the unorthodox theories of the chal-
lengers are significant. Expressed schematically, the resulting pattern of the
development of the extraterrestrial Alien presence both in science fiction and
in science seems to be a synergistic loop: Given a normal psychological mechanism of discrimination of the Other in earlier natural and prescientific supernatural forms, the interest of the scientist in ETI, once caught by reading
science fiction, feeds into her or his theory of the nature of the universe, which
in turn feeds the imagination of the science fiction writers, thus stimulating
further interest by the scientist who reads science fiction. This schema certainly suggests an explanation for the continuing and perhaps escalating interest in aliens in science fiction among certain scientists, certain science
fiction writers, and large numbers of science fiction readers.

Nevertheless, the scientific contribution to the presence of the Alien in science fiction leaves a great deal unaccounted for. Among scientists themselves,
with or without reference to science fiction, the topic of the Alien appears to
arouse an inordinate degree of reaction—and visibly emotional reaction, at
that. If anything, therefore, scientific interest in the Alien increases the evidence for human fascination with the idea of the Alien without doing anything to explain that fascination.

In particular, it fails noticeably to account for the reaction by those
uniqueness-hypothesis supporters who, although vehemently rejecting the existence of ETI and hence the possibility of contact with it, cannot merely reject the topic as a null hypothesis and leave it alone. The passion involved in

certain responses is peculiar and not easily attributable to rhetorical strategy. Nor is it likely to be simply a result of scientific contempt for the wrongheadedness of other scientists and the ignorance of the nonscientific public. For if scientific anger and contempt were directed solely at wrongheadedness and ignorance, there are other instances of both which are far more prevalent, far more immediate, and far more far-reaching in their effects on humans and should by rights be receiving the full brunt of passionate and conflicted scientific attention, but are noticeably not doing so. Nor can the enthusiasm of the contact optimists be at all easily accounted for, since they, who should understand better than nonscientists the true magnitude of the odds against contact with ETI, odds that are demonstrable from the mathematical calculations of the Greenbank equation, still persist in their optimism. Consequently, scientific theory, although it clearly contributes to the existence, understanding, and increasing sophistication of the Alien in science fiction, does not explain the essential need that created the concept.[10]

THE PSYCHOLOGISTS, THE PSYCHOCRITICS, AND THE OTHER

The theory of the Alien as a manifestation of psychological forces in the human spirit has its foundations in the twentieth-century development of psychology, with the concomitant spread of psychological theory into general knowledge. This spread has run parallel to the development of science fiction as a genre, although the knowledge is diffuse and not always accurate. Psychocriticism, the application of psychological theory to the study of literature, offers obvious opportunities in the discussion of the Alien, particularly as a way of explaining its nature. That science fiction and psychology have both come to maturity in roughly the same time span, however, does not imply any special relationship between them: Science fiction deserves appropriate and accurate psychocritical study no less and no more than any other form of fiction in the twentieth century. In general, however, both psychologists and lay psychocritics have failed to make full use of the opportunities offered. Although a number of the "professional" psychocritics (i.e., psychologists and psychiatrists who write literary criticism) discuss UFO narratives (see Baker, *The Aliens among Us*) and literature, they do not for the most part address science fiction. The large number of "lay" psychocritics (literary critics who use psychological approaches to literature) who address literature in general—particularly modern literature—seem to avoid science fiction. In avoiding science fiction, however, psychocriticism is perhaps simply following the example of the founders of the major schools of psychology of the early twentieth century: Alfred Adler, Harry Stack Sullivan, and Sigmund Freud do not address the topic of the Other directly. Freud himself has one study of otherness in "Das Unheimliche" ("The 'Uncanny'" 1919), a discussion of the uncanny in literature that does not address science fiction concepts.

Nevertheless, there are occasional exceptions among both professionals and nonprofessionals. Among professional psychocritics (since she is an MD and publishing in *Psychiatric Quarterly*, I assume she is a psychiatrist), Ednita Bernabeu offers a rigorously Freudian approach to the topic of science fiction ("Science Fiction: a New Mytholos," 1957). Taking it more seriously than many other critics of the subject, she cites de Camp's *Science Fiction Handbook* (1953) as her source for the definition of science fiction. In addition, among her examples of how psychological patterns in the human mind appear in the narrative patterns of the texts of science fiction she includes a solid paragraph on Ray Bradbury's *The Martian Chronicles* (1960), in which she discusses how

> the "Martians" can assume the shapes of the explorers' dearest kin, and by illusion, create around them the places in the past the explorers loved best. By this device the "Earthmen" ... are easily trapped. The reliving of these "happiest moments" is evidently in this author's plot a form of autistic gratification for which the condign punishment of the "explorers" is their destruction. (529)

Although she mentions "Martians" here and elsewhere (531), as well as "other life forms" and "other species" (529), she does not examine the Alien in any detail. She does, on the other hand, include some discussion of robots, noting particularly that "the detached inhumanity characteristic of much science fiction, which centers around robots and the 'science of robotics,' is offset by the painful struggle to reach or maintain a feeling of aliveness ... an expression of the struggle against schizoid feeling of self-alienation or estrangement" (531). Although the phrasing of "robots and the 'science of robotics'"—particularly the latter—might suggest a familiarity with Isaac Asimov's robot stories, she does not mention him by name, and it is more likely that she is quoting from de Camp. Her general opinion is that science fiction offers "schizophrenoid fantasies" (533) and that "[t]he mechanisms predominantly displayed are those of the earliest ego. ... It is postulated here that the oedipal conflict is more threatening and is met by severe regression to primitive ego mechanisms and pregenital libidinal levels, antedating those found in other types of escape literature" (534). She is careful to add, however, that "[n]o implication is intended or believed that readers and writers of this fiction are schizophrenic, which would be as mistaken as to assume that all the authors and readers of detective fiction are potentially homicidal" (534), a caveat not all psychocritics were willing to issue. Bernabeu's discussion, although an interesting example of psychocriticism of science fiction, also illustrates its dangers.

Another exception to the general silence of professional psychocritics is Robert Plank (a fellow of the Orthopsychiatric Association and an MSW). Plank is the author of a number of papers on various aspects of science fiction, of which "The Reproduction of Psychosis in Science Fiction" (1954) anticipates Bernabeu to some extent, although based on dynamic psychology rather than Freudian psychoanalytic theory. This paper was the subject of a special note in Groff Conklin's review column in the February 1955 issue of *Galaxy*, in which he commented that "I finished reading it with a feeling that the author thought most science fiction writers (and by implication readers too) were bugs. 'Schizomorph' is what he calls the stories, thus accusing the writers of having schizoid personalities, 'especially of the paranoid type'" (106). Conklin's response was entirely understandable. Unlike Bernabeu, Plank failed to include a disclaimer of any such implication. In Plank's paper, according to its author, "[t]he hypothesis is advanced that science fiction is, to a higher degree than other literature, morphologically similar to schizophrenic manifestations of the paranoid type" (420). The hypothesis, for whatever reason, does not include aliens and is chiefly concerned with what he describes as "[t]hree leading motifs—space travel, survival after a catastrophe, and influencing machines" (420). Like Bernabeu, he draws on examples of science fiction, which, unlike her, he identifies specifically, and he uses both short stories—Raymond Jones's "Discontinuity" and Jack Vance's "The Potters of Firsk" (1950), Frank Robinson's "The Hunting Season" (1951), J. T. M'Intosh's "Mind Alone" (*Galaxy*, 1953), and Milton Lesser's "Tyrants of Time" (1954)—and novels, including Jules Verne's *A Journey to the Center of the Earth* (1965), Jack London's *The Scarlet Plague* (1915), James Hilton's *Lost Horizon* (1933), and George R. Stewart's *Earth Abides* (1949). His references to secondary studies of science fiction are limited to J. O. Bailey's *Pilgrims through Space and Time: Trends and Patterns in Scientific and Utopian Fiction* (1947).

For consideration of the Alien, however, Plank's most important discussion of science fiction appears in *The Emotional Significance of Imaginary Beings* (1968)—subtitled "A Study of the Interaction between Psychopathology, Literature, and Reality in the Modern World"—in which he devotes some space to the Alien. In this study, Plank acknowledges that "even if we cannot yet understand the widespread desire to meet 'aliens,' the longing for the epiphany of the humanoid, we must assume that yearning to be powerful" (46). He points to conflicting attitudes about the constitution of the universe by the philosophers Blaise Pascal and Emmanuel Kant—both indicating, he notes, immense depth of feeling—as attitudes that find a satisfaction in the myths of imaginary beings of one sort or another. Plank suggests the further contribution to the myth of imaginary beings of such emotional factors as the "widespread 'existential' discomfort in our civilization . . . [and] the sinking feeling of individual importance in the face of superindividual [*sic*] forces" and suggests that "by inventing nonhuman monsters . . . it becomes possible to deny human responsibility"; that is, the Alien functions as a defense mechanism against the outcome of humanity's own behavior (91). But the creation of the imaginary being can also be a positive thing—a developmental mechanism: "Heterotopia transcends realism. . . . We can create imaginary beings, not as a mere play of fantasy, not only to identify with them, but to form a world by which our world can be measured and oriented" (170). Plank neither overestimates nor underestimates the significance of the Alien in the present century, and he describes its positive and negative characteristics evenhandedly. In general, he appears to view the creation of the imaginary being as one among many psychological mechanisms.

As a characterization of the Alien in science fiction, however, the study presents some problems. To begin with, Plank is, as his subtitle suggests, discussing the imaginary being manifested not only in the psychopathology of mental patients but also in scientific theory, in the documents of UFO believers, and in fiction. The science-fictional Alien, therefore, is the topic of approximately one quarter of his discussion. Moreover, he distinguishes his categories by applying the criterion of awareness of the imaginative process: If the process of imagining aliens is "scientifically disciplined" (81), the results become part of xenobiology; if not, they become at best fiction, for those who are aware of their imaginary nature, and at worst delusion, for those who think they are real. In the study of science fiction, however, it is quite evident that "scientifically disciplined" is an entirely relative factor: Some science fiction is as disciplined as anything that appears in a scientific journal and some is only one remove from pure fantasy. In addition, Plank's use of the term *fiction* when dealing with imaginary beings does not clearly distinguish science fiction from speculative fiction as a whole. Finally, his sample of science fiction stories is extremely small. For example, in his discussion of the relationship of the Alien to the development of space travel in the twentieth century, his sample of short stories is drawn from a single anthology (*The 7th Annual of the Year's Best SF 1952*). Only a handful of novels are referred to elsewhere in the study, not all of them directly concerned with aliens. His study is, therefore, severely limited in its usefulness.

Nevertheless, in spite of these limitations of the study as a study of science fiction, the psychological factors Plank suggests as important in the study of imaginary beings in general do have a considerable bearing on any study of the Alien as a psychological manifestation. *The Emotional Significance of Imaginary Beings*—although it must continue to be viewed, as Mark Hillegas suggests in "Victorian 'Extraterrestrials'" (1975), as among the "first attempts" (391) at a psychological explanation for the popularity of other worlds and imaginary beings—is, within its limits, a constructive and suggestive contribution to the problem of the fascination of the Alien.

Perhaps most usefully, however, Plank's general theory of imaginary beings provides a critical framework in which the topic of the Alien may be more thoroughly and perhaps even conclusively argued by psychocritics, professional or lay. It is neither necessary nor desirable, however, to agree with either Bernabeu's or Plank's conclusions about the allegedly "schizophrenic" nature of science fiction in order to conduct such an argument. Plank's theory of the imaginary being as a psychological reflection of the besieged individual in a clearly difficult world, for example, lends credence to Eric Rabkin's theory, argued in "Fairy Tales and Science Fiction" (1980), of the Alien as a coping device—a response to "the elemental need for fiction to deal with the beasts we feel in our world" (83), a character in the "subjective drama" of psychological development (84), and an element of "yet newer ways of coming to deal with our lives" (90). In making this argument, Rabkin argues that "science fiction functions in precisely the way Bettelheim suggests that fairy tales do, providing not so much logical answers as satisfying ones" (84). The Alien, therefore, functions appropriately within the pattern of literary manifestations of internal dramas. Like Plank's contribution, however, Rabkin's discussion, although it contributes to explaining the fascination of the Alien, does not complete this explanation, and Rabkin is not a psychologist.

The theory of the Alien as a psychological manifestation also allows for specific images to appear and be identified. Plank himself identifies the image of the guardian, a "being of superior power, wisdom, and goodness," similar to those traditional in religious belief but "essentially natural rather than supernatural" (101), and he offers Overlord Karellen in Arthur C. Clarke's *Childhood's End* (1953) as his example of the new, natural protector who replaces such figures as the guardian angel or the fairy godmother. The second image that can be identified by this theory of the Alien as psychological manifestation is the image of the companion. Mark Hillegas, in the passage I have cited commenting on the fascination that "aliens and other worlds" have for readers, introduces the theory of the Alien as companion: "Whether or not one accepts the theories of these and other psychologists, the fact seems indisputable that many people have had a deep need to find that we are not alone" ("Victorian Extraterrestrials" 391). Plank, too, implies in the course of describing the writer of fiction that the Alien fulfils this or a similar function: "If a man has the gift to draw delight and succor from his fantasies while clearly recognizing them as fantasies . . . he may assuage the anxiety of being alone by merely imagining that he is not" (82). Even Rood and Trefil pay perhaps unconscious tribute to image of the Alien as companion in the title of their collaboration on the contact debate—*Are We Alone?* The image of the companion and the loneliness that evokes it, however, are as far from universal and as far from explaining the overall nature of the Alien as is the image of the guardian. Nevertheless, none of these images can be ignored.

All these pieces of psychocriticism so far, however, identify only one particular psychological manifestation as the Alien, and singly and together they fail to account for the multiplicity and multifariousness of the Alien. Gardner Dozois, however, a writer and editor of science fiction, not a lay or professional psychocritic, points out that the Alien plays a very large number of possible roles in science fiction, each one occurring over and over again in different variations in different stories:

> Sometimes they are benevolent space brothers, sometimes sinister monsters,
> sometimes they love us, or collect us, or keep us as pets, or teach us, or learn

from us; sometimes they don't care about us at all—sometimes they don't even notice us, brushing us aside like insects. . . . Sometimes alien and human can interact, merge, form partnerships, and strike bargains, dicker, learn to love each other, perhaps even have sex with each other. (*Aliens!* x)

If we compare the few images so far identified by psychocriticism with this list of possible interactions, it is clear that many of them do not fit into the categories of psychological manifestation identified by the psychocritics. To say, for example, that the Alien is a response to our need not to feel alone is not only inadequate to account for the range of possible relationships but totally inappropriate as an explanation for the multiple versions of the alien invasion that destroys or attempts to destroy the human race either wholly or in part.

Psychocriticism so far has done little serious work with the figure of the Alien. It has served to identify a few recurrent individual images and functions, and, by pointing to the psychological roots of certain of those images, it has accounted for some of the "charge" that appears to attach itself to the Alien. To this extent it usefully directs subsequent critics to certain lines of inquiry. On the other hand, however, it has failed to ground itself securely in any particular psychological theory or theories, it has not attempted to account for the findings of other critical approaches, and it has not addressed itself appropriately to the task of offering a complete theory of the Alien. Consequently, what has been said so far by psychocriticism is, although useful as a starting point, incomplete as an explanation for the fascination of the Alien.

A more convincingly complete accounting for the fascination, persistence, strangeness, and increasing complexity of the Alien, however, can be brought about by the application of the theories of a contemporary of Freud and an equally great psychological theorist: C. G. Jung. Jung's analytical psychology, although not the most obvious or popular choice as an interpretative tool for a study of science fiction, nevertheless offers significant opportunity for the discussion of the Alien.[11] Carol Schreier Rupprecht, in her article "Archetypal Theory and Criticism" in *The Johns Hopkins Guide to Literary Theory and Criticism* (1994), asserts that previously identified problems with Jung's work may be the result of misunderstanding, since the practice of archetypal criticism is still developing: "Archetypal criticism, then, construed as that derived from Jung's theory and practice of archetypal (analytical) psychology, is a fledgling and much misconstrued field of enquiry with significant but still unrealized potential for the study of literature and aesthetics in general" (89–90). The most assertive supporter of archetypal/Jungian criticism is, however, Clifton Snider, who in one of a series of three articles on this form of criticism, written for the *Psychocultural Review*, explains:

> Literary criticism based on Jungian analytical psychology can add a new dimension to literary art. It can show . . . how literature contributes to the psychic balance of a community. . . . Examining a literary work in Jungian terms can show why the piece is structured as it is. The value of Jungian criticism is that it sets literature in its proper place in a human context as a representative of the psyche without, at the same time, getting away from literature's intrinsic worth as an art form. ("C. G. Jung's Analytical Psychology" 99–100)

Moreover, although in "Analytical Psychology and Literary Criticism" (1980) one of Jung's close colleagues Marie-Louise von Franz cautiously describes the position of Jungian psychology with respect to literary criticism only as "ancillary" (124), she makes clear at the same time the hermeneutic nature of its participation in the process of understanding literature:

> The word *hermeneutics* comes from Hermes, the name of the messenger who commutes between the world of the gods (the archetypes of the collective unconscious) and the world of man. He is forever versatile and a master of the word (*logos*). He quarrels and makes friends with his brother Apollo, the god of art (and of medicine), and is, like Apollo, the "*musagetes*," the lover of the muses. The artist's eternal but heavy task is to bring into form that which assaults him from the depths of the psyche. Hermes, the herald, helps the artist to communicate it. (125)

These arguments for the application of Jungian theory to literature have been made in terms of literature in general, without reference to science fiction. Nevertheless, they translate easily to the application of Jungian theory to the study of science fiction.

Several approaches to bringing science fiction and Jungian theory together have been made. A paper proposing an archetypal/Jungian study of science fiction, entitled "Science Fiction, Archetypes, and the Future," was originally presented at the Clarion Workshop in 1973. Its author, R. Glenn Wright, proposes such a study from a point of view much like that of Snider, on the grounds that literature, including science fiction, "contributes to the psychic balance of a community" (Snider, "C. G. Jung's Analytical Psychology" 99). Wright further says that science fiction is one of "the two genres in which archetypal patterns are presented most starkly and unambiguously" (175) and that in the face of a science that is increasingly difficult to understand, there is "a way into the problem of 'scientific translation': through art, specifically . . . through that sub-genre of the literary art, science fiction, for it is science fiction that has met the power, glory and horror of science, scientists, technology and technocrats head on" (177). Moreover, it is science fiction, because of its archetypal content, that will enable the future, because "[w]hen a culture is *in extremis* . . . and must either make a kind of inductive leap into its next phase of development or die, I believe that manifest archetypal drives are extremely important in determining whether that culture will make its leap or not" (178). In some ways, perhaps, Wright oversimplifies the function of art in general and science fiction in particular, but his point is well taken. Two years later, in "Victorian 'Extraterrestrials,'" Mark Hillegas mentions Jung's "book on flying saucers" in the same breath as he suggests that "[s]tories of aliens and other worlds had . . . and still have a very great fascination, and for this I believe there must ultimately be a psychological explanation" (391). The idea was, however, not taken up by other Jungian psychologists or psychocritics at the time, and Hillegas's suggestion was left only to psychocritics such as Carl Malmgren, in "Self and Other in SF: Alien Encounters" (1993) and *Worlds Apart: Narratology of Science Fiction* (1991), and also Kenneth Golden in *Science Fiction, Myth, and Jungian Psychology* (1995).[12]

The applicability of archetypal/Jungian theory to science fiction is supported by science fiction writers. The most prominent of these is Ursula Le Guin, who in talking about her own work and that of her colleagues consistently uses archetypal/Jungian ideas and terminology, whether in extended discussion, such as her papers on "The Child and the Shadow" (1975) and "Myth and Archetype in Science Fiction" (1976), or casual references, such as the remark that "I wish I had known Jung's work when I wrote [*The Left Hand of Darkness*]: so that I could have decided whether a Gethenian had *no* animus or anima, or *both*, or an *animum*" ("Is Gender Necessary? Redux" 1976, 169). In a response to an article by David Ketterer on *The Left Hand of Darkness*, Le Guin wrote:

To me a myth is a living element, a symbolic constellation, in Jung's terms, within my own psyche; and my job as an artist is to create a way, a thoroughfare, to and from it, by means of my art, so that both the image and some sense of its meaning can come up into consciousness and be communicated to other consciousnesses. I fully accept Jung's definition: "The symbol differs essentially from sign or symptom, and should be understood as the expression of an intuitive perception which can as yet be neither apprehended better, nor expressed differently." (138)

Although Le Guin's support for the validity of Jung's theory of archetypal symbols in considering her own work must carry weight, that support need not be confined to her own work. It extends beyond it to the whole genre of science fiction (and of fantasy fiction) and must carry similar weight there.

Jungian criticism is, therefore, acceptably if unexpectedly appropriate in the reading of the science-fictional Alien. It is unexpected because, although he was extraordinarily widely read, Jung's acquaintance with science fiction was clearly limited—his only direct discussions of science fiction texts are of Fred Hoyle's *The Black Cloud* (1957) in "Flying Saucers: A Modern Myth of Things Seen in the Skies" (1969) and of John Wyndham's *The Midwich Cuckoos* (1957) in "On Flying Saucers," the supplement to that paper. In discussing Hoyle, Jung explicitly limits himself to a psychological interpretation of the encounter with the black cloud, which turns out to be a sapient being,[13] and of the failure to acquire the knowledge that it attempts to convey:

Understood psychologically, the story is a description of fantasy-contents whose symbolical nature demonstrates their origin in the unconscious. . . . What then—psychologically speaking—is the meaning of this cosmic, or rather psychic, collision? Obviously, the unconscious darkens the conscious, since no *rapprochement*, no dialectical process takes place between their contents. (CW 10:*817–18*:430)

Similarly, also limiting himself to strictly analytical psychological interpretation, in discussing Wyndham's novel he focuses on the mysterious children,[14] suggesting that their "peculiar parthenogenesis and . . . golden eyes denote kinship with the sun and characterize the children as divine progeny" and that "[i]t is obvious that the sun children, miraculously begotten, represent an unexpected capacity for a wide and higher consciousness, superseding a backward and inferior mental state" (CW 10:*823–24*:432–33). This discussion is couched completely in terms of the identification of the archetypal significance of the children. The criticism of the novel that immediately follows—that "[n]othing is said, however, about a higher level of feeling and morality, which would be necessary to compensate and regulate the possibilities of advanced perception and intellect" (CW 10:*823–24*:432–33)—does not, moreover, constitute *literary* criticism, since it ignores possible literary reasons for Wyndham's omission of what to Jung himself is the *necessary* advanced morality that will compensate for advanced intellect. For Wyndham himself, however, and for his readers, the absence of the higher level of feeling is precisely the locus of the children's strangeness: that it is possible to be a sapient being without these particular components in the psyche. What is sapient and what is human, Wyndham suggests, are not necessarily precisely congruent.

Jung himself, moreover, acknowledged that he was not a literary critic. In a letter to Herbert Read in October 1948, acknowledging his pleasure at receiving a copy of Read's *The Green Child* (1935), Jung writes: "I feel not naturally drawn to what one calls 'literature,' but I am strangely attracted by genuine fiction, i.e., fantastical invention" (*C. G. Jung Letters* I: 509). Furthermore, he goes on immediately: "Inasmuch as fantasy is not forced and violated by and subjugated to an intellectually preconceived bastard of an idea, it is a legitimate and authentic offspring of the unconscious mind and thus far it provided me with unadulterated information about the things that transcend the writer's conscious mind. Most writers hate this point of view" (*Letters* I: 509). This comment by Jung does not, I believe (in spite of his attachment to the rules of "intellectually preconceived" science) derogate from the application of Jungian theory to science fiction—at least not with regard to the figure of the Alien, which, as I shall argue, is in *essence* a product of the untrammeled unconscious, although not so in *detail*. Indeed, Jung commits himself only with extreme caution to the idea that analytical (archetypal) psychology may be used as a tool of literary critics, and with the proviso that it should be by others rather than himself. When he added a head note to "*Ulysses*: A Monologue" at the time of its inclusion in *Wirklichkeit der Seele: Anwendungen und Fortschritte der Neueren Pyschologie* (1934), he wrote: "This literary essay . . . is not a scientific treatise. . . . I have included it in the present volume because *Ulysses* is an important 'document humain' very characteristic of our time, and because my opinions may show how ideas that play a considerable role in my work can be applied to literary material" (CW 15:*163*:109*n*).

At the beginning of one of his two papers on psychology and literature, "On the Relation of Analytical Psychology to Poetry," he was careful to point out that "when we [analytical psychologists] speak of the relation of psychology to art, we shall treat only of that aspect of art which can be submitted to psychological scrutiny without violating its nature" (CW 15:99:66). In addition, he acknowledged bluntly that "there is a fundamental difference of attitude between the psychologist's approach to a literary work and that of a literary critic. What is of decisive importance and value for the latter may be quite irrelevant for the former. Indeed, literary products of highly dubious merit are often of the greatest interest to the psychologist" (CW 15:*136*:87–88). It is for this reason, paradoxically, that his archetypal psychology is so peculiarly appropriate in the context of science fiction—particularly in the reading of the Alien.

The paradox arises because science fiction has been persistently marginalized and because, when some science fiction texts were received into the alleged center, it was and is still almost inevitably true, as Sturgeon pointed out bitterly in 1953, that in general "science fiction was the only category [of literature] that was judged by its worst examples rather than its best" (Gunn, e-mail). Jungian psychology, however, itself to some extent still a marginalized theory,[15] does not need to consider the literary status (good or bad, best or worst) of the material with which it deals. The text's literary status per se is immaterial when the literature is examined as the locus of ideas and not judged as the locus of literary value, particularly as literary value is strongly, in modern literature, derived from the writer's psychological and social insight into his or her own culture. A Jungian approach may therefore be able to discriminate—in terms of *relative* success and failure only—among all examples of science fiction in terms that are appropriate to and designed for it, rather than for something else, and therefore it may produce a "truer" reading of the Alien, reaffirming that, like *Ulysses* in Jung's own view, science fiction texts are *documents humains*.

THE OTHERNESS OF THE OTHER

The Alien, it will have become clear by now, is a problematic and elusive concept. The approaches of scientific and psychological theory do not account for a presence characterized, as I shall go on to demonstrate, by fascination, persistence, strangeness, increasing complexity, and almost overwhelming numbers. Scientific theory, although it clearly contributes to understanding the existence and increasing sophistication of science-fictional approaches, does not do anything to explain the essential need that created the concept of the Alien. Similarly, psychological theory, although it has explained assorted images and functions in different aliens and suggested useful approaches to be followed up in understanding the need for, the fascination with, and to some extent the multifariousness of the Alien, has not yet come up with a coherent theory that accounts for its strangeness. But if each approach alone falls short of accounting for what it is that makes the Alien such an attractive and richly rewarding topic for study, together they may offer something more. It is, therefore, possible that an approach that uses elements of both to read the science-fictional Alien may be more productive. But even so, a third theory must also be considered. Alongside the scientific theory and the psychological theory of the Alien there exists the theory of the Alien as an element in a text—a literary phenomenon—and this theory is complex and problematic.

NOTES

1. Wood also recognizes what I term the "inner stranger" in her definition of the stranger:

> The stipulation . . . that the contact shall be a first one between the people concerned separates our concept of the stranger [from] another current one, that of the person who is socially isolated from the members of his group even though he is in daily contact with them. . . . These persons are thought of as strangers to their groups because in certain respects their situation is comparable to that of the individual who has entered the group for the first time; they are in the group but not of it. (43)

2. See Edwin O. Reischauer, *The Japanese* (1981), in which he notes that there has been

> a long time for racial mingling and the development of cultural homogeneity. This process was no doubt aided by the artificial seclusion of Japan from the seventeenth to the nineteenth century and has been further fostered by strong centralized rule since then. But long before this the Japanese had developed a picture of themselves as a racially distinct and pure group, often portrayed in terms of a single great family (35),

and this cultural homogeneity is responsible for the fact that "[t]he foreigner [*gaikoku-jin, gaijin*] in Japan . . . is treated very politely, but always as an outsider" (405). See also Mark Siegel's article "Foreigner as Alien in Japanese Science Fantasy" (1985).

3. The spread of disease is a negative effect as well as an indicator of this increase in globalization. In "Globalization, Development, and the Spread of Disease" (1995), the Harvard Working Group on New and Resurgent Diseases refers to the "sporadic cases of travellers being struck down by tropical diseases" as a concern alongside "[t]he large-scale movement of goods and people around the globe [that] increases the probability of vectors . . . and nonhuman carriers of disease being introduced into areas where neither previously existed" (quoted from website). SARS and avian flu are recent cases in point. More positive, however, is the phenomenon of the FIFA World Cup of Football, the final match of which in 2002 was estimated by television network executives to have been watched by approximately one and a quarter billion people—almost a quarter of the world's population.

4. It is in this context of the human stranger that Julia Kristeva's Freudian study, *Étrangers à Nous Mêmes* (1988; translated as *Strangers to Ourselves*, 1991) operates. It is a study of the psychological stranger *within* the individual, in the context of theories of social alienation, as well as a psychosocial discussion of historical strangerhood as this relates to the issue of the integration of immigrants into French society in the critical years following World War II.

5. It is usually cited as "Yes, Virginia, There Is a Santa Claus!" but the actual title is "Is There a Santa Claus?"

6. The well-known writer of supernatural fantasy, H. P. Lovecraft, opened "The Call of Cthulhu" (1928) with the sentence "The most merciful thing in the world is the inability of the human mind to correlate all its contents" (45). Merciful or not, it is certainly common. Many people who do not admit to being believers in the supernatural can be observed behaving as though they are.

7. It is often argued that the alleged extraterrestrial aliens of the UFO debates are merely survivals of the supernatural Alien masked by technological decoration, often by borrowing from science fiction rather than science. Contempt for adherents of UFO beliefs is widespread, although not universal, among members of the science fiction community. For example, in *The Creation of Tomorrow*, Paul Carter's "Genealogy of Magazines Cited" includes *Other Worlds* (1949–1957) and comments that it "changed [its] name in 1957 to *Flying Saucers from Other Worlds*, and thereupon ceased to be a science fiction magazine" (x). This contempt is not always appreciated outside the science fiction community: George W. Earley, in his preface to *Encounters with Aliens* (1968), an anthology of stories about "UFOs and Alien Beings in Science Fiction," makes the singularly idiosyncratic claim that "to judge by the reactions of many in the science fiction field, the idea of visiting aliens in the here-and-now is

more than disquieting: it is downright frightening" (19). Earley offers no evidence in the form of specific references, other than anecdotal, for this assertion. Whether or not the aliens in encounter narratives are merely masked supernatural others, they have very little in common with the aliens of science fiction, as they are, unlike those in science fiction, stereotypically repetitive in form and behavior.

8. Even Stephen Hawking was at least acquainted with Kingsley Amis, Aldous Huxley, C. S. Lewis, William Golding, and John Wyndham, according to his biographers (White and Gribbin, *Stephen Hawking: A Life in Science* 10).

9. "This legislation was buried in a batch of regulations very few members of government probably bothered to read in its entirety, and was slipped onto the books without public debate" (Lyster 1).

10. Similar passion, however, *is* generated in anthropological circles over human ancestry (see Roger Lewin's *Bones of Contention: Controversies in the Search for Human Origins*, 1987) and human genetic inheritance as depicted by sociobiology (see Andrew Brown's *The Darwin Wars*, 1999). There is a curious symmetry in the way so much passion is devoted to the past (unchangeable) and the future (unknowable), whereas the present—living and changeable—is carefully distanced as far as possible from any passion at all.

11. Numerous arguments have been raised against its use as a critical approach to literature in general, and on both theoretical and practical grounds. As James Baird points out in "Jungian Psychology in Criticism: Theoretical Problems" (1976), "The intrusion of Jung upon the field of full critical authority has been answered to in our time by indifference and more often fury" (18). But although Baird himself identifies problems, beginning with what he sees as "the problem of the anagogic" (4) fundamental to Jung's ideas, even he is prepared to admit that Jung's theories have their uses.

12. I shall return to Golden's book in chapter 7.

13. A black gaseous cloud enters our solar system and starts to occlude the sun, threatening the survival of all life on Earth. Scientists discover it to be sapient, enter into communication with it, and persuade it to move on, removing the threat. As it leaves, an attempt is made to transfer some of its advanced knowledge into the mind of one of the scientists, but the attempt kills him by overloading his brain.

14. During a mysterious blackout of the village of Midwich, all women in the area are simultaneously impregnated by an unknown force. They later all simultaneously give birth to ostensibly human children with strange golden eyes, children who possess

high-level *psi* powers of compulsion and destruction, which they use to terrorize the original inhabitants of the village. In the end, however, they are destroyed.

15. This marginalization began to narrow, as Rupprecht points out in "Archetypal Theory and Criticism" (1994), "with the rise in the 1980s of reader-response theory and criticism" (39).

Nailing Jelly to a Tree: Theorizing the Alien

Given the particularity of the way it is written, science fiction needs to be read not as anomalous mainstream fiction (as it has so often been) but as a separate genre (sui generis), so that its most popular trope, the Alien, would then be read in an appropriate context. Unfortunately, it is not easy to identify science fiction so that it can be read as science fiction, for its texts (not least those short-story texts with which I am concerned here) are, like Freud's infant, "polymorphously perverse" ("Transformations of Puberty" 1965, 139).[1] Under the tent of a literary theory of science fiction, some critics use the traditional (prestructural and structural) tools of novel criticism and some use the new (poststructural and postmodernist) tools. Neither group appears to be truly comfortable with the problematics of the genre, which have been additionally increased because, like a cat in the clutch of an affectionate toddler struggling to escape capture without forfeiting its place in the household, science fiction wriggles and squirms to except itself from the clutch of theory without forfeiting its recognition as part of the literary spectrum. In general, however, critical approaches to the extraterrestrial Alien up to the mid-1980s divide into three categories: those using pre-poststructuralist (traditional) theories, those using poststructuralist (postmodernist) theories, and those using feminist theories.[2] All theories of the Alien, however, require the Alien to function as a trope for encoding meaning within a text.

THE TRADITIONAL CRITICS AND THE OTHER

Prior to 1968, because of the marginalization of the genre, critical studies of science fiction other than book reviews were rare and were largely carried out on an ad hoc basis as far as theoretical positioning is concerned, as is the case in one of the earliest and most influential studies—Kingsley Amis's *New Maps of Hell* (1960). The traditional critics of science fiction tend to be structuralist in orientation, and they state or imply that the Other, in the natural but ex-traterrestrial form of the Alien, operates as a trope, whether for entertain-ment, for literary effect, for didactic purposes, for heuristic experiment, or, sometimes, for two or more of these purposes simultaneously. These ap-proaches are employed, implied, or explicitly described by academics, writers, and readers alike. Unlike the hypotheses of scientists, traditional critical ap-proaches do not concern themselves to any great extent with the possible real existence of aliens, and, unlike the hypotheses of the science fiction commu-nity (writers, editors, and fans), they do not usually concern themselves with the inherent strangeness of the Alien.

Common to all theories of the Alien as a trope of whatever sort, however, is the assumption of a structuralist narratological approach to science fiction. In this approach, the literary trope is part of a theory that considers a narrative as a structure of movable parts susceptible of exchange, substitution, ordering, reordering, interpretation, and so on. The early (structuralist) twentieth-century narratology that invaded the understanding of the nature of science fiction, not only by critics but also by writers, derived principally from Vladimir Propp, Victor Shklovsky, Claude Lévi-Strauss, and Tzvetan Todorov. Narratology is Stanislaw Lem's approach, therefore, in "On the Structural Analysis of Science Fiction" (1973), and is important in Darko Suvin's con-struction of science fiction, subsequent to his characterization of it as *"the lit-erature of cognitive estrangement"* ("On the Poetics of the Science Fiction Genre" 1972, 4; original emphasis)[3] and as a literature of metaphor and para-ble in *Positions and Presuppositions in Science Fiction* (1988).[4]

Although a generalized theory of science fiction as literature was late in ap-pearing, when one did so it became very influential within a short time. Suvin's "On the Poetics of the Science Fiction Genre" gave the genre a significant boost toward academic and critical respectability. In this article Suvin argues for "a def-inition of SF as the *literature of cognitive estrangement*" (372; original emphasis), grounding his argument for *estrangement* on Victor Shklovsky's term *ostranenie*, modified by Brecht's observation that "[a] representation which estranges is one which allows us to recognize its subject, but at the same time makes it seem unfamiliar" (Brecht, "Short Organon for the Theater" 1948; cited in Suvin 1972, 374), so that "the look of estrangement is both cognitive and creative" (374). Suvin, moreover, includes a strong and explicit claim in the article that

> [science fiction] is an educational literature . . . irreversibly shaped by the pathos of preaching the good word of human curiosity, fear, and hope. Significant SF . . . demands from the author and reader, teacher and critic, not merely specialized, quantified positivistic knowledge (*scientia*) but a social imagination whose quality, whose wisdom (*sapientia*), testifies to the maturity of his critical and creative thought. (381)

Suvin's theory of science fiction as "an educational literature" provided a substantial directive for subsequent critics to circumscribe the genre in terms appropriate to such pedagogical (in the widest sense) function.

Until Suvin's article achieved its effect of making science fiction respectable, however, the notion of the science-fictional Alien as an entertainment trope was the most frequently offered. According to C. S. Lewis in "On Science Fiction" (1977), the entertainment provided by the Alien is a "keen, lasting, and solemn pleasure" (129). In "Biologies and Environments" in *The Visual Encyclopedia of Science Fiction* (1977), however, Brian Ash, commenting on Stanley Weinbaum's "A Martian Odyssey" (1934), suggests merely amusement rather than pleasure in mentioning the story's "catalogue of bizarre lifeforms" (93). For Jack Williamson, also in *The Visual Encyclopedia,* in his contribution on "Exploration and Colonies," the Alien seems to be one among many of the tropes for the satisfaction of curiosity found in science fiction: "[W]e all long to see what lies beyond the hill" (78). In general, discussions of the Alien as an entertainment trope do not provide any more information about the nature of strangeness than the fact that strangeness entertains the reader.

In those theories in which the Alien is considered to function straightforwardly as metaphor, the Alien is the signifier for a signified that can vary from text to text, from author to author, and from critic to critic. As early as 1953, in his introduction to *Space Space Space: Stories about the Time When Men Will Be Adventuring to the Stars,* an anthology of science fiction in which six of the ten stories involve aliens, William Sloane announces that "[a]lthough some of the characters in [the stories] are beings from other worlds, if you look at them closely enough they will prove to be alive only insofar as they are derived from what the author has learned about himself and the rest of us. People are people, and all we know is in some way or other a reflection of ourselves" (11–12). The Alien in this and similar discussion is no more than a metaphor for other kinds of people, or even other people. Similarly, Paul Rice in a cogent discussion of the Alien as a metaphor, "Metaphor as a Way of Saying the Self in Science Fiction" (1983), considers the Alien as a proleptic metaphor of the human self: "It may be that through the suggestion of selves not human we are glimpsing human possibility" (14). For Ursula Le Guin, however, the Alien is a metaphor for the unconscious. In her essay, "Science Fiction and Mrs. Brown" (1976), using the example of what happens when Virginia Woolf's naturalistically portrayed Mrs. Brown is introduced into the context of the highly conventionalized science fiction narrative, Le Guin discusses the problem of reconciling science fiction and naturalistic fiction:

> Could it be that Mrs. Brown is actually, in some way, too large, for the spaceship? That she is, you might say, too *round* for it—so that when she steps into it, somehow . . . the sinister and beautiful aliens suddenly appear to be, most strangely, not alien at all, but mere elements of Mrs. Brown herself, lifelong and familiar, though startling, inhabitants of Mrs. Brown's unconscious mind?[5] (103)

In effect, Le Guin here not only points to the Alien as a metaphor for unconscious energy or material but also implies that the Alien is *always* a metaphor. Peter Nicholls, in his introduction to *Science Fiction at Large* (1976), the collection of articles in which Le Guin's piece appears, makes the same point: "The importance of science fiction can only be that it speaks to us of the real world. . . . Science fiction works primarily through metaphor. To read it literally is not to hear its profoundest and most disturbing reverberations" (8). For him, in fact, the Alien appears to be only one of the submetaphors of a genre that is as a whole metaphoric.

In asserting the metaphoric nature of science fiction, however, Nicholls could point to the detailed arguments of Suvin's second substantial and influential discussion of the prosaics of science fiction, *Positions and Presuppositions in Science Fiction* (1988), in particular to the conclusion, "SF as Metaphor, Parable and Chronotope (with the Bad Conscience of Reaganism)," as an authoritative contribution to the discussion. Patrick Parrinder in

"The Alien Encounter: Or Mrs. Brown and Mrs. Le Guin" (1979), however, stops short of this, arguing that "[t]he choice of alien features is always meaningful, whether or not it carries an openly satirical, ironic or didactic reference to human life; aliens in literature must always be constructed on some principle of analogy or contrast with the human world. It follows from this that aliens in SF invariably possess a metaphorical dimension" (52). Parrinder's argument is important in that it distinguishes, as other arguments do not, between individual aliens and concept of the Alien. That any individual alien may be read as metaphor is obvious—that the class "alien" is metaphor less so. Indeed, if handled carelessly, treating the Alien as a metaphor can be reductive in the extreme, since it may ignore or exclude or blur much of what makes the Alien strange and fascinating.

In theories of the Alien as metaphor, moreover, metaphor (in the sense in which it is used in such theories) becomes problematic because it is essentially a closed system. Metaphor requires equation: $A = B$; the Alien is a "reference to human life" (Parrinder, "The Alien Encounter" 1979, 52). The danger of this theory of the science-fictional Alien as metaphor is perhaps that if everything in science fiction becomes metaphoric discourse, the value of metaphor as a specific interpretative trope for particular elements such as the Alien (an element Rice in fact draws attention to) is lost.

Closely related to metaphor and also used in discussion of the Alien is the icon. More persuasively than the advocates of the Alien as metaphor, Gary Wolfe, in *The Known and the Unknown: The Iconography of Science Fiction* (1979), discusses the Alien as icon: "Like a stereotype or a convention, an icon is something we are willing to accept because of our familiarity with the genre, but unlike ordinary conventions, an icon often retains its power even when isolated from the context of conventional narrative structures" (16). By treating the Alien as an icon, Wolfe is able to account for much of what treating it as a metaphor does not: The icon can be a structural device that involves cultural and psychological significance as well as literary effect. He relegates the Alien, however, to subordinate status as part of the more comprehensive icon of the monster: "However civilized or technological they may be, science fiction aliens clearly partake of the icon of the monster" (202). The fascination of the Alien as monster, he implies, is due to our fear: "The unknown becomes the more fearsome through the knowledge that it contains an intelligence other than our own. . . . Even to conceive of an alien intelligence is to conceive, at some deep level, of an invasion of one's own personality by outside forces, or a violation of one's community by strangers" (205). Wolfe's use of strongly emotive terms (*fearsome, invasion, violation*) argues for a very strongly felt and very specific response to the icon of the Alien. It is not at all clear, however, that such a response is common to all, or even to the majority, of science fiction readers, and it does not account for the constant recurrence of certain types of alien: the guardian or the companion, for example. Consequently, although by defining the Alien as icon rather than as metaphor Wolfe substantially increases our understanding of its compelling fascination, by subsuming it into the category of monster he imposes an unnecessary constraint upon its field of significance.

More general functions of the Alien are, however, also identifiable. To begin with, from the point of view of the nonspecialist reader and the writer, the science-fictional Alien has a considerable practical utility, as Brian Ash points out. In his definition of "aliens and extraterrestrials" in *Who's Who in Science Fiction* (1976), in fact, he suggests that the usefulness of the Alien as a structural device for creating conflict is its primary importance: "The interaction between humans and aliens is the basis of many plots. They may fight, cooperate, or sometimes simply ignore each other" (12). Ash also draws attention to its allegorical and didactic possibilities as "[a] ripe area for allegories of human behavior and speculative treatments of the nature of perception and communication. It also provides scope for illustrating the relative importance or insignificance of Man when he encounters beings of lesser or greater intelligence" (12). This utility has probably had considerable influence on the popularity of the Alien in science fiction, most strongly perhaps in the early years of the pulp magazine tales in which the preferred stories were "action stories" in which effective plot devices were in considerable demand. The first editor of *Astounding*, F. Harry Bates, mentions this in an editorial piece, "Additions—Improvements" (1933), announcing a change of emphasis in story requirements for the magazine:

> Finally, hereafter, we are going to require our authors to put more science in most of the stories they write for you. We have come to feel . . . that the greater number would be pleased if we departed a little from our established "action" story policy in the direction of one embodying more science. It will not be easy

to get this new kind of story, for we will not allow anything to clog the flow, to retard the pace, to interfere in any noticeable way with the *story* values we have always given in our fiction. (420–21)

The increasing sophistication of science fiction as it moves away from the early emphasis on action stories has to some extent also reduced the emphasis on plot. Nevertheless, the popularity of the Alien has not been similarly reduced.

Equally, however, the Alien appears in critical discussion as a moral trope, revealing by its nature and presence a moral truth. Gardner Dozois takes this approach in his introduction to *Aliens!*: "[J]ust as a distorting funhouse mirror can sometimes present the clearest picture of a man, so it may be that we see ourselves most plain and most instructively when we look into the face of the Alien" (xi). The Alien as moral trope, in the form of a mirror presenting ways of recognizing inherent and important truths about humans (such as relationships between human beings of different sorts), has, like the Alien as practical warning, as much usefulness in general terms as any other moral trope.

Moral lessons certainly and probably practical lessons also, are, however, selectively targeted in science fiction. Ursula Le Guin, for example, argues in her essay "American SF and the Other" (1975) that serious political discussion or speculation is absent from science fiction. Although the reader can easily find the sexual, social, cultural, and racial Alien in science fiction, she points out, there is at least one noticeable omission: "the social Alien . . . 'the proletariat'. . . . Are they ever persons, in SF? No. . . . The people, in SF, are not people. They are masses, existing for one purpose: to be led by their superiors. From the social point of view most SF has been incredibly regressive and unimaginative" (98). Science fiction, it is implied here, could function as a form of political manifesto by engaging itself with the notion of what Le Guin terms the "social Alien." (There are, no doubt, other similar gaps that no one has yet identified in science fiction's engagement with human aspects in alien disguise.) But neither Le Guin's identification of the missing proletariat or "social Alien" nor the possibility of other missing aliens does anything to address the actual concept underlying what we call the Alien and/or alterity.[6]

The theory of the Alien as a didactic trope is also popular, in part at least because it agrees well with the notion of science fiction as a form of instructional literature. This notion has been evident although not always agreed with by writers and readers in the field from an early stage in its history. In the early pages of *Astounding*, for example, its second editor, F. Orlin Tremaine, introducing a new feature called "Science Discussions" in the December 1936 issue, announced:

> We have always faced an unwarranted bias on the part of a large portion of the educational world against "pulp" magazines as a class. . . . I am going to break down this opposition bit by bit until we are recognized as a distinct corollary of the sciences. . . . Our fiction weaves a spell by projecting, through logic, the basic truths presented factually through the various education media. . . . We must so plan that twenty years hence it will be said that *Astounding Stories* has served as the cradle of modern science. (152)

Although he does not mention the Alien specifically in this remark, he clearly indicates that science fiction in general should have a truly practical function as what might be called extracurricular science lessons, and it may be assumed that the topic of extraterrestrial intelligence would have been for him as valid as any other science topic included in the magazine's pages. In the same line of direct instruction, Robert Silverberg, writing a blurb (a brief introduction) for Randall Garrett's "The Best Policy" (1957) in *Earthmen and Strangers* (1968), offers the Alien as a practical warning about future human behavior: "When human beings begin to encounter strangers in the universe, conflict is likely to erupt. Earthmen, by and large, are an aggressive sort of people, and it would not be surprising to run into a race of equally aggressive, militaristic creatures Out There. This could produce a nasty crash as one culture meets the other in a head-on impact" (46). Allowing for a certain amount of exaggeration (not confined to Silverberg) on the subject of human aggressivity, there is enough evidence in history to suggest that such a practical warning might be valid and necessary in general terms.

At its most extreme, the use of the image of the alien as a didactic trope is found in those anthologies of science fiction compiled for use as readers in various academic disciplines. Such volumes as *Introductory Psychology through Science Fiction*, edited by Harvey A. Katz, Martin H. Greenberg, and Patricia S. Warrick (1977); *Sociology through Science Fiction*, edited by John W. Milstead, Martin H. Greenberg, Joseph D. Olander, and Patricia S. Warrick (1974); *Anthropology through Science Fiction*, edited by Carol Mason, Martin H. Greenberg, and Patricia S. Warrick (1974); *Apeman, Spaceman: Anthropological Science Fic-*

tion, edited by Harry Harrison and Leon E. Stover (1968); *American Government through Science Fiction*, edited by Joseph D. Olander (1974); and *Marriage and the Family through Science Fiction*, edited by Val Clear (1976), can be found on university library shelves and in university bookstores as teaching aids in the various social sciences for which they are designed. For the teaching of philosophy, also, *Philosophy and Science Fiction*, edited by Michael Philips (1984), and *Thought Probes: Philosophy through Science Fiction Literature*, compiled by Fred D. Miller Jr. and Nicholas D. Smith (1989), are available. How useful they are to the instructor concerned must be the business of the instructor, but the portrayal of the Alien in stories included within them can only be diminished by this relentless insistence on science fiction's utility as a classroom adjunct.

The theory of the science-fictional Alien as a heuristic rather than a didactic trope is less frequent. Basically, in a heuristic text the writer sets up a ficton or a narrative in order to find out what inferences may be drawn from it, whereas in a didactic text the writer sets up a ficton or narrative in order to teach a lesson that is already known or decided upon. It could be argued that once a heuristic text is written and published, it becomes didactic, but I am not convinced by such an argument, and even if it were valid, the initial distinction would not be eliminated. The heuristic trope is explained by Le Guin, in her essay "Is Gender Necessary?" (1976), in the course of making clear that her own creation of Gethen and its androgynous inhabitants (from *The Left Hand of Darkness*) was not to serve as a model for humanity but to explore certain possibilities of gender:

> I was not recommending the Gethenian sexual setup: I was using it. It was a heuristic device, a thought-experiment. . . . The experiment is performed, the question is asked, in the mind. . . . [M]y Gethenians . . . are simply a way of thinking. They are questions, not answers; process, not stasis. One of the essential functions of science fiction . . . is precisely this kind of question-asking: reversals of an habitual way of thinking, metaphors for what our language has no words for as yet, experiments in imagination. (163)

Le Guin's point that the Alien is only one of many heuristic tropes in science fiction is well-taken. In fact, in the novel she introduces the idea that the Gethenians may be the result of genetic engineering experiments from a proto-stock that has elsewhere produced humans, which changes the nature of the experiment. On the other hand, however, Greg Benford, in discussing the creation of aliens in "Aliens and Knowability: A Scientist's Perspective" (1980), sees this particular heuristic experiment of Le Guin's as in fact no more than a didactic trope:

> The sexual strangeness of the Gethenians in Ursula Le Guin's *Left Hand of Darkness*, for example, is a distancing trope, a way to examine our own problems in a different light. In countless lesser works aliens are really stand-in humans . . . quasi-human, with emotions and motivations not much different from our own. Aliens as mirrors for our own experiences abound in science fiction. (54)

Benford's comments, however, merely reflect the fact that the line between the heuristic trope and the didactic trope may be a little blurred in specific instances. Even he does not seem to be claiming that the science-fictional Alien is always a didactic trope, for elsewhere in the same essay he indicates that the science-fictional Alien can indeed operate as heuristic trope. In his discussion of Hal Clement's novel, *Mission of Gravity* (1978), he points out that one of the things the Mesklinites of the novel (like other science-fictional aliens) illustrate or explore is a general theory about the biological roots of psychology: "This 'biology as destiny' theme occurs often in science fiction, but, like the Mesklinites, the aliens of such stories commonly speak like Midwesterners of the 1950s and are otherwise templates of stock humans" ("Aliens and Knowability" 54). His complaint that the strangeness of the Mesklinites is limited to the directly demonstrable effects of their biological strangeness on their psychology is to some degree valid. But it cannot be construed to imply that no heuristic experiment is going on—simply that the heuristic experiment of the Mesklinites as Clements carries it out in his novel is flawed.

As a heuristic trope, moreover, the Alien is used in a wide variety of experiments by a number of different authors and may be used to explore philosophical, psychological, and other problems. Robert Plank, for example, using Philip José Farmer's *Strange Relations* (1960) as his example, suggests that the Alien can be used by writers to speculate about the roots of behavior important to individuals: "[F]antasy about the role of sexuality in the relationship between men and alien species, however, is not particularly concerned with intercourse, but goes beyond it in two directions: in exploring the question of mutual sexual attraction, and the question of fertility" (*Imaginary Beings* 96). Heuristic experiments may be performed on topics concerning societies as well as individuals. Frank Herbert, like Ursula Le Guin, looks at his own work, and, writing in "The ConSentiency—And How It Got That Way" (1977) about his novels and stories set in the multispecies universe he calls the ConSentiency, he describes the aliens who populate it as deliberate heuristic experiments. He explains that his experimentation was initiated when he looked at some of the important cultural determinants current in contemporary human democracies: "I began taking out and examining some of my most dearly beloved assumptions: That Law will always bring justice provided you perfect the Law. ... Delays are bad. ... Red tape is evil. ... Small is inefficient and ugly" (6). He goes on to point out that the novels are experiments in which aliens of different sorts test those assumptions by virtue of their alienness: "McKie's universe is peopled by various sentient beings who function to hold those *beloved assumptions* up to a crueler examination" (7). Herbert's assumptions are located in the realm of the practical, but more abstract problems are explored by other writers. In *Alien Encounters* (1981), Mark Rose discusses the theme of a story by Cordwainer Smith in which a young man falls in love telepathically with the female purebred cat who is his mental partner in fighting the psychic menace of the "dragons." Rose points out that "the transfer of the cats from the category of the nonhuman to the human in 'The Game of Rat and Dragon' involves the appearance of the alien in the form of the nameless monsters of the void" (190). For Rose, one of the everpresent themes of science fiction is just this distinction between the human and the nonhuman. As he describes Smith's narrative strategy in the story, it is clear that, consciously or unconsciously on Smith's part, the alien "dragons" become the instrument of a heuristic experiment in the definition of human and nonhuman categories.

The Alien as heuristic trope suffers, however, to some extent like the Alien as didactic trope, from the disadvantage that the end is implied in the nature of the trope. The nature of the results of each experiment is implicit in the way the experiment is designed and in the choice of what is chosen for experimentation. But unlike the didactic trope, the heuristic trope is at least open to a range of possible ends. Theories considering the Alien as a heuristic trope go further toward developing the understanding of strangeness per se than theories of the Alien as didactic trope, but do not solve the problem altogether.

The Alien is also seen by mythopoeic critics considering science fiction as a part of the larger literary continuum as one of the characteristics of that larger continuum translated into specifically science-fictional terms, although not specifically as a didactic or heuristic trope. Fredericks, Rose, and Rabkin, therefore, all consider the Alien in terms of the characteristics of science fiction as a romance-mode narrative. In his article, "Revivals of Ancient Mythologies in Current Science Fiction and Fantasy" (1977), for example, S. C. Fredericks, in considering science fiction's mythopoeic nature, sees the Alien as a trope of displacement. Fredericks claims that in Stanley Weinbaum's stories, "the planets Mars and Venus, filled with alien and unpredictable life-forms, ripe for exploration and adventure, provide a displacement in science fiction terms of the ancient *Odyssey*'s fairytale lands" (51). The Alien functions similarly for Mark Rose in his discussion, in *Alien Encounters: Anatomy of Science Fiction* (1981), of the displacement characteristic of the romance mode in science fiction's thematic treatment of the human and the nonhuman: "The nonhuman in science fiction may be conceived positively. . . . Alternatively, the nonhuman may be conceived negatively as a form of the diabolic in dystopias and some alien invasion stories" (41). Eric Rabkin implies a very similar function in his discussion of the relationship between fairy tale and science fiction. His major point is that the fairy tale's talking animal is matched in science fiction by the Alien: "Science fiction writers, giving us back Adam's innocence, often allow their protagonists communication with animals, especially animals in the guise of aliens—and yet, with all of imagination to choose from, these science-fictional animals are typically just revisions of the fairy tale stereotypes" ("Fairy Tales and Science Fiction" 1980, 86–87). I shall return later to these discussions by Rose and Rabkin.

The traditional criticism identifying the science-fictional Alien as a standard encoding trope is common, if not ubiquitous, in exploring its nature. A standard encoding trope (as I have already noted) exchanges two senses, so that X = Y, as the textbooks illustrate it. *Alien*, however, is not a term that has a specified sense to be exchanged but a symbol for the unknown: Any trope in which *alien* appears as one term must have "?" as the other. At issue here is the question of strangeness.

There are other substantial disadvantages to considering the Alien as a trope of the standard kind. If, on the one hand, it is done without taking into account such other special features of the genre as the entirely nonliterary requirement for scientific propriety, the result may well be of dubious value, since this requirement may skew the presentation of the nature of the Alien in a way that may totally obscure the real metaphoric or iconic significance of the particular alien being considered, or cloud the moral issue being presented. If, on the other hand, the requirement *is* taken into account, the tropic significance of the Alien is often revealed to be not very interesting—a straightforward mask for a variety of human aspects or activities. Moreover, considering the Alien as trope does little to explain its compelling quality, for, as a metaphor, it appears to have little more compelling power than other metaphors. But the real objection to theories reducing the science-fictional Alien to a form of didactic trope is that a didactic trope is something which by its nature can teach us only that which is already known at least to the one who tries to teach it. The end is implied in the nature of the trope. Furthermore, considering the Alien merely as a trope for teaching, whatever the lesson (practical, moral, or other), necessarily evades the issue of the kind or extent of the Alien's strangeness. If it is sufficiently strange, it is not available to teach us anything very useful, whereas if it is not sufficiently strange, it will not attract enough attention to be effective.

Consequently, it is evident that although all traditional theories of the Alien as a literary trope address to some extent one or another of its qualities, all of them fall short of accounting fully for all of those qualities. The strangeness (above all), the persistent fascination, and the increasing complexity of the Alien in science fiction ultimately escape being pinned down by accounting for the Alien in terms of traditional literary approaches.

THE POSTSTRUCTURAL THEORISTS AND THE ALIEN

Some of what happened to science fiction in the wake of the tsunami of poststructuralist theory that broke over North America's academia in the form of the international conference entitled "The Languages of Criticism and the Sciences of Man" at the Johns Hopkins University in October 1966 should not have happened to a bug-eyed monster (*bem*).[7] Nearly all critical discussions of science fiction that postdate this event, however, are either postmodernist (however that may be defined) or feminist (with the latter incorporating much of the former's methodology) in approach, although some critics of science fiction, empowered by the distinguished theorists behind a particular theory, have made forays into such other esoteric poststructuralist activities as exo-semiotics (Sofia) and suture theory (de Vos). In 1989, Samuel R. Delany, a well-known writer of and theorist about science fiction, addressed the subject of literary theory and its relation to science fiction in a three-part article in the *New York Review of Science Fiction*: "Neither the Beginning nor the End of Structuralism, Post-Structuralism, Semiotics, or Deconstruction for SF Readers: An Introduction" (February, March, April 1989). Somewhat later, Damien Broderick, also a writer and theorist, wrote two important studies addressing the question of critical theory and science fiction: *Reading by Starlight* (1995) and *Theory and Its Discontents* (1997). Delany and Broderick, both working from a practical grounding in writing science fiction, do a great deal to illustrate the practice of theory in relation to science fiction. On the purely theoretical side, the relationship of critical theory to science fiction is subject both to summary articulation, such as that by Istvan Csicsery-Ronay in "Postmodernism's SF/SF's Postmodernism" (1991) and by Brian McHale in "Science Fiction," in *International Postmodernism: Theory and Literary Practice* (1997), and to extended discussion such as that by Barbara Puschmann-Nalenz in *Science Fiction and Postmodern Fiction: A Genre Study* (1992) and by Carl Freedman in *Critical Theory and Science Fiction* (2000). Michael Swanwick's "A User's Guide to the Postmoderns" (1986), however, is a discussion of personalities active in the development of cyberpunk and other science-fictional styles, rather than a discussion of the theory involved.

Postmodernism established itself as the theory of preference for the academic discussion of science fiction almost immediately after the arrival of poststructuralism (of which it is a major component). In "Postmodernism's SF/SF's Postmodernism," his editorial introduction to the November 1991 issue of *Science Fiction Studies*—a special issue on science fiction and postmodernism—Istvan Csicsery-Ronay claims that

> [l]inking postmodernism and SF is hardly a new thing; many of SF's most sophisticated commentators have been doing it for the past 15 years. . . . What is it about these two shadowy concepts, postmodernism and SF, that draws them together? Postmodernism has been defined and re-defined enough times to have taken on a shape, a silhouette—but it is the silhouette of an enigmatically protean form. Every discipline seems to have a different focus, drawing on different sources for support—sometimes texts, sometimes artwork, sometimes empirical phenomena. SF has an advantage over most other disciplines in that it has had something like a theory of postmodernism ingrained in its futurism for many years. (305)

This positioning of the participants, however, gives the impression that science fiction has finally been given its proper due and been belatedly acknowledged as real literature: the peasant outsider bringing vigor and vitality into the aristocratic but enervated elite. While making a similar claim for postmodernism as the theory of choice in the discussion of science fiction, Brian McHale positions the same two participants differently. In "Science Fiction" (1997) he writes forthrightly and in overt metaphorical terms: "'Discovered' only belatedly, science fiction (SF) is today being actively colonized by the discourses of postmodernist theory and criticism" (235). He goes on to say, moreover, that

> [i]n effect, by the 1980s the intertextual network through which popular SF motifs, imagery, "ideas," etc. circulate among SF texts—and about which the SF community, writers and fans alike, are impressively knowledgeable and self-conscious (see Delany 1988)—had merged with the intertextual field of "high-art" postmodernist fiction to such an extent that materials, motifs and discourses now circulate nearly as freely between popular SF and postmodernist fiction as they do within the SF genre proper. Nevertheless, the strata remain functionally and institutionally distinct; this is not a case of "convergence" so much as symbiosis. (237)

In spite of the difference of perspective, however, both Csicsery-Ronay and McHale are agreed on the significant intersection of science fiction and "'high-art' postmodernist fiction" and on what specifically science fiction brings to that intersection. The contribution, which McHale in the preceding quotation calls "material, motifs and discourses," is described by Csicery-Ronay as "a treasury of powerful metaphors and icons capturing the reality of insecure borders: the Female Man, xenogenesis, the cyborg, the simulacrum, viral language, cyberspace, Mechs and Shapers, and many others" (306). In his list of metaphors and icons and his "body of privileged allegories" (305), however, Csicsery-Ronay does not include the Alien (unless this is what he means by xenogenesis). McHale, too, ignores this particular motif in his article. He does mention aliens in *Constructing Postmodernism* (1992), but only in the context of an argument for "an enduring angel-function," which "[i]n our own time . . . has been largely 'science-fictionized,' ceded to aliens from outer space" (202). In his note to this point, however, he includes, alongside the science fiction aliens of Stanislaw Lem's *Solaris* (1961) and Stanley Kubrick's classic space film *2001: A Space Odyssey* (1968), the "everyday-or-garden-variety aliens which are the staple of *National Enquirer* UFO stories" (299), without any distinction between their ontological status as fiction (in the former case) and "urban myth"/folklore (in the latter). In support of this identification, however, he cites Joanna Russ as having "explicitly made the connection between angels and aliens in her story 'Souls' (from *Extra(Ordinary) People* 1984)" (299). This marginalization of aliens in the postmodernist approach to science fiction is not surprising in view of the condition of humanity that postmodernist literature purports to reflect and reveal and postmodernist theory purports to interpret. Although postmodernism seems to be susceptible of endless and iterative definition, I do not propose to redefine it here. Instead, I will appropriate (a good feminist if not a good postmodernist critical tactic) Csicsery-Ronay's observation that it is an "an enigmatically protean form" (305), and proceed by interrogating within science fiction's self-acknowledged characteristics those earmarks (or what Linda Hutcheon, in *A Poetics of Postmodernism*, 1988, calls "common denominators"; 612) by which postmodernist literature is generally identified for the edification of students and other curious people in the critical wilderness. Here, therefore, I deliberately, in the italicized phrases, quote from the standard and simplified description in well-known student guides, Holman and Harmon's *A Handbook to Literature* (1986) and Chris Baldick's *Concise Oxford Dictionary of Literary Terms* (1990), as well as from Hutcheon.

Presenting itself postmodernistically in many texts, science fiction is, like postmodernist fiction in general, *characterized by a superabundance of disconnected images and styles* (Baldick 1990, 174), since in terms of textural style (cadence, diction, vocabulary, syntax)—if that word means anything still—writers of science fiction are, until they develop personal styles (idiolects), all over the map from Rider Haggard to Margaret Atwood, via J. R. R. Tolkein, Ernest Hemingway, and Raymond Chandler. Furthermore, like postmodernist mainstream fiction texts, individual texts of science fiction can display themselves, to borrow Baldick's characterization, as *self-consciously "depthless" works of fabulation, pastiche, bricolage, or aleatory disconnection* (Baldick 1990, 175). Moreover, considered in terms of Linda Hutcheon's definition, they can exhibit *reflexivity* and *irony*, as well as the *mixing of popular and high art forms* that she suggests are characteristic of postmodernist fiction (Hutcheon 1988, 612). I would also point out that they are governed by "extratextual referentiality" as a sine qua non—a work that fails to establish explicitly accurate reference to extratextual scientific knowledge in particular is, as I have previously noted, not science fiction; and they practice intertextual referentiality (with other science fiction texts as well as fantasy texts and the texts of mainstream fiction) naturally, casually, incessantly—and purely for fun—and they acknowledge influence liberally (the "anxiety" of influence would seem absurd to most science fiction writers).

Science fiction, however, presents not only as postmodernist and nonpostmodernist but also as modernist and nonmodernist. Presenting as modernist texts, science fiction texts, therefore, create within themselves *an ordered universe* (Holman and Harmon 1986). They *construct intricate forms.* They *interweave symbols elaborately.* They *oppose some established present order.* They exhibit *historical discontinuity.* But the way in which they conform to the characteristics of modernism seriously deforms the definitions of those characteristics. The ordered universe that science fiction texts create—referred to usually as "the future"—is a universe without ontological status, and its order may throw our notions of order into disarray (a *contraterrene* or *antimatter* universe, for example, or a universe whose chronicity runs contrary to our own); the established order they subvert by the invention of the future universe is the whole of the past and present universe; and the historical discontinuity they adopt is dissociation from time. As well as exhibiting the "normal" historical discontinuity that characterizes mainstream texts, science fiction texts also exhibit the "special" historical discontinuity of the discontinuity of future from past (with the actual present as their past) and hence from history, although paradoxically many science fiction texts are deeply concerned with the nature of time, especially although not exclusively in time-travel scenarios, and with the lessons of history. Nevertheless, unlike modernist texts, science fiction texts do not seem to offer much in the way of *asocial individualism, solipsism,* and *existentialism,* being, on the contrary, largely social and optimistic.

It is beyond my mandate here to analyze in detail the problems science fiction as a genre poses in terms of the application of literary theory. The problems do not arise because there is a fault in science fiction or because there is a failure of theory. Privileging the novel—as Hutcheon in *A Poetics of Postmodernism* acknowledges she does by confessing that "this book (like most others on the subject [postmodernism]) will be privileging the novel genre" (6)—through the assumption that all longish prose fiction texts are novels will allow any experienced critic with sufficient understanding of a particular theoretical approach to the novel (structuralism, or suture theory, or whatever) to apply that theory without problems to any mundane (in Delany's sense of the word) or non–science fiction text such as *Moll Flanders, Moby Dick, Hard Times, Mrs. Dalloway, Riders in the Chariot,* or *The Diviners.* The inclusive approach to texts is understandable, for if all texts of prose fiction are novels and all theory is "novel theory" (which inspection suggests is the case), novel theory works perfectly every time because the attributes of the novel are established and understood. "Novel theory" does, however, create problems with science fiction texts because, although they share with other kinds of fiction the quality of being prose fiction, they are not always part of the collectivity we know as the novel. Science fiction differs from mundane fiction in terms of the determinants that operate within it, setting it apart from the mainstream in the way it must be read, as Samuel Delany argues cogently albeit controversially in "Generic Protocols: Science Fiction and Mundane" (1980). When the science fiction text is treated as a novel and read using any kind of "novel theory," the results are satisfactory only if the absence of any real recognition of its science fictionality is acceptable. Science fiction as a genre is a different collectivity—differing from the collectivity of mundane fiction as an pine forest differs from a rainforest—and just as people who examine one tree at a time cannot see the forest for the trees (and usually get lost), critics who persist in studying one science fiction text at a time using "novel theory" cannot see the collectivity of science fiction and miss the difference that the nature of that collectivity imposes upon individual texts. Writers of science fiction, admittedly, may imitate mundane textual forms and patterns without noticing or committing to mundane ideology and "novel theory," and many of them claim specific literary influences. As a group they do not claim theoretical approaches, although some individuals do so (although not necessarily with theoretical rigor: If a science fiction writer distinguishes *modern* and *postmodern,* for example, it is likely to be as a chronological distinction in which *modern* means post-1900 and *postmodern* means post-1950). The most explicit debates on the theory of science fiction have been those over New Wave and cyberpunk as types of science fiction.

Compounding the problem is that academic postmodernist approaches to science fiction seem to suffer from a form of critical tunnel vision that privileges the recent subgenre of science fiction that has come to be known as *cy-*

berpunk. They marginalize or mute, consequently, other established subgenres such as "hard science" science fiction, social science fiction (utopias and dystopias), and space opera. Moreover, following the emphases that postmodernist studies of mainstream literature had already established, postmodernist studies of science fiction ignore or despise the short stories by privileging the novel (actually the later, post-1970 novel, in fact). A high proportion of magazine stories predate cyberpunk (and by no means all of those contemporary with cyberpunk are in themselves identifiable as cyberpunk), and there are very few extraterrestrial aliens in cyberpunk—whether novel or short story. One exception is *Psykosis* (1995), the third novel of a cyberpunk trilogy by Wilhelmina Baird; the two previous novels, *Crashcourse* (1993) and *Clipjoint* (1994), do not refer to the aliens, although set in the same ficton. The stranger or other or outsider in cyberpunk tends, in fact, to be the psychological stranger, the one who is a stranger to her/himself, whose strangerhood is inner and invisible to others, often, as it were, merely a science-fictional analogue of Colin Wilson's *The Outsider* (1956). From my point of view, postmodernism is problematic in its selectivity about which texts it will acknowledge in its discussion, and, for one reason or another, it has little to say about the extraterrestrial Alien.

To these problems may be added, first, the problem (from the literary scholar's point of view) of science fiction's need for compliance with *scientific* theory, and, second, the initial and continuing strong resistance by those inside the genre to assigning "literary" quality, values, and status to science fiction. The former constitutes a difficulty in that errors in science may, from the science fiction community's point of view, damage the science fictionality of the novel, so that any attempt to discuss it as science fiction from a literary point of view may simply be aberrant. The latter, evident in the antiacademic trend in some science fiction quarters, carried to the point in some cases of deliberately evading the purposeful scrutiny of scholars who might have earlier determined this differentiation and dealt with it, is summed up in Dena Benatan's aphorism: "Let's get science fiction out of the classroom and back in the gutter where it belongs" (cited in Gunn, *The New Encyclopedia of Science Fiction* 28).

Science fiction's polydiscoursive nature cannot be fitted into the poststructuralist mold, any more than a polygonal peg can fit in a square hole. Attempts to qualify science fiction as a postmodernist genre/literature, therefore, emerge with either the essential nature of postmodern theory or the essential nature of science fiction (or, occasionally, the critic) seriously bent out of shape.

THE FEMINIST CRITICS AND THE OTHER

Feminism is at least as protean if not as enigmatic as Csicsery-Ronay determines postmodernism to be ("SF's Postmodernism/Postmodernism's SF" 305), so that feminist literary theory, depending on the position of the critic, is also protean. Natalie Rosinsky, in *Feminist Futures* (1984), explains the effect:

> [A]s recent theorists demonstrate, feminism is not one cohesive viewpoint but rather an ideological framework which contains a range of views. These diverging beliefs may be articulated politically (for example, socialist vs. capitalist feminism) as well as in more general philosophical terms. It is in this latter, more fundamental sense that I analyze the feminist ideologies that shape the content and form of much recent speculative fiction. (ix)

But whatever shape it takes, it is something distinct—feminist literary theory is not a subset of traditional theory, or even of poststructuralist or postmodernist theory: It may appropriate their tactics and strategies for examining literature, including science fiction, but it is autonomous and has its own extended history. Moreover, although feminist critics are less likely to issue summary statements about either science fiction or postmodernism or the convergence of these ideas, the relationship of feminism to science fiction is significantly developed, and there are a number of authoritative feminist critics of science fiction, including Jenny Wolmark, Marleen Barr, and Robin Roberts, and a substantial number of important books and articles. Feminist critics may, therefore, have differing notions of science fiction's value to feminism, but many of them address themselves to it in some detail.[8]

Earlier feminist critics dealing with science fiction employ traditional (pre-poststructuralist) general theories of science fiction, and in doing so they commit themselves to traditional concepts of the Alien. Some feminist critics adopt the notion of science fiction as one of the didactic modes. Joanna Russ, a distinguished writer-practitioner and critic of science fiction, for example, considers that science fiction is always didactic, and, when offering her "reasons why critical tools developed with an entirely different literature in mind often do not work when applied to science fiction" in "Towards an Aesthetic of Science Fiction" (1975), proposes first "[t]hat science fiction, like much medieval literature, is *didactic*" (113; original emphasis). Critic Rachel Blau DuPlessis in "The Feminist Apologues of Lessing, Piercy, and Russ" (1979) considers the didactic function of science fiction specifically to be a new inclusion in the traditional mode of the *apologue* or *teaching story*:

> Women writers have found their poetics in discovery . . . , in the appropriation and consolidation of the power to analyze one's own life . . . , in a critique of the rules of the world, and in a representation of the world as it could be. Especially these last two interests inform some fiction by women which challenge the world as we know it by a resolute imagination of other times and other customs. These works are speculative fictions—teaching stories or apologues. . . . Teaching stories contain embedded elements from "assertive discourse"—genres like sermon, manifesto, tract, fable . . . these usually guide or inform the action. (1)

Neither Russ nor DuPlessis deals with the nature of the Alien in their respective discussions, however, and the Alien's function as a didactic trope remains only implicit. In *A New Species: Gender and Science in Science Fiction* (1993), Robin Roberts also sees some value in characterizing science fiction as didactic:

> Feminist science fiction's long history may provide clues to how feminism itself can continue, even in inhospitable climates. Feminist science fiction can teach us to rethink traditional, patriarchal notions about science, reproduction, and gender. Only in science fiction can feminists imaginatively step outside the father's house and begin to look around. Feminist science fiction also provides lessons about popular culture and gender. (2)

But Roberts, as the title of her study suggests, is directly and essentially concerned with the topic of the Alien. For her, the teaching story teaches something specific by its inclusion of the Alien, which functions almost exclusively, therefore, as a didactic trope, with all the associated problems of this didacticism that I have previously identified among traditional critics.

Like traditional criticism, however, feminist science fiction criticism is less restrictive in the works and types of works it covers than nonfeminist postmodernist criticism. It deals not only with cyberpunk but also with social science fiction and space opera. Marleen Barr does not even restrict her discussion to science fiction. In *Alien to Femininity* (1987) she considers all forms of speculative fiction ("I use the term [speculative fiction] to include feminist utopias, science fiction, fantasy, and sword and sorcery" xv *n.*) because they have "in recent years been enlivened by the contribution of new female (often feminist) voices. Because these writers are not hindered by the constraints of patriarchal social reality, they can imagine presently impossible possibilities for women. Their genre is ideally suited for exploring the potential of women's changing roles" (xv). In practice, however, in *Alien to Femininity* Barr discusses only writers who are at least marginally writers of science fiction rather than of pure fantasy or sword-and-sorcery, and there is nothing in the definition of a utopia, at least, that excludes it from being science-fictional.

Moreover, again like traditional critics and unlike many poststructuralist and postmodernist critics, some feminist science fiction critics acknowledge some of the internal conventions of the genre. In her preface to *Women World-walkers* (1985), for example, Jane B. Weedman refers to the distinction of science fiction and fantasy in her discussion:

> [S]cience fiction concerns the exploration of actions and events that have not yet occurred within the realm of human experience but conceivably might, whereas fantasy centers around events and characteristics that apparently cannot happen. We may, through scientific extrapolation, accept the possibility that there are aliens, some type of intelligent beings who exist on other worlds, but few, if any, of us believe that elves commonly populate earth. (6)

The introduction of the illustration comparing aliens and elves as examples of the possible and the not-possible Other reflects Weedman's concentration on the anthropology of science fiction in this collection of essays, and, as I shall discuss later in this chapter, also perhaps reflects the considerable interest of feminist writers and critics in general in reading the alien-feminine nexus.

But feminist science fiction critics also draw attention to the inadequacies (for feminists) of traditional criticism. Veronica Hollinger, for example, says, in "Feminist Science Fiction: Construction and Deconstruction" (1989), her review of Sarah Lefanu's *Feminism and Science Fiction* [*In the Chinks of the World Machine*] (1988), that

> [i]t seems to me that too often we confine ourselves to New Critical or humanist readings which are limited in the ways that they can produce meanings from texts. Such readings often separate form from content and privilege the latter.

One result has been the neglect of texts which do not easily lend themselves to character or plot analysis; another has been the reduction of quite disparate textual positions to one overarching position termed "feminist SF."[9] (223)

The emphasis on content apparent in much traditional "New Critical and humanist" criticism of science fiction is also a part of the case against relying on it exclusively. Elsewhere, however, there is some opposition to the concentration not merely on these points specifically but on content in general. In "Re-Theorizing Textual Space: Feminist SF (and Some Critical Limitations)" (1996), Lucie Armitt begins by claiming that "despite the growing body of feminist scholarship accruing around the science fiction narrative, until recently critics have placed so much emphasis upon the significance of its political content that the importance of politicising the narrative has almost entirely been overlooked" (37). She goes on to argue, however, that not merely the feminist criticism of science fiction with its appropriated tools, but feminist science fiction itself as a result of its symbiosis with or entrapment in the patriarchal matrix of the genre, particularly in the magazines, has failed to recognize the signs of entrapment in the generic identity of science fiction. Quoting W. R. Irwin's definition in *The Game of the Impossible* (1976), she identifies the problem as "the notion of narrative closure":

It is important to recognize, when dealing with SF, that a conventional work of fantasy functions via "an intellectually closed system," a point that some fantasy critics remain unwilling to accept. Thus although it may present the reader with a fictional world in which certain (or even many) of the conventions of empirical reality are challenged (perhaps irrevocably), it does so in a manner that prioritizes internal coherence and allows for the consolationist possibilities of narrative closure which keep fantasy on a safely distanced level. Evidently, any critic wishing to claim that feminist SF is endowed with special revolutionary properties simply because it is feminist SF will, therefore, either have to overlook this issue of closure altogether, or make claims for radical content as an intrinsically destabilizing narrative trope that challenges even the bonds of the formula mode. There is an element of truth in the latter, insofar as closure is at least partially dependent upon narrative consolation for effect. (37)

Armitt's general argument—that a politicizing of the narrative structures as well as of the content has to take place in women's science fiction—is an important one.

Nevertheless, it is not necessary to take Irwin, who is not dealing with science fiction so much as fantasy (as his title indicates), as gospel and to dismiss out of hand the claims of some science fiction, feminist or not, to be open-ended. Even some nonfeminist science fiction does not require writers and/or readers to deal in closed structures. Much depends on the quality of the particular fiction under discussion. Those within the science fiction subculture—the practitioners—tend to be making their claim in the context of advice to writers to strive for perfection. The short stories of the magazines frequently end in questions, and Theodore Sturgeon's contention that science fiction should always "ask the next question" is not an idle remark. Stephen Baxter more recently says that science fiction "explores the next dilemma," and, as some anonymous aphorist has observed, you cannot solve a dilemma by shifting from horn to horn. If science fiction stories are indeed presenting real dilemmas, they are not presenting real closures as I understand Armitt to be defining them. On the one hand, the story line in science fiction stories of aliens typically poses a problem of one sort or another to which the solution is simply a new problem, which remains unanswered. On the other hand, closure may be dismissed as undesirable by other writers. In the foreword to *N-Space* (1990), Larry Niven addresses closure in science fiction as follows:

> When every page has been read, and the book has been put down, is the story over? Some stories flow onward through the reader's imagination. Some authors leave playgrounds for the reader's mind. That was what charmed me about Andre Norton's stories: all the endings were wide open. I could close the book and continue moving further into the unknown. As I grew older I began demanding endings. (26)

Niven implies here that stories have to have endings but not closure. Given the important concept within the genre of the Future History and the concomitant multiplicity of trilogies, series, sequels, prequels, collaborations, and franchises, I am inclined to suspect that the ending of an individual piece of fiction (short story, novella, or novel) may be limited to the end of plot or narrative trajectory but not of the fiction. The fiction is embedded in a ficton constructed by the writer, and a ficton by its very definition is open-ended.[10]

The question of narrative closure in the narrative in which the Alien is presented, however, may be of only peripheral relevance to the discussion of alien nature itself. Whether it appears in a "consolationist" and closed narrative or in an open and "destabilized" narrative, an alien may be effective or ineffective as an alien for reasons that have nothing to do with the nature of the narrative as closed and stable or open and destabilized. I would argue, however, that the Alien per se is "radical content" in Armitt's sense of the term and therefore constitutes "an intrinsically destabilizing narrative trope that challenges even the bonds of the formula mode" (37), so that in and of itself it tends to destabilize any fiction in which it occurs.

Feminist science fiction extends its methodological borrowing to the theories of poststructuralism and postmodernism. Jenny Wolmark in "The Postmodern Romances of Science Fiction" (1995) points out that one of the specific qualifications of feminist science fiction as postmodernist is that "[f]eminist science fiction uses the codes and conventions of both science fiction and romance fiction, and as such it acquires that postmodern ambivalence described by Linda Hutcheon, whereby it is 'doubly coded' because it is 'both complicitous with and contesting of the cultural dominants within which it operates'" (158). According to Robin Roberts, moreover, feminist postmodern texts allow for paradigms of the future different from those identified by postmodernist critics in cyberpunk:

> [F]eminist postmodernist science fiction contains worlds that are optimistic, disruptive, and contradictory; they take the visions of the nineteenth- and twentieth-century feminist utopias and make them theoretically complex. By using narrative experimentation, pastiche, self-reflexivity, the breakdown between genres cultures catastrophically disrupted, and a critical approach to language, recent feminist writers test the flexibility of the science fiction tradition. (*A New Species* 1993, 139)

Such borrowing of techniques is not unique to feminist science fiction and more and more characterizes the genre as a whole as it seeks to expand beyond previous boundaries. But it is the feminist science fiction writers who give the expansion its impetus and flexibility.

In addition to its methodological borrowings from other theories, feminist theory also, of course, brings to the understanding of science fiction its own toolbox of original strategies and tactics. Its discussion of science fiction, therefore, often requires the procedures described by Lefanu in *Feminism and Science*

Fiction of *recovery, appropriation, revision,* and *inscription* (9). Feminist writers of science fiction, therefore, *recover* tropes and other devices, which have been taken over by the patriarchal usage, and return them to feminist usage: "[I]n feminist science fiction, the figure of the witch and many other overly sexist tropes are recovered for feminist purposes" (Roberts, *A New Species* 1993, 8). They *appropriate* poststructuralist strategies and tactics for approaching science fiction—like most postmodern critics, for example, feminist critics of science fiction repeat the "treasury of motifs" approach of the postmodernists (see Lefanu, *Feminism and Science Fiction* 1988, 5; and Wolmark, *Aliens and Others* 1993, 2), as well as the theories of metaphor (Wolmark, "The Postmodern Romances" 1995, 158). Roberts, in addition, points out that "[w]omen writers appropriate the female alien, utopias, and the woman ruler and transform them into feminist models" (*A New Species* 1993, 3). Furthermore, they *revise* interpretations: "In *The Last Man*, Shelley provides another paradigm for feminist revisionists: the redemptive power of art reworked through the feminine" (22). Revision is a particularly potent procedure for psychological interpretation of the Alien, according to Roberts, who points out that "[t]raditional science fiction like 'The Lovers' reveals that mothers and mothering characterize women as Alien, threatening, central, and powerful. These pejorative descriptions, however, have been transformed by women writers into pictures of feminine strength" (10) and that in the science fiction magazines, "[t]he cover art and cover stories, reveal that the female alien and the woman ruler were transformed in the pages of the pulp science fiction magazines in a way that rendered them available for feminist appropriation" (11). Feminist critics *inscript* or *inscribe* their new interpretations on what is usually considered to be an overwhelmingly masculine genre so that "[l]ike the feminist utopias of the 1890s and the 1970s, the feminist SF of the 1980s depicts worlds in which women write their bodies, worlds in which feminine powers and female monsters become revered models for alternative societies and sciences" (Roberts, "Post Modernism and Feminist Science Fiction" 1990, 136). In their interpretative inscripting they carry out a process of writing or inscripting the feminine, for "female aliens 'write the body' by altering its size and adapting its powers to a less robust patriarchal symbolic order" (Roberts, "Post Modernism and Feminist Science Fiction" 1990, 46). In doing so, they can and sometimes do produce new concepts of the alien.

Significantly, however, while using both its own tools and those of postmodernism for its own postpatriarchal agenda, only feminist theory, among all the various pre-poststructural and poststructural theories, has chosen to address in any substantial way the figure of the Alien in science fiction. When Judith Hanna writes at the beginning of her paper "The Greenskins Are Here" (1985) that "[f]or the purposes of this paper at least, I want to assert that the concept of 'the alien' is a, if not *the*, dominant theme in sf" (126; original emphasis), from a feminist perspective her qualification is barely necessary: The Alien *is* always "a, if not *the*, dominant theme in sf" (my emphasis). Through a process of double-coding or transcoding, feminist science fiction focuses on the extraterrestrial Alien and through the manipulation of this figure engages above all with the dilemma of feminine identity.[11]

The issue of feminine identity is, for most feminist critics and writers, cast in terms of the dichotomy of the Self and the Other. Defining "Self/Other" in *The Encyclopedia of Contemporary Literary Theory* (1993), Melanie Sexton writes:

> The Self/Other opposition posits that at the Center of personal experience is a subjective self, which constructs everything alien to it as "other." The opposition, sometimes phrased in different terms such as centre/margin or dominant/muted, has played an important role in feminist criticism since Simone de Beauvoir employed it to explain the power imbalance between men and women. . . . In *The Second Sex* (1949), Simone de Beauvoir argued that man is the subject, woman is the Other. Whereas man's experience is central and absolute, woman's is perceived as inessential, alien, negative. (620)

Feminist science fiction criticism, however, departs from the simple binary encoding of man as subject, woman as Other, in favor of a system of double-coding or transcoding. In the historically determined androcentric Western culture, as Judith Hanna sums it up, "A woman is defined in terms of her gender; a man is simply human. Which brings us again to the assertion: if a woman isn't human, she must be alien" (126). In this binary encoding (man(*Self*))?(woman=alien(*Other*)), which I will refer to as the androcentric (male-centered) encoding, *human* is understood positively, *alien* is defined with extreme negativity (the woman/alien is monstrous—a source of contamination and destruction), and ? indicates opposition.[12] Under the new rules, so to speak, the double-coding/transcoding/feminist encoding pursued in feminist science fiction is contingent upon the authoring of the text: Whereas in texts by male writers the *apparent* text may be read, if not literally, at least with the androcentric key,[13] the subtext must be read with an inverted function in that key—an inversion which reads the Alien, however apparently "monstrous," as fascinating and powerful: empowered rather than negated or marginalized or muted by difference. In feminist writing, however, the second term of the androcentric binary encoding (woman/alien(Other)) is reassigned (woman/alien(alien/Self)), where alien is defined positively as *difference*. "The 'Alien,'" writes Judith Hanna in "The Greenskins Are Here" (1985), "is difference personified, walking about on however many legs, swimming, flying, crawling, or however it gets about (or not) as the case may be" (126). Moreover, for feminist writers and critics, the oppositive ? is replaced by the appositive +, giving the feminist key (man=human(Self))+(woman=alien(alien=Self)). I distinguish with some care between *oppositive* and *appositive*. The encounters of men and women are historically determined as (to say the least) *oppositive*—with that word's secondary sense of *adversative* included, and probably irretrievably so. But although the sexes stand in opposition to each other, this relationship should not carry over to our joint human encounter with the extraterrestrial Other, the Alien with whom a relationship could therefore be *appositive* (neutral). The feminist writers' appropriation of the extraterrestrial Alien, redefining it positively, is their entitlement to replace the *o*ppositional symbol with the *a*ppositional.

In *A New Species*, Robin Roberts uses this feminist key in decoding the strategies of feminist science fiction writers. She begins by pointing out that "too often" traditional (male) science fiction "has been dismissed by critics and reader as fundamentally conservative and hence oppressive to women" (1)—those critics and readers who read it in terms of what I call the simple androcentric binary encoding (man=human(Self)) ? (woman=alien(Other)). She then goes on to claim that "[a]s a careful reading of selected science fiction texts shows, however, the genre has always acknowledged the power of the feminine through its depiction of the female as alien" (1), and for this reading the feminist encoding (man=human(Self)) + (woman=alien(alien(Self)) is brought into play as the writer's and critic's stance. Consequently, Roberts argues, in the writing of Mary Shelley, "*The Last Man* appears to be, like *Frankenstein or the Modern Prometheus* (1985), a novel without important female characters, but reading the novel as codedly feminine reveals its feminist warning" (21). In this new formulation, it is possible to see aliens as *disguised* women: "Women in disguise as aliens or in disguise as 'women' turn up in SF written by women quite interestingly" (Russ, unpublished letter, cited in Lefanu, *Feminism and Science Fiction* 18).

Although this feminist key, which enables the transmutative power of *appropriation, recovery, revision,* and *inscription,* appears to produce the standard trope that, as I have argued earlier in this chapter, exchanges two senses, it does not do so. Instead, it produces a significantly transmuted trope that removes the Alien from the status of mere metaphor. *Alien,* as I have pointed out, is not a term which has a specified sense to be exchanged but a symbolic or algebraic notation for the unknown. Consequently, it is a special-case trope. Feminist science fiction uses woman (today's actual woman) as the basis for *appropriation, recovery, revision,* and *inscription,* but, as Judith Hanna (1985) points out, "One of the basic insights of feminism, that branch of sociology which is women studying women, might be phrased as the hypothesis that women are an alien race who have been colonized (or perhaps even domesticated as pets) so long that we've never known what it might be to live in other than a Man's World" (129). "Alien" in feminist science fiction, signifies, therefore, a new feral (non-colonized, nonenslaved, nondomesticated) woman: woman(self). Not only, as Hanna asserts, have today's women "never known what it might be to live in other than a Man's World," but also, having known life in "a Man's World" (domestication, slavery, colonization), can never know, although they can speculate and imagine, what it is to have never been colonized, enslaved, domesticated—even if they are liberated. The implications of this are exemplified, Wolmark points out, in Gwyneth Jones's *White Queen* (1992), in which Jones

> uses the familiar SF motif of an alien-human encounter to explore the collapse of stable boundaries between self and other, human and alien. The cultural construction of "otherness" is a central concern of the novel, and the mutual incomprehension of gender relations and identities on the part of both humans and aliens is used to ironic effect to suggest that the binary framework is wholly inadequate for an understanding of difference. ("The Postmodern Romances" [165])

The standard trope is binary, in keeping with the apparent binary framework of male/female difference; the revised trope is split-ended. The Alien in the feminist science fiction text, however, is coded (woman/alien(alien/Self)) not for the known woman but for the feral woman—woman(self)—which is as unknown as the unknown Alien itself.

The new trope of the Alien is used in feminist science fiction's heuristic experiments. Veronica Hollinger in "(Re)reading Queerly: Science Fiction, Feminism, and the Defamiliarization of Gender" (1999), for example, sees James Tiptree Jr.'s stories as heuristic experiments in examining gender through the Alien: "I read Tiptree's feminist stories as explorations of some of the more dismal exigencies of a naturalized heterosexuality, (re)constructed as a kind of inescapable heterosexual bind. . . . In these stories, sex and death are co-extensive" (27). It can be argued that it is hard to read "Love Is the Plan, the Plan Is Death" (1973) as anything other than a meditation upon human sexuality. I would not argue that this reading is appropriate if the alien in the story is seen only as a metaphor, whether in the androcentric or feminist encoding. My point is that whatever the alien encodes metaphorically, it does so from the standing of a fully realized otherness. Moggadeet may perform metaphorically for woman(other), but only if "it" is doubly encoded for the unknown and speaks in the text as that unknown does it perform heuristically for woman(self).

The Alien as subversive of genre and society is essential to the heuristic experiments of feminist science fiction according to Roberts, who notes in *A New Species* that "[p]aradoxically, the genre's obsession with Woman as evil allows women writers to subvert the overtly sexist paradigms of science fiction" (3). According to Cathy Peppers, in Octavia Butler's Xenogenesis Trilogy (collected as *Lilith's Brood*), for example, the alien within is heuristically invoked by feminist science fiction using the new version of the Alien: "It is this desire for the alien, the other, for difference within ourselves which, more powerfully than forsaking origin stories altogether, can allow us to recognize the value of origin stories while resisting and changing them from within" ("Dialogic Origins and Alien Identities in Butler's *Xenogenesis*" 1995, 60). The purposes of these heuristic experiments may vary from writer to writer, but the protocols by which they proceed are significantly shifted from the old androcentric encodings toward the new feminist encodings. Both in metaphor and beyond mere metaphor, woman(self) informs all narratives of the Alien in feminist science fiction.

Feminist encodings of science fiction are, perhaps, not the complete answer to the problem of the nature of the extraterrestrial Alien. The Alien as feral woman or woman(self) is appropriately "unknown" and therefore uncanny, often powerfully so, but its effect is often hindered by the use of the retro techniques of feminist literary theory identified and used by feminist writers and critics of science fiction: *recovery, appropriation, revision,* and *inscription* (Lefanu 1988, 9). By *retro*, I mean that the technique requires an implicit reiteration of the nonfeminist original in order that the original may be revised or recovered or appropriated or reinscribed as new and feminist. Although denying the original validity, however, the feminist writer is simultaneously forced to hold it up for scrutiny, and this procedure, which might be called frustrated denial (rather than pretended or suppressed denial, or true *apophasis*), runs the risk of muddying the reader's response to the new form. Although feminist appropriation and differentiation of the trope of the Alien make significant contribution toward reading the Alien, they still do not completely account for it.

CONCLUSION

The standard criticism of science fiction incorporates discussion of the figure of the Alien by treating it as a standard encoding trope (metaphor, motif, and icon) or as an extended encoding trope (by appropriation, revision, recovery, inscription), which together can account for the position and the nature of the Alien in science fiction. Nevertheless, a trope, by definition, is what happens when a mind compares the superficies of two naturally occurring phenomena in a psychic (mental or psychological) process and, assuming an identity from the comparison, represents one by the other. The Alien (a relatively naturally occurring phenomenon—i.e., a fictive or imaginary one), however, represents the unknown, and the unknown is not a phenomenon but an unphenomenon or nullity. A comparative process for accounting for the unknown in a literary text, therefore, should require a differentiation in the nature of the trope.

By working with Jungian archetypal theory, I shall introduce a further differentiation of the Alien—the Alien as archetype—which, although it has affinities with standard theories of the Alien as trope, nevertheless leads to a fuller accounting for the Alien's essential strangeness and fascination. This further differentiation is approached, in my next three chapters, through examining the particularity of the creation of alien form, alien psychology, and alien society by the writers, their editors, and their fans. Like almost everything else to do with science fiction, however, their discussion of alien creation is conducted in terms that remove it from the context of literary criticism and places it squarely in the context of the scientific enthusiasm which characterizes much of the twentieth century.

NOTES

1. In 1985, for example, when it was suggested to Margaret Atwood on the publication of *The Handmaid's Tale* that "you could almost call it science fiction," she replied, "You could, but it's not science fiction of the classic kind. There are no martians. There are no space machines" ("There's Nothing in the Book That Hasn't Already Happened" 1985, 66). In 1986, however, "science fiction of the classic kind" or otherwise, it won the first ever Arthur C. Clarke Award—an annual award set up in honor of one of the most distinguished writers of "classical" science fiction—for the best science fiction novel published in Britain. The vast difference between possible views of science fiction (represented by Atwood and her interviewer on the one hand and on the other by the jury of science fiction writers and editors who made the award) reveals elegantly how problematic science fiction has always been.

2. Beginning in the late 1980s, the discussion of the Alien begins to focus more frequently on gender (Queer Theory) or on artificial intelligence (AI). The question of otherness and gender is hardly substantial in comparison with otherness and the extraterrestrial Alien, since male and female humans are intrinsically part of the same genome. The question of AI as a form of the Other is not something I can engage in here.

3. Suvin notes that "the first version of this essay crystallized out of a lecture given in the seminar on fantastic literature in the Yale University, in Spring 1968" ("On the Poetics of the Science Fiction Genre" 1972, 372). A modified version of this discussion appears as "Science and Cognition," the introductory chapter to *Metamorphoses of Science Fiction* (1979).

4. In 1991, poststructuralist narratology is applied to science fiction in Carl Malmgren's *Worlds Apart: Narratology of Science Fiction* (1991). I shall return in chapter 6 to the Alien as *actant*, which forms part of his discussion in *Worlds Apart*.

5. Woolf's discussion of Mrs. Brown first appears in the essay "Mr. Bennett and Mrs. Brown" (1923) and then in the longer and more substantial "Character in Fiction" (1924). I shall return in chapter 6 to the theories of Woolf, Le Guin, and others, on the question of character in science fiction.

6. I am not here calling into question the accuracy or the value of Le Guin's point about the lamentable lack of political consciousness evident in much science fiction, merely suggesting that it does not directly address the question of the nature of the extraterrestrial Alien.

7. The conference proceedings, edited by Richard Macksey and Eugenio Donato, were published as *The Structuralist Controversy: The Languages of Criticism and the Sciences of Man* (1970).

8. I am not deliberately excluding feminist-sympathizing male critics. Marleen Barr cites Peter Fitting's "'So We All Became Mothers': New Roles for Men in Recent Utopian Fiction" (*Science Fiction Studies* 1985), but otherwise I have found none whose work pertains to the figure of the Alien.

9. I concur with her observation that Lefanu's book "really is required reading for anyone interested in the intersections of SF and feminism, an area which has not always been well served (when it has been served at all) by Anglo-American SF criticism" (223).

10. I'm using the term in Spider Robinson's definition as cited in my introduction: fictons are "invented space-time continua which are *imaginary but viable*, different from but plausibly related to this one" (*Melancholy Elephants* 1984, xiii; original emphasis). Robinson attributes the creation of the term to Robert A. Heinlein.

11. Since I am concerned not with the cyborg (the machine-human blend) but with the natural extraterrestrial Alien, I have to leave to one side Donna Haraway's influential and important work on that kind of Other.

12. Texts in which the androcentric coding is simply reversed—usually humorous, parodic, or satiric texts—must be read with the key (woman=human(Self)) (man=alien(Other)).

13. Male science fiction writers did exclude human women from their texts, but they represented the feminine through the female alien (see Barr, *Lost in Space* 1993, 62).

II

WRITING THE ALIEN

3

A Question of Shape: Alien Form

Since the differing shape or physical form of the Alien is the most obvious indicator of its otherness (although not of the nature of that otherness) and constitutes both its most obvious link with and its most clear-cut disjunction from earlier versions of the Other in folklore and in human psychic history, it is on the form of the Alien that the magazine stories tended to focus in what space they had for the discussion of aliens. Nevertheless, even in the earliest years, the aliens from short science fiction texts, whether possible or impossible, have amounted to somewhat more than a proposition or educated guess about what could be imagined in the way of nonhuman people. Consequently, over the period from the beginning to the present day, they provide a more than ample selection of material from which may be inferred in part the conceptual framework of alterity that has accumulated in the genre and that reveals the underlying archetype of the Self in the Other.

At first glance, however, it is not obvious how archetypes of the unconscious could be incorporated in fictions that involve conscious design according to scientific principles. But, according to Jung, however subject creativity may be to the rational processes of the conscious mind, the engagement with the archetypal unconscious is never lost. In discussion of the creative process in "On the Relation of Analytical Psychology to Poetry," Jung draws a clear distinction between two types of creative activity, and it is the second of these that is applicable to science fiction. For Jung, a writer of the first type "is wholly at one with the creative process" (CW 15:*109*:72)—unconscious and conscious blend as it were, and the archetype and its embodiment in the fiction are not separated. But a writer of the second type "is not identical with the process of creation; he stands outside it" (CW 15:*110*:73)—the unconscious mind provides creative process and archetypal presence, but the conscious mind provides the rational application of technique. It is reasonable to suppose, therefore, that the science fiction writer, who sets out to acknowledge and incorporate the scientific basis of a plausible alien being, should belong in the second group, consciously manipulating the archetype of the OtherSelf, sharing the unconscious impulses that lead to writing fiction of any kind, but consciously applying design principles as part of his or her technique. In this way, the archetype of the OtherSelf can be accommodated in even the most the rigorously hard-science science fiction.

The most prevalent underlying assumption of science fiction stories about aliens and of discussion by science fiction writers and readers about the design of the alien is that form is not merely the obvious indicator of an alien's alterity but the significant one. As mentioned previously, the working principle for the design of the alien sapient was laid down by Campbell during his long tenure as editor of *Astounding/Analog*; he instructed writers for the magazine to "give me a creature that thinks like a man but is not a man" (cited in Theodore Sturgeon's "Galaxy Bookshelf" 1974, 92). The challenge to the science fiction writer, therefore, is to design a creature of nonhuman form and be able to demonstrate that such a creature could indeed think like a human. As far as hard-science science fiction was concerned in Campbell's day, plausible aliens could be created by the application of sufficient imagination and a clear understanding of the principles of biological science—specifically biomechanics, as illustrated by de Camp's and Campbell's own articles on the topic. But although de Camp and Campbell may not have known, or have wanted to know, about the archetype underlying the Alien, they were not exempt from its influence.

THE PRINCIPLES OF ALIEN DESIGN

The foundation of the discussion of alien design in science fiction rests upon the previously suggested requirement of science fiction that scientific principles and knowledge be respected. Science fiction was, however, slower to accord this privileged status to biology than to physics or to chemistry. Although this laggardly recognition has more recently provoked attempts to redress the balance, in the early years imagination, fueled by the fascination with which writers, artists, and readers alike approached the challenge of alien form, often outran plausibility.

The first formulation of the principles for the scientific design of alien sapients was that by L. Sprague de Camp, in his two-part article "Design for Life" in *Astounding* in May and June 1939—a formulation of the subject that has never been surpassed in thoroughness or clarity by subsequent writers. In part 1 (in the May issue), moreover, de Camp also formulated one of the earliest and most succinct statements of the primary constraint or principle, pointing out that the intention of conscientious science fiction writers is "not to go contrary to known fact, however thinly we may spread our speculations about the unknown" (1:107–8). The first part of the article sets out the general theory of the biological underpinning of morphology: "How do these imaginary life-forms stack up against what we know about the nature and limitations of life? . . . Which would a biologist admit to be plausible, and which would he damn as phony?" (1:103). In order to achieve these standards, he suggests, it is necessary to "proceed by looking at life on the one planet whereof we do have firsthand information, to see what principles, if any, we can derive as to how life on other planets might evolve" (1:104), remembering that "[t]rying to imagine a plausible animal that will succeed in earning its living in a given environment is something like a problem in engineering" (1:104). In part 2 (June issue), de Camp theorizes about the detailed anatomy of alien beings and suggests "the probable specific shape and structure" of an alien (2:103). He reiterates the importance of taking evolutionary principles into consideration:

> In my former article I mentioned the resemblance of the evolutionary process to one of engineering design. A phylum—line of descent—of animals is faced with the problem of adopting a shape that will enable it to survive in competition with other phyla, in the face of climactic difficulties and the ceaseless attacks. . . . Given the problem, the phylum normally has a choice of a limited number of *practical* solutions. (2:103; original emphasis)

The comparison of evolutionary principles to engineering theory is important. Engineers—respected as hard-headed and more practical than scientists confined to the laboratory—were frequent heroes in early science fiction (see, for example, Colin Kapp's stories about the Unorthodox Engineering Corps); Willy Ley's 1941 article on the development of technology was entitled "Prelude to Engineering," not "Prelude to Science." The editorial blurb to part 1 of "Design for Life" confirms the overall goal of de Camp's articles: "Life-forms don't happen—they're designed on sound mechanics" (1:103).

The general theory of alien design was next addressed by Willy Ley in "Let's Build an Extraterrestrial!" (1956). Although much less detailed, Ley's discussion is nevertheless useful, not only because it drew people's attention to de Camp (which was essential for a new, post-WWII generation of science fiction readers) but also because he reinforces de Camp's underlying principle by asserting that "you obviously cannot produce a biologically possible or even believable creature by the (random or artistic) combination of separate parts" (Ley, "Let's Build an Extraterrestrial!" 1956, 49). Even the phrasing of his title "Let's Build . . ." seems designed to continue de Camp's introduction of the concept of engineering on sound mechanical principles. Like de Camp, however, Ley goes back to the first principles of the underlying physics, chemistry, and biology necessary for life, dealing briefly with the questions of size and bipedality. His approach, although very similar to de Camp's, adds a historical dimension to the issue by linking alien design back to the design of the "gods, demons or just outlandish creatures" (49) in such texts as Kepler's *Somnium* (1634), Konrad von Gesner's *Historia Animalium* (1551–1587), Sebastian Münster's *Cosmographia* (1544), and Christiaan Huygen's *Kosmotheorus* (1692). Ley is much more focussed on life-forms in general, however, than on aliens in particular.

Although de Camp and Ley chose to write in the primary forum of the magazines, discussion of the topic was not restricted to the magazines. In September 1963, a panel discussion at the Discon Science Fiction Convention in Washington, DC, addressed the question, "What Should a BEM Look Like?" The distinguished panelists who argued the question, under the chairmanship of George Scithers, included not only de Camp and Ley but also Isaac Asimov, Leigh Brackett Hamilton, Fritz Leiber, and the science fiction artist Ed Emsh. Before discussing the appearance of *bems*, the panel spent some time discussing the nature of intelligence. In the course of this discussion, de Camp, referring back to his "Design for Life" articles in light of more recent discoveries about dolphin intelligence in the absence of manipulative limbs, confessed, "I am a little bit baffled and beginning to wonder if maybe some of the astro-blobs and giant amoebas and things like that, which I simply discarded as so much nonsense back in 1940 [*sic*], might not have something to them after all" ("What Should a BEM Look Like?" 1964, 88). Saying, "I think intelligence is as intelligence does" (88), Asimov dismissed this remark as mere caviling, as did Willy Ley, who told de Camp flatly: "I would like to take the opportunity of saying that your whole article is still correct" (92). The discussion also included the topic of "whether—assuming a gravity roughly comparable to Earth's—the large six-limbed form ever could evolve; that is, on the plan of the centaur, or the angel" (95). The conclusion reached was that it could not. But in looking at the discussion with hindsight, it seems clear that the thinking of the participants was biased by the introduction of the term *centaur*, for knowledge of this mythological creature's nature immediately focused on the discussion of whether a sapient herbivore could evolve. Had the term *gryphon* been introduced as an alternative ("on the plan of the gryphon or centaur") instead of *angel*, which the participants ignored completely, some discussion of the evolution of a sapient six-limbed carnivore might have been enabled. Six-limbed sapients do often appear in science fiction.

But the most unusual contribution to the discussion, and one not apparently covered in the magazines before this point, concerns the aesthetics—the artistic principles—of alien design. It was put forward by Fritz Leiber: "I think the bug-eyed monster ought to be beautiful. . . . I feel that even the thing that evokes an initial feeling of revulsion will seem beautiful if it is a living being and looked at in the proper way . . . and especially perhaps in the case of intelligent living beings" (89–90). Since this is a discussion of science fiction, Leiber is naturally concerned with the scientific underpinning of beauty, which he describes as a matter of mechanics: "If the supporting limbs look too thin or unnecessarily thick for the mass, I think we see this as an ugliness of proportion as well as something wrong from the standpoint of biological engineering" (90). Both de Camp and Brackett agreed with Leiber, although the topic was not pursued as extensively as it perhaps deserved—perhaps understandably given the constraints of the occasion.

Since audiences at science fiction conventions were limited in numbers (although often influential then as now—members of the audience at Discon included Hal Clement, Katherine MacLean, Mike Resnick, and Dick Eney), discussion continued further in the magazines. Just as Ley had taken the discussion, along de Camp's lines, to the readers of *Galaxy*, Ben Bova was taking it to the readers of *Thrilling Science Fiction* in articles appearing in 1973 through 1975. In "Extra-terrestrial Life" (October 1974), for example, Bova takes as the subtitle of his article "An Astronomer's Theory," and he sets out what he postulates from an astronomer's point of view as

> the universal requirements for life . . . the requirements that hold true no mat-ter what environment we care to discuss.
>   1. *Life needs a building block* (a chemically active ingredient, almost certainly carbon as on Earth) . . .
>   2. *Life requires a solvent* (medium for chemical reactions, water on Earth) . . .
>   3. *Life needs some form of energy exchange reaction, and a healthy supply of the reacting substance* (on earth, a heat producing biochemical reaction involving hydrogen and oxygen). (59–60; original emphasis)

This discussion emphasizes physical and chemical requirements of life. But except to set up and demolish the hypothetical example of a Hollywood-style extraterrestrial in the form of a "Giant Lobster" (53), Bova does not extend his discussion to include details of biology and morphology.

The next major contribution to the basics of alien morphology came from Hal Clement in a symposium on *The Craft of Science Fiction*, under the title "The Creation of Imaginary Beings."[1] Like de Camp, Clement is interested in basic principles, and when he is working he starts from the very beginning, as he makes clear in describing his method: "As it happens, I get most of the fun out of working out the physical and chemical nature of a planet or solar system, and then dreaming up life forms which might reasonably evolve under such conditions" (Clement, "The Creation of Imaginary Beings" 1974, 262). Clement made a major contribution to the field when he introduced the notion that, given careful theoretical underpinning, it might be possible to evade some of the postulates that de Camp had set out, producing a much more extensive range of biological and morphological possibilities: "The Hunter in *Needle* was a deliberate attempt to get around [de Camp's] minimum-size rule. *Mission of Gravity* complicated the size and speed issue by variable gravity" (Clement, "The Creation of Imaginary Beings" 1974, 271–72). Moreover, Clement (a teacher of science for many years) not only encourages experimentation but in the course of his discussion also suggests ways of thinking experimentally. In a discussion of human senses and variations on them, he suggests, for example, that "[s]cent seems to have all the disadvantages and none of the advantages, as a long-range sense" (Clement, "The Creation of Imaginary Beings" 1974, 270). He goes on to refer to his story "Uncommon Sense" (1945), in which he experimented with scent, but for nonsapient aliens only, and then adds: "Granting the intelligence, it would have been—would still be, indeed—interesting to work out their cosmology. . . . Then, of course, the intelligent speculator starts wondering what essential details are missing from *our* concept of the universe, because of our lack of the sense of (you name it)" ("Invention" 1941, 270). The illustrations from his own work are typical of Clement's approach, for he has no reservations about sharing his methodology with his readers, thus encouraging them to follow his example. In fact, when *Mission of Gravity* first appeared as a four-part serial in *Astounding* in 1953, an article by Clement titled "Whirligig World," in which he explained in precise detail how the Mesklinite world had been conceived and constructed, appeared in the June issue alongside the third installment (and was subsequently reprinted in the 1978 edition of the novel as the "Author's Afterword: Whirligig World," 216–31). Consequently, Clement's contribution to the literature on alien design had even greater impact because he could point to his own successful published experiments in the creation of imaginary beings alongside this practical exposition.

Not all successful designers of aliens, of course, work in the same way. It is clear from Frank Herbert's article on the aliens of the ConSentiency, for example, that his aliens were designed by much more intuitive methods—or, at least, if they were designed as methodically as Clement's, Herbert was not about to admit it. In "The ConSentiency—And How It Got That Way," which appeared in *Galaxy* in May 1977, Herbert describes the genesis of the Taprisiots, who are "an almost perfect means of communication, but they put you in peril when you employ them" (7), as he explains where he gets his ideas:

> I get my ideas from different sources for different stories. For the McKie stories, the origin is a Taprisiot I attempted to use as firewood. He did, after all appear to be a stubby brown log with limbs short enough to go into my fireplace. Seeing my intention, the Taprisiot proposed a bargain: Ideas in exchange for his life. He also explained that he was extremely low in British Thermal Units. (5)

In the same article, he describes the "Pan-Spechi, a five-gendered race which can mimic almost any other sentient form" (5), the "Calebans"—"You see them as the visible stars" (5)—and "Wreaves, who carry the insect analogy a bit further [than the Pan-Spechi]" (5). But although Herbert is willing to describe the inhabitants of the ConSentiency, he remains silent on the process of their design.

By the time Hal Clement's article appeared in *Astounding*, moreover, other contributors to the debate were already beginning to feel the need to address individual problems in alien design. One of these is the problem of whether or not a carbon base and an oxygen-reduction metabolism is necessary for intelligent life. Although in his previously mentioned article, "Extraterrestrial Life: An Astronomer's Theory" for *Thrilling Science Fiction*, Ben Bova, like de Camp before him, had taken care to deal explicitly with the justification of an oxygen-based metabolism for extraterrestrial intelligence before going on to consider other questions of design, the question nevertheless persisted. It was in fact most recently revisited in October 1984 by Stephen Gillett, who discussed in considerable detail the possibility or impossibility of chlorine- and fluorine-breathing aliens in an *Analog* article entitled "Those Halogen Breathers." Gillett concludes with considerable reservations about these alternative forms of metabolism for intelligent life.[2]

Increasing specificity of scientific approach to the potential of alien sapients in the universe prompted increased attention to biology as a science in science fiction. Ironically, in view of the fact that de Camp's initial test of the an alien form's plausibility had been its satisfaction of biomechanical principles ("Design for Life" 1:103), biology was often overlooked. By the early fifties, dissatisfaction had been evident among biologically inclined readers for some time, and some biologists were particularly irritated by the appearance of "plant men"—sapient plant-analogues, deriving the energy to function by photosynthesis of sunlight. In the October 1956 issue of *Astounding*, in his article "Those Impossible Autotrophic Men," therefore, V. P. Eulach had already discussed the possibility of such aliens from a biologist's standpoint:

> Every now and then in science fiction the more or less human beings arriving from outer space turn out to be green. Like plants, they contain chlorophyll, and like plants they are independent of outside sources of food—that is, they are what biologists call autotrophic organisms. Unless we want to let our science fiction roam into the realm of the completely fantastic and impossible, the question arises as to just how probable such humans or other animals could be. (98)

He reminds readers that "[n]o very large, very advanced, or very complex animal [on Earth] is in any way autotrophic" (Eulach 1956, 99), and he concludes that, where other planets are concerned, "we can be pretty sure that there will be something comparable with our plants. We can also be sure that there is no planet populated with photosynthetic animals of any size or complexity" (102). If Eulach's argument did not entirely eliminate the appearance of autotrophs in science fiction, it at least ensured that writers were forced to consider the scientific *rationale* for what they were doing in introducing them. Moreover, it was the first discussion to include a specific biological component in a general scientific rationale for the design of aliens.

This need for a specifically biological rationale was, however, slow to catch on. Fifteen years after Eulach had made his point, biological understanding and accuracy in science fiction was still so low as to draw a forceful lecture from a knowledgeable reader. In a letter to *Analog* in the June 1969 issue, Matt Cartmill writes:

> I want to register a gripe that I've been nursing for several years now. Science
> fiction writers and editors are fairly careful about keeping up with informed
> opinion in those sciences which are relevant to hypothetical technologies—
> physics, chemistry, astronomy, molecular biology, and so on. . . . In the biologi
> cal sciences, however, writers and editors are not so careful. I'm moved to write
> this letter because of irritation with two stories published in Analog in the last
> year which embodied gross biological whoppers. (170)

The misuse of biological science in the two stories that aroused Cartmill's wrath concerned anatomy and genetics, respectively, and his letter drew an approving editorial response of "Valid points!" from Campbell.[3]

Biochemistry may have been implicitly subsumed in biology at this point. But in 1980 Greg Benford, lending his authority as writer and scientist to the biologists, raised the issue directly by pointing out that writers need to deal with the fact that "[e]ven if, for example, we found alien plants we could stomach, anything they contained resembling sugar could easily have the wrong sense of rotation from Earthly ones and thus would be unusable as food. Proteins, trace minerals—all would almost certainly be incompatible with our organic systems" ("Aliens and Knowability," 55). He goes on to point out that, unlike difficulties with FTL (faster than light) travel (and, I might add, communication), the difficulty with ecology is consistently ignored in science fiction, and he suggests that, whatever may be the reasons for ignoring it, "the problem is worth the attention of the critics" (55). Benford's contribution to improving the plausibility of science fiction set in multispecies galaxies is, therefore, important regardless of whether or not it turns out to be correct—he speaks, after all, only of loose probabilities—because he sets out a possibility that, regardless of whether the writer of a story agrees or disagrees, has to be taken into account in any presentation of humans in an alien planetary environment and has to be provided for with some kind of thought-out justification.[4] But in the stories and fact articles in the magazines, biochemistry became only lately a matter of concern.

Possibly as a result, however, of the cumulative pressure of opinion represented by de Camp (initially) and later Cartmill, Lambe, and Benford, the biological sciences in general began to receive more respectful consideration in the literature on alien design. One of the earliest indications of this occurred in "Making Sense of Extraterrestrial Senses" (*Analog*, January 1979), in which Kenneth Rose took up Clement's challenge to the "intelligent speculator" on the subject of further consideration of alien senses. Rose argues, from a biologist's point of view and on the basis of a number of terrestrial examples of exotic senses, for the existence of aliens who will operate with a sensorium very different from our own.

The next major theory to appear in *Analog* that was comparable to de Camp's prewar article—systematic, extended, and scientifically based—on the biological underpinning of alien design, however, did not emerge until the 1980s when a group of articles on xenobiology began to appear in the pages of the science fiction magazines. Robert A. Freitas Jr. contributed articles on alien biology, psychology, sex, and other topics to the pages of *Analog*. In "Extraterrestrial Zoology" (*Analog*, July 1981) he begins by pointing out that

> [x]enobiologists have formulated a simple rule, called the Assumption of Mediocrity, which says, in essence, that Earth should be regarded as "typically exotic." The unusual solutions devised by evolution on this planet to cope with the problem of survival will find their parallels, though not necessarily their duplicates, among the living species of other worlds. As biologist Allen Broms once remarked, "life elsewhere is likely to consist of odd combinations of familiar bits." (53)

Freitas then proceeds to review various terrestrial forms of zoological life and to offer speculative alternatives that might provide a basis for the design of alien sapients. Although Freitas's contributions—unlike those of his predecessors in the debate—are not explicitly addressed to those who need assistance in alien design or who need to be persuaded to be scientific about it, but are offered simply as a review of the topic, they are clearly intended to offer *current* information about scientific theories of zoology and biology.

Discussion of alien design in the magazines continues through the 1980s and 1990s, although to a much lesser extent. More recently, material on the design of aliens directed to new writers appears in the relatively new medium (to the genre, at least) of "how-to" books. In 1996, for example, in a science fiction writing series under the general editorship of Ben Bova (a former editor of *Analog*), Stanley Schmidt (current editor of *Analog*) published *Aliens and Alien Societies: A Writer's Guide to Creating Extraterrestrial Life-Forms*, in which he includes both basics (chapter 4 is entitled "Biochemical Basics") and advanced design topics (chapter 11 is entitled "Farther Out: Life Not as We Know It"). It is accompanied in the same series by Stephen Gillet's *World Building: A Writer's Guide to Constructing Star Systems and Life-Supporting Planets*. By 2000, however, as a result of the process of mediated discussion of biological theory over a long period, certain basic principles of alien design were established and are available to the community of science fiction writers to put into practice in their work. The challenge to the science fiction writer, therefore, is to design a plausible alien of nonhuman form and, in doing so, to demonstrate the achievement of standards of scientific plausibility by the application of sufficient imagination to a thorough understanding of the principles of biological science.

THE BODY/BRAIN/MIND/BEHAVIOR NEXUS IN ALIEN DESIGN

Although from the beginning writers, editors, and readers all spent a lot of time arguing about the design of alien bodies (morphology), they did not spend nearly as much considering the brain that could be part of that body and could be assumed to be the seat of alien as of human sapience. This omission may have occurred because the acknowledgment of biology as a hard science lagged among those concerned with science fiction. No attention appears to have been paid to the relationship between the brain and the intelligence, which was the principal concern.

Essentially, the consensus on the alien brain is easily explained because of a fairly clear scientific, philosophical, and popular understanding of the *body* (including brain) already existed, thus providing a referent for the science fiction writer's use. In the early years, therefore, de Camp's discussion of the intelligent brain appears to have been sufficient for most writers. In the first part of "Design for Life" (1939) he discusses the brain, but only in terms of its size, noting that "a man has about nine billion neurons in the cortex or outer layer of his cerebrum or fore-brain. . . . So it is a reasonable inference to say that our e.-t. couldn't think unless he had a number of neurons comparable to that of man. . . . As long as the animal is big enough to carry around a brain of 1,000 cubic centimeters or more, it doesn't matter how big it is" (1:114–15). In part 2, references to the brain are mostly in the context of the demands that might be made of it by differences in form.

After de Camp, no major contribution to the specific subtopic of the alien brain appeared until very late in the design debate. In 1984, however, in "Sentience and the Single Extraterrestrial" (*Analog*, February 1984), Tom Rainbow sets out the arguments for a particular view of the nature of the brain and speculated about its potential for sapient aliens. He begins with a detailed consideration of brain structure and neural organization in humans and mice as this relates to the size of brains necessary for sapience. He suggests that

> humans seem to have a higher neuronal density than other mammals. . . . I also assumed that there is no minimum number of neurons that's required to produce self-awareness. Obviously, a one-neuron being is unlikely to be self-aware, regardless of how small its body is. . . . The smallest known hominid brain belongs to *Australopithecus*, estimated to have had a 500g brain. (47)

Rainbow goes on to examine the implications of brain size and complexity for physiology (48), body size (49), anatomical structure and the possession of hands (54, 50), metabolism (50), and prenatal and neonatal development (49). He also briefly discusses the implications of the alien's biology for its behavioral patterns. More speculatively, however, as an implication of the kind of brain he envisages as the "sentient" (i.e., sapient) brain, he introduces the question of the problematic relationship between intelligence/sentience and self-awareness:

While it is clear that to be sentient you have to be intelligent, it's not obvious that to possess hominid-level intelligence you have to be self-aware. Self-awareness might be akin to the operating system of a computer, something that's required to integrate a variety of disparate cognitive functions. Or it may be something that evolved to facilitate social interactions among hominids. Regardless, it's plausible to imagine that there are intelligent species for whom it is merely an option. (56–57)

On this point, Rainbow demonstrates clearly that even a biologically rigorous foundation, focusing exclusively on the brain, allows for free-wheeling speculation about the nature of aliens.

The question of the emergence of a nonmaterial consciousness given the presence of a material brain was largely ignored. There may not have been any discussion of the process because physiological theories of mind-body interaction were and still are extremely complex and controversial, and in addition entail complicating psychological and philosophical extensions. I suggested in my introduction, with respect to the mind of the writer, that we can infer from the phenomenological concept of Embodiment in its most basic formulation ("that perception and understanding of the world are partly a function of the fact that consciousness is not 'pure', but exists within a membrane of flesh and blood" [Poole 1988, 264]) that each such membrane of flesh and blood contains only one individual. My observation suggests that in the short stories themselves the consensus on the body-brain-consciousness-mind relationship does not appear to go beyond this level. In theoretical discussions of alien intelligences, where it might seem obvious that it should come into play, the topic is missing: John W. Campbell writes about the characteristics that support intelligence without reference to the terms *mind* or *consciousness* in his *Analog* editorial "The Nature of Intelligent Aliens" (October 1967). In this particular editorial he does not refer to the so-called large brain required for intelligence, although this was a fairly common factor in theories of alien design. In the practice of alien design, the focus is on the boundary between nonsapience and sapience. There are sufficient stories in the magazines to suggest a bias in the consensus toward dualistic explanations, including stories that imply that psyche and soma are actually separable, but they do not involve questions of the alien psyche. One obvious exception to the avoidance of the mind-body problem is Herbert's Pan-Spechi, a species in which a single

"ego" circulates among five brains in separate bodies; Pan-Spechi first appear
in his short story "The Tactful Saboteur" (1964) and later appear in his novel
Whipping Star (1970). In his novel *Mayflies* (1979), Kevin O'Donnell introduces an alien whose "mind" moves into a human body at birth, obliterating
the original human mind since there can be, as the narrator observes, only
"one per customer" (212–13). Both writers seem to assume the highly controversial notion that consciousness is not merely distinct from the brain but de-
tachable, although neither uses the term *consciousness*. In regard to the design
of plausible aliens, the relationship of body and mind (and the subsequent
psychology of the alien) appears to have developed as a matter of simple inference from the observed nature of the phenotype, without regard to psychological or philosophical theory.

But even in the absence of contributions on the theory of consciousness
and its relation to the brain, paralleling Rainbow's on the brain itself, not even
the most naive of the early writers practicing alien design would have been
likely to suppose that mind just arrived out of the blue when the brain reached
a certain size and/or capacity—or even neuronal density. The most obvious
solution to the problem was to take the path of least resistance and assume
that the process would have been the same in all sapient species as it has been
in humanity—whatever that might be. The problem with this solution, however, is that the bridging mechanism between presapience and sapience in the
human species is subject to periodic reinterpretation. The authority of *Analog*
in general—and Campbell in particular—in the science fiction field had
much to do with the rise in interest in the design of aliens and with the increased professionalism that resulted from publication of material instructing
readers of science fiction how to write it. As a result, when theories of the evolution of alien intelligence surface from time to time in *Astounding/Analog*'s
pages, they tend to have a disproportionate—and to some extent, a skewing—
effect on the field. What de Camp—and to a lesser extent, Ley—had concluded as a matter of rational scientific exposition and argument on the
question of alien morphology was subsequently restated in much more
polemical terms by Campbell. As I have pointed out, his editorial, "The Nature of Intelligent Aliens" (*Analog*, October 1967), completely ignores the
mind-body problem and presents a theory of alien morphology as the biological foundation for the nature of intelligence in a nonhuman sapient. Without going into the basic physics, chemistry, or biology of the issue, he begins

by discussing the "intelligent alien" in general morphological terms entirely consistent with de Camp's exposition, although, unlike Ley, he does not refer directly or indirectly to de Camp's "Design for Life" articles. Campbell's argument about the morphology of the intelligent alien asserts that "some things remain fairly universal probabilities," and, after some discussion of particulars, he goes on to interpret this assertion, in a way that is entirely consistent with de Camp, to mean that

> the aliens will be fairly large bipeds, omnivorous, thin-skinned, with no natural armor except around the central nervous system, where it will also serve as part of the endoskeletal support structure. Their sensory organs will be of the very best quality, tending more to acuity and precision than to raw sensitivity. They will have binocular vision, and binaural hearing, with fixed mounted ears having a complexly creased and folded external ear structure, or an equally complexly structured lens system internally. ("The Nature of Intelligent Aliens" 1967, 7)

He then moves from morphology of the species to ecological status: "Our intelligent alien will, of course, be the most dangerous fighting animal—*purely as an animal*—on his planet" (172) because "until a species becomes so ferociously deadly as pure animals that it doesn't have to spend all its energies avoiding would-be consumers and/or managing to catch dinner themselves— they don't have the leisure to develop intelligence" (172). Having made his point about morphology and ecological status, Campbell makes a sudden leap to the topic of alien psychology. He derives his conclusions from the analogies he has asserted between the intelligent alien's morphology and human morphology, and his analogies in turn have much to do with the anthropological theory, current at the time, of humans as "the Killer Ape," originally proposed by Raymond Dart in "The Predatory Transition from Ape to Man" (1953) and widely popularized by Robert Ardrey in *African Genesis* (1961) and *The Territorial Imperative* (1966). Campbell goes on to assert, explicitly, that "these factors that apply to why we are what we are physically apply equally well in a less popular area—what we are behaviorally" (173). His argument, however, evades the issue of *how* or why intelligence develops in a species once it has the leisure. Moreover, he does not examine the implications of the theoretical underpinning of his position, which, although it in some ways appears to anticipate the concepts of sociobiology, predates E. O. Wilson's *Sociobiology: The New Synthesis* (1975) by almost a decade and might be characterized as a

blend of social Darwinism à la Herbert Spencer and behaviorism. It is easy to
see Campbell's position reflected in *Analog*'s stories and to some extent in stories in other magazines.

Since *Analog* continued to be the locus of theory on the subject of alien
morphology even after Campbell had been succeeded by other editors, it is in
Analog that subsequent theoretical positions about the nexus are implied—
these positions focus particularly, although not entirely, on sociobiology. Following the publication of E. O. Wilson's *Sociobiology*, Ben Bova, Campbell's
immediate successor, first introduced the subject to readers of *Analog* in October 1976 by writing an editorial on the subject entitled "Ideas and Ideologies" and by publishing Thomas Easton's article, "Altruism, Evolution, and
Society," in the same issue.[5] In a later issue (*Analog*, May 1977) he devoted the
whole of the letter column ("BrassTacks") to the correspondence that resulted
from the editorial and the article.[6] Neither Bova's editorial nor Easton's article, however, directly address the implications of sociobiology for the design
of alien beings.

The major postwar and post-Campbell scientific contribution to alien construction, that of Robert A. Freitas, had been almost entirely morphological in
emphasis. But Freitas's contributions were also postsociobiology, and given
the new enthusiasm for the biological underpinning of alien design, it was not
long before the relationship of brain and mind (in general terms only, without reference to the mind-body problem) in aliens came under Freitas's
scrutiny. In the same year as Rainbow's article on brain structure and intelligence, in an article entitled "Xenopsychology" (1984), Freitas began to consider specifically what might reasonably be inferred to arise in the brain of a
biologically probable alien:

> Obviously even a creature that looks vaguely human may or may not act hu-
> man. How vastly more difficult must it be for us to understand extraterrestrial
> beings who may look like nothing we've ever seen before? Certainly we shall
> be at least as surprised by alien behavior as we are by earthly minds. But evo-
> lution is even more important than physical appearance, especially where
> alien psychology—xenopsychology—is concerned. All living creatures,
> whether of this world or another, are survivors in an endless chain of "win-
> ners," organisms whose behavior and sentience allowed them to succeed and
> increase their numbers. (41)

In making his argument, Freitas, in addition to discussing the Papez-MacLean theory of the "triune brain" and using Gödel's Theory of Incompleteness to suggest the limits of human thinking and the possible differences of alien ways of thinking, also includes a section entitled "Extraterrestrial Sociobiology." This section is a discussion of sociobiology as it might affect the nature of possible sapient aliens if alien life paralleled human life in its relationship between body and mind, and Freitas is referring primarily to what he describes as Wilson's "suggestion that human social patterns are shaped by evolutionary processes" ("Xenopsychology" 1984, 44). For him, the utility of Wilson's theory is that "intelligence and civilization are not intrinsically linked to hominoids. Only by an accident of evolution on earth were our social characteristics linked to the anatomy of bare-skinned, bipedal mammals and the peculiar qualities of human nature" (46). Hence, sociobiological theory provides acceptable grounds for designing alien sapient beings: They can be sapient and non-"hominoid." When Freitas offers these speculative, scientifically based opinions about a biologically based psychology for alien sapients, he provides the last link in an important chain. Biology is unequivocally established as a science in science fiction on an equal footing with the sciences—physics, chemistry, and astronomy—that have been recognized from the beginning.[7]

It is a little difficult to qualify the difference the emergence of sociobiology made to alien design. Most science fiction writers had adopted a notion of a relationship between body and mind that in some ways resembles sociobiological theory but is more akin to a simple extrapolation from de Camp's discussion of the way life-forms evolved physically, refined after 1984 by Freitas's contribution. In the provocative and relevant guest editorial "An Alien Viewpoint" (1987), for example, C. S. Bushnik (adopting the nonhuman persona of a terrestrial snake) states flatly that "physical differences inevitably shape our philosophies, attitudes, and ways of life" (5). He illustrates the way such differences might work by framing a question in his last footnote: "[A]nd while I've got your attention down here, what do you suppose a snake calls a 'footnote'?" (186). Certainly, this question could be assumed to suggest nothing more biologically specific than the simple analogies with which writers had been working from the beginning—Charles R. Tanner's Shelk in "Tumithak of the Corridors" (1932) and "Tumithak in Shawm" (1933) look like spiders and drain their human feedstock of blood and life, because that is what the spider appears to do to its insect victims and hence what the spider-shape connotes at least subliminally in the human psyche. Bushnik's other assertion, however, that "physical differences inevitably shape our philosophies, attitudes, and ways of life" (5), may be either no more than this kind of simple morphological theory of behavior patterns or, given the date of the editorial, a possible acknowledgment of sociobiological theory. Without knowledge of the writer's intention, the issue remains unresolved.

In science fiction, therefore, in regard to the design of plausible aliens, the relationship of body and mind (and the subsequent psychology of the alien) appears only to require internal consistency within the design and to have developed as a matter of simple inference from the observed nature of the phenotype. It does not necessarily imply a commitment on the part of the writer to the tenets of sociobiology, and, in many cases, such commitment was not at issue, since the discussion and design of many such biologically consistent alien psyches (and indeed, sociocultural gestalts) predated the emergence of sociobiology in 1975. It operates, since that point, if at all, merely as useful hypothesis, alongside other hypotheses, for the design of alien minds in alien bodies.

THE PRACTICE OF ALIEN DESIGN

In the early days, especially before de Camp's articles appeared, the form of the alien in a science fiction magazine story was often without any apparent coherent *rationale*. In fact, in July 1931, only the second year of *Astounding's* history, one of its readers, Arthur H. Carrington, wrote a letter to the editor in which he is already commenting wryly on the form of the aliens in its pages:

> And then low forms of life such as crabs and alligators with very highly developed scientific knowledge! A few issues ago, octopi were in the lead! . . . And those Martians! Sometimes they are ant-like, and other times worms, and again human freaks! (I still prefer the silver-green messenger I saw on the stage twenty years ago. He was a gentleman and a scholar and no one yet has improved upon him.) . . . Maybe all your stories won't be weird and full of monstrosities. Science is full of beauty and culture, you know. (131)

Naturally, de Camp's articles did not immediately result in the biologically sound design of every alien in science fiction. They did, however, flag the question of alien morphology as a professional question for the dedicated and intelligent science fiction writer. The vast majority of stories subsequently, therefore, at least raise, even if they do not always answer, the question of alien morphology, for aliens fascinate writers as well as readers. Moreover, in spite of limitations of space in the magazines, many writers manage to create interesting sapients of one or other kind. Some writers also deliberately raise important issues in the relationship of form and sapience in a nonhuman sapient, whereas others are more casual.

Nevertheless, in some stories about aliens the question of morphology is simply not raised in the discussion of alien characters. For whatever reason, the writer either deliberately withholds information about the form of the alien or accidentally fails to provide any. On the one hand, nothing at all is said about the aliens in Frank Robinson's "The Maze" (1950) and Walter Miller's "No Moon for Me" (1952), and it is not possible to speculate reasonably in either case. In Kevin O'Donnell's "Low Grade Ore" (1977) it is possible to infer multiple forms, possibly monstrous, but the author does not specifically discuss alien form—their hostility is independent of their form. In Winston P. Sanders's "The Word to Space" (1960) and Sterling E. Lanier's "Join Our Gang?" (1961), given the nature of the stories, it is possible to infer anthropomorphic aliens by their lack of specificity—but there is no actual evidence in either of them; that is, they are not actually designed and presented as anthropomorphic. In none of these stories, moreover, does the limitation of morphological information seem to be a conscious decision. On the other hand, however, in Timothy Perper and Martha Cornog's "Guz's Place" (1988) the lack of description is clearly purposeful—the point of the story being that human response to Guz's appearance, if he/she/it were to be seen, would be one of such fear and repulsion as to make a relationship between its species and humans impossible. But although various degrees of indeterminacy exist for various reasons, stories in which the form of the alien is not a consideration form a small minority of the whole group of stories about aliens.

Yet even the most casual of writers has to make some kind of initial decision, and this initial decision involves a limited number of morphological choices. The aliens resulting from these choices may be described as *homologous* (like, but not identical to, human form), *analogous* (like some familiar animal or bird or reptile or plant form), *heterologous* (unlike any specific form), or completely *exotic* (unclassifiable). The use of these groups is not intended to present a rigid taxonomy of alien morphology but is simply invoked to avoid repetitive definition. From group to group, however, the level of otherness introduced and the potential for full alterity is different, and even where either of these is missing, the reasons for the lack are significant and often interesting and by no means always detract from the value of story as story. *Anthropomorphic* aliens, aliens who are almost identical to human form, often appear, particularly in earlier stories, but they do not offer any design issues, although *anthropomorphism* is involved in the literary modeling of aliens.[8]

Oddballs

Homologous aliens—oddballs somewhat like but not identical to the human in form—represent a serious commitment by the writer to the concept of alien form as a primary trope to convey otherness. There is an attempt to imply biological differences that, unlike those of merely anthropomorphic aliens, are more than superficial or cosmetic. It is possible, moreover, to argue that the commitment to biological difference implies at some level a decision to turn away from the supernatural precursors that are still faintly implicit in the use of anthropomorphic aliens.

The basic design parameters of the homologous alien can be linked directly to de Camp's (1939) article, "Design for Life." Certainly, what he begins by saying in part 1 sounds like a justification for a merely anthropomorphic alien: "There are good reasons for thinking that it would probably look *something* like a man, at least at a sufficient distance" (1:103). As his argument proceeds, however, his schematic moves the parameters further and further away from the purely anthropomorphic alien, until he is able to conclude at the end of part 1 that in general terms the alien would be "an active multicellular land-animal with a weight between forty pounds and a ton, made of carbon compounds and operating on an oxidation-reduction metabolism" (1:116), which would suggest, contrary to his opening remark, that the alien could well be *nothing* like a "man" at any distance. In part 2 he concentrates on "the probable specific shape and structure" of an alien (2:103). He refines his description (of "an active multicellular land-animal," etc.) to provide the alien "with a head, two arms, and two legs" (2:110–11), and he argues persuasively for warm-bloodedness (2:111), "good keen senses," especially the "remote-acting senses" of sight, hearing, and smell (2:111), with two eyes (2:113) and two ears (2:114). At the end of part 2, he concludes that a sapient alien "would probably be an active biped between a siamang . . . and a grizzly bear in size, with or without a balancing tail, with or without hair, possibly a hopper, but more probably a runner, with arms ending in from three to seven fingers, with a head bearing mouth, nostril or nostrils, a pair of ears, and two or possibly more eyes" (2:114). Here he has clearly returned to parameters much closer to "something like a man" (1:103) and has specifically included bipedality—one of the factors that is considered crucial in scientific discussion of the development of human sapience (see Michael C. Corballis's *The Lopsided Ape*, 1991). Additionally, in this second part of the article, de Camp is careful to include a discussion of possible adventitious characteristics (furry or naked, runner or hopper, for example) and encourages the use of scientifically based imagination on other features: "a certain amount of frills in the way of color, hair-distribution, flaps of skin, and so forth" (2:114). He concludes, moreover, with the careful warning that "[n]o matter how manlike our e.-t.s are, they will . . . be the results of millions of years of independent evolution" (2:115). Undoubtedly, de Camp's argument for what might be called the generic scientifically plausible alien will, if attended to seriously by a writer, tend toward the design of homologous aliens.

Given the strong scientific underpinning offered by de Camp for the homologous alien, the use of homology in the design of an alien character offers much more opportunity for the writer in search of otherness than the use of anthropomorphism, and it encourages the provision of descriptive detail about the alien's form, varying widely in amount. At one extreme, for example, only a suggestion of the otherness of the alien is put before the reader with "flash-card" speed.[9] In Raymond Jones's story "Tools of the Trade" (1950), in which Joe, the Terran engineer-owner of a spaceship repair facility, is being tested by an alien galactic administrator for his potential as a galactic official, the reader is introduced to the Radalian administrator by this method: "The Radalian was a sleek creature who seemed covered with bright green velvet. Great wild eyes shifting at random in the bulging sockets. Scanning vision, Joe thought. He had seen it twice before, but didn't know it was in the Radalians" (84). Putting minimal detail before the reader almost as a single impression (holistically) encourages the reader to assimilate it quickly, and, by its minimality, encourages the reader's participation in the construction of the alien's form. Moreover, by keeping the reader undistracted by questions of form, it serves more efficiently the story's purpose in which such questions are subordinate to questions of intellectual ability.

At the other extreme is the "flooding" technique, in which a mass of information is provided in an extensively and minutely detailed description of the alien. Flooding is used in Randall Garrett's story, "Needler" (1957), in which the otherness is explicitly set out as a series of parallels between alien and human form:

> The Enlissa weren't quite as tall, on the average, as a human being. The skeletal structure was a little heavier, and the section corresponding to the human rib cage was a series of armor plates that completely enclosed the viscera. The pale blue-violet of their skins came from the cobalt-protein complex that carried the oxygen through their blood, performing the same function that hemoglobin does in the human animal. They were noseless; breathing done through the mouth. . . . The eyes were solid black . . . somewhat larger than human eyes, but . . . set in front of the skull, allowing stereoscopic vision. Their protective covering might have been called hair. . . . [It] consisted of ribbons of thin chitinlike material. The ribbons weren't much thicker than human hair, but they were nearly a sixteenth of an inch in width. (89)

In this and similar examples the detail, although fascinating in itself, appears to be detail for its own sake and does not serve the intent or the flow of the narrative, which is a simple story of the capture (and its consequences) by a human space-force ship of the first living Enlissa, their alien enemy. Some details may even be questioned on grounds of common sense if not actual scientific plausibility: No one, for example, who has had to eat a meal or two while suffering from a heavy cold, with its inevitable nasal congestion, is likely to consider "breathing done through the mouth" evolutionarily efficient. Paradoxically, in fact, the "flash-card" technique of suggesting otherness in Jones is more effective than the "flooding" technique employed by Garrett because the latter forces comparison rather than leaving it open. Moreover, the arrangement of contrast and comparison in Garrett is designed syntactically in a pattern of parallels to an existing human standard, all forcing the response that "this other being is like me—but different" (e.g., "the Enlissa weren't quite as tall, on the average, as a human being"), enabling readers to relax, having been provided with answers for their questions and thus not being provoked to further thought. Otherness should force a response of "this other being is different from me—how can it be known?"—leaving the reader without answers and forced to continue questioning. The result of this dependence on a reference to a human standard, therefore, is to undercut otherness and render it, if not ineffective, at least less effective than might be desired by the writer.

As a narrative strategy, homology can work in either of two ways in the design of aliens. On the one hand, it allows the deliberate subordination of considerations of alien form to other considerations in the story. Stories that take this approach include, in addition to Jones's "Tools of the Trade," Harlan Ellison's "Blind Lightning" (1956), in which Kettridge, a former biochemist working as a searcher for a drug company looking for new materials on other planets, is captured by one of the native inhabitants, Lad-nar. Lad-nar is presented initially in a cascade of fragmentary images: "The thing rose nine feet on its powerfully muscled legs. It had an iridescent, glistening fur, and it resembled a gorilla and a Brahma bull and a Kodiak bear and a number of other Terran animals. But it was none of these creatures" (169). The key factor—power—is presented directly in the comment "powerfully muscled," and its general homology; in de Camp's terms this creature is something like a man, suggested by "legs" and "fur." Size is added and homology increased by the comparison with the "gorilla," and size is reiterated in the comparison with "bear" and "bull." But the focus is immediately blurred by the throwaway phrase "and a number of other Terran animals" and then contradicted by "none of these creatures." Finally, the whole description is discounted as being "as inaccurate and brief as Kettridge's last moment of horrified awareness" (70). What Ellison has put into the reader's head is an image of this alien as kaleidoscopic and unreliable as that which Kettridge himself has. Then, after an interval, we see through Kettridge's eyes "the dreadfulness of the huge creature's head with its wide, blunt nose . . . three flaring nostrils . . . massive double-lidded eyes . . . a high, hairy brow, and . . . black half-moons under its cheekbones" (170). Here the face of the alien becomes visible—as I have pointed out, the alien will have a face, as animals do not—to us as to Kettridge. The alien presence of Lad-nar is powerful and convincing, as is the subsequent narrative of the redemption of Kettridge through sacrifice. Apart from his size and strength, however, his particular form is not a significant issue in the story—Lad-nar offers no metaphor or foundation for morality. In such stories, the more-than-minimal otherness of homology supports and strengthens the story, but it does not make the story.

On the other hand, homology can be an extremely useful metaphoric or symbolic strategy. Poul Anderson, for example, uses it subtly and effectively in the portrayal of the two contrasting alien species in his classic story of cultural interference, "The Helping Hand" (1950). The Cundaloans, whose cultural independence is destroyed by their acquired economic and technological dependence on humanity, are almost perfectly anthropomorphic: Anderson, using the voice of his protagonist—a well-meaning human government official—deliberately draws attention to the similarity between human and Cundaloan, and plays briefly with the notion of "strangeness" in introducing them: "People—yes, the folk of Cundaloa were humanoid enough, mentally and physically, to justify the term. Their differences were not important, they added a certain charm, the romance of alienness, to the comforting reassurance that there was no really basic strangeness" (6). He describes the Cundaloan ambassador as

> typical of his race—humanoid mammal, biped, with a face that was very man-like, differing only in its beauty of finely chiseled features, high cheekbones, great dark eyes. A little smaller, more slender than the Earthlings, with a noiseless feline ease of movement. Long shining blue hair swept back from his high forehead to his slim shoulders, a sharp and pleasing contrast to the rich gold skin. (6–7)

The Skontarans, although also "bipedal mammals," are sharply differentiated from the human:

> Under a wide low forehead and looming eyebrow ridges, the eyes of Skorrogan [the Skontaran ambassador] were fierce and golden, hawk's eyes. His face was blunt snouted, with a mouthful of fangs in the terrific jaws, his ears were blunt and set high on the massive skull. Short brown fur covered his muscular body to the end of the long restless tail, and a ruddy mane flared from his head and throat . . . the acrid reek of his sweat hung about him. (6, 10)

The contrast between the two aliens, in which human beauty is associated with the Cundaloan and animality with the Skontaran, supports the ambivalence of the human attitudes toward the two species of which Anderson is concerned to illustrate the effects. The beauty of the Cundaloans is, although attractive, nevertheless weak—almost childlike, something Anderson suggests by denying it, in speaking of "the gentle deference of Cundaloa, which in no way indicated weakness" (7)—and provides a clue to their vulnerability to cultural interference and leads in the end to their existence as a tourist attraction with living exhibits. The animality of the Skontarans, on the other hand, is repulsive but tough, and provides, symbolically or metaphorically, a clue to the strength with which they will maintain their independence and extort the respect of the humans at the end of the story. Homology here nuances the otherness implied in the description of both Cundaloans and Skontarans, but because that otherness is subordinated to the symbolic requirements of Anderson's fable about American cultural imperialism, it remains sufficiently effective for its purpose. That same subordination, however, prevents the otherness of the aliens from developing into alterity, since the implied comparison to human norms is always kept in play.

Homology is, therefore, however subtly introduced and used, and for whatever purpose, not wholly safe as a trope for expressing otherness. Although it introduces (or can introduce) more than a minimal otherness into a story, the constant dependence on reference to a human norm, which is implicit in the patterns of comparison and contrast that homology requires, can serve to undercut difference rather than to extend it. Homology, in fact, tending to operate metaphorically or symbolically, works to suggest otherness to the reader rather than to create it explicitly. But although it can do so with considerable success in some stories, it does not always do so, and this tendency therefore constrains its potential for producing alterity.

Talking Animals

An alien who is recognizably drawn to resemble something among the spectrum of terrestrial fauna or flora—either singly or in a blend of two or more—in form and behavior may be referred to as an *analogon* or *analogue* of the human (similar in functionality to a human but not in form) or *analogous* to it. But whereas the anthropomorphic alien is drawn from the terrestrial human in the same way as the supernatural Others of folklore and religious belief, and the homologous alien is drawn in terms of direct equivalency with the human form, the analogous alien is drawn by analogy with forms not human but nevertheless terrestrial in origin. As such, the analogous alien is a product not only of the writer's conscious choices but also of what its originary form represents in the human psyche, generally speaking. It therefore has to be discussed in terms of psychological theory about the symbolizing activity of the unconscious psyche as it is manifest in folklore, in literature, and in the individual's dreams.

A constantly recurring symbolic figure of folklore, literature, and dreams is the talking animal. At its most basic, the talking animal reflects in somewhat distorted fashion human encounters with actual animals, and this continued set of encounters, although dwindling in the face of the increasing mechanization of the world, has also given rise to a wide array of common beliefs and superstitions about animal nature. "Animals are yet, to many people, little furry parables," says Bergen Evans in *The Natural History of Nonsense* (1947, 29). There is also a biblical tradition of talking animals, evident in the intervention of Balaam's ass—considered in the narrative in Numbers 22:21–35 to be an astonishing event, with important moral and allegorical implications—and in the serpent speaking to Eve in the Garden of Eden (Genesis 3:1–6). But significantly for the antiquity of the tradition of the talking animal, the behavior of the serpent—unlike that of the ass—is not described in the narrative as causing Eve any surprise, and, equally, her matter-of-fact response has attracted little or no attention in later generations: The Genesis story, it may be inferred, originates in a context in which talking animals were not exceptional.[10] Richard Heinberg in *Memories and Myths of Paradise* (1989) quotes Ginzberg's *The Legends of the Jews* (n.d.) as saying that "in all respects, the animal world had a different relation to Adam from their relation to his descendents [*sic*]. Not only did they know the language of man, but they respected the image of God, and they feared the first human couple, all of which changed into the opposite after the fall of man" (65). In other religions, too, there are similar traditions of talking animals. In *David Thompson's Narrative of His Explorations in Western North America, 1784–1812* (1916), for example, Thompson records that the stories of the Nahathaway Indians "all refer to times when Men were much taller and stronger than at present, the animals more numerous, and many could converse with mankind, particularly the Bear, Beaver, Lynx, and Fox" (90). In *Psychology and Alchemy* (1953), Jung refers to a similar belief among the Pueblo Indians, who identify "with human and animal ancestors" (CW 12:*171*:131). Moreover, there is also the Eastern European story-telling tradition that begins a folktale, not with "Once upon a time . . ." but with "Once, in the days when the animals could talk . . ." Discussing the motifs common to both science fiction and folktale in "Fairy Tales and Science Fiction," Eric Rabkin has commented that "one that functions equally strongly in both fairy tales and science fiction is that of talking animals" (86–87).[11] The familiar talking animal of folktale is the most immediate

ancestor of the analogous alien, and so familiar a figure is it that we hardly notice its subtle influence. Yet the motif of the talking animals goes back beyond
the manifestations of art, literature, religion, and folklore to the common root
of all imaginings—to psychic activity in the individual human mind.

In the Jungian theory of the unconscious, animal symbolism plays an important role in individual psychological development and self-understanding,
and it is a particularly important topic. Jung's discussions in "The Phenomenology of the Spirit in Fairytales" and elsewhere of "theriomorphic spirit symbolism" (CW 9(i):425:233), shed a great deal of light on the topic of analogous
aliens in science fiction. "In a dream," says Jung, for example, "the animal symbol points specifically to the extrahuman, the transpersonal" ("On the Psychology of the Unconscious" CW 7:159:98) or is "a representative of the
unconscious" (*Symbols of Transformation* CW 5:503:327), and he also notes
that in mythology "the unconscious is portrayed as a great animal . . . a whale,
wolf, or dragon" (*Mysterium Coniunctionis* CW 14:277:210). Particularly significant, with respect to the portrayal of aliens as analogous to terrestrial
fauna, is Jung's identification of the "helpful animals" of folktale as manifestations of the archetype: "They act like humans, speak a human language, and
display a sagacity and a knowledge superior to man's. . . . [T]he archetype of
the spirit is being expressed through an animal form" ("The Phenomenology
of the Spirit in Fairytales" CW 9(i):421:231). Moreover, as he makes clear, such
a figure has "magical powers and . . . spiritual authority [that] suggest that, in
good and bad alike, he is outside, or above, or below the human level. Neither
for the primitive nor for the unconscious does his animal aspect imply any de-
valuation" ("The Phenomenology of the Spirit in Fairytales" CW 9(i):420:230).
Like the transpersonal archetype of the Self or Spirit, the personal archetypes
of the unconscious can be symbolized by animals, so that Jungian analyst
Irene Claremont De Castillejo, in *Knowing Woman: A Feminine Psychology*
(1973), records an instance of the animus being symbolized by a frog (80). In
Jungian terms, therefore, the theriomorphic form of the Alien is a signal, although not the only signal, that it may appropriately be considered as an archetype (a point I shall return to in my final chapter). The attribution of a
symbolic and archetypal nature to animal forms involves the concomitant attribution of psychic energy (libido) characteristic of all Jungian archetypes
(and to some extent of other unconscious systems). An archetype charges,
so to speak, its symbolic manifestations with psychological energy, and the

psychological energy and traditional history of the talking animal are therefore significantly implicated in the fascination that the analogous theriomorphic alien has for readers of science fiction.

The creation of analogous aliens is, however, attractive to writers because,
in addition to being driven by both cultural sanctions and psychological impulse, it is technically simple. The narrator of Poul Anderson's novel *World
without Stars* (1967) explains to the reader that "[t]here is an old game in
which you show a picture of a nonhuman to your friends and ask them to describe the being. No xenological coordinates allowed; they must use words
alone. The inexperienced player always falls back on analogy" (54). In similar
fashion, perhaps, some writers of science fiction, given the absence of such
"xenological coordinates," might be said to fall back by default on the use of
analogy in creating fictional aliens. This results, particularly in stories written
before de Camp's "Design for Life" articles (1939), in aliens simply referred to
by compounding the name of the creature with the word *men*. Edmond
Hamilton in "Within the Nebula" (1928), for example, offers a group portrait
of the "Council of Suns" almost entirely in terms of analogy and compounded
names:

> Creatures there were utterly weird and alien in appearance, natives of the
> whirling worlds of the Galaxy's farthest stars—creatures from Aldebaran,
> turtle-men of the amphibian races of that star; fur-covered and slow moving be-
> ings from the planets of dying Betelgeuse; great octopus-creatures from mighty
> Vega; invertebrate insect-men from the races of Procyon; strange, dark-winged
> bat-folk from the weird worlds of Deneb. (93)

The process of choosing a particular species of terrestrial fauna and rendering
it sapient is, in fact, so simple and so popular a method of designing an alien
people that the roll call of analogous aliens in science fiction short stories resembles a catalog of terrestrial wildlife. In addition to Hamilton's *turtle-men*,
octopus-creatures, *insect-men*, and *bat-folk*, readers have encountered sapient
analogues of *crocodiles* (Hamilton, "The Monsters of Mars" 1931), *apes* (Fyfe,
"Protected Species" 1951), *monkeys* (Asimov, "Gentle Vultures" 1957), *frogs*
(Chilson, "Hand of Friendship" 1983), *large bears* (O'Donnell, "Information
Station Sabbath" 1977), *small bears* (Iverson, "The Road Not Taken" 1985),
large cats (McDevitt, "Black to Move" 1982; Anvil "Experts in the Field" 1967),
lizards (Hamilton, "The Stars My Brothers" 1962), and *caterpillars* (Garrett,

"The Asses of Balaam" 1961). This list is by no means exhaustive. Blends of
two or more species are also frequently encountered. The use of analogy combined with blending produces, for example, Tarvish, who looks "pretty much
like a koala . . . except where it's like an anteater" (180) in Anthony Boucher's
"The Star Dummy" (1952); Coeurl, who is "catlike" with "shoulder tentacles"
(9, 8) in A. E. van Vogt's "Black Destroyer" (1939 and later incorporated in the
opening chapters of *The Voyage of the Space Beagle*, 1963); and the "octo-
pussies," as humans on Sandaroth have nicknamed the Darotha, who combine
elements of octopus, shark, and tiger, in Johnathan MacKenzie's "Overproof"
(1965, 72). Blends are usually more remarkable for their ingenuity than their
credibility.

Ingenuity rather than credibility, moreover, dominates the construction of
some aliens designed as analogues (or blended analogues) of fauna—both before and after de Camp's suggestions. William Tenn's L'Payr, who is the protagonist in "Party of the Two Parts" (1954), is a sapient amoeba analogue in
an entertaining story about what crime has been committed where and by
whom. The alien L'Payr is a Gtetan criminal who is fleeing charges of distrib-
uting pornography—explicit pictures of amoebae reproducing—on his home
world of Gtet. He steals a spaceship, runs out of fuel, and crash-lands on
Earth, which is a protected world and has no knowledge of the wider galactic
civilization. In order to buy fuel to get away, he sells the pictures to human
schoolteacher Osborne Blatch, for whom they are not pornography but provide superlative illustrations for a biology textbook, in exchange for his fuel
which is a chemical that Blatch as a science teacher can easily get for him.
Once the deal is complete, L'Payr escapes but is arrested, although for importing contraband, not pornography, since the material on which the original pictures are printed is illegal on Earth. Blatch is taken into custody as a
material witness. Like Clement's Hunter in *Needle* (1949), L'Payr defies de
Camp's principle that "the minimum size of an intelligent animal is thirty
pounds" ("Design for Life" 1939, 2:110) and his comment that a thirty-pound
amoeba would be "puddled" in normal Earth gravity (1:103). Ben Bova later
emphasizes the problem in "Extraterrestrial Life: An Astronomer's Theory"
(1974): "Weight . . . increases with the *cube* of size. The strength of a supporting structure (legs or skeleton), depends upon its cross-section, and therefore
increases only with the *square* of size" (63). Tenn, however, makes no serious
effort to make his protagonist plausible: L'Payr, although not microscopic, is

not only much smaller than the thirty-pound minimum for sapiency but also both sapient and still able to function normally in Earth gravity.

The trend toward emphasizing or deploying ingenuity at the expense of plausibility can be seen even where the description is limited to mere suggestion, as, for example, in Eric Frank Russell's "Dear Devil" (1950), in which a "minor poet" from a Martian spaceship crew deliberately maroons himself in order to take charge of the feral children who are the only survivors of a catastrophic plague on Earth; Russell's description is limited to suggestions of color (blue), outline (a ball), and the possession of eyes and tentacles, but although the outline is sketchy, it is unmistakably a sketchy outline of some animal analogue (most probably an octopus). In "The Blattids" (1931), Morrison Colladay offered sapient "giant roaches" (844), faithfully drawn as upright and human-sized cockroaches by the artist, in defiance of the "the familiar rule of squares and cubes" (de Camp, "Design for Life" 1939, 1:116). Similarly, although by implication only, the alien visitor to Earth in Neil W. Hiller's "Peace Feelers" (1986), which is specific only about antennae—the "feelers" punningly alluded to in the title—and a sensorium that has no visual sense, suggests in context something insect-like but at least approaching normal human size. An attempt to extend the possibilities of microscopic aliens produced Ralph Farley's sapient "filterable virus" in "Liquid Life" (1936) and Eric Frank Russell's Glantokians, who are an "intelligent virus" in "Impulse" (1938), but both are examples of the kind of hive-minds or multi-organismic creature whose potential for intelligence Isaac Asimov discusses in his *Astounding* article, "Beyond the Phyla" (1960), not of individually microscopic sapients.

Other writers, moreover, were prepared to move from the animal to the plant kingdom and to enroll flora as well as fauna in the ranks of sapient beings. In T. R. Stribling's "The Green Splotches" (1927), previously mentioned, the Earth is visited by "Mr. Three"—a mobile plant being whose sinister plans for Earth are thwarted by a heroic group of scientists. Murray Leinster introduces sapient, mobile, and carnivorous plants in "Proxima Centauri" (1935), and in Nat Schachner's "The Saprophyte Men of Venus" (1936), Earth is invaded by sapient mushrooms. But although sapient fungi like Schachner's reappear at least as late as 1976 in Lee Overstreet's "Angel of Destruction" (*Galaxy*, January 1976), they are, for perhaps obvious reasons, even rarer than sapient plants. It is not clear which, if any, of the earlier examples, V. P. Eulach had in mind while writing his article "Those Impossible Autotrophic Aliens," but any one of them would have served his purpose. Moreover, in spite of Eulach, writers have still not given up on sapient plants. James White, in *Star Surgeon* (1963), one of his Sector General hospital novels, introduces the "AACPs, a race whose remote ancestors had been a species of mobile vegetable" (33), who plant "themselves during their sleep period in specially prepared soil" (38) instead of eating: Their plausibility is enhanced by White's careful explanation of how they function, but because they are kept very much in the background it is not clear whether or not they succeed in evading Eulach's judgment. Going even further beyond the familiar animal kingdom, however, at least two attempts have been even been made to introduce aliens designed by analogy with inorganic originals. P. Schuyler Miller introduces mobile sapient mineral forms in "The Tetrahedra of Space" (1931), and D. G. James's protagonist in "Philosophers of Stone" (1938) encounters sapient rocks. But such inorganic aliens (who must be distinguished from the fairly common nonphysical aliens) remain unlikely, and, by de Camp's and Clement's standards, no more than fanciful.

Analogues of fauna, therefore, predominate, as though in science fiction, in attempting to accommodate the archetypal impulse toward the OtherSelf, the powerful psychological impulse for animal symbolism already present in myth and folklore manifests as unthinking preference for analogous aliens. Michael Gordon, in fact, in a letter to *IASFM* (February 1985) about Gillett's "Viewpoint: the Fermi Paradox" in a previous issue, expresses a conscious preference in the matter while simultaneously admitting its unlikelihood: "I personally prefer a 'Star Trek' universe full of warm-blooded, furry mammals and feathered avians, having adventures and intrigues" (18). Significantly, although Gordon does mention avians, he does not include reptilian or saurian aliens. In fact, in keeping with de Camp's discussion of the theory that poikilotherms are, biologically speaking, less likely to develop sapience than mammals, there are relatively few serious attempts at saurian (reptile or amphibian) analogues in magazine science fiction. It is tempting to suggest that limitations on the length of magazine fiction may make it more difficult to establish a serious saurian analogue, since sapient saurian species have appeared in recent novels.[12] Similarly, there are very few developed avian analogues, with the exception of Poul Anderson's Ythrians in the stories that form part of *The People of the Wind* (1973) and *The Earthbook of Stormgate* (1978). The Ythrians are painstakingly designed to meet de Camp's stipulations in "Design for Life"

(1939) about sapient avian aliens: "We might stretch things a bit and say that if the minimum size of an intelligent animal is thirty pounds, and the maximum size of a flier is the same, intelligent fliers are possible. But that seems a rather marginal case, so let's call it 'very doubtful' and leave it at that" (110). There may be other more random factors at work here in the resistance to sapient birds than difficulty of making them plausible and convincing. Many people are allergic to feathers, for example, and the birds with which most modern urban humans are most familiar are, on the one hand, pigeons (a particularly messy and unattractive species as their nickname of "flying rats" suggests) and starlings, or, on the other hand, domesticated birds, which are not particularly intelligent.[13] Furry pets (cats, dogs, hamsters, gerbils, ferrets, etc.) are certainly the most common, even though many people are allergic to fur, but they do not seem to inspire sapient analogues any more than do turtles and goldfish, and size may be a factor here. The relative scarcity of terrestrial marsupial species in North America and Europe probably accounts for the absence of marsupial analogues in magazine science fiction.[14] In general, however, Gordon's statement of preference reflects a general bias in science fiction's portrayal of analogous alien, at least in short stories, toward the phylum in which humans are located taxonomically—the mammals.[15]

In spite of its simplicity and naturalness, the disadvantage of constructing an alien by analogy is that the process familiarizes something that ought to be as strange as possible within the limits of comprehensibility. In short fiction, analogy may become even more of a problem. Randall Garrett, for example, in "The Asses of Balaam" (1961), uses analogous aliens (large caterpillar analogues) in a story of first contact between this species and humans, seen from the point of view of an alien wildlife service agent, Dodeth Pell:

> With the careful precision of controlled anger, Dodeth Pell rippled a stomp along his right side. *Clop*clopclop*clop*clopclop-*clop*clop-clop*clop*clopclop . . . Each of his twelve right feet came down in turn while he glared across the business bench at Wygor Bedis. . . . The ripple was a good deal more effective than just tapping one's fingers, and equally as satisfying. (70)

In this particular example, the problem arises from Garrett's shift into (human) omniscient narrator with the sentence beginning "The ripple . . . ," which needs to stay within the limited point of view of Dodeth Pell's alien thought patterns to be effective by avoiding the very (though not necessarily uniquely) human action of finger-tapping. On a larger scale throughout the story, this approach makes Dodeth Pell sound so much like a harried bureaucrat that the otherness of his form barely registers appropriately, although it is actually crucial to the plot, since the multiple legs (the biological structure common to all species on this particular planet) and high-frequency vocalizing of his species are responsible for his failure to recognize human beings as sapient. It could be argued that this effect is a deliberate attempt to distract attention in order to increase the surprise of the surprise ending, but the argument is not particularly convincing. Garrett's story is ingenious and entertaining, but it is not as effective as it was clearly intended to be. Consequently, it serves to demonstrate the major disadvantage of analogy—that producing humanlike sapient behavior in a biologically familiar nonsapient form works to the detriment of otherness.

The advantage of constructing an alien by analogy, paradoxically, is that the process limits the incomprehensibility of the totally unknown. This advantage is effectively demonstrated by Robert Chilson in his story "The Hand of Friendship" (1983), in which his protagonist is sent to the Trill planet on a semidiplomatic mission from Earth. The Trills are an alien species of frog analogues: "Trills look rather like frogs. . . . Thick throat, wide mouth, big black-and-silver eyes, skin a gray-green color" (136). Beyond this initial statement, however, Chilson limits physical description of the Trills to the "trilling" vocalization for which the humans have named them, and their hands: "Trill hands are long, lacking a finger, and claw-tipped" (143, 136). Nevertheless, from his basic analogy Chilson builds up a fully realized and fully nuanced portrait of a completely alien species. The reproductive pattern that they share with terrestrial frogs changes family and social structures, for example, up to and including their notion of government. Equally, however, it eliminates much of what psychologists identify in humans as affect, as well as interpersonal empathy—and any possibility of friendship between humans and Trills is ruled out. Consequently, Bunundig, the Trill whose life the protagonist has saved out of human feelings of friendship, can only tell him in response:

> "Friendship is an emotion totally alien to Trills. Even I who have studied it cannot comprehend it. And so is enmity. You react to me not as if I were a thing, but a person like yourself. But I am not a person like yourself. I am the only person I

recognize. All others, Trill or nonTrill, are but things to me. . . . *We don't want to be your friends.* We don't want to be your enemies, either. We only want to be"—and here he used a word usually translated as "citizens." It means, literally, "members of the community." (Chilson, "Hand of Friendship" 1983, 158; original emphasis)

The process of building up to this point is done so thoroughly that the culmination of the story in this description of Trill nature by Bunundig produces not merely a genuine otherness but—albeit briefly—a genuine alterity.

Analogy as a tool for constructing aliens is, therefore, at best a two-edged blade. John J. Pierce makes an obvious point when he says of James White's Sector General Hospital stories that "after a while, one begins to wonder *why* aliens should look like caterpillars, sea urchins, and the other Earthly analogues favored by White" (*Great Themes of Science Fiction* 1987, 7). Although this remark is not altogether fair to White, it does nevertheless point to an underlying problem. It may not be possible for the human mind to imagine something it has never seen, except by some sort of analogy. This particular problem is raised by Greg Benford in "Aliens and Knowability" (1980). In the course of his discussion of Hal Clement's *Mission of Gravity* he complains that the Mesklinites, in spite of their small size and centipede-like form, "commonly speak like Midwesterners of the 1950s and are otherwise templates of human stock" (54). The most effective otherness suggested by analogy, in spite of the occasional tour de force, such as "Hand of Friendship," is where the analogy is covert. For if its ease and simplicity are deployed appropriately—with skill and restraint— it produces otherness that is genuine and fascinating.

Like Nothing on Earth

Otherness is further increased in the heterologous alien. Unlike the analogous aliens designed from terrestrial species or combinations of species, heterologous aliens are without terrestrial models, except insofar as they are things that can be visualized. To some extent, however, the initial description of such an alien depends upon the principle of analogy, although the analogy may be to something other than a species of fauna or flora. The techniques of description are often the key to the success of presenting a heterologous alien.

Direct continuous description of heterologous aliens with a flood of detail (similar to the pattern of usage in presenting some homologous aliens) occurs most commonly in the early years, although it still appears occasionally today.

Among the group of heterologous aliens introduced by this technique of flooding are aliens from some of the classic stories, such as the Mother in Williamson's "The Moon Era" (1932). Williamson, in a straight word sweep of description somewhat akin to Garrett's description of the homologous Enlissa, describes the alien Mother fully on the hero's first encounter with her:

> Its body was slender, flexible as an eel. Perhaps five feet long, it was little thicker than my upper arm. Soft, short golden down or fur covered it. Part of it was coiled on the sand; its head was lifted two or three feet. . . . Aside from red mouth and dark eyes, the head had no human features. Golden down covered it. On the crown was a plume or crest of brilliant blue. But strange as it was, it possessed a certain beauty. A beauty of exquisite proportion, of smooth curves. Curious wing-like appendage or mantles grew from the sides of the sleek, golden body, just below the head. Now they were stiffened, extended as if for flight. They were very white, of thin soft membrane. Their snowy surfaces were finely veined with scarlet. (311)

Unlike Garrett, however, Williamson avoids the effect of repetitive comparison, and by focusing on the head and relating that alone—and not the extreme otherness of the rest of the creature—to the human, he succeeds in suggesting that here, as with humans, is where the selfness of the creature is most prominent. In addition, he succeeds in presenting the Mother, whether or not she is morphologically plausible, as not only Other but beautiful. (It is a little surprising that no one pointed this out to Fritz Leiber when he raised the point of alien beauty at Discon.) If there is a problem with this presentation, it is simply that the Mother's appearance is not integral to the story's narrative development.

When thoroughly integrated, however, detailed description is more effective. In "The Sack" (1950), William Morrison manages to accomplish a thorough integration. Like Williamson, he introduces his alien protagonist, a marooned traveler from a tremendously advanced civilization, with straightforward description, although somewhat more economically:

> The Sack . . . rarely deviated from the form in which it had made its first appearance—a rocky, grayish lump that roughly resembled a sack of potatoes. It had no features, and there was nothing, when it was not being asked questions, that might indicate that it had life. . . . It ate or moved by fashioning a suitable

pseudopod, and stretching the thing out in whatever way it pleased. When it had attained its objective, the pseudopod was withdrawn into the main body again, and the creature became once more a potato sack. (79)

But Morrison integrates his description by explicitly linking the Sack's form with its function in the story: "[T]he Sack was stuffed with information, and beyond that, with wisdom" (80), and its wisdom is shown at the end in its refusal to provide any more information on the grounds that if it does, humans will lose the ability to think for themselves. Like Anderson with his homologous Skontar, Morrison is using otherness metaphorically, but unlike Anderson, he produces a real otherness, rather than a nominal one, by introducing life and sapience in a form that is familiar—most of Morrison's original readers would know what a potato sack looks like—but not remotely connected with life or sapience. Form is not random, even for heterologous aliens, as the more careful authors were quick to insist.

Suggestion alone, rather than full description, is sometimes used to great dramatic effect to produce the impression of real and literal otherness in heterologous aliens. In a classic story of alien encounter, Damon Knight's "Stranger Station" (1956), the repeated word *golden*, which characterizes the secretion produced by the alien—as "goldenly agleam there, half alive" or "golden elixir" or "chill gold" (123)—although not used to describe the alien itself, nevertheless describes it by association. But some of the sense of strangeness comes from that fact that although this elixir is golden and life-enhancing, it is nevertheless "sweat" or "gook" (128, 129). The alien's form, too, we see, as does the protagonist Wesson himself, briefly and fragmentarily, and only as "something massive and dark, but half transparent, like a magnified insect—a tangle of nameless limbs, whiplike filaments, claws, wings," with "great clustered eyes . . . [and] coiled limbs" (127, 129). The impact of the otherness that results from the use of suggestion in "Stranger Station" is acknowledged by Robert Silverberg in his introduction to the story in *Earthmen and Strangers*: "a chilling portrayal of a weird relationship between man and nonman. Few stories have captured the sense of differentness in an alien being as awesomely well as this one" (113). The alien's sapience is not at issue here: The issue is the impingement of the two individuals of different species, both sapient, upon each other simply as a result of presence without interaction. There is no communication between them, not even visual or radio contact, and they do not share the same space in any real sense (the two sides of the station are completely walled off from each other). The alien is manifestly sapient, since its people have somehow bargained with the Earth authorities to exchange the elixir for whatever it is that it gets from the exchange (the unspecified nature of this adds to the story's tension). But there is nothing about it that could lead the human protagonist to recognize it as sapient in the encounter, and what he loses in that encounter seems to be his own sapience, as indicated by the loss of his ability to communicate with the AI (artificial intelligence) in charge of the station. The alien seems to suffer in a similar way, and the elixir is only a by-product of its participation in the encounter, not something it brings to it. There is some implication, here, since its movements become random and uncontrolled, that the alien, too, might be suffering loss of sapience. "Stranger Station" and "Rule Golden" (1954) by the same author are quite different in treatment and in effect, but between them they illustrate how wide the range of possible results of putting two species into close proximity could be.

Heterologous aliens, therefore, constructed by the techniques of suggestion and understatement, can offer—where the techniques are appropriately deployed and integrated into the point of the story rather than merely random—effective experiences of otherness, although the experience almost never approaches experience of the alien as a person. The effectiveness of the minimalist techniques in presenting the heterologous alien might be used to argue that the relative brevity of the short story form is to the advantage of the presentation of the heterologous alien, as is not the case for aliens designed analogously.[16] Certainly, heterologous aliens are relatively scarce in novel-length works—or at least scarcer than one would expect—where minimalist techniques are a disadvantage in the complex and extended interactions that characterize the novels. They remain rare, however, both in the short story and the novel, perhaps because of the extreme difficulty of constructing sapient creatures heterologously without violating de Camp's design principles.

Exotica

Exotic aliens are those that do not possess a morphology in the strictest sense of the term, and they cannot be related to any discrete entity in terrestrial experience. I use the term *exotica* to include aliens on de Camp's list in "Design for Life" (1939) of "animated crystals, the gaseous and electrical beings, and the disembodied intelligences"(1:104), as well as a few that de Camp may not have envisaged. In his discussion he rules these out of consideration as being without any appropriate rationale, shaped by "the purest of random guesswork" and hence "unproductive" (1:104). Some of them can be loosely described as *shape-changers, phasing forms, discorporate beings,* or *energy beings,* but a great many of them are simply unclassifiable. When de Camp chose to ignore them, however, he effectively challenged some skilled and careful writers to prove him wrong by ingenious design, although other writers simply used them without regard to their plausibility. Consequently, exotic aliens appear in stories sufficiently often to require some mention here, however scientifically implausible they may be.

The shape-changing alien is less exotic than most since it has analogues in folklore (the werewolf). The shape-changer is the alien figure in John W. Campbell's "Who Goes There?" (1938), in which something or somebody invades an Antarctic research station by disguising itself sequentially as various members of the staff. Here the effect produced is one of pure menace, but although a response to that menace is effectively evoked, the alien hardly comes across as having a personal existence—the nature of the otherness distances it too greatly. The degree of strangeness in the exotic alien is possibly such that it evokes a primitive response of fear that ingenuity in storytelling is unable to avert, thus impeding its personalization. On the other hand, in stories where the shape-changer is apparently without menace, such as Larry Niven's "The Meddler" (1968), the comedic effect seems to cancel out the remoteness too well. In this tale of an alien private detective under cover on earth in order to catch up with a shape-changing alien criminal who has taken refuge here, the alien comes across as insufficiently strange. On the basis of these examples, simple oddity of different sorts and strengths may be all that a shape-changer is capable of.

The phasing-form alien (the alien whose form changes according to the phase of its life) is less simplified but equally remote. Anne McCaffrey writes a story involving phased-form aliens. In "Velvet Fields" (1973), human colonists settling a planet fail to recognize the aliens in their vegetative phase and go ahead planting crops and raising livestock; by doing this and consuming the crops and meat they harvest, they remove large quantities of the planet's substance from use by the inhabitants, causing them to be born in their humanoid phase horribly mutilated. Such a species must be considered exotic rather than analogous because, although the principle of changing form at different times in a life is familiar to anyone who has studied terrestrial biology (tadpoles change into frogs, caterpillars into butterflies), McCaffrey's notion of phasing from a plant form to an animal form requires not only some stretching of the process of phasing but also of the meaning of the term *analogy* in alien construction. Such phasing aliens are also found in Sydney Van Scyoc's upbeat fable, "Skyveil" (1974), about moral behavior in the face of the unknown, but they are less exotic than McCaffrey's since there is no plant form involved. In both these stories, the effect of otherness of person in the alien is interrupted by the shift from one form to the other since, for example, the problem of continuity of consciousness between phases is not addressed. Exotic aliens such as these need not necessarily contradict de Camp's guidelines, but stories that try to use them do not always make them very plausible.

The discorporate alien is the alien who has no physical form. Usually this state is only temporary, and the alien manifests as a mind-controlling psychic parasite in a borrowed host body. In William Tenn's "Firewater" (1952), where they are a manageable nuisance, and in Frederik Pohl's "We Purchased People" (1974) and Spider Robinson's "User Friendly" (1986), where they are sinister and callous in their handling of their human symbionts, their physical bodies are elsewhere and their occupation of human bodies merely a way of acquiring functionality (transport and interspecies relations), as well as information and entertainment on Earth. Discorporate aliens can be used with great power to subtle effect, as Pohl and Robinson both demonstrate, in spite of their implausibility, but they remain, like other exotica, remote and without personality as sapient beings.

The energy being—the alien who exists in the form of an energy field—does not necessarily have mind-controlling abilities and is, therefore, both less threatening and less simple than other exotic aliens. The response evoked in Fredric Brown's "The Waveries" (1945), for example, in which the energy beings nicknamed *waveries* are attracted to Earth by the presence of radio waves and subsequently consume all electrical energy as soon as it is generated (hence returning the Earth to a nostalgically presented pastoral existence), must to some extent be dependent on the individual reader's response to the idea of a world without electricity. Most engagingly, however, energy beings appear as alien anthropological observers in temporary imitation human bodies in Theodore Sturgeon's "The [Widget], the [Wadget], and Boff" (1955), which is a story about difference in humans but which, apart from the notion of alien observers on Earth, includes very little to do with the otherness of aliens about whom we know nothing: Here strangeness is almost entirely lost to the parodic form of the first-person narration in which one of the aliens recounts the process of the experiment. Terry Carr's aliens, too, in "The Dance of the Changer and The Three" (1968), are attractively strange—even slightly funny—but, as the narrator finds out, their strangeness holds unpredictable dangers for the humans involved with them. This story, too, is a story that involves energy beings, but as in the stories of Sturgeon, Blish, and Knight, the aliens are present to explore the idea of knowability rather than to act as examples of how exotic aliens might be expected to exist.

Unclassifiable exotic aliens produce, again, a simplified effect of strangeness. It may be an effect of comedy or something more serious (usually didactic). In Katherine MacLean's "Pictures Don't Lie" (1951), for example, the aliens are used for didactic effect. The point of the story is that after a long and difficult process of establishing contact, humans on earth, having guided the aliens to a "safe" landing on an airfield, discover that by doing so they effectively destroyed them, since the ship is microscopic and is now out there somewhere among acres of blades of grass, smaller than a needle in a haystack. MacLean makes a serious comment on the danger of making assumptions in the absence of all the evidence. But in their didactic context, the aliens themselves are not detectably personalized or strange.

Even where comedic rather than didactic intent is involved, however, some aliens offer no more than a certain strangeness about them, but it is insufficient even to suggest alterity. Such comedic aliens include, for example, the Wub, who becomes any life-form that eats it in Philip K. Dick's "Beyond Lies the Wub" (1952), and the sapient planet in Edward Wellen's "Tar Baby" (1974), who captures all the spaceships that approach it because it wants company. In these stories, there is only a slight oddity involved. In a third story, Frederik Pohl and Cyril Kornbluth's "Gift of Garigolli" (1974), sapient microscopic visitors from space are stranded in somebody's kitchen but finally get away, leaving behind a gift in the form of a substance that biodegrades plastic. Their leader, who is the voice in the first-person narration, is somewhat personalized but also more human than alien, and the attraction of the story is in its humor rather than its presentation of alien nature.

The exotic aliens who contribute most to the understanding of alterity are curiously the most exotic of all. James Blish and Colin Kapp—both careful thinkers and skilled writers not content with easy solutions—introduce aliens who are unclassifiably exotic to address the issue of knowability and alien sapience. In "Common Time" (1953) and "Ambassador to Verdammt" (1967), respectively, Blish and Kapp, as I shall discuss in chapter 4, test the knowability of extreme otherness. Paradoxically, therefore, it is these exotic aliens—the least consistent with de Camp's suggested parameters—who contribute the most extreme real and literal otherness to the range of otherness, but who also, by their extreme otherness, dilute the notion of the Self in the Other.

CONCLUSION

The discussion of the theory and practice of the physical design of aliens—alien morphology—in the examples I have cited is essentially a discussion of otherness, not of alterity, partly because otherness, although necessary to produce alterity, is not sufficient to do so and partly because otherness of form is only one component of this necessary otherness (the other being otherness of psyche or mind). In designing aliens, therefore, writers construct the physical element of the Alien's otherness that makes the possibility of alterity more or less likely to emerge. If they design the otherness of their aliens according to the design parameters suggested by de Camp, Ley, and others, the likelihood of alterity is increased, although not necessarily assured.

In the design of an alien, the writer gives what might be called a "local habitation and a name" to a unique manifestation of the archetypal Other as a creature which is based, as humans are based, in a physical organism (a body) that is possible within the physical nature of the universe and the constraints placed upon the possibilities of biological organisms within that universe. The presentation of aliens in the short stories of the magazines suggests that such physical or morphological otherness, whether it appears in anthropomorphic, homologous, analogous, heterologous, or exotic aliens, may be either nominal or real and may function either literally or symbolically. Whatever the particular nature of its otherness, however, given an appropriate context, the possible alien—the alien consistent with current biological knowledge and theory—is a creature whose body provides a shaping habitation for the otherness of its psyche (mind)—and from the quality of its mind its alterity (OtherSelfness) may be in part determined.

NOTES

1. In the symposium, however, a separate article by Poul Anderson, entitled "The Creation of Imaginary Worlds: The World Builder's Handbook and Pocket Companion" (1974, 235–57), contributed the introduction to planetary backgrounds for sapience.

2. It is rather curious, however, that on this particular point, some scientists are rather more optimistic than the science fiction writers writing in the magazines. Robert Shapiro and Gerald Feinberg in "Possible Forms of Life in Environments Very Different from the Earth," their contribution to the proceedings of a 1982 conference under the title *Extraterrestrials: Where Are They?*, devoted careful attention to this point. In the abstract to their paper, they write:

> Speculations concerning extraterrestrial life-forms have generally assumed that their basic physical processes will be similar to those employed by life on Earth. . . . We have considered the requirements for life from a broader point of view and find them to be less restricting. What is required is a flow of free energy, a system of matter capable of interacting with the energy and using it to become ordered, and enough time to build up the complexity of order that is associated with life. These conditions maybe met in a variety of environments, some very different from Earth. They may give rise to life forms using solvents other than water, chemical systems making little use of carbon, and even forms based on physical interactions, rather than molecular transformations. It is possible that life is very prevalent throughout the Universe." (113)

In their conclusion, they suggest that the universe should be seen not as a "desert, sparsely populated . . . but as a botanical garden with countless species" (119).

3. The story involving anatomy is "Skysign" by James Blish (May 1968), in which a young woman, kidnapped by aliens and implanted "under the right mastoid process" with a "sleep-inducer" to control her, disposes of the aliens and frees herself and a companion, explaining, "I ordered a tough steak, and I got a sharp knife along with it. . . . So I cut the gadget out" (161). The story involving genetics is John Phillifent's "The Rites of Man" (November 1968), which is about humanoid aliens who want to swap genes, among other things, with humans (120), apparently by interbreeding rather than gene-splicing.

4. The point, however, was not altogether ignored in science fiction. It had, for example, been involved in a novel by David J. Lake, *The Right Hand of Dextra* (1977), and a year after the article was published Benford himself and his collaborator Gordon Eklund touched on this and related problems in their novel *Find the Changeling* (1980).

5. De Camp's article "The Breeds of Man" (1976) does not make any reference to sociobiology.

6. Bova's editorial "Genetic Politics" (1976) does not refer back to sociobiology but is concerned only with the issues surrounding recombinant DNA and the Asilomar guidelines.

7. The references include both Wilson's *Sociobiology* (1975) and Dawkins's *The Self-ish Gene* (1976), but the article makes no attempt to evaluate the validity of Wilson's theory.

8. See chapter 6 for the discussion of literary modeling.

9. A flash card is "a card containing a small amount of information, held up for pupils to see, as an aid to learning" (*Concise Oxford Dictionary*, 10th ed., 1999). It is used particularly in teaching reading.

10. The question of talking animals was recently revisited in a story in one of the supermarket tabloids of a couple who allegedly met a talking bear and who were so startled that they ran away.

11. It is even more common in modern fantasy. See Monk, "Goddess on the Hearth" (2001).

12. They appear, for example, in W. T. Quick's *Yesterday's Pawn* (1989) and as the focus of Robert J. Sawyer's trilogy *Far-Seer* (1992), *Fossil Hunter* (1993), and *Foreigner* (1994). There is, moreover, a notable nonfictional development of a sapient saurian in a single chapter in Dale Russell's otherwise nonfictional study of dinosaurs, *Odyssey in Time* (1989), which may have influenced novel writers.

13. Work being done with an unusually intelligent grey parrot, Alexander, recorded in Peter J. Snyder's "Uncovering the Intellectual and Emotional Lives of Birds: Common Sense, Science and the Problem of Anthropomorphism" (2000) may require revision of theories of intelligence in this particular species, although not necessarily of the bird world in general. Although Alexander has appeared on television, there has been nothing in recent science fiction to suggest that he has impacted upon writers of science fiction any more than the general population.

14. Again, however, there are good examples in novel format: Gordon Dickson's Ruml in *The Alien Way* (1963) and, more recently, Rebecca Ore's Gwyng in the *Becoming Alien* (1988), *Being Alien* (1989), and *Human to Human* (1990). The latter writer also offers striking examples of avian aliens (although the principal avian character is flightless).

15. But even among the mammals that are incorporated into the aliens of science fiction, there is undoubtedly some hierarchy of psychological responsiveness involved, in

agreement perhaps with Desmond Morris's observations in *The Naked Ape* (1967), which led to his formulation of "the first law of animal appeal [which] states that 'The popularity of animal is directly correlated with the number of anthropomorphic features it possesses'" (201), so that amongst all animal species, the animals that children are most responsive to are those that have "hair," "rounded outlines," "flat faces," "facial expressions," "the ability to manipulate small objects," and "rather vertical" postures (200).

16. Even at short-story length, however, this technique can backfire. For example, in James Schmitz's "Lion Loose" (1961), as a result of the minimal information about the heterologously designed carnivorous Hlat, the protagonist's encounter with it as it stalks some of the inhabitants of a hotel on a space station resembles being stalked by an animated hearthrug rather than an experience of otherness or strangeness.

The Thought That Counts:
The Alien Psyche

In the alien form, so science fiction postulates, manifests the alien psyche—like the human psyche, and hence sapient, and yet also unlike because it manifests in an unlike form.[1] Similarly, the discussion of the theory of the design of the alien psyche—alien psychology—is essentially a discussion of otherness in the psyche, not of alterity, partly because otherness, as I have already suggested, although *necessary* to produce alterity, is not *sufficient* to do so, and partly because otherness of psyche is only one component of this necessary otherness (the other being the otherness of form already discussed). In designing alien psychologies, therefore, writers construct the second element of the alien's otherness, which makes the possibility of alterity more or less likely to emerge. They are in quest of the truly alien nonhuman psyche, conscientiously trying to eliminate all unconscious assumptions and finding that psyche to be, in complex but not difficult senses of the words, knowable, recognizable, comprehensible, and compatible.

ALIEN SHRINKAGE: THE THEORY OF THE ALIEN PSYCHE
Discussions about the theory of the sapient alien's psyche are largely missing from the magazines and other forums where the theory of the sapient alien's form was regularly and eagerly discussed. No one in the early years of science fiction, that I can discover, attempted to produce a scientifically grounded discussion of principles to be observed in the design of the alien psyche that

could be put alongside de Camp's discussion of alien form ("Design for Life" 1939). In *Astounding* and *Analog*, admittedly, John W. Campbell wrote occasional editorials that introduced questions of intelligence (that is, *sapience*). In the September 1957 issue, his editorial discussed the question of how humans can learn and why they fail ("Learning Patterns"), and in the September 1959 issue, the editorial "What Do you Mean . . . Human?" addressed the topic of a "workable definition" of human, suggesting for consideration "[a] human is an entity having an emotional structure, as well as a physical and mental structure" (162). Additionally, in the July 1965 issue, Campbell introduced Lawrence Perkins's story "Delivered with Feeling" with a direct although brief comment on the term *intelligence*: "While 'Intelligence' may be an actual, identifiable entity, our one sample of 'intelligent life-form' is a very narrow base for conclusions. We might not recognize what another race used for 'intelligence.' And neither, remember, would a third alien do any better!" (133). No larger discussion of the subject was forthcoming immediately in *Analog*, possibly because a survey of psychological theory similar to de Camp's biological article would have run counter to Campbell's manifest hostility to psychology as a science evinced in such editorials as "The Modern Black Arts" (December 1970). In fact, the first serious offering on the topic in *Analog*, Robert Freitas's previously cited article "Xenopsychology," did not appear until 1984, under the editorship of Ben Bova. The background theory of psychology for alien sapience as it manifests in stories is, therefore, very much a matter of ad hoc choices based on individual knowledge or otherwise of current psychological theory.

The working principle for the sapient alien was, as I have previously noted, apparently laid down by Campbell when he instructed writers for the magazine to "give me a creature that thinks like a man but is not a man" (cited in Theodore Sturgeon's "Galaxy Bookshelf" 1974, 92). Campbell's focus on thinking, is, of course, of ancient lineage in describing human as opposed to animal intellect, going back to Seneca's assertion that "[m]an is the reasoning animal" (Seneca 1934). Even if considered in the more politically correct wording—used by Spider Robinson in a back-cover blurb for Rebecca Ore's *Becoming Alien* (1988): "Write me a creature than thinks *as well* as a human, but not *like* a human" (277)—Campbell's formulation, however useful and succinct as an operating principle for his writers, nevertheless still does not provide the basis for a definition. This principle for the creation of appropriate alien psyches for stories to be published in *Analog* owes its success to the fact that it was—at least after Campbell had been editor for a few years—in large part an ex post facto formulation, since the writers he was dealing with, having read stories already published by him in the magazine, knew what Campbell meant without need of more precise instruction, just as Campbell knew what he needed to buy to satisfy his readers without a more precise definition. Consequently, Campbell, his writers, and his readers were all working pragmatically and intuitively in their understanding of sapience and in their creation of the psyche of the knowable alien.

Within science fiction, therefore, in the continued absence of a specific definition of sapience, later writers have continued to take their cue from Campbell in the introduction of alien psyches into their work. His formulation is open, perhaps deliberately so, to multiple interpretations, and the writers have taken advantage of the open-endedness to be as sloppy or as precise, as rigid or as flexible, as they choose, according to their individual temperaments. At one extreme, among the novels of alien contact where more space is available for development, can be found the theory of sapience put forward by the psychologist in H. Beam Piper's *Little Fuzzy* (1962), who considers precisely enumerated and technical criteria such as "true mentation" (159) in his fairly complicated ruminations on the subject.[2] At the other extreme can be found the rule laid down for Janet Kagan's investigators in *Hellspark* (1988), which imposes only the broad triple condition of having "art, artifact, and language" (147), interpreted with extreme flexibility by various characters in a deliberate and conscientious effort to avoid possible error. In magazine stories, however, such extended consideration was never really achieved. Yet over time a consensus—brought about by borrowing from ethology, primatology, anthropology, psychology, sociology, and whatever else came to hand—has established certain rules of thumb about what an alien species must be able to accomplish in three areas of behavior—language, culture, and tools (technology)—before it achieves sapient status. Given, moreover, that these three markers for alien sapience were developed, as I shall demonstrate later in this chapter, almost from the beginning, it is surprising that there is not also from the beginning widespread discussion of general theories of psycholinguistics, of culture, and of technological development.

Of the three, language was discussed relatively frequently: often interestingly, but always in isolation, and sometimes repetitively. Like intelligence in general, language was considered in Campbell's editorials: In the June 1941 issue, for example, he points out the deficiencies of telepathy in alien communication ("Interpreters May Still Be Needed" 6), and this point was used later by G. R. Shipman to introduce his article "How to Talk to a Martian" (October 1953). But Shipman, although he begins by discarding telepathy, is actually making a more practical argument for a scientifically based approach to alien languages in science fiction:

> If Twentieth Century science can already suggest a way to talk to Martians, science-fiction writers have an obligation to base their fantasies of the future on the knowledge of the present. Science fiction, to be enjoyed by an intelligent reader, has to be plausible. Recently I read a story that was spoiled for me because of one elementary error. An extraterrestrial character in it spoke English with a phony foreign accent in which all the *t*'s became *s*'s. Yet this outlander, who couldn't manage our *t*-sound, had one in his own name! You don't have to be a Ph.D. in linguistics to see the howler. (120)

Almost two years later, Charles F. Hockett, in "How to Learn Martian" (May 1955), also argues for a more scientifically based approach to interspecies communication and a greater awareness of the variety of problems that might arise. It may or may not be relevant to the general attitude to linguistics, that whereas similar articles on alien form were often if not always followed by a list of related items for further reading, no such list is provided by either Shipman or Hockett for his article. When Lawrence Perkins, whose story "Delivered with Feeling" (1965) had been introduced by Campbell with a comment on intelligence although the story had been about the nature of language, followed it up with the article "Target: Language" (1967), Campbell said in introducing the article: "One of the distinguishing characteristics of an intelligent race is the use of an abstract-symbol communication system. But we know so little about even our own language . . . and less about the abstract concept 'language'" (81). At the time the article was published, however, more was known about language than Campbell seems willing to acknowledge. Perkins's highly idiosyncratic account of the nature of language provoked a great deal of correspondence, showing that readers were eager for discussion of linguistics, but it is clearly not state of the art for the date of its publication: The texts listed for further reading were all in the region of twenty years old at the time the article appeared, and there is no mention of the research of such an important linguistics expert as Noam Chomsky[3] or of the kind of research that led up to Eric E. Lenneberg's massive *Biological Foundations of Language* (1967). It is hard to escape the conclusion that if Campbell and other editors and writers had been as scientifically minded in their approach to language as they were in their approach to other disciplines such as physics and chemistry, Perkins's article might have been required to be more up-to-date in its research, even if it could not wait for publication until the appearance of *Biological Foundations of Language*, so that *Analog*'s readers might have more recent approaches to language drawn to their attention. In later years, outside the pages of *Analog*, Larry Niven in "The Words in Science Fiction" (1976) and Sheila Finch in "Berlitz in Outer Space" (1988) contributed helpful discussions of alien linguistics from the point of view of the professional writer, and Marvin Minsky offered an authoritative discussion from the point of view of the artificial-intelligence expert in "Communication with Alien Intelligence" (1985).

The theory of alien culture fared even less well than the theory of alien linguistics as a topic for discussion in the magazines.[4] In *Astounding* and *Analog*, Campbell's hostility to sociology as a science was as manifest as his hostility to psychology ("The Modern Black Arts," *Analog*, December 1970). Arthur J. Cox contributed "Varieties of Culture" to *Astounding* (December 1950) and included citations (as other science fact articles did) at the end (among them Ruth Benedict and Margaret Mead—the former being the focal point of Cox's discussion), but this was an isolated occurrence.[5] Cox's citations, moreover, reveal him as fairly conservative in his position, and although he does not mention it specifically, the Universal Culture Pattern (UCP) constructed by Clark Wissler in *Man and Culture* (1923) clearly plays a part in his approach. In the development of the consensus, too, there is clearly a considerable reliance—whether recognized or not—on this Universal Culture Pattern. It was standard fare in secondary and postsecondary educational curricula, and was, for example, summarized by social anthropologist Leon Stover in the afterword to *Apeman, Spaceman: Anthropological Science Fiction* (1968), the anthology he developed and edited, in collaboration with the well-known science fiction writer Harry Harrison, for university use. The UCP is perhaps somewhat outdated by current anthropological thinking, even in the revised version of Felix Keesing (1958, 1962), but it would have nevertheless been sufficiently widespread in the general public perception (and therefore part of the ambient cultural knowledge) to form some sort of standard for the writers over the period from Wissler's original publication.

The lack of social science theory beyond that of human societies did not go unnoticed. In the February 1976 issue of *Galaxy*, Jerry Pournelle, by that date a respected writer of science fiction with science articles also to his credit, reviewed *Cultures beyond the Earth: The Role of Anthropology in Outer Space*, edited by Magorah Maruyama and Arthur Hawkins, which he found so disappointing that he points out its shortcomings in no uncertain terms: Of the writer of the only article included on possible alien cultures, for example, he comments that she is "described as 'interested in alternative lifestyles.' She is also interested in alternative physics" ("A Step Further Out: *Cultures Beyond Earth*" 39). He reasons that it is worth writing a negative review because "it's important. There is a crying need for speculative social science, for an examination of the role of anthropology in outer space. This book pretends to be it, and that's what makes me angry: not that it attempts and fails, but that it doesn't attempt at all. It merely pretends" (42). He goes on to argue, from a standpoint completely opposite John Campbell, that

> attempts to use the methods of the exact sciences in the study of man and society have failed, often disastrously, and a good case can be made that they'll always fail. I happen to believe there's far more intuitive understanding of man and society in literature than scientific knowledge about the same; that there is "an operation called Verstehen" that eludes the most meticulous rat-runner with his Skinner box in the most scientific of psychology departments. But though I believe introspection may be more valuable than mathematics for understanding the nature of man, it does *not* follow that we can discard the hard knowledge we have from other disciplines. . . . The "anthropologist of outer space" simply cannot afford ignorance of elementary physics. (42–43)

Pournelle is clearly arguing in this review for the importance of intelligent understanding of social science as well as physical science to the lives and thinking of an audience much wider than only the readers of *Galaxy*. More directly addressed to writers and readers of science fiction is the article he coauthored with Larry Niven, "Building *The Mote in God's Eye*" in the previous issue (*Galaxy*, January 1976) as a follow-up to the publication of their collaborative novel *The Mote in God's Eye* (1974). After making the clear assertion that "in

The Mote in God's Eye . . . we built not only worlds but cultures," they go on to explain that

> [f]rom the start *Mote* was to be a novel of first contact. After our initial story conference, we had larger ambitions: *Mote* would be, if we could write it, the *epitome* of first contact novels. We intended to explore every important problem arising from first contact with aliens—and to look at those problems from both human and alien viewpoints. That meant creating cultures in far more detail than is needed for most novels. (100)

In the final section of the article, after discussing technology and its limitations in the ficton, they discuss the "kinds of interstellar organizations" that will be compatible with it, including the unambiguous statement that "*Mote* is supposed to be entertainment, not an essay on the influence of science on social organization. (You're getting *that* here)" (110). In view of the general lack of articles on social science in the science fiction magazines, this article plus Cox's article and Pournelle's own earlier remarks amount to almost *all* the information magazine readers were going to get.

Discussions of the theory of alien technology and the science that was its foundation could be said to be, however, omnipresent—albeit implicitly—in the discussions of human technology. This omnipresence is the result of the assumption, fundamental to science (and hence to science fiction), that the basic physical and chemical nature of the universe, which results in technology as we know it, is established and unvarying. Consequently, apart from scattered references, such as those suggesting that aquatic cultures would not be likely to develop metal-working capabilities, there are few articles directly addressed to the question of how specific alien cultures would shape a technology. In 1981, Bernard Campbell presented a conference paper, "The Evolution of Technological Species," which, had it been made available to science fiction writers in a form more accessible to general readership than the published proceedings of the conference, might have had a considerable interest for and impact on writers concerned with the issues of alien technological development. Perhaps, since the stories themselves are filled with discussion, albeit on a case-by-case basis, of how aliens of differing forms and habitats might shape an appropriate technology, the absence of direct theory of technology was less significant than the absence of theory in the other two areas:

The stories *are* the theory, so to speak, of the alien psyche's dealings with technology.

In a very real sense, moreover, discussions of alien psyche faced a problem that simply did not arise in discussions of alien form. Essentially, the operation of the consensus on the design of the alien form—its body—is easily explained because a fairly clear scientific, philosophical, and popular understanding of what *body* is exists to provide a referent for the science fiction writer's discussion. But there does not seem to be any similar fundamental agreement about mind.[6] Therefore, whereas even quite small children can learn from simple observation of form which creatures among those it meets are human beings and which are not, even psychologists and philosophers have considerable difficulty agreeing on what is psyche and what is not. The constitution of the human psyche was and is not nearly so well understood as the constitution of the human form.

A variant of the anthropic principle (that theories of the universe are constrained by having to allow for the presence of humans as observers in it) seems to be in operation here: Theories of the human psyche are constrained by having to allow for the fact that it is the human psyche that is constructing the theories. This philosophical conundrum also lies behind what I have suggested earlier is the problem of defining sapience. Charles Hampden-Turner, in the introduction to his compilation of the historical and philosophical schemata of the structures of the psyche, *Maps of the Mind* (1981), describes this fundamental problem as follows:

> "What is the mind?" is a question that has intrigued people from the earliest times—indeed, for as long as man has considered the possibility of mind at all. It is the first truly philosophical question which comes with the dawning of self-consciousness. Yet it stumbles on the vexing question: How can that which knows, know itself? Each representation of the known which lacks the knower is necessarily incomplete. (8)

It follows, however, that if Hampden-Turner is right in asserting that we cannot know ourselves and that our representations of the human psyche are "necessarily incomplete" (8), then we cannot know other (nonhuman) psyches either. If, moreover, we do not know what we are looking for, it is going to be very difficult for us to recognize it when we find it, since theories of sapience will also have to be considered to be constrained by the fact that the theorizers are themselves sapient. Nevertheless, even hedged about with these constraints, the science fiction writer seizes, over and over again, the opportunity to explore the knowability, recognizability, comprehensibility, and compatibility of the alien psyche, and, given the huge number of stories in which alien sapience is an issue (contact stories), it is possible to construct, through the consensual rules of thumb, the concept of otherness in psyche and sapience that writers link to their concept of otherness in form.

DESIGNING MINDS—THE PRACTICE OF ALIEN PSYCHOLOGY

The science fiction writers' passion for designing alien psyches, although it may not be the only motive for writing stories of alien contact, is nevertheless strong enough to produce contact stories in sufficient numbers to allow the identification of distinct scenarios. *First-contact* stories postulate first encounters between humans and another sapient species, whether these happen accidentally or as a result of deliberate search, and they focus on the process of recognizing sapience. *Established-contact* stories postulate the existence of repeated or long-term encounters between humans and another sapient species, and the focus is on the process of understanding the nature of a previously determined alien sapience through experience of a specific difference or differences between human and alien psychology. Both these scenarios involve direct encounters with aliens and are given a full range of treatment from extreme realism to extreme romanticism. *Hypothesized-contact* stories and *blind-contact* stories offer indirect contact only. The former postulate the discovery of unoccupied alien artifacts or worlds as evidence for the existence and nature of an alien species (usually but by no means always from the human point of view), and the latter postulate a situation in which two sapient species come into contact but do not know that a contact has taken place. Blind-contact stories can be distinguished from stories that consider the problem of knowability, however, for whereas in the latter the narration is ambiguous about the alien, in the former an omniscient point of view of the narration often clearly indicates that both sides are sapient and perhaps mutually knowable; they simply do not see what—or who—is there. Of these four scenarios for contact, the two most significant for the consideration of sapience are *first contact* and *established contact*, but the issues and problems of alien sapience may be foregrounded in any of the four.

Is Anyone There?—Knowability

The primary question in stories of alien contact, therefore, is knowability—whether or not humans can meet and understand the sapient alien (assuming, of course, that such aliens exist) in any rational sense of the word *understand*. Knowability has rarely been addressed by writers and even more rarely by critics of science fiction. Greg Benford (a scientist and a writer and critic of science fiction) starts to address knowability in "Aliens and Knowability" (1980), pointing out that "[a]liens do occasionally appear in science fiction as distant, inexplicable things, often ignored by the human characters. Making them objects of indifference does not exploit or illuminate the philosophical problems involved, though" (56). He identifies two particular problems: first, language, asking, "how can beings be strange and still communicate with us easily?" (56). And, second, categorization, asking how we can avoid being like the hero of Benford's own novel, *If the Stars Are Gods* (1977)—"trapped, by his own use of human categories, into a fundamental ignorance of the aliens" (56). At its most extreme, Benford points out, "irreducible strangeness" in the alien would require writers to acknowledge that "true aliens would be fundamentally unknowable" (57).[7] What his argument seems to assert at this point, however, is that "irreducible strangeness" would render the aliens imperceptible—that is, that they would exist in a manner in which they could not be perceived as entities (although, presumably, they might appear as objects or forces). The implied notion that unknowability is or could be an extension of strangeness is, however, problematic. *Strangeness* is measurable, and, although it may be described as "essential" or "irreducible," it may also be described otherwise, so that even if the yardstick of strangeness were infinitely long, it would still be the same strangeness and the same yardstick. *Unknowability*, on the other hand, is, like pregnancy, not measurable or a matter of degree but an absolute: Something is either knowable or unknowable. In "Effing the Ineffable," presented at Aliens: The Anthropology of Science Fiction, the Eighth J. Lloyd Eaton Conference in 1986, Benford repeats the idea of "irreducible unknowability": "Of course, we all know that one cannot depict the totally alien. This is less a deep insight than a definition. Stanislaw Lem's *Solaris* asserts that true contact and understanding is impossible. It was a vivid reminder twenty years ago. As genre criticism, it seems nowadays ponderously obvious" (14–15). Moreover, depicting the totally alien is not really what science fiction is trying to do. The pursuit of the Alien in science fiction is the pursuit of strangeness (through otherness to alterity), not the pursuit of the unknowable.

It may be useful at this point, therefore, to consider briefly how we know or do not know anything. *Know* is a problematic word and, hence, so is its derivative pair *knowable/unknowable*. But in its most general sense, the twofold definition put forward by James Ward for the root verb seems to allow for a crucial distinction in the knowability/unknowability of the alien. Ward writes that "[t]o *know* may mean either to perceive or apprehend, or it may mean to understand or comprehend" (Ward, *Encycl. Brit.* XX. 49 s.v. *Psychology*; cited in *OED2*). If, therefore, we can know either *perceptually* ("perceive or apprehend" without forming a concept) or *conceptually* ("understand or comprehend" by forming a concept of something perceived), an alien might fall into one of three kinds of (un)knowability: It might be perceptually *and* conceptually unknowable (which would correspond to Benford's "irreducibly unknowable"), *or* perceptually knowable *but* conceptually unknowable, *or* perceptually *and* conceptually knowable. The intrinsic nature of storytelling clearly requires, however, that the attempt to represent the Alien, if the Alien is the writer's interest, go forward as though even the perceptually and conceptually unknowable alien might be representable, as the other categories are. Although the aliens in the vast majority of short stories clearly fall into the final category, perceptually *and* conceptually knowable, there are a number of stories which deal with those in the middle group.

Strategies for the representation of the perceptually *and* conceptually unknowable ("irreducibly unknowable") alien in science fiction are limited. What goes on in Benford and Eklund's own novel, for example, is not a discussion of the "irreducibly unknowable," since the protagonist knows the aliens perceptually at least, but the exploration of the state of mind of the protagonist—his conceptual "unknowingness" (entering at some level, the "cloud of unknowing" of the mystics) in which he is aware of his perception of the aliens but cannot form any concept of them (as though all the category receptacles in his psyche are round and the nature of the alien is square), so that the aliens keep sliding out of his psyche.[8] The problem of *knowability* in this basic sense of being perceptible to another species is therefore addressed in magazine short fiction only rarely—and successfully addressed even more rarely.

Strategies for the representation of the perceptually knowable but conceptually unknowable alien are also limited. One strategy most frequently used for this kind of alien in short stories is that of *alien room*. *Room*, here, is used in the sense of "space" taken up by an object and imagined to be left behind by it when it is removed, as in the old put-down "Better your room than your company"; in mainstream fiction, the strategy's most notable example is Virginia Woolf's *Jacob's Room* (1922), in which the protagonist's character and life is derived from an examination of the room in which he lived. The strategy produces *hypothesized-contact* stories, which offer only indirect contact and do so by postulating the discovery of alien artifacts as evidence for the existence and nature of an alien species. Such stories focus on the investigative process of collecting and interpreting the evidence, whether this is a single artifact or a whole abandoned world. The empty artifact appears in William E. Bentley's "The Dip Stick" (1954) and A. E. van Vogt's "Enchanted Village" (1950); the empty world is featured in Jack McDevitt's "Black to Move" (1982), although only one city is presented. Usually this scenario postulates humans investigating nonhuman artifacts, but not always: In Leo Szilard's "Grand Central Terminal" (1952) and C. J. Cherryh's "Pots" (1985), empty Earth is being studied by alien archaeologists. Stories following the hypothesized-contact scenario are more often than not "hard science" stories, with a considerable emphasis on forensic procedures and technology, as in Hal Clement's "Technical Error" (1943), in which the officers and crew of a crashed human spaceship on an uninhabited planet discover an abandoned alien spaceship and attempt to get it in working order in order to be able to leave the planet on it.[9] Not all stories that postulate conceptual unknowability employ the "room" strategy in this almost literal sense.

In other stories that postulate conceptually unknowable aliens, the strategy adopted tinkers with what humans consider universal constants by exploring how far knowability might be dependent on some kind of common experiential matrix for the participants. A story about an attempt to *understand* knowable aliens through the identification of the nature and purpose of an artifact depends upon the provision in the story's setting of a shared experiential matrix—an environment common to both parties to the encounter in which at least one of them is at home, although the other may or may not be—such as a strange planet or an abandoned spaceship. Stories in which the investigation of the *knowability* of aliens is foregrounded, however, may exploit the possibilities of a common experiential matrix. One classic example of such an investigation is James Blish's story "Common Time" (1953), in which the protagonist is on the test flight of a new form of space drive designed to carry humans over interstellar distances. In the course of this flight he is thrust into an experience in which he loses all normal frames of reference (exemplified specifically by the loss of contact with the passage of time that underpins all normal human existence) and, in the awakening which follows a long period of unconsciousness, finds himself swamped in confusion over what he is experiencing:

> The thing (or things) which had restored him to consciousness, however, was— it was what? It made no sense. It was a construction. . . . No it wasn't a construction, but evidently something alive—a living being organized horizontally, that had arranged itself in a circle about him. No, it was a number of beings. Or a combination of all these things. . . .
>
> Its voice, or their voices, came at equal volume from every point in the circle, but not from any particular point in it. Garrard could think of no reason why that should be unusual. . . .
>
> The creature said . . . "You are the being-Garrard. We-they are the clinesterton beademung, with all of love.[10] (51)

The effect of strangeness produced by the *clinesterton beademungen* is so extreme that the reader shares the narrator's confusion about what he is encountering and even, significantly, his confusion about whether or not he is actually encountering anything at all except a figment of his own imagination. It is clear that Blish's protagonist, like Benford's in *If the Stars Are Gods* (1977), knows the aliens perceptually at least, but in a much more emotionally immediate mode, conveyed by his fumbling attempts to name to himself, to corral in language his perceptual knowingness, and to correct his conceptual unknowingness. His inability to stabilize his perceptions of the aliens in complete utterances (a complete utterance would contain a concept) creates loopholes for the aliens as they slide out through the spaces between the words, leaving their "room" behind them.[11] Paradoxically, moreover—and in defiance of the commonly received wisdom that the unknown is something that will arouse fear (and hence hatred)—at the limit of knowability love casts out fear: The narrator is quite unafraid of what is happening to him, and only on his return to Earth is the question raised uneasily by another earthbound character as to whether the *clinesterton beademungen* pose any kind of threat to humanity. The problem with knowing the sapient alien, implies Blish in "Common Time," is that, although it may be perceptually knowable in the absence of a shared experiential matrix but conceptually unknowable, if we only perceive it without being able to conceptualize our perception, we may never know whether we have actually perceived something/someone or not.

Also a part of the problem of knowability is the problem of how far perceptual knowability can extend in the absence of conceptualization. In Colin Kapp's "Ambassador to Verdammt" (1967), the problem of knowability is addressed in a context that also questions how far the experiential matrix is actually common to both alien and human and whether such a matrix is necessary to communication. The protagonist arrives on a planet where the aliens manifest themselves to humans as sounds—of feet running over the roof of his shelter and of maniacal laughter—without visible bodies, and hence they are only perceptually knowable; his attempt to find them, and hence know them conceptually, leads to delirium, which, it is implied, would have ended in insanity had he not been rescued. Eventually, he manages to stabilize himself long enough assess his experience:

> Later, some more rational part of his mind re-appraised the sensations and thrust upon him the half-formed concept that he was factually motionless and that these quasi-environments were actually being created and dissolved around him.
>
> He remembered that Prellen had defined intelligence with reference to the Unbekannt as the conscious ability to manipulate environment. (83)

If the Unbekannt are actually manipulating environment, then the experiential matrix of space-time is different for them than for him; for him it is a constant, whereas for them it is a variable. They may not be on the planet in anything like the same way he is—even the concept of being "on" a planet might not be part of their experiential matrix (if the planet is a shared experiential matrix, then it is so in an extremely stretched meaning of the word *shared*, at least as far as space is concerned). On the other hand, the Unbekannt do seem to share a common time-matrix, and Gale Asch makes this point in a letter to *Analog's* editor in which he questions Kapp's postulate that the aliens were "incomprehensible" (*conceptually unknowable* in my terminology):

> This story postulates a being so alien as to be incomprehensible to humans. It also postulates that these were intelligent beings; that they changed their envi-

ronment. This yields the conclusion that they were aware of their environment and of themselves.

Therefore, these beings are not incomprehensible to humans, as follows: I think, therefore I am. I think, therefore I remember. I remember, therefore I was. I was and now am, therefore there is past and present. In the past there was future. If there was future, there is future. If there is past, present and future, existence is in sequence of past, present and future. That which perceives its existence perceives past, present and future.

This was implied in the development of the story.

There is inherently a common ground of awareness between all sentient beings. Sensory methods may differ.[12] (167–68)

The extent of the "common ground" Asch identifies is indicated by the fact that the Unbekannt have managed to communicate at least the concept of the exchange of infants as "ambassadors" or intermediaries between them and the humans: The details of this communication are not laid out, but clearly imply that communication can exist in the absence of conceptual knowledge. In the exchange of ambassadors, moreover, Kapp makes the point that the conceptually unknowable may be knowable or become knowable to those whose psyches are not already set in patterns of knowing: The adult psyche, once formed by its experience of knowing, cannot reform itself to accommodate new forms of knowing. Living provokes specific modes of conceptualization and these cannot be replaced later by other modes. The ambassador—the human who will learn to communicate by forming experience in contact with, and therefore including, the conceptual modality of Unbekannt—is a newborn infant. The Unbekannt are perceptually knowable, even in the absence of a reliably shared experiential matrix, although their knowability, like that of Blish's *clinesterton beademungen*, strains even perception.

In these two stories, the perceptually knowable but conceptually unknowable aliens lie at the extreme of strangeness or otherness. Both the *clinesterton beademungen* and the *Unbekannten* are truly exotic aliens, as I noted in my previous chapter on alien form, lying completely outside de Camp's guidelines, and this exoticism, given the effectiveness of both stories, suggests that it might be possible to argue that an extreme of otherness supports alterity. But it is not possible on the evidence of either or both of them to decide whether alterity *requires* conceptual unknowability.[13] Moreover, alterity, in terms of my Jungian approach, requires the Other as a Self, and there is no indication of "selfness" either in Blish's story, which seems either to rule out the notion of Self as we understand it or to imply a plural Self, or in Kapp's. The comparative rarity of stories about perceptually knowable but conceptually unknowable aliens, moreover, indicates that although writers of short stories may appreciate the issues of knowability/unknowability, they prefer to address the questions of recognizability, comprehensibility, and compatibility in the conceptually knowable alien.

First Contact—Recognizability

The first-contact story is the most generally recognized as the appropriate context for determining the recognizability of sapience in the conceptually knowable alien. So popular are first-contact stories that Gary K. Wolfe considers that "writing a 'first contact' story . . . becomes somewhat like a pianist's adding Liszt or Scriabin to his repertoire" (*The Known and the Unknown* 1979, xii), so that sooner or later nearly every writer, even a writer with only a mild interest in aliens, produces one. The initial recognition of sapience in a hitherto unknown but conceptually knowable species is a large subcategory among first-contact stories, and it is usually carried out in the form of an argument about the precise interpretation in this particular set of circumstances of the rules of thumb. The resulting hypothesis implies that a xenologist stranded on an unexplored planet circling a remote star who encounters a creature emerging from the local flora can, if he/she/it has the presence of mind to remember the rules of thumb and to check for the existence of sapience-markers, easily decide whether the creature is one of the local fauna or one of the local immigration officers.

Systematic checking for the use of sapience-markers appears early in the chronological development of first-contact stories. In Weinbaum's classic story "A Martian Odyssey" (1934), the human hero, having landed on Mars, leaves his companions and his ship and sets out to explore the area where they have landed. Almost immediately he meets and rescues a Martian creature and quickly notices "a little black bag or case hung about the neck of the bird-thing!" and infers that the creature is "intelligent . . . or tame" (6) because the bag is "a manufactured article" (7). The possibility of communication is suggested to him by the creature's going "into a series of clackings and twitterings and [holding] out its hands toward me, empty," which he takes to be "a gesture of friendship" (6). Given this initial evidence to arouse his suspicions of sapience, he attempts to establish it by exchanging names. After success with this first step—the Martian understanding Dick's naming of himself and returning his own name as Tweel—the linguistic exchange falters: "[H]ere we stuck! . . . [T]ry as I would, I couldn't get a single word! Nothing was the same for two successive minutes, and if that's a language, I'm an alchemist" (7). Although he has failed to achieve satisfactory linguistic communication with the alien, he has established to his own satisfaction that Tweel is a language-using entity. Dick moves on to try another sapience-marker: "After a while I gave up the language business, and tried mathematics. I scratched two plus two equals four on the ground, and demonstrated it with pebbles. Again Tweel caught the idea, and informed me that three plus three equals six. Once more we seemed to be getting somewhere" (7). The use of number, Weinbaum suggests, is important, but in isolation it may be limited, for the protagonist immediately has to go beyond it by trying to establish Tweel's understanding of graphic symbolism. He draws a map of the solar system in the sand: "Tweel understood my diagram all right. He poked his beak at it, and with a great deal of trilling and clucking, he added Deimos and Phobos to Mars, and then sketched in the earth's moon" (7–8). His conclusion, after Tweel follows up this evidence of sapience by apparently meaningless antics with the completed diagram—repeatedly leaping up and landing on his beak in the center—is that "[w]e could exchange ideas up to a certain point, and then—blooey! . . . Yet, in spite of all difficulties, I *liked* Tweel, and I have a queer certainty that he liked me" (8–9). What they can exchange, in fact, goes little beyond the recognition of the other's sapience indicated by the presence of the markers, and this exchange becomes what is meant by initial recognition of sapience in an alien species.[14]

The primary marker that flags the entity as a possibly sapient entity may be its activity rather than its possession of an artifact. In Anthony Boucher's story "Star Dummy" (1952), previously mentioned, the protagonist Paul Peters is told about the strange creature in the wombat cage at the local zoo and goes to look at it: "He could see the thing now, and it was in body very much like an outsize koala. . . . But it was what it was doing that fascinated Paul. It concentrated on rubbing its right forepaw in circles on the ground, abruptly looking up from time to time at the nearest wombat" (180). Paul recognizes a possible sapience-marker, the use of graphic symbolism, and as a gesture of response himself draws a diagram of the solar system (demonstrating his own sapience by so doing) on the ground in the cage. His diagram is recognized, and he knows that he is dealing with a sapient creature: "An animal who can draw, an animal who can recognize a crude diagram of the solar system, is rational—is not merely a beast like the numbly staring wombats" (181). He and the alien, Tarvish, then exchange number symbols. Boucher's treatment of first contact in "Star Dummy" is an example of sapience recognition demonstrably linked with Weinbaum's treatment, although his story is quite different.

What Weinbaum establishes in "Martian Odyssey" is a protocol of first-contact sapience recognition that other writers have found acceptable and convenient to follow, especially in accidental encounters such as he describes. In contrast to the accidental on-planet first contact, however, is the deliberate on-planet first contact. In stories of the latter, the narrative follows the process of seeking out an alien species and attempting to prove its sapience. The simple markers in such stories usually become part of a formal protocol, including precontact preparations, and some discussion of the contact protocol is often included in the story. Precontact preparations are often elaborately detailed in the story, even where the story is of the contact itself. In Michael Kube-McDowell's story "Slac//" (1981), for example, the narrator, a member of "the Service" specializing in alien contact, explains to the reader: "The crucial step was to monitor the communications of the inhabitants from orbit, and . . . use a linguacomp to crack the language. Or . . . plant a selection of sight-sound peepers. . . . Then, language in hand, simply go meet the inhabitants. When a new animal approaches you speaking your language, it gives you pause" (145). What is represented here is a codification or rationalization dependent on one of the three basic markers suggested by Weinbaum—language. The codification is further revealed when the contact team, which has already established sapience in one species on a planet, finds another that shows the same markers, as one of the team tries to explain to her skeptical leader:

"Well, they have language."
    "Many species communicate with sound."
    "Captain, some of these creatures speak Semu."
    "Mimicry is not unknown, is it?"
    Gritting her teeth, Wells continued. "They're socially organized."

"So are bees. Are they tool-makers? Do they have writing."

"No. Not that I've seen so far. But—"

"Aren't those the prime determiners?" (162)

Of Weinbaum's three suggested markers, in fact, only the use of number is missing in this discussion, although, for the purposes of the particular story, a new one ("socially organized") has been added. In this particular story, in spite of its comparatively recent composition, the codification remains very simple in order to permit the narrative of discovery of sapience to proceed unimpeded by complications in the concept of sapience.

The triple conditions initiated in Weinbaum's story persist and are incorporated by later writers, such as Lee Killough, into even the most complex concepts of sapience. In Killough's story "Sentience" (1973), the action involves the hearing of a "sentient-species claim" filed under a "Federation law [that] held that all sentient beings—whether mammalian, reptilian or anything else— were people, and therefore not to be warred upon" (104). In Killough's ficton a planet proposed for colonization is studied for "four years" by an inspection team, whose "first and foremost task" (105) is to determine whether or not the planet has a sapient life-form. Moreover, the process of determination introduced in this story is not a matter of ad hoc observation. Those who perform it must have a "professional competence" based on "degrees in biology, pananthropology and psychology . . . [and] specialist training in sentience evolution" (105). The inspection team works with a specific definition of sentience as "conscious perception, integral to intelligence" (107), occurring in a physical form that conforms to de Camp's design principles—large enough to have a brain "above the critical minimum" size and with "grasping limbs of some type—hands, tentacles or claws" (108).

Killough, however, introduces a crucial distinction between markers and proofs in the identification of sapience. The grasping limbs of a sapient are necessary because it "must be able to use tools if it is to evolve" ("Sentience" 1973, 108), but because some animals use tools, as Ley pointed out (Ley, "Prelude to Engineering" 119), tool use actually constitutes "only a possible indication of intelligence, not proof" and may be acquired "fortuitously" ("Sentience" 1973, 109). An "advanced social structure," too, constitutes a marker rather than a proof because, like tool use, it is also found among animals (108). What constitutes a proof is "[l]anguage, certainly, and construction" (109). But even a proof may be qualified by its context and require interpretation: "Unfortunately we know that primitive species exist which are not yet capable of the latter and in which the former is still so rudimentary as to be hard[l]y recognizable" (109). The ultimate proof, however, is

> the only behavior we have been able to safely consider unique to rational beings is what has been variously termed creativity or synthesis. It is the ability to take two or more unrelated items and combine them to produce a useful or esthetic result. An animal that discovers a useful object or a beneficial method of performing a task will continue to apply that discovery the same way and no other time after time. . . . An intelligent creature will experiment to see what else can be done with a method or object. (109–10)

In Killough's story, because Cian Buurn can prove that the shree do indeed use daggerthorns not only for hunting but also as weapons—by poisoning them with plant juice to kill miners employed by the company that is working on their planet—he is able to prove "creativity" (112). Consequently, he is able to win at least a temporary reprieve for them. Moreover, this concept of "creativity" cannot be discounted as the mere improvement of tools, which, Ley points out in "Prelude to Engineering" (1941), is also found in a limited way among animals (119).

In her exploration of the nature of one of the traditional markers, moreover, Killough actually improves the concept of the simple sapience-marker. A simple marker such as tool use, she demonstrates, does not exist in isolation—it is part of a complex. The absence of this marker allows the possible presence of the others suggested by Weinbaum (language and number) in the shree to remain untested: The inspection team has not looked for language or number in the shree because it has no reason (in its opinion) to do so. The simple markers, therefore, Killough implies, are only markers, and even if proving actual sapience has to begin with examination of the same markers, they have to be treated as markers only (not proofs), as ambiguous, and as a complex rather than as separable items. The markers are necessary but not sufficient.

At the same time as Killough changes the concept of the sapience-marker, moreover, she improves the requirement for proof. The ambiguity of the sapience-markers requires that they must be questioned in a protocol of testing. Killough's investigator regards language as proof, although this assertion is qualified by the recognition that species exist with languages too primitive to be assessed, yet the investigation has not looked for such primitive languages. In Poul Anderson's "The Master Key" (1964), however, the reliability of language ability as a proof of sapience is explicitly questioned:

> "The key to this problem is the Lugals. You have been calling them slaves, and there is your mistake. They are not. They are domestic animals."
>
> Per sat bolt upright. "Can't be!" he exclaimed. 'Sir. I mean, they have language and—"
>
> "*Ja, ja, ja,* for all I care they do mattress algebra in their heads. They are still tame animals." (154)

Even language, Anderson implies here, is only a marker of sapience in isolation—it must be taken in the context of other indicators. The Lugals, moreover, demonstrate tool use—another marker which in this context is also quite misleading. In fact, markers may be suspect for a number of reasons. In on-world encounters, the ambiguity of the simple markers of sapience may be compounded by the question of form: In "Skyveil" (1974), for example, Sydney Van Scyoc demonstrates that the presence of familiar markers such as language and tool use prevents the recognition of the fact that the apparently human inhabitants of a particular planet are merely one intermediate and nonsapient stage in the development of an entirely alien life-form, which is only truly sapient in its final form. It is not necessary, therefore, to accept Anderson's implied assertion in "The Master Key"—that "wildness" is an intrinsic part of sapience and something that distinguishes sapients from nonsapients—in order to understand why his proposition for the necessity of questioning even the basic markers in any given context comes to the fore in many contact stories.

Weinbaum's protocol requires the acceptance of the axiom that the existence of sapience in any species will be flagged by certain external markers, which he identifies as tools, language, and number, any one of which may provide the initial signal. These external markers are broadly defined: *Tool* covers any artifact, *language* covers any symbolizing communication system, and *number* covers any mathematical demonstration. From the point of view of the observer within the story, they are, however, *simple* markers in the sense that they can be used and identified individually in a particular encounter.

They are, also, broadly speaking, markers of intellect (intellectual capacity), but they do not by and of themselves constitute intellect, although they will always be involved in it. The general concept of "intellectual capacity" holds good, moreover, even if different writers cannot agree on precise definition. Furthermore, although they are usually considered as discrete abilities, each of them in turn incorporates a set (not the same set necessarily) of individual faculties or abilities (pattern recognition, time binding, memory, symbolizing capacity, problem solving, and so on). The basic sapience-markers, it appears to be agreed, are only the tip of the iceberg as far as sapience is concerned: They do not constitute sapience, although they confirm its existence.

Yet the concept of sapience-markers is problematic in that it introduces qualitative judgment into the assessment of sapience. The use of them implies a recognizable boundary—a specific line that can be drawn—between sapient and nonsapient creatures. The narrative of Killough's "Sentience" ends with the end of the hearing of Cian Buurn's claim on behalf of the shree, before the final verdict is handed down but not before the lawyer whose clients will be dispossessed if the shree are judged sapient has managed to emphasize the point raised by the original inspector that the sapience-marker of tool-using may not have spread beyond a few individuals nearest to the mining camps and thus under the greatest pressure to adapt. The story of the shree, their exploiters, and their defenders is continued in *The Monitor, the Miners, and the Shree* (1980), which further develops these points. Killough's point about the development of sapience had previously been raised in Philip J. Farmer's "Prometheus" (1961), where specimens of an avian species recognized as "the Galaxy's most intelligent non-sentient beings" about whom there is "even speculation they might be advanced enough to have a language" (9) are being held in a local zoo while a scientific team tests the species on their home planet for evidence of sapience. The protagonist, infiltrating the avians on the planet on behalf of the scientists, looks for the basic markers, noting that one of the avians wields "a club" (92) and another uses a gourd-shell as a container (94). In particular, however, he searches for "the beginning of a language" and a capacity for "symbolic thinking" (96). The question of placement of the boundary for any particular marker further contaminates the simplicity of the simple markers.

Even more significantly, it is possible to infer from Killough's story that the absence of markers must be questioned. Although in this story it is entirely possible that the shree, still developing sapience, have not yet reached the stage of language, the fact that no one has noticed it does not mean that it does not exist. In the search for sapience, absence of evidence is not, prima facie, evidence of absence. Consequently, in the absence of evidence, the investigator is obliged to be suspicious.

The stories by Weinbaum, Boucher, Killough, and Farmer, moreover, all demonstrate the idea that the existence of a common or shared experiential matrix in stories of contact normally preempts the issue of the knowability of the alien and allows the issue of the recognizability of sapience to be addressed directly. In all of them, there is a planetary environment common to the investigator and the subjects. Weinbaum's encounter takes place in the middle of a semidesert on Mars where neither Dick (totally removed from his own Earth environment) nor Tweel is completely at home. Nevertheless, although the desert context may be foreign to both of them, it is undeniably common to both of them. In Boucher's story, too, a context exists that is common to both parties, although because it is more complex it is misinterpreted by one of them. As a result of his misunderstanding of the complex foreign context of Earth, Tarvish, looking for "rational" (sapient) creatures on Earth, tries to establish communication with lions and wombats because, although they have the "waves" (182) that mark creatures which might understand him, he fails to recognize the context (zoo) in which he finds them (it is not clear why Earth's nonrational animals have waves and humans do not—nor even why Paul is an exception among humans in having them). Here, nevertheless, as in other stories, the potentially problematic nature of the planetary environment is turned into an advantage by being exploited for dramatic enhancement of the narrative.

Space, on the other hand, is sometimes considered the ideal shared experiential matrix for first-contact encounters since it provides instant proof of sapience through the possession of advanced technology implied in the construction of such a complex artifact as a spaceship. The simple markers of planetary environments are subsumed in the *compound* marker of space technology, since all the basic identifiers of sapience are required to achieve technology at that level. Murray Leinster's "First Contact" (1945) involves space as the common environment shared by the crews of two spaceships—one human, one not, meeting in space far removed from the home world of either—and there is, therefore, no problem for either party in recognizing the sapience of the other, although the problem of *comprehending* the other is not thereby avoided.

Nevertheless, space, too, has the potential to be problematic for first contact with aliens, and even there the recognition of sapience in spacegoing aliens is not always automatic. This particular aspect of recognizability is explored in Poul Anderson's classic story "Hiding Place" (1961). Here, the human protagonists board a drifting interstellar spaceship of an unknown type, only to find that its cargo consists of alien creatures collected from many different planetary environments as zoo specimens and that the crew of the ship seems to have hidden among the animals. The problem presented to Nicholas van Rijn and Captain Bahadur Torrance is that they know sapient aliens must be present (the ship requires more than one crewmember) but not in what physical form, and they therefore have to separate the crew from the cargo by examining the caged creatures in a process of elimination—ruling out one species after another on grounds of their physical incapacity for operating the ship. Although the unusual situation and the change in testing process make this a special case, nevertheless, in Anderson's story, as in most other first-contact stories, what is being addressed is the recognizability of sapience in another species.

Taken as a group, therefore, first-contact stories imply a consensus on the recognizability of sapience in different species by the identification of sapience-markers. Moreover, implicit in that consensus—however loose—is the markers' status as universal constants (that is, constants that will appear in all conceptually knowable sapient species).[15] Implicit, also, in what is said about the basic markers is the recognition that they present themselves as a *set* or *gestalt*. As a group, first-contact stories also suggest that you need language *and* math *and* artifacts—or language *and* construction *and* creativity—or whatever the writer's preferred terms for the set of markers is; one marker alone does not qualify. Appropriately, however, writers of first-contact stories are not in lockstep agreement over the precise nature of the sapience-markers—and no one so far has tried to propose a formal protocol on the subject. Nevertheless, they do seem to be in agreement that individual sapience-markers add up to a gestalt greater than their sum, and consequently the gestalt may be considered a matter of consensus, albeit a loose one.

First-contact stories, it may be concluded, have developed a set of conventions according to which they describe initial encounters between representative individuals or groups of two different sapient species—one of which is usually human—and the narrative unfolds with the characters sharing a common experiential matrix. The encounter described may be accidental or the result of a deliberate search. In either case, the narrative is structured by process: It traces the process of recognizing sapience in a totally unknown entity, or the process of establishing sapience in a suspected species, or the process of testing an already known species or individual for the reality of its sapience. The narrative usually incorporates some discussion of the nature of sapience, explicitly or implicitly, postulating a core of sapience-markers that form the gestalt we call sapience, and it will often lay out a specific contact procedure. In accidental encounters the criteria are usually basic when humans are checking nonhumans; when nonhumans are checking humans, the criteria are sometimes more unusual if not downright bizarre. The dramatic potential of the first-contact scenario is emphasized by the fact that humans are examined for sapience, with increasingly bizarre criteria, much more frequently in first-contact stories than in any other scenario. The first-contact scenario is also most suited to the short-story form, although in some instances the combination of the emphasis on strangeness and the limited room for development results in something that might be more appropriately called the "first-impact" story. First-contact stories concern themselves with the conceptually knowable alien and with the issue of recognizability.

Feeling Things Out—Comprehensibility

Whereas first-contact stories pursue the concept of recognizability and the process of recognition, established-contact stories pursue the concept of comprehensibility—and hence the possibility of substantial and significant interaction with sapient aliens. The recognition of the gestalt produced by the sapience-markers, of course, itself implies some degree of comprehensibility. Essentially, stories of interaction with sapient aliens depend on the hypothesis that, given the knowability of the alien in general and given proof of sapience in a specific alien creature, that alien should be comprehensible: Humans will understand aliens well enough for interaction because we will find common factors between ourselves and the alien in question, although complete understanding may be impossible and even partial understanding fraught with difficulty and frustration (generally speaking, in the magazine stories the closer the alien is to the limit of knowability, the more likely it is to be truly incomprehensible). Consequently, just as first-contact stories set up protocols and conventions of recognizability, established-contact stories set up similar protocols and conventions to explore comprehensibility, essentially (true to science fiction's association with scientific method) in the form of a consensus hypothesis—the hypothesis of comprehensibility.

Much of the exploration of comprehensibility depends upon a set of assumptions about human psychology—actually a popular and eclectic version of psychology rather than any specific or officially sanctioned psychological theory. The assumptions common to most established-contact stories seem to be that human psychology is a gestalt of discrete innate factors that together constitute an intellect-affect core, out of which develop behavioral systems such as art, cosmology, education, game-playing, law, logic, medicine, philosophy, politics, religion, social codification, technology, trade, and war. It is then postulated that just as the marker traits of sapience are universal constants,[16] so also are other factors that contribute to sapience—and that therefore the intellect-affect core (which together constitute the psyche) and the behavioral system-set that arise in a given sapient species are merely particular, specific, and local manifestations of constants that will occur elsewhere in the universe among other conceptually knowable aliens, although they will be subject to differentiation as the result of biological and environmental factors. Consequently, sapience can be approached as part of the "typically exotic" status attributed to Earth under the Assumption of Mediocrity rule by xenobiologists (Freitas, "Extraterrestrial Zoology" 1981, 53; citing Allen Broms). In any encounter between human and alien, the two psyches will exist side by side in such a way as to produce what might be called an interface between them. Comprehensibility, therefore, can be addressed by looking not only at what might occur in the way of analogues in a similarly sapient but biologically different alien but also at what might not occur—at both the parallels and the mismatches in the interface.

Of the factors in the intellect-affect core, alien intellect has received by far and away the most attention. Although there are many established-contact stories which either assume as the default that intellect is a constant (humans and aliens will think alike) or point out deliberately the existence of specific parallels between human thought processes and those of the most exotic of aliens,[17] established-contact stories that explore the way in which alien intellect would differ from human intellect are by far the more common, suggesting the prevalence of the attitude in science fiction circles. David Brin's experience, recorded in "The Dogma of Otherness" (1986), tends to confirm the existence of a widely held belief that the human mode of intellect is not the only one—not even the only one on Earth. In discussing the possible sapience of dolphins with lecture audiences, he comments that repeatedly

> I'd patiently describe the brilliantly simple experiments of Herman and others which had forced *me* to abandon my own early optimism that it was only a matter of time until we learned to understand dolphin speech.
>
> But this only seemed to deepen the questioners' sullen insistence that there must be *other varieties of intelligence*.[18] (5; original emphasis)

It should be noted that by the time Brin comes to write this article, scientific thinking has already moved away from the position advocated by Campbell and cited at the beginning of this chapter, that "[w]e might not recognize what another race used for 'intelligence'" (Blurb for Perkins 1965, 133). According to Sam Moskowitz, the possibility of other varieties of intellect (to borrow Brin's phrase) was introduced into science fiction by Stanley Weinbaum in "Martian Odyssey" as early as 1934 (from where, possibly, it was recognized as a principle by Campbell): "The author placed great emphasis on the possibility that so alien a being would think *differently* from a human being and therefore perform actions which would seem paradoxical or completely senseless to us. This novel departure gave a new dimension to the interplanetary 'strange encounter' tale" ("Dawn of Fame" 1974, viii–ix.). In his blurb for "The Best Policy" (1957) by Randall Garrett in the anthology *Earthmen and Strangers* (1968) Robert Silverberg, too, asserts that "one feature of alien beings is their alienness: they are not likely to think the way we do" (Silverberg, *Earthmen and Strangers* 1968, 46). Garrett's story exploits the way in which the human captive of the alien Dal is able to mislead his captors in a lie-detector test by exploiting ambiguities between his own language and the language of his captors that enable the answer to any question put to him to be both completely truthful and completely misleading, depending on the definition of the terms within it. Both the human and the alien Dal work cognitively with the binary logic of either/or—either truth or falsehood—but only the human, it seems, has capability to avoid or evade binary logic and go beyond it to multivalent logic and the concept of an utterance which is simultaneously both true and false. Similarly, in "Now Inhale" (1959), Eric Frank Russell postulates a society where game-playing is valued to the point where a condemned prisoner can postpone his or her execution by playing the game of his or her choice until an outcome is decided. In these circumstances, the superior exercise of logic as a defensive weapon is illustrated when the game used here by the condemned human prisoner is the game of piling rings on spikes according to certain rules of order, as "played by the priests in Benares . . . [for] about two thousand years" (133). The protagonist's knowledge and application of the potential of this game to continue indefinitely allows him to postpone his execution until rescue arrives and the alien society is defeated.

But variations in the use of logic may take a backseat to other capacities of the psyche of a sapient species. In another story in the same anthology, "The Gentle Vultures" (1957), Isaac Asimov writes about an invasion force on the moon who are waiting for Earth to destroy itself in a nuclear war before moving in to enslave humans: They are constitutionally pacifist and vegetarian, and when in the psyche of the human they trap for study they see themselves metaphorically identified (in a vivid pictorial image they receive telepathically) with vultures, they are so horrified and inhibited that they abandon their base and leave Earth to its own devices. This story prompted Noel Keyes, when he was including the same story in *Contact* (1963), to suggest in his introduction (as part of a discussion of science fiction as metaphor about the unknown) that "the power of human metaphor to subvert an alien mind, may well be man's best, though unwitting, defense" (9). In both these stories, the human wrests advantage from a difference in modes of thinking between the human and the alien species. There is clearly, moreover, a conflict between the difficulty of conveying a different intellect and the desire to do so, since in both stories the similarity is stronger than the difference. In Garrett's story, the aliens are (in spite of biological difference) very humanlike in their psychology, and in Asimov's story the Hurrians are even similar biologically, although they are "little-primate" and "tailed" ("Gentle Vultures" 1957, 98), rather than "large-primate" (104) and tailless as humans are. But in neither story does the difference in mode of thinking between human and alien affect mutual comprehensibility.

Often, moreover, even where intellect is directly considered, the kind of intellect is not the issue. In William Morrison's previously cited story "The Sack" (1950), for example, the almost omniscient alien admits that he may be doing humans a disservice by answering their questions because "[t]he process of coming at the truth is as precious as the final truth itself. I cheat you of that. I give your people the truth, but not all of it, for they do not know how to attain it of themselves. It would be better if they learned that, at the expense of making many errors" (92). The alien's concern clearly springs from past experience of the effects of informational spoon-feeding on less gifted races: The process of learning is not only a necessary part of understanding information properly, but the ability to learn is itself a faculty that needs to be exercised. In making this point, he is making a point made over and over again in human thinking about learning—that whether as children in school or adults at work, humans understand better what they have learned if they have learned it by working things out for themselves. Even superior intelligences, the story of "The Sack" implies, will operate on this principle. More intellect is not necessarily different intellect, and the huge difference in biology of the Sack itself (see previous chapter) is completely irrelevant.

Affect (emotion, feeling) is also often a focus for discussions of comprehensibility in alien species. Although, as Brian Ash remarks, "the likelihood of human emotions existing in an utterly nonhuman metabolism is not particularly strong" (*Faces of the Future* 1975, 165), there seems to be a consensus that there will be feeling of some kind. Rob Chilson's "The Hand of Friendship" (1983), which as previously pointed out explores the nature of an alien without apparent capacity for that particular kind of affect we might call *liking*, is exceptional in its premise, and even there Chilson does not seem to be suggesting that the Trill necessarily have no affect at all. Moreover, because affect, much more than intellect, seems in humans to be related to although not determined by biology, the biology of the alien will provide sufficient clues to make the affect that it gives rise to at least minimally comprehensible. Feeling may even be more significant than intellect: Frank Herbert's "Try to Remember" (1961) suggests that the ability to understand (through intellectual self-examination) its own affect may be what makes a species truly civilized and hence truly sapient. In many stories, therefore, comprehending the affect produced by the alien biology solves the problem of the alien's overall comprehensibility. Consequently, stories that suggest that the alien may be totally incomprehensible—or even only *almost* totally incomprehensible—from the point of view of affect are rare.

Nevertheless, although most writers agree that the Alien is conceptually knowable, recognizable, and, usually (as a result of a theory of sapient behavior based on the idea that humanity is psychologically "typically exotic") comprehensible at least in part, some writers seem prepared to accept the idea that a knowable alien might present a specific aspect that is totally incomprehensible. The extent and quality of alien comprehensibility is the focus of a very large proportion of established-contact stories, which therefore present directly or indirectly the issue of the comprehensibility of the alien sapient by examining a specific aspect of its behavior. More often than not it is presented as a puzzle to be solved in order to facilitate further interaction. On the one hand, the aliens' behavior may present only mild strangeness and the puzzle is easily solved. In Bruce Stanley Burdick's "Q.E.D." (1984), for example, the protagonist demonstrates humans' right to be considered sapient by demonstrating elementary geometry. On the other hand, it may present a quite specific point of incomprehensibility and the puzzle remains unsolved. A comprehensive exploration of the latter extreme is offered in Ray Brown's "Getting Even" (1982). Brown floats the original and attractive concept of "Interspecific Co-agency," which is a property of interspecies relations and means that "you don't have to understand a sentient creature to deal with it" (32). The protagonist, therefore, looking back on his attempts to find out from a Cleph informant who might have attempted to commit genocide against the Cleph, recalls, "I never was sure how well we were communicating at any time, and it's possible that we never really 'understood' each other at all" (31). He solves his case, but he never really understands how the Cleph think or feel about it. This story demonstrates a point of conceptual unknowability within a conceptually knowable species—perhaps even a specific point of "irreducible strangeness" (Benford, "Aliens and Knowability" 1980, 57)—but the Cleph are certainly knowable and comprehensible in all but that one aspect.

The matching of characteristics at the interface is, however, not inevitable. Mismatches—points at which the comprehensibility of the aliens fails because parts of the interface do not correspond—may occur. Generally speaking, these errors may be the result of biological factors (I use *factor* here as something causative but not determinant). References to the importance of being aware of the significance of biological factors are therefore frequently made in the magazines as hints to readers and writers to broaden their outlook. In the introductory blurb to "Initial Contact" by Perry Chapdelaine, for example, a story about first-contact problems in dealing with compound species which appeared in *Analog* in 1969, John W. Campbell writes: "In getting the meaning from an alien's message, it isn't hard to get math and physics. The problems start with terms like 'I' and 'mine'! Wonder what a bee's idea of 'I' is?"

(143). One of John Brunner's scientists in his novel *Total Eclipse* (1974) makes explicit the argument for the effect of biological factors on comprehensibility, in the course of an angry exchange with an interfering bureaucrat. Trying to defend his team's lack of progress in the investigation of a planet whose sapient aliens have become extinct, he draws a parallel with Earth, saying,

> La Paz after a century, tumbledown, covered with creepers, the home of wild animals and snakes and butterflies and birds—how much could you tell about the way of life of a human family by burrowing into the rubble and rotting leaf mold, hm—if you were from another planet and had never seen a live human being? . . . Here's a piano frame—but you have no ears, you never imagined music! Here's a tableknife—but you don't eat, you only drink liquids! Here's a sewing machine—but you have fur and don't wear clothes! After one century, how much sense would you make of what remained? (63)

Brunner's argument is not that "biology is destiny"—a concept that bedevils many stories about aliens—but an extension of the biologists' general rule that form follows function in a living organism and of embodiment theory as I have discussed it in the previous chapter. On these points, for example, Canadian palaeontologist Dale A. Russell writes:

> It is biologically possible for creatures with human brain-body proportions to exist, because they (we) do exist. For the purposes of the thought-experiment, what might some anatomical consequences be for the existence of such brain-body proportions within the body plan of a small theropod dinosaur? They would not be arbitrary, for if they possessed no functional purpose they would not be targeted by selective pressures. (*Odyssey in Time* 1989, 214)

Whatever its complexities and controversial aspects, the theory has arisen because the most obvious fact about the human mind or psyche is that it is found only conjoined with the human brain in the human body. And, as the quotation from Brunner suggests, the mechanisms of embodiment are of less concern to the writer than the result of assuming soma and psyche as conjoint parts of a whole, however that conjoining takes place. The brain (the "membrane and blood") is housed in a container—the human body. Since the brain contains all information necessary to manage (to use a rather simple metaphor) the body that contains it, it is itself to some extent "not innocent" of its container (Poole, "Embodiment" 1988, 265). This will be as true of the alien as of the human. So, Brunner seems to be arguing, just as the form of a sapient creature evolves under the constraints of its ecological role, so its tools and artifacts will be created by its mind under the constraints of its physical form. Since humans cannot know in advance what biological factors may have shaped the different psychology of the alien, they should be prepared to make cautious reasonable guesses from any available evidence—or, at the very least, be on the alert for the possibility of mismatches.

Paradoxically, the mismatch that offers the most formidable challenge to comprehensibility is the nonsapient in human form: anthropomorphic or humaniform animals. Edmond Hamilton's "The Stars, My Brothers" (1962) and Johnathan Blake MacKenzie's "Overproof" (1965) both attempt to address the problem of human response to nonsapient beings in human form and sapients in nonhuman form. In "The Stars, My Brothers," the protagonist, Reed Kieran—a space-frozen scientist—is, a century after his accidental freezing, kidnapped and resuscitated by political activists (calling themselves the Humanity Party) who expect him to support their attempt to prevent the Sakae, the sapient nonhumans of the planet Sako, from treating the humaniform animals of that world as the animals they are. Kieran expresses the crucial point of the story explicitly: "If your Sakae are intelligent and the humans of Sako aren't, then the Sakae have the rights on that world, don't they?" (117). Hamilton supports Kieran's remark by presenting him convincingly, and with a touch of irony, as a man who has undergone a transformation. Originally a science teacher, he has gone into space as a scientific observer as the result of a Swiftian revulsion from humanity (specifically in the form of Gertrude Lemmiken, a student with continual head-colds who sniffs all the way through his physics classes). He has since then been totally isolated from humanity in a century of suspended animation as a result of a freak accident, and in his isolation he has learned about himself and humanity, as he explains to Bregg (one of the Sakae):

> I was in darkness for a hundred years. . . . I've told you how I feel, yes. But I haven't told you what I think. . . . [T]he people out there in the corral have my form, and my instinctive loyalty is to them. But instinct isn't enough. . . . Reason tells me that you . . . who are abhorrent to me, who would make my skin creep if I touched you, you who go by reason—that you are my real people. (142)

His background as science teacher and scientific observer is emphasized, since science fiction equates the scientist with the rational person, and what he has learned is expressed in terms of the primacy of rational thought over animal instinct. Further emphasis is given to the clash between instinct and rationality by making the alien Sakae "lizardoid" with its obvious connotations of cold-bloodedness and snakiness.

Rationality is also the key to MacKenzie's story "Overproof." In it, a similar point is made by demonstrating what follows when an investigative team consisting of a biologist and his anthropologist wife attempt to establish that the Iachu (anthropomorphic creatures) of the planet Sandaroth are sapient, not the animals that the Garotha (analogous sapients) on the planet claim they are. MacKenzie's Garotha are presented in more detail, both physical and cultural, than Hamilton's Sakae, with vividly pictorial emphasis placed on the physical elements that create the initial instinctive revulsion: "The body was vaguely feline in shape, with legs that might have been a blend of panther and frog. The head might have been part tiger, part shark—although there were only four sharp, tearing teeth; the rest were grinding molars, showing that the creature was omnivorous. The eyes were large, saucerlike, and heavy-lidded" (77). Carefully, however, MacKenzie makes the additional point that "the Darotha had, individually and collectively, reacted with both fear and loathing when they first saw a human being" (77), as a result of their experience with the behavior of the Iachu. He also makes explicit the reference to Swift's comments on humanity, which was left implicit in Hamilton's story, in designing and explaining the name *Iachu*—which, the narrator says, is "of English derivation. The preliminary scientific expedition which had first seen the humanoid natives of Sandaroth had immediately dubbed them 'Yahoos'" (77)—*Iachu* being the Garothan pronunciation of Yahoo. But it is the Garotha, however alien their form, who are the species in which rationality exists on Sandaroth, and the Iachu who are, as the investigating anthropologist is forced to acknowledge, "*just not human*"—that is, just not sapient (77)—in spite of their form. Consequently, both in this story and in Hamilton's, the point that emerges is that the rational capacity to override instinct and accept sapience in other than human form—across the boundaries of species and in spite of dramatic alterity in the aliens—is one (though not the only) significant test of human sapience. Equally, the stubbornness by which some of the humans in each story, unable to comprehend what they can clearly see, cling to their attempts to demonstrate the sapience of nonsapients in human form, demonstrates another version of the strangeness of sapient life.

The hypothesis of comprehensibility set up in established-contact stories requires that human sapience be considered as a gestalt of innate psychological factors constituting an intellect-affect compound, out of which develop behavioral systems such as art, cosmology, education, game-playing, law, logic, medicine, philosophy, politics, religion, social codification, technology, trade, and war. It postulates that human behavioral systems of these sorts are merely particular, specific, and local manifestations of the universal constants, and that other forms of the same universal behaviors will exist in creatures elsewhere in the universe—aliens. Borrowing some of its assumptions, and some of its authority, from discussions of physical evolution, it also postulates that the psychology of the Alien—a product of a process of physical and social evolution comparable to that of humans although different from it in specifics—will consist of a similar gestalt and include analogous factors. Although the Alien's basic psychology may be inferable from its physical nature and behavior, however, just as basic human psychology is to some extent inferable from human physical nature and behavior, there will nevertheless be a margin of error. The margin of error is introduced by the presence of biological factors in the alien psychology. Because, given alterity of form, the basic biology of the two species is different, a significant proportion of the biologically determined factors *either* will be only loosely analogous in both species *or* will be completely "wild"—so different as to be unimagined or unimaginable by the other. This hypothesis of comprehensibility allows a psychic (psychological) alterity to be envisaged and explored, focusing the exploration, within specific stories, on the helps and hindrances to mutual comprehensibility created by interspecies differences in particular kinds of interaction. The factors brought into a relationship of any sort constitute the *interface* of the encounter that is a specific although not an exclusive focus of difference between two species. Depending on the author's choice, the difference explored may be something that contrasts analogous factors and the systems they produce or something that examines the problems arising from "wild" factors.

Getting Together—Compatibility

The foundation of all contact stories is the hypothesis that aliens will be conceptually knowable, recognizable, and, to some extent at least, if not wholly, comprehensible. For purposes of storytelling, however, it is further postulated that they will almost certainly be compatible—in the sense that interaction of some sort will be possible—because a sapient species will be social (sociative), however its sociality (defined by Michael Carrithers in *Why Humans Have Cultures* (1992) as "a capacity for complex social behavior") manifests (34). Although a major difference between knowability/recognizability/comprehensibility on the one hand and compatibility on the other exists, in that compatibility is a matter of affect rather than intellect, the complexity of the nature of compatibility is also substantially different.

We are barely at the point of identifying what constitutes our own sociality. Many, if not all, science fiction writers and readers would probably agree with R. D. Laing's assertion that

[i]t's difficult to get down to what universal constants of behavior exist in any one species. . . . I can entirely agree with the last chapter of Lévi Strauss' *The Savage Mind* (1966), where he says that we cannot naively adopt any particular form of total world view or *Gestaltian* meaning our mind happens to find plausible. We can, however, place all these views—all of which display dramatic characteristics, reduced by Lévi-Strauss to diachronic transformation of binary elements—within the general framework of a world view. (quoted in Evans, *R. D. Laing: The Man and His Ideas* 1976, 7)

In fact, however, and despite Lévi-Strauss's stricture on "naively" adopting "any particular world view," humanity has begun to move toward an understanding of its own universal cultural constants. The evidence for this exists in the form of what is popularly known as the Declaration of Human Rights or the International Convention on Human Rights, but is more properly identified as the two "Human Rights Covenants [the *International Convention on Civil and Political Rights* and the *International Convention on Economic, Social and Cultural Rights*] . . . unanimously adopted by the UN General Assembly Res[olution] 2200/XXI on Dec. 16, 1966," which "entered into force in 1976" (Osmańczyk 356, 359). The covenants, merely by asserting as universal (in the sense of applying to all human beings) those rights they spell out, assert that what is protected by those rights is also universal. They incorporate in their various provisions, therefore, what may be viewed as at least a preliminary encoding of universal human cultural constants. The difficulty of understanding universal human constants is not in failing to recognize them for what they are, but in digging them out from the multiple strata of mere "local bylaws" under which they are buried.

For the science fiction writers of the magazine stories, however, difficulty is not the same as impossibility, in spite of the fact that Laing's remarks clearly imply not only that human universal constants are difficult to pin down but that the universal constants of multiple species must be correspondingly more difficult to pin down. Naively or not, by Lévi-Strauss's standards and with the implicit support of the human rights covenants, consequently, science fiction writers are prepared to assume that some constants of behavior are identifiable with a fair degree of probability, even across species boundaries where sapient species are concerned, at least for the purposes of creating fictions.

Compatibility has been rather less prominent in the magazine discussions of the nature of aliens than knowability or recognizability. Whereas the latter issues are both matters of intellect, compatibility is a matter of affect and specifically of affect as it concerns interpersonal behavior among individuals: the quality known as sociality. It is clear that in alien encounters the human species' cultural constants as encoded in the human rights covenants are going to be of little if any practical use. The problem of compatibility seems to have been raised in the scientific community, however, as early as September 1956, in a paper by Andrew G. Haley entitled "Space Law and Metalaw—A Synoptic View" delivered at the Seventh International Astronautical Conference in Rome. Haley points out that the "Great Rules" (by which he refers to the different versions of the so-called Golden Rule in various world religions) are all framed anthropocentrically and that this must be revised in multi-species contexts:

> To metalaw we can project only one principle of human law, namely the stark concept of absolute equity. . . . Under the concept of absolute equity we must project the possibility of an indefinite number of natures, and therefore of an indefinite number of frameworks of natural laws. . . . The maxim of metalaw which inexorably follows is "*Do unto others as they would have you do unto them.*" . . . During all the long centuries of human civilization no law giver has framed the Golden Rule in the language of the Great Rule of metalaw. . . . It is a law for one frame of existence. But with equal positiveness the Golden Rule has no application in the field of metalaw. In metalaw we deal with all frames of existence—with sapient beings different in kind. We must do unto others as they

would have done unto them. To treat others as we would desire to be treated might well mean their destruction. We must treat them as they desire to be treated. This is the simply expressed but vastly significant premise of metalaw. (436–37; original emphasis)

At this point in his argument Haley is addressing the question of natural law and the moral foundation of legal codes both criminal and civil, not the legal codes themselves. Metalaw was subsequently introduced to science fiction readers in G. Harry Stine's article "How to Get Along with an Extraterrestrial ... or Your Neighbor" (1980). Stine argues for the adoption of "metalaw" as proposed by Haley, with the addition of a number of other principles: of due care, of self-defense, of survival, of free choice, and of free movement (44). Metalaw is for all sapient beings according to Haley, and Stine therefore presents an ad hoc definition of an intelligent (sapient) being: "a system having *all* of the following characteristics: Self-awareness . . . Possessed of a time-binding sense . . . Creativity . . . Adaptive behavior . . . Empathy . . . Communicative" (40–41).[19] Stine's selection of characteristics, however, although providing a handy selection of traits necessary for sapient compatibility, do not quite add up to a full definition of sapience itself. Nevertheless, his presentation of Haley's concept and his expansion of it offered a useful stimulus to later writers.[20]

The prominence of the Golden Rule and metalaw in science fiction does not exclude other concepts of a foundation for moral interaction. Willard Marsh's "The Ethicators" (1955), for example, takes a somewhat different tack. It features bilateral symmetry as the biological key to sapience:

The missionaries ... had no real hope of finding humans like themselves in this wonderously [sic] diversified universe. But it wasn't against all probability that, in their rumaging [sic], there might not be a humanoid species to whom they could reach down a helping paw; some emergent cousin with at least a rudimentary symmetry from snout to tail, and hence a rudimentary soul. (55)

The implication is that bilateral symmetry in a nonsapient species will permit the development of sapience (identified here as "a rudimentary soul") manifesting as a "moral law of give and take" (59) in the evolved descendants. Any species that is bilaterally symmetrical and reaches the level of sapience, it is postulated, will achieve moral law, which will thus appear as a universal constant of sapience. In Marsh's story, give and take is reflected in literal transactions of small objects in conversation but is clearly analogous to the more abstract human concept of fair play.[21] Similarly, other desirable virtues of human intraspecies sociality, such as gratitude, loyalty, and responsibility, may have analogues, which may be more or less comprehensible and compatible across the species boundary, so that social interactions may take place.

On the other hand, many vices of intraspecies sociality, such as callousness, ingratitude, and selfishness, may also be present and comprehensible, although neither necessary nor desirable in interspecies interactions. Edward Bryant's "Dancing Chickens" (1984) and Pat Cadigan's "Roadside Rescue" (1984) both explore interspecies potential for the cruelty of sexual exploitation. According to the consensus, therefore, especially in more recent years, the shadow side of human sociality will also have its analogues.

Certain issues of sociality have, however, over the years been repeatedly considered in terms of what will happen if they are carried over from intraspecies to interspecies relations. The microbonds of individual behavior between members of a single species will carry over into encounters between individuals across the species boundary. They become, if encounters are multiplied, therefore, macrobonds between the species. Discussion of certain of these constitute important topoi of interspecies sociality: acceptance, empathy, and cooperation.

Acceptance of aliens as people is a crucial point. It is present even in the classic story of alien encounter, Weinbaum's "A Martian Odyssey." Weinbaum makes this point when Dick is describing his initial meeting with Tweel by having him say, "We could exchange ideas up to a certain point, and then— blooey! . . . Yet, in spite of all difficulties, I *liked* Tweel, and I have a queer certainty that he liked me" (8–9). The experience of the narrator with the Cleph in Brown's "Getting Even" may be described as mutual incomprehension, but it does not result in a lack of acceptance of the Cleph as persons in the narrator's mind. Whatever else the effects of frustration and difficulty of comprehension in encounters may be, they do not necessarily rule out acceptance of the alien as a person.

Nevertheless, acceptance is by no means a given in a new encounter. The fear of strangers is very basic in human psychology, and at the moment of meeting the alien for the first time, the human sees a living creature that has no analogues, real or imagined, in his or her mental catalogue. At Discon, Fritz Leiber raised the point that the alien would seem beautiful, however strange, because like the creatures we already know it would be functional for its environment and survival, and humans in the encounter would recognize this good engineering and find it aesthetically acceptable. This point was visited with a different emphasis the novel *The Game of Fox and Lion* (1986) by Robert Chase, in which Chase introduces the idea that the human response to the appearance of aliens will be different from the response to humans whose appearance is different—in this case, genetically engineered into animal-human hybrid forms: "Benedict had never seen a Bestial at close range before. . . . Closer examination disclosed signs of human heritage . . . the human traces in some ways made the overall effect even more unsettling. A totally alien creature could have been accepted on its own merits" (65–66). The assumption that a "totally alien creature could have been accepted on its own merits" is, however, not entirely safe according to other writers. Bob Shaw, for example, in *Orbitsville* (1975) articulated the principle of the "arachnid reaction":

> The revulsion that most people get when they see spiders—arachnids—is so strong and widespread it has led to the theory that arachnids are not native to Earth. . . . But if the arachnid reaction is what some people think it is—loathing for something instinctively identified as of extraterrestrial origin—then we might be in trouble when we make the first contact with an alien race.
>
> The worry is that they might be intelligent and friendly, even beautiful, and yet might trigger off hate-and-kill reactions in us simply because their shape isn't already registered in a kind of checklist we inherit with our genes. (95)

The "arachnid reaction" is implied and illustrated in a number of alien stories in the magazines from the early days. In Charles Diffin's "Dark Moon" (1931), the hero encounters on another planet a large nonsapient creature, which appears to him as "a thing of horror" (181), and he immediately compares it to the most horrible thing he knows: "Spider! He had named it unconsciously. But the name was inadequate, for here was a thing of horror beyond even a spider of prodigious size. This peaceful valley!—and here was its ruler, frightful, incredibly loathsome!" (182). The similar and stronger reaction by the hero to the aliens he meets in Gerald Vance's "Monsoons of Death" (1942), however, omits the comparison and focuses on the reaction. The protagonist, a scientist by the name of Ward, newly arrived on the planet, is informed by the senior investigator on the site, Halliday, that "[t]his area is inhabited by a species of creature which I do not believe has been classified. I do not know if they are human or if they possess intelligence. . . . But I know that there is something very repellent and fearsome about them. I *felt* that much" (214). Halliday's actions and reactions to these mysterious aliens seem to Ward to be unsatisfactory. When Halliday confesses to being too scared to find out if they can be killed, Ward feels "a cold anger against this man" (214) and goes out to confront them. When he encounters them, his reaction is entirely in keeping with Shaw's description of the arachnid reaction:

> There was one nauseous, sense-stunning instant of incredible horror as his eyes focused on the nameless monstrosities that were revealed in the gray mists of the monsoon . . . an instinct a billion years old, buried beneath centuries' weight in his subconscious, suddenly writhed into life, as pulsing and compelling as the day it had been generated.
>
> The lost forgotten instincts of man's mind that warn him of the horror and menace of the unknown, the nameless, the unclean, were clamoring wildly at his consciousness. . . . Without conscious thought of volition his legs suddenly churned beneath him and he lunged forward. (219)

The same reaction is echoed in Damon Knight's "Rule Golden" (1954) at the point where the human protagonist meets the alien, Aza-Kra: "I was trembling. I had fallen into a crouch without realizing it, weight on my toes, fists clenched" (17). Here the reaction is less violent, possibly because Aza-Kra is already caged and apparently under human control. Knight also suggests the arachnid reaction in the more distant encounter of the human and alien in "Stranger Station" (1956). But although the reaction is important, the majority of stories from the beginning to the present day suggest that the reaction is not inevitable.

At the opposite extreme from the arachnid reaction to the alien is *empathy*. In human psychoanalysis, psychology, philosophy, and aesthetics, empathy is variously described and defined as "projective identification" (Rycroft 1972, 42–43), or "an unverbalized, covert communication process whereby attitudes, feelings and judgements are passed from person to person without ever being publicly articulated" (Reber 1985, 238), or "[p]rojection (not necessarily voluntary) of the self into the feelings of others or, anthropomorphically, into the 'being' of objects or sets of objects" (Seymour-Smith 1988, 268). Although Seymour-Smith's comes closest, none of these definitions really approximates the science-fictional use of the term, where it varies from being "a restricted kind of telepathy . . . in which only feelings and not thoughts may be perceived" (*Grolier SF*, "Esp") to a generalized affect involving feelings of kinship and friendship.[22] The notion of empathy is, however, foregrounded in Gordon R. Dickson's "Lulungomeena" (1954), which introduces the alien Dor Lassos, of a species called Hixabrod, into a community of humans on board a spaceship, to whom he narrates an anecdote of the death of "several Micrushni" on one of his previous voyages. The human narrator comments on the incident:

> I had had some experience with Hixabrodian ways; and I knew that it was not sadism, but a complete detachment that had prompted this little anecdote. But I would see a wave of distaste ripple down the room. No life form is so universally well liked as the Micrushni, a delicate iridescent jelly-fish-like race with a bent toward poetry and philosophy. The men at the table drew away almost visibly from Dor Lassos. But that affected him no more than if they had applauded loudly. Only in very limited ways are the Hixabrod capable of empathy where other races are concerned. (347)

Dickson's point, however, is that even the limited empathy of the Hixadbrodian is sufficient for him to empathize with the longing of one of the characters for home—the Lulungomeena of the title—contrary to the expectations of the other characters. But whereas for Dickson different species will have different levels of capacity for empathy, for van Vogt empathy is more basic. In "Cooperate—Or Else!" (1942)—later incorporated, together with the other four stories in the series, "Repetition" (1940), "The Second Solution" (1942), "The Rull" (1948), and "The Sound" (1950), into the novel *The War against the Rull* (1959)—van Vogt describes how humans and the alien ezwals come to an agreement on mutual cooperation in the face of the hostile Rull. After a number of shared adventures, the human protagonist, Trevor Jamieson, and his ezwal counterpart confront each other directly when it is necessary for the latter to reveal that it is an intelligent being and not an animal: "They were two intelligent beings facing each other; and though the ezwal realized it only vaguely, he [Jamieson] felt the kinship that exists between all intelligence once it is in communication" (*The War against the Rull* 1959, 114). For van Vogt, it

appears, the ability to empathize (to feel kinship with another) across species
boundaries will characterize any interaction between intelligent species. On
the whole, the kind of optimism about the generality of empathy between
species, shared by Dickson, van Vogt, and the other writers who show it in action, does much to counteract the possibility of the "arachnid reaction."

The capacity for empathy across species boundaries is related to the issue of
cooperation. Extrapolating from the intraspecies experience of cooperation,
interspecies cooperation is seen as a possibility. Van Vogt's humans and ezwals,
for example, can cooperate as a result of the "kinship" or empathy they share.
But empathy is not essential to cooperation. Even the Trill of Chilson's "The
Hand of Friendship," who are lacking in intraspecies empathy, are able to cooperate in work and government, and therefore also—to a limited extent—in
interspecies situations.

In addition to empathy, cooperation between different sapient species will
require adaptivity, since one of the big problems of human international
travel and communication is culture shock, and this is assumed to increase at
the interspecies level. Culture shock, according to Alvin Toffler, "is the effect
that immersion in a strange culture has on the unprepared visitor. . . . It is
what happens when the familiar psychological cues that help an individual to
function in society are suddenly withdrawn and replaced by new ones that are
strange or incomprehensible" (*Future Shock* 1970, 10–11). In an editorial for
Analog (September 1982), entitled "The Relativity of Emergency," Stanley
Schmidt writes that "[t]he severity of an emergency—whether a set of conditions is 'critical' or 'livable'—depends very largely on what you're used to and
prepared for" (8). Schmidt's editorial deals with emergencies of physical environment, but it is equally true of social environment. Finding oneself alone in
a foreign culture may be difficult but may be mitigated by preparation; finding oneself alone in an alien culture may be impossible in the absence of any
way of preparing. F. M. Busby's "The Learning of Eeshta" (1973) explores the
painful process of an alien's adaptation to human culture. Similarly, Frank
Herbert's "The Tactful Saboteur" (1964) explores the problems of interspecies
relations after the initial culture shock is assumed to be over and the different
species of the ConSentiency have supposedly become accustomed to each
other, at a time when more covert differences arise. Few of the short stories in
the science fiction magazines have space enough to deal with the problems
that arise from immersion, but even in initial encounters the escalation from

intraspecies culture shock to interspecies culture shock is assumed by science fiction writers to be extreme.

Empathy and cooperation, moreover, allow a sapient species to develop informal social protocols (codes to express interpersonal values), and these too, therefore, may also operate across species boundaries. The protocols may be similar to human protocols or completely different. In "Dutchman's Price" (1985), Joel Rosenberg explores the interpersonal social obligations of friendship and community roles in a society based on communal care of the eggs and hatchlings (since the aliens are oviparous reptiloids) and where the primary social unit is the work guild. Yet despite what seems like an enormous difference, there exist similar issues of loyalty and treachery for individuals of the species. Frederic Brown's "Puppet Show" (1962) introduces the protocol of shape equality: After successfully passing a number of tests for possible admittance to the postulated galactic federation, the humans being tested stumble by expressing their belief in the superiority of the human shape and revealing their capacity for prejudice in this "shapism." Arthur Clarke's "Rescue Party" (1945) introduces an example of interspecies disaster relief. In "Sanctuary" (1988), James White suggests that the protocol of offering shelter to strangers, which humans have derived from the biblical declaration of Jesus that "I was a stranger and ye took me in" (Matthew 25:35, King James Bible), may be a universewide protocol among civilized sapients and a key to acceptance into the galactic organization.[23] Proper understanding of alien social protocols, in addition to proper deployment of human social protocols, it is postulated, may be one of the important keys to interspecies compatibility.

Stories about compatibility, in particular, often seem to be stories of ethics. In fact, the prevalence of the concepts of acceptance, empathy, cooperation, and adaptivity confirm that from the beginning, regardless of the primacy of the science in science fiction, ethics have their place in alien encounter.

CONCLUSION

As interaction with the idea of the Alien proceeds in the stories, examining as it does so the otherness of psyche that is encountered, modified by issues of knowability, recognizability, comprehensibility, and to some degree compatibility, and present in otherness of form, some suggestion of the underlying encounter with the Jungian archetype appears. Although the writer is constructing the psyche of the Other, developing it by whatever process on the foundation of biological otherness (the necessary foundation of an extreme otherness out of which alterity may arise), at this stage inevitably the creative process is drawing on the writer's own internal experience of Self, the ultimate archetype, and the existence of that Self in a body. To a very considerable degree the created alien therefore invokes that same archetypal experience in the reader. Although the fascination with the idea of the Alien felt by both writer and reader is initiated by a curiosity about its form, it is much more developed by a curiosity about its psyche as a nonhuman person.

Most aliens who feed this curiosity, according to the consensus identifiable in the stories from the magazines, are therefore at least conceptually knowable, recognizable, comprehensible, and to some degree compatible. All four processes are expected to be mutual: As we humans will know, recognize, comprehend, and accept (find compatible) others, we will in our turn be known, recognized, comprehended, and accepted. But this will have to be accomplished in interaction. Humans are individual Selfs, but live socially—in societies or communities with other Selfs. Therefore, writers have identified another major challenge presented by the Alien: the challenge of *commensality,* that is, unconstrained (or relatively unconstrained) coexistence. Once the existence of conceptually knowable, recognizable, comprehensible, and compatible aliens—OtherSelfs—had been postulated, a hypothesized context for coexistence and interaction between humans and OtherSelfs became necessary, and this context was soon created in what became known as the multispecies galaxy.

NOTES

1. *Psyche* was Jung's preferred term for the nonsomatic component of a human being. I therefore follow him in my Jungian approach to the construction of alien personalities, using *psyche* in the sense of "the animating principle in man and other living beings, the source of all vital activities, rational or irrational" (*OED2*). The use of this term and of the derived adjective *psychic* are not, however, intended to imply anything supernatural about sapience. Moreover, although Jung touches on the mind-body problem in the papers included in *The Structure and Dynamics of the Psyche* (CW8), he does not commit himself to a specific theory of their interaction.

2. Given the book's publication in 1962, this handy discussion of the nature of sapience was in fact available to writers and readers of science fiction, and, although it was not within the pages of the magazines where other sorts of theory were being discussed, might have had almost as wide a distribution.

3. Chomsky's *Current Issues in Linguistic Theory* (1964), *Aspects of the Theory of Syntax* (1965), *Syntactic Structures* (1965), and *Topics in the Theory of Generative Grammar* (1966) had recently appeared, of which the first at least might have provided interesting reading for anyone thinking about alien linguistics.

4. Occasional articles appeared elsewhere. "Alien Sociology" (1975), by A. R. Manser, was part of a group of articles under the general title "Science in Science Fiction" in *The Advancement of Science.*

5. It may have been prompted by the fact that when Bernard I. Kahn's story "A Pinch of Culture" (1950) had been published in August of the same year, it was accompanied by a letter to the editor (published in the letter column), in which Kahn drew attention to the cultures on which he based his alien culture, saying, "You might be interested in the background of this story . . ." (160) and citing Ruth Benedict's *Patterns of Culture* (1946) as a source. Certainly, the culture that Kahn uses (that of the Dobu) is one of those featured in Cox's "Varieties of Culture." Cox spends some of his time discussing theories of culture in general.

6. As previously noted in chapter 3, even the *Oxford Companion to the Mind* (1987) does not include a definition (usually the product of a consensus) about what *mind* is, a fact acknowledged by the editor.

7. He revisits this topic of alien knowability and strangeness again in "Imagining Other Minds" (1998), which was written as part of a series of three about Benford's participation in the design of the mission marker to be included in the Cassini unmanned spacecraft mission to Saturn in 1997. In it, and in the third of the series, "A Portrait of Humanity" (1998), Benford brings some of his previous arguments to the fore in his discussion of how to design a marker that hypothetical aliens would be able to decipher, and, in doing so, he presents some valuable insights into the process of constructing aliens as that process might take place in the psyche of the writer.

8. It is significant that Benford's example is from a novel and not from a short story (either his own or someone else's). Representation of perceptually and conceptually unknowable aliens seems to be limited to novel-length treatments. Some theorizing by critics also seems to equate knowability with comprehensibility. Such an equation is certainly not shared by most writers of first-contact stories, who readily distinguish between the two. In general, science fiction writers seem to agree that even an incomprehensible alien is knowable in the very basic sense of being apparent to human perception as an entity.

9. This scenario is developed at full length in Arthur C. Clarke's *Rendezvous with Rama* (1973), in which humans investigate a mysterious spaceship that enters the

solar system. A detailed comparison of Clement's story and Clarke's novel provides interesting material for understanding not only what constitutes a real hands-on hard-science story ("Technical Error" 1943) and one that is merely scientifically correct (*Rendezvous with Rama* 1973), but also a strong realism about knowability contrasted with a weaker realism.

10. Since, as Garrard reflects, "the plural of *beademung* is *beademungen*" (53), when he is being addressed here it is by all of them (*we*) acting for the moment as a single entity (a *beademung*).

11. Gavin Hyde's "Sparkie's Fall" (1959) and Theodore Sturgeon's "The [Widget], the [Wadget], and Boff" (1955) provide further examples of this loophole technique.

12. In the middle paragraph, I have edited the text into run-on form instead of the original list form in order to save space.

13. A requirement for "irreducible unknowability," moreover, would require some redefinition of the locus of the unknowing. The writer cannot unknow what he/she is imagining, and although he/she can create a fiction about unknowing, he/she does not include actual unknowing in his/her fiction.

14. That Tweel's intellect is, ironically, superior to Dick's is examined in Rosemarie Arbur's paper, "Teleology of Human Nature *for* Mentality?" (1983) in which she notes that

> [t]he retrospective thematic attitude exists as a result of readers' and writers' looking back on what seemed to be naive science fiction and finding in it real tension and ambiguity. Stanley Weinbaum's 'Martian Odyssey' (1934), as it is read today and perhaps as it was read when it was first published, is a good example." (75)

She also points out that it is *only* in this retrospective reading that Tweel's superiority is visible.

15. *Universal* presents some difficulties and may be a loaded term. Given the wide distribution of knowledge of the UCP as background anthropological material for the writing of science fiction, it retains its validity in discussions of science fiction where the patterns considered are considered at species level, although clearly contemporary anthropological and sociological research might disagree that any particular psychological trait or cultural behavior is universal at the intraspecies or individual level. The term I use for specific activities that seem to be "universal" constants in the consensus is *commonality*.

16. At present, scientific evidence for the sapience-markers depends on evidence from human beings. So far, then, because every human is sapient, every human evi-

dences potential for language, number, and tool use, although it seems to require other humans to activate these potentials, and obviously there are individuals who are brain-damaged in whom these specific potentials cannot be activated. Sometimes the search for sapience identifies only the potential for sapience, and the alien may be designated presapient, a scenario that involves its own protocols and conventions.

17. Brian Ash's discussion of alien intellect in *Faces of the Future* (1975) implies that the existence of so many stories of parallelism may be due to the difficulty of conveying alien ways of thinking: "It *is* difficult to conceive of an intelligence which functions on entirely different principles to our own; but it is a probability which we should sensibly accept as we approach that historic meeting" (165; original emphasis). Whether the assumption of parallelism is attributable to such difficulty of concept or to simple failure of imagination or to the need to foreground other qualities, however, such stories usually do not present questions of comprehensibility.

18. About the *level* of dolphin intellect, Brin comments that "the basic problem-solving skills of even the brightest porpoise cannot match those of a human toddler. I'm afraid if we want 'other minds' to talk to, we're going to have to look elsewhere . . . or construct them ourselves" (5), and "I've listened to recorded dolphin 'speech,' transposed in frequency. The sounds are repetitive, imprecise . . . clearly filled with emotional, not discursive [*sic*] information" (5).

19. He defines *time-binding* as the "ability to consider optional future actions and to act upon these considerations" (7). Writing as Lee Correy, Stine subsequently laid out his definition of metalaw in greater detail in the prefatory note to *A Matter of Metalaw* (1986).

20. Almost immediately, for example, Wayne Wightman in "Do Unto Others" (1980) addresses the application of the Golden Rule itself in an interspecies context and finds it severely wanting.

21. Since its publication antedates E. O. Wilson by twenty years, the story is clearly not a serious hypothesis along sociobiological lines suggesting that human virtues have biological origins by asserting that "fair play" has a biological determinant in biological symmetry. It belongs with those stories, cropping up from time to time, that aliens who have been stranded on, marooned on, deported to, or who have merely visited Earth somehow either become the original humans or alter existing hominids toward sapience.

22. Many stories discuss the effects of empathy. For example, Raymond Z. Gallun's "Mad Robot" (1936), Malcolm Jameson's "Alien Envoy" (1944), Thomas Easton's "Mood

Wendigo" (1980), Reginald Bretnor's "Without (General) Issue" (1981), Madeleine Robins's "The Boarder" (1982), and Alexander Jablokov's "The Place of No Shadows" (1990) all show individuals of different sapient species communicating across species boundaries on a basis of shared feelings of empathy. But very few stories address the nature of empathy directly.

23. Similar exploration of protocols revealing patterns of likeness in unlikeness characterize Randall Garrett's "Asses of Balaam" (1961), Alexander Jablokov's "The Place of No Shadows" (1990), and Bernard Kahn's "Pinch of Culture" (1950).

Sleeping with the Alien:
The Society of the Alien

The only sapient inhabitants of the universe we know of with scientific certainty are humans. Yet, that universe provides (as the Assumption of Mediocrity more recently developed by scientists seems to confirm for the readers and writers of magazine science fiction stories from the earliest days) a highly plausible context for possible other inhabitants. If it has produced humans, the science-fictional argument runs, then it will surely have produced many other species of knowable, recognizable, and to some degree comprehensible sapients, all of whom will have a wide range of sociocultural gestalts to be explored. Because they will surely be Selfs like us, they will offer the opportunity for a wide range of possible interactions with each other—interactions that in turn offer new sets of problems and issues of the same kinds (moral, ethical, social, and legal) that humans have always faced—as well as interspecies interactions with humans.

Alien societies constitute an important aspect of the Alien as an emerging archetype.[1] In the early years of the magazines, with some exceptions (as I have already noted), guidance on construction of alien societies was less directly available to writers than guidance on the design of aliens. Nevertheless, some writers view the society of which an alien is part as an important extension of the otherness—or the alterity, where this is achieved—of the individual aliens, and consequently the society is foregrounded and designed as rigorously as the alien itself. Often, however, the otherness of the individual alien is not developed into the otherness of an alien society, whether because the nature or structure of the narrative does not require it or because the writer is unable to follow through effectively. In this chapter, I am less immediately concerned with archetypal implications in the fictions than with the direct representation of the sociality of aliens—that is, with how aliens, individually Selfs as humans are individually Selfs, engage in communal activities that may or may not be comparable to those of their human counterparts.

The major construction principles of the commensality of aliens are similar to those of alien design. But the frequency with which they are employed differs considerably. Just as alien biological forms constructed by analogy (analogous aliens) offer less potential for alterity than heterologous aliens, so alien sociocultural gestalts constructed by analogy with human sociocultural gestalts also offer less in the way of alterity. But whereas heterologous and exotic aliens are relatively common because they are almost as easy as analogous aliens to construct, heterologous social structures seem to present much more difficulty for practical and convincing achievement. (This difficulty becomes even more marked when writers tackle the question of interspecies organizations.) Although the fictional multispecies galaxy of such stories presents a rich context for exploration of the nature of otherness within species, the otherness presented is often contaminated with likeness and thus fails. Nevertheless, it is worth exploring the reasons for that failure as well as for the exceptional successes.

THE COMMONALITIES OF SAPIENT SOCIETIES

Science fiction hypothesizes, to a very large extent, that each extraterrestrial species in a multispecies galaxy will constitute an autonomous society, whether it remains on its world of origin or has spread to several. By extrapolating from a principle later specifically given voice by biologist Allen Broms (cited by Robert Freitas in "Extraterrestrial Zoology" 1981) who speculates that extraterrestrial life is, biologically speaking, "likely to consist of odd combinations of familiar bits" (53), writers have taken the opportunity to speculate that extraterrestrial societies can similarly be extrapolated from known terrestrial human societies. Human sociocultural patterns are identified by broad terms such as education, medicine, government, law, war, games and play, trade, religion, and art. Together they are assumed to constitute a *civilization* or whatever the sociocultural gestalt of a species should be called.

Among all sapient species, therefore, writers speculate that the sapience result-ing from a similarly evolved intellect and allied to a similarly evolved system of affects within a species produces an analogous range of sociocultural features that can be identified and understood across interspecies boundaries as a civ-ilization. As I have argued in chapter 4, many writers adopt the notion of a re-lationship of "consistency" between body and mind that much resembles the sociobiological theory of Wilson and others, but which is merely a useful hy-pothesis for the design of aliens minds in alien bodies. To a certain extent, this consistency principle is given extended application in the design of alien soci-ocultural patterns, and in some stories the sociocultural pattern is set out as consistent with the hypothesized evolution of the bodily form of the alien, whereas in others such consistency is ignored. Those specific human sociocul-tural features that are extrapolated into alien cultures in stories (whether these extrapolations are to be explicitly considered or merely implicitly present) constitute what science fiction writers consider the commonalities of inter-species sociocultural patterns. Although it is implied that there may be pat-terns that do not have analogies among different species, there is very little attempt to go beyond the spectrum of human patterns and to hypothesize so-ciocultural activities that have no human analogues, direct or indirect. Even the commonalities are, by and large, approached very conservatively.

Education

The consensus about alien civilizations seems to assume that in order to maintain the development of a society, especially a technological society, a sapient species will have developed a system of education to make sure that knowledge is passed on to each new generation of offspring. This assumption draws its rationale, perhaps, from the fact that even nonsapient terrestrial an-imals pass on to their offspring information necessary for survival. Neverthe-less, in spite of the importance of education, conceptualizations of alien education are rare in magazine science fiction: Stories featuring students or teachers or professors as protagonists are quite frequent, but the education process itself is rarely foregrounded.

At first sight, this does not seem to be the case. Alien education is fore-grounded, for example, by R. A. Lafferty in "The Primary Education of the Camiroi" (1966). But Lafferty's major purpose is satire, and the structure and process of Camiroian education are subordinated to an exuberant presentation of curriculum and the extent to which the knowledge of Camiroian children in primary school is superior to that of educated human adults. The actual process of this education is unexamined. A closer look at what is available in the way of stories about education involving aliens shows that what is going on is nearly always less a conceptualization of alien education and more an adaptation of human education processes to the education of aliens.

It is mostly in this form that education has received considerable attention from such writers as are interested in it. In most of Mary Caraker's stories, for example, as collected in *Seven Worlds* (1986) after earlier original magazine publication, the process of alien education is virtually identical to human educative processes (though not necessarily to in-classroom processes) since the aliens are importing a human teacher—Caraker's protagonist. There is nothing in the stories, however, to imply that it must necessarily be so, and some hints about alien education processes may be discerned. Later, in the ironic "Innocents" (1989), for example, and "Suffer the Children" (1995)—both by the same writer using other protagonists—the alien processes of education are very surprisingly different, but the education process itself is not foregrounded; both stories are cautionary fables about not taking anything for granted where aliens are concerned. Similarly, Harry Turtledove, in the stories collected as *Earthgrip* (1991) after previous magazine publication, chooses an academic—a professor of literature whose specialty is science fiction—as protagonist (although the action does not allow her to stay in the classroom for very long). But these stories are problematic in terms of alien education: Although Jennifer Logan's classroom as described in the longest of the stories, "The Foitani" (serialized in *Analog* in 1991 as "The Unknown"), includes students of different species, she herself is human, and her classroom activities, as well as the university that exists as the context of her preparation and preoccupations in her teaching career, would be familiar to any academic in a North American university of the 1990s. The basic consensual hypothesis on education as evidenced by these and other writers, therefore, is that teaching and hence learning will proceed in any species along the same lines, although the curriculum may be different.

Education is the least likely of the commonalities to be suggested by science fiction writers as a process connected to or derived from the biological evolution of form in the aliens concerned. Even in a rare exception such as James White's "Combined Operation" (1983), one of his many Sector General Hospital stories, it is not the education process that is foregrounded. White's discussion of the education process in this story occurs peripherally in the protagonist's speculations on the nature of the life of an alien stranded in space after its ship collided with "a large natural object" (152), probably an asteroid. The alien in question is an enormous segmented creature whose segments constitute the entire race and who, as it turns out, spends part of its time with the segments joined and part with them separated. As White describes it, the alien's

> brain forms part of the central nerve core which during fusion is linked to the brains of the individual ahead of and behind it via the interfaces at each end of the body . . . so that an individual segment learns not only by its own experience but from those of its predecessors farther up the line. This means that the larger the number of individuals in the group, the smarter will be its male head and forward segments. Should the head segment, who is the elder of the group and probably its decision maker, die from natural or other causes, the male next in line takes over. (177)

But, peripheral as this comment on the education of the young (the new segments) is, it is clear that White has devoted enough attention to the creation of his alien to remember or conclude that its education process could be as consistent with its biological structure as any other part of its life. He also implies that this education process is not limited to education for survival at the most basic level but also is sufficiently sophisticated to allow for the development of technology.

The scarcity of stories dealing with alien education may reflect the scarcely veiled hostility to schools and teachers that surfaces from time to time in editorials and letters in the science fiction magazines, thus confirming the point that Lafferty makes in his story. What appears to be a hostility to the teaching profession at the postsecondary level is evident from time to time in such articles as Lloyd Biggle's striking and strident essays on the topic of academics and science fiction in "Science Fiction Goes to College: Groves and the Morasses of Academe" (1974) and "The Morasses of Academe Revisited" (1978). This hostility suggests one possible explanation for the relative absence of stories about alien education, since it would clearly have rendered writers who might be interested in writing about alien forms of education reluctant to insert themselves into the line of fire. Jack Williamson, in his article "Will Academe Kill Science Fiction?" (1978), however, strikes a more positive note, answering the question posed in his own title as follows: "I don't think so. The effects of our late welcome into the ivory tower will probably be mixed, but SF is a sturdy young giant with a history of survival" (69), and he cites discussions in *Analog* editorials by Ben Bova and James Gunn evaluating the possible effects. More recently, however, science fiction seems to be becoming less hostile to postsecondary education as the universities' role in information processing and storage becomes more evident and more high-tech. Consequently, since education is fundamental to the development of technology, education in most alien societies remains implicitly present though seldom foregrounded for explicit examination and generally unspecified.

Medicine

Medicine, one of the sociocultural features of human civilization that is highly dependent on education, is another commonality usually present at least implicitly in stories. A sapient species, the consensus postulates, will have to have learned to maintain the health of its population by a system of medicine in order to insure against the destruction of the society by disease. Beyond this, however, the consensus more often than not merely postulates forms of alien medicine that are more advanced than, rather than actually different from, human medicine. Much more infrequently, stories postulate that alien medicine is less advanced for some reason than the human, and occasionally attitudes to medicine rather than the nature of medicine are addressed.

The consensus on medicine as a sapient commonality produces widely differing stories. William Morrison's ironic tale "Bedside Manner" (1954), for example, postulates a race so advanced in the practice of medicine that they can restore to full health a human who has been almost totally destroyed in an accident—with results that are not quite what either the doctor or the patient expected. In Arthur Porges's "Emergency Operation" (1956) the Ilkonan doctor, Dr. M'Lo, a sapient of microscopic size, enters a human patient to remove a "tiny particle . . . of plutonium" (333), but any cognitive estrangement or otherness here is merely constituted by the difference in size of doctor and patient: what is actually done medically speaking is humanly conceived. In

Thomas R. Dulski's "In Whose Name Do We Seek the Quark?" (1983), the ability of the advanced species known as the Teydurax to cure certain kinds of mental illness becomes an issue only because the Teydurax are prepared to use their ability as either bribe or coercion to ensure that the protagonist, a human negotiator, will sign certain interspecies agreements. More often than not, as here, alien medicine, although important, is not defined with sufficient specificity to enable its otherness to be examined.

Medicine as a commonality of sapient species is most strikingly and thoroughly explored by James White through its use as the primary issue of interspecies relations. In the future history that he imagines, a series of hospitals have been set up in various parts of the galaxy to offer advanced medical services on an interspecies basis. In his continuing series of novels and stories focused on one of these hospitals, Sector Twelve General Hospital, White not only explores, deliberately and in depth, the protocols, practice, and theory of interspecies medicine in a hospital setting, but he occasionally articulates directly the principles that a sapient species will practice in caring for its members. A responsible sapient species, for example, will equip its starships with a distress beacon for emergencies, and, as hospital psychologist O'Mara puts it in *Ambulance Ship* (1979): "If a species advanced enough to possess starships did not make this provision for the safety of its individuals . . . then I would prefer not to know them" (8). Moreover, White also postulates that a species' ability to interact with other sapient species may well be most efficiently carried out through medicine. Another remark by O'Mara made in the course of comparing the hospital's success rate with that of the official Cultural Contact Group makes it clear that Sector General itself operates according to this policy:

> I mention the Cultural Contact group's three successes simply to make the point that within the same time period this hospital became fully operational and also initiated First Contacts, which resulted in seven new species joining the Federation. This was accomplished not by a slow, patient buildup and widening of communications until the exchange of complex philosophical and sociological concepts became possible, but by giving medical assistance to a sick alien. . . . But the fact remains that all of us, by giving medical assistance, demonstrated Federation's good will towards e-ts much more simply and directly than could have been done by any long-winded exchange of concepts. (6–7)

Given the centrality of O'Mara to the Sector General fiction, White may be assumed to be using him at this point (and possibly at others) as a viewpoint character (to speak for White himself), and behind O'Mara's objectively phrased valuation of medical assistance because of its usefulness is (possibly) White's less objective and more passionate implication that the giving of medical assistance is more essential to interspecies relationships than conceptual exchange.

Although interspecies medicine is foregrounded in White's fictions, the otherness of alien medicine is subordinated. White's primary focus is the potential for interspecies bonding through the practice of medicine, and Sector General is in many ways very conservative. Although the doctors, nurses, psychologists, pathologists, and support staff are from numerous species, as are the patients, the medicine practiced and the care received fall into categories familiar to any large modern hospital: obstetrics, pediatrics, geriatrics, surgery, internal medicine, and so on. When cracked Melfan carapaces and broken human bones are repaired, the medical procedures involved, although different in detail, are very similar or at least analogous, and White makes explicit comments to this effect from time to time.

Nevertheless, at the same time, White's chief protagonist in most of these fictions, Dr. Peter Conway (whose career we trace from Junior Physician up to the highest rank of Diagnostician without learning his first name until after his final promotion), is never limited to the more conservative medical practice of his colleagues. The typical scenario of a fiction involving Sector General Hospital faces Conway with a hitherto unknown alien in a first-contact situation complicated by the fact that the alien is probably although not necessarily injured, sick, or mentally disturbed. As White points out in "The Secret History of Sector General" (1979), "[M]y problem in recent years has been that, when I dream up a really alien alien, it promptly falls sick or gets itself damaged in an accident and ends up becoming a problem for Sector Twelve General Hospital" (xvii). Examination of the topic of alien medicine continues throughout White's writing career as his ideas and experience expand. Often, especially after the introduction of the ambulance-ship Rhabwar in *Ambulance Ship*, the action moves out beyond the confines of the hospital and introduces alien societies and their associated medical problems in situ. Recently, new protagonists from species other than human—Cha Thrat in *Code Blue—Emergency* (1987) and Lioren in *The Genocidal Healer* (1991)—

have been introduced, and narratives of interspecies medicine are attempted from alien points of view. What emerges from the fiction as a whole, if White's writing about the hospital is traced from the first novelette "Sector General" (1962) to the final novel *Double Contact* (1999), is a repeated, albeit sometimes unsubtle probing of the concomitant new relationships between body and mind as new versions of body are encountered.

Government

It is further postulated in the consensus that in order to maintain a stable (or at least reasonably stable) social environment for the pursuit of education (to support the development of technology) and the practice of medicine, a species will have developed a third commonality—government. Some system of government, loosely defined as any form of organized cooperation based on ideology and operating at a group or specieswide level, will therefore exist in other species. In general, however, the *theory* of government (political theory) is given short shrift in science fiction. In "American SF and the Other" (1975), discussing both shorter fiction and novels, Ursula Le Guin condemns science fiction for its failures in this respect. According to her observations of science fiction,

> [t]he only social change presented by most SF has been toward authoritarianism, the domination of ignorant masses by a powerful elite—sometimes presented as a warning, but often quite complacently. Socialism is never considered as an alternative, and democracy is quite forgotten. Military virtues are taken as ethical ones. Wealth is assumed to be a righteous goal and a personal virtue. Competitive free-enterprise capitalism is the economic destiny of the entire Galaxy. (99)

Le Guin implicitly contrasts this political "brainless regressivism" (99) with the way science fiction was able to at least "inch its way out of simple racism" (99)—a progress she attributes to Cyril Kornbluth, Theodore Sturgeon, and Cordwainer Smith, "among others" (99). Her analysis accurately accounts for much—if not "most" as she claims (99)—of science fiction (up to the date of her discussion) in which a political stance of any sort can be determined. Perhaps the most apposite example of Le Guin's summation is Harl Vincent's "Parasite" (1935), which finishes on a note of "brainless regressivism" about interspecies relations when the protagonist reflects on the human genocide of the sapient alien parasites that have invaded Earth: "Gordon thought hard for a moment, an unaccountable nausea sweeping over him as he reflected upon the stupendous truth that a civilization had been or was being wiped out. Resolutely then he turned his mind to other and more pleasant things. Their own civilization had been saved" (107). The story is thoroughgoing in its naive political insularity at a time of increasing international instability, but some readers of science fiction may have preferred the insular approach. The writer of a letter to the editor of *Fantastic Adventures* several years later (December 1943) in an even greater time of international instability certainly appears to do so: "I was disappointed in the Luvium story. Nazis again. Ye gods, why does the war always creep into science-fiction. I'd like nothing better than to see a nice, twenty-thousand word novel of the future in *Fantastic Adventures*, preferably by one of the following authors. . . . It seems some of the above are too busy in military occupations to bother writing" (Gruebner 1943, 195). Even Robert Heinlein, possibly the most politically minded of SF writers, tends to be less imaginative and speculative politically than he is in any other area, although *Starship Troopers* (1959) with its oligarchical human government of veterans is a notable exception. Yet the alien "Bugs" in this novel are a standard "hive-mind" species, with government entirely unseparated from mere insect-style cooperation, and we know even less about the allied aliens referred to simply as "skinnies." In most if not all stories in which the alien encounter is the chief focus, new concepts of political organization, political theory, or even political awareness tend to be invisible, and alien systems seem to repeat human systems.[2]

There are, of course, some stories that might qualify as exceptions to Le Guin's charges. Poul Anderson's Ythrians—the winged species who figure in many of his stories in *The Earthbook of Stormgate* (1978) and *The People of the Wind* (1973)—are, according to one of the human characters in "The Problem of Pain" (1973), "incapable by instinct of maintaining what we'd recognize as a true nation or government" (32). What Anderson portrays, however, is not a pure anarchy, as the character seems to imply, although he does not spend much time discussing the nature of the system that does exist, and certainly there is nothing to suggest any kind of correlation between the biology of a winged form and its inability to form a government. Curiously enough, it is Isaac Asimov, not usually thought of as a politically active writer, who offers an interesting example of a form of government—if it can be considered a form of government—that is literally a matter of biology in his story "Green Patches" (1950, as "Misbegotten Missionary"). Here Asimov postulates the ultimately cooperative alien species:

> All life on Saybrook's planet is a *single* organism . . . each organism has its place, as each cell in our body does. Bacteria and planets produce food, on the excess of which animals feed, providing in turn carbon dioxide and nitrogenous wastes. Nothing is produced more or less than is needed. The scheme of life is intelligently altered to suit the local environment. No group of life forms multiplies more or less than is needed, just as the cells in our body stop multiplying when there are enough of them for a given purpose. When they don't stop multiplying, we call it cancer. And that's what life on Earth really is . . . one big cancer. Every species, every individual doing its best to thrive at the expense of every other species and individual. (55)

Certainly, there is a sinister quality to the political agenda of the Saybrook's planetary cooperative in its determination to include Earth and all its life-forms willy nilly. Given the biological underpinnings of the cooperation described in the story, the distinction between the multi-organismic state and the communist state is plausible, but it is a nice distinction. Asimov, however, makes it quite clear, if not in the story itself at least in a later article, that he himself sees this level of cooperation as distinct from human (or single-species) totalitarianism of the sort Le Guin suggests.

Cooperation on a similar scale, Asimov argues, when he returns to the topic outside his fiction, may nevertheless be the next step in the evolution of sapience in humanity. In his article "Beyond the Phyla" (1960), having previously discussed what he describes as the phylogenetic development of intelligence (i.e., sapience) in "The March of the Phyla" (1960), he goes on to speculate what might be the future development of intelligence. It would take the form, he suggests, of "multi-organismic" intelligence—the cooperative integration of multiple organisms into a single intelligence—of which the "only possible ancestor . . . is man" (102). Asimov acknowledges the problems with considering multi-organismic intelligence from the point of view of a single-organismic intelligence: "It is, of course, repugnant to a human individual at the present stage of his development to think of himself as a mere unit in a multi-organismic society, without will of his own and whenever necessary, liable to be sacrificed cold-bloodedly, to the overall good" (104). Nevertheless, he argues, using an analogy with the existence of cells in a multicellular organism, "In a multi-organismic society, the individual may well retain a good deal of mental and physical independence. He may think for himself and have his own individuality; and *also* be part of the greater whole" (104). He concludes, bracingly, "[B]y analogy, who knows what unimaginable sensations, what new levels of knowledge, what infinite insights into the universe will become possible for a multi-organismic society" (105).[3] The impact of this argument is perhaps greater than its validity, but even Asimov's argumentative powers do not leave his readers embracing it eagerly, and he does not return to the point.

Even to Asimov, however, political cooperation among single-organismic beings was a problematic form of government. More typical of his approach to political ideas is another story, "The Gentle Vultures" (1957), which followed "Green Patches" but preceded "Beyond the Phyla." Here the galactic cooperation of different species, in which each species contributes the particular goods of its own world to the small-primate Hurrians in return for being rescued by them from the aftermath of nuclear war, emerges clearly as nothing more than high-tech feudalism, as the Hurrians are assisted by their "eugenic analyzers," which help them to "direct matings and sterilizations to remove, as far as possible, the competitive element in the remnant of the survivors" (106). The human to whom the system is explained, as the Hurrians wait for nuclear war to break out so they can come to the rescue, is rightly appalled. Unlike "Green Patches," however, "The Gentle Vultures" lacks any suggestion of a biological underpinning for the political structure: It is not demonstrated why the evolution of small primates (monkeys) to sapience should result in noncompetitiveness whereas the evolution of large primates results in competitiveness. For all the reader can tell, it depends on whether or not the species has a tail. Any ambivalence is lost, and "The Gentle Vultures" remains a statement entirely within a human context.

Ecological cooperation, as distinct from the multi-organismic cooperation which seems to be the principle of "Green Patches," is also a possible form of government. Two stories by S. Kye Boult (a pseudonym of the relatively little-known William E. Cochrane) explore this possibility: "The Habitat Manager" (1971) and "The Safety Engineer" (1973). Both stories feature the alien governmental operative, Jme, and the governmental system itself features the cooperative interdependence of multiple species in support of their planetary ecology. That all the major species on the one planet should develop cooper-

atively is consistent with the biology he postulates for them, but the simultaneous evolution of more than one sapient species on the same planet, although encouraging, may be less plausible, at least in terms of Campbell's
suggestion that the "Intelligent Alien" will be the "unchallengeable most-
dangerous-animal on the planet" ("The Nature of Intelligent Aliens" 1967,
177). The organizing principle of the ecology appears to be the food chain,
and although Boult handles this very deftly, it is clear that the admission of
any species into the interdependence and its role there might well depend on
its position on the food chain. Consequently, Boult's view of the ecological cooperative might be on the optimistic side.

Other examples of explicit speculative political theory occasionally emerge,
although they are not usually foregrounded in the shorter forms of magazine
fiction. Robert Chilson's "Hand of Friendship" (1983), for example, implies a
suitably imaginative and speculative alien government system consistent with
the biology of the alien. The froglike Trill, we are told, "don't have a government" (136) at all in the human sense. Nevertheless, they have achieved the
equivalent of a planetary government:

> I knew the sound that means "association" in Trill. It is an important word to
> them. It means, loosely: incorporation, marriage, confederation, union, part-
> nership, local government, business company, gang of robbers—it means any
> kind of voluntary relationship between two or more Trills. The planetary gov-
> ernment is technically an "association of associations." (137)

It is implied that it is the Trills' evolution as egg-layers and fertilizers that has
resulted in a species without the capacity for relationships other than self-
interested cooperation (and as previously discussed, they lack the emotional
capacity for familial love or friendship between individuals). Bunundig, the
human protagonist's Trill contact on the planet, explains to him that "[n]o
Trill helps another, or associates with another in any way except out of self-
interest. To end an association is not betrayal, since we are not bound together
by strong emotions, as other races seem to be" (140). The "association" principle works as a government by allowing individuals to form associations out
of self-interest, and each of these associations publish their arguments on a
particular topic or issue. Then, at a given time, each member of the community begins to "sound off" (140), "singing" or "trilling" its vocal contribution
to the chorus from the top of the tree around which its residence is built. Each

member of an association sings the sound pattern of its most powerful member until the pattern of one association predominates and the others fall silent. If translated into human terms, it might be hard not to describe this system as "regressive," since it seems to shift merely from "might is right" to "vocal might is right" or even "government by filibuster"—neither of which seems to equate with democracy, even if it were a workable system for human vocal apparatus and lungs. This form, in its presentation of the effects of carrying individuality and self-interest to the extreme, is probably diametrically opposed to the cooperation proposed by Asimov and Boult.

One political idea that did find an early niche in science fiction dealing with alien relations is the idea of interspecies negotiation by means of "conferences." Conferences of political leaders for purposes of treaty negotiation have a long history on Earth, and the speculative use of it in discussion of interspecies relations is perhaps a natural step. Science fiction assumes that the concept of the conference is comprehensible among sapient species as an appropriate forum for negotiating solutions to political differences. One of the earliest presentations of such a conference is found in Raymond Z. Gallun's "Hotel Cosmos" (1938). The conference in this story, however, exists merely as a background to an attempt on the life of one of the delegates and the protagonist's thwarting of this attempt; there is no discussion of how a conference of different species might work in specific detail. It is not, however, assumed as applying universally: To members of a species like Larry Niven's Kzin, where a diplomat may be known by his profession as "Speaker-to-Animals" (*Ringworld* 1970, 13) and where "[i]n challenging a kzin, a simple scream of rage is sufficient" (*Ringworld* 1970, 14), the concept of a conference to negotiate treaties would not come easily—if at all. Ironically, moreover, "Hotel Cosmos" was written in 1938 at the very moment in twentieth-century history when the international treaties laboriously negotiated in international conferences after World War I were collapsing into the preliminaries to World War II.

Other uses of the concept of the conference for interspecies interaction have occurred more recently. Frederik Pohl's story "Sitting around the Pool, Soaking up the Rays" (1984) uses the same premise as his earlier "We Purchased People" (1974)—that alien intelligences project themselves into human hosts—although in the more recent story, there is a single agenda common to all the alien species and directed toward the acquisition of Earth's nuclear wastes rather than the purchase and use of individuals for individual projects. In Spider Robinson's "User Friendly" (1986), however, the aliens take over humans at random in order to be present at an interspecies conference the purpose of which is completely opaque to humans, who are not allowed to be present in their own right as a species but only as (literally) hosts and warm bodies for the extraterrestrials to occupy. Both stories focus on the helplessness of the humans at the hands of aliens, and if they make a political point at all, other than the use of a political trope that is considered a sane and civilized way of settling differences, it is that even where a species may understand the trope of negotiation, the understanding does not mean that they will use it in a way that humans would consider sane and civilized.

The concept of the conference as a negotiating forum may be extended to include the use of the "constitutional conference" to establish the relationship of individuals or of groups to the state and to each other—a variation more familiar to Canadian readers of science fiction, perhaps, than to others. This type of conference is illustrated in Barry Longyear's "Savage Planet" (1980), in which democracy is introduced to a politically underdeveloped species in order to permit them to establish sovereignty over their own planet and ward off human exploiters. The use of American-style theory of democracy, although it challenges the blanket nature of Le Guin's complaint that democracy is "quite forgotten" ("American SF and the Other" 1975, 99), does not of itself constitute any exceptionally speculative notion of political theory. The time lag between her essay and Longyear's story is significant. Even fifteen years after the absence of political thinking in science fiction is pointed out, there are few serious examples of political and governmental otherness to be found.

Law

Law, including conflict resolution generally defined, is also postulated as a commonality. A sapient species composed of individuals will have to have developed some system similar to the sort humans have developed and know as law—both civil and criminal—for mediating or judging disputes among its individual members and among different groups of individuals, providing justice, or, if justice is impossible, at least conflict resolution. Unlike systems of government, legal systems, questions of law, and the nature of justice are often foregrounded in stories of interspecies interaction.

Early magazine stories take the commonality of law much more for granted than later ones and assume much more in the way of compatibility of systems.[4]

One of the very early stories of first contact, Malcolm Jameson's "Alien Envoy" (1944), for example, presents law as a commonality and assumes, although indirectly, its compatibility across species boundaries. Jameson appears, in the procedures and actions of his characters, to be making the assumption that, although the alien has to be taught, slowly and painstakingly, the basics of human language (i.e., American English), once communication is established the compatibility of its legal system can be taken for granted. It is assumed that not only will its system of government include such concepts as the sovereignty of nation-states and of diplomacy (for the alien here is an ambassador, with all the legal ramifications that the title implies)—but also that its system of law will include concepts such as delegated authority (he is acting on behalf of his species) and contracts (for he is empowered to negotiate and sign a treaty with Earth). Since the interest of the story is focused on the language-using ability of the alien, not on the potential legal hazards of interspecies interaction, Jameson's assumptions are aesthetically if not actually justified.

Subsequent and more sophisticated discussions of law as a commonality not only tackle the topic directly but usually avoid making such unjustified assumptions. One of the major themes among writers focusing directly on the commonality of law is the existence of different species-specific systems of law within the multispecies galaxy and the effect on individuals of the coexisting or overlapping systems and jurisdictions. The concept of law as the producer of justice becomes problematic when legal systems are multiplied as the result of the involvement of multiple species. At its most basic, this multisystem effect poses the problem of what, in any particular instance, constitutes a criminal or civil wrongdoing. It seems to be safely assumable in the consensus that individuals of a given species are entitled to justice according to the law of their own species where the act is committed within the jurisdiction of that species, even in the context of the multispecies galaxy. It might be assumed that, by analogy with international law on extradition, in cases of such behavior, individuals of one species might be subject to the law of another species if the behavior were committed within the jurisdiction of that other species. Within the human species, this system works reasonably well. Jonathan Brand's "Long Day in Court" (1963), however, explores the potential for an interspecies justice system where an act considered normal by one species may be considered criminally aberrant by another and demonstrates immediately that this arrangement does not even begin to address the possible problems.

The action in this particular case takes place on "Transit Station J" (a space station in orbit around Jupiter and under the Earth government's jurisdiction) between a couple named Daap-daap from Fomalhaut, when the male beats up his wife. He is entitled to do this in order to punish her for something that he has done, since the "Fomalhaut Ethology Handbook" that the judge consults tells him that "[p]unishment for wrong-doing is customarily inflicted on the females—wife, or, if unavailable, mother, or, if unavailable, female guardian" (147). But the male concedes that this same beating breaks an "Earth law . . . concerning Grievous Bodily Harm and Assault" (148). As summarized by the Earth judge to Daap-daap, the issue at this point is

> You admit to beating your wife, and recognize that this is illegal under Earth law. Your defense against the charge of Assault is Justification with Racial Mores, and within your code of mores the justification is that your act of Assault was a legitimate punishment for a wrong which you had committed, or, at least, for an act which was illegal according to the laws of your domicile place; that wrong being the same act of Assault. The situation so far is simple. . . . However, your explanation is unsatisfactory in this particular, that under Earth law punishment may not be inflicted before the crime is committed. Therefore the same act cannot be both crime and punishment. (149)

The defendant, however, insists that the crime and punishment were the same: "We deny that punishment was inflicted before the crime was committed. Nor was it inflicted afterwards. It was simultaneous" (149). Given this denial, the judge is now in a paradoxical situation: "[I]f Daap-daap was to be excused for hitting his wife, then he had done no wrong—and justification no longer applied. For how could he justifiably [sic] be hitting his wife if he had nothing for which to punish her? You get in the same mess, only the other way round, Mark thought, if you find them guilty" (150). After further consideration he realizes that this is a "test case to decide if Earth law should continue to hold on the Station" and "the very statement of the charge and the defense tampered with the structure of the law itself" (151). Finally, the judge is able to escape the paradox by means of a joke which, translated "simultaneously to every group in the room" (153), settles the case: "Mark realized that his job was done. Like the wind over a plain of grass a change ran over the room. . . . All round the room it was the same. Everyone reckoned the case was happily resolved" (153). It is perhaps significant that the judge at this point reflects that "[a] soft answer turneth indeed away wrath" (153), linking the action of law with the familiar biblical code of behavior (Proverbs 15:1, King James Bible).

Even given the compatibility of the concept of a crime across species boundaries and legal systems, the concept of punishment may not translate, or, if the concept of punishment for convicted criminals is equally compatible, ideas about the nature of that punishment might differ radically. Larry Niven's "Cruel and Unusual" (1977), therefore, introduces speculation about the nature of punishment. When on Niven's future Earth, humans kill a chirpsithtra, "it is not denied by humans that Diplomat-by-Choice Ktashisnif died in the hands of the . . . kidnappers" (167) because they had no medication for her allergy to humans, and it is further agreed between the human narrator and the chirpsithtra with whom he is discussing the case that "there are no accidents in the commission of a crime" (167). Under chirpsithtra law, the kidnappers are charged with "murder by slow torture" and convicted (167). They are subsequently punished, also according to chirpsithtra law: "For three days the world had watched while chirpsithtra executioners smothered four men slowly to death" (168). There is a measure of agreement between humans and chirpsithtra on the crime (murder), although the two species differ on details (murder is defined according to the method in chirpsithtra law but not by human), and there is agreement between the species that crime is punishable. The difference is that for humans "cruel and unusual punishment" is not acceptable, whereas for the chirpsithtra the punishment must match the crime exactly: "cruel and unusual punishment" fits "cruel and unusual crimes" (168). The story seems to imply that, although the chirpsithtra system is more strictly logical than the human system, the systems on the whole mesh well. But it is left unclear whether the result of a specific cross-species crime and its punishment can produce that which both species can equally call justice. Elsewhere the degree of compatibility of systems of law is much more variable than Niven's story might imply. In William Tenn's "Party of the Two Parts" (1954), previously discussed, the problems facing the officers of the legal system are far from being as clear cut: As a result of the involvement of more than one species, the nature of the crime (the production and sale of sexually explicit photographs), the reality of its commission, and the existence of the perpetrator are all in doubt from a legal point of view by the end of the story. Although the issue is the same, however, the contexts are not: In Niven's story the galactic organization is merely an extremely loose cooperative, whereas in Tenn's story, the galactic organization, although not described in detail, seems to be more tightly knit in its structure, and the existence of complex codes for settling interspecies legal disputes is explicitly mentioned.

Where a galactic organization exists, moreover, the problems are inevitably compounded or eased by the degree to which the organization has harmonized the systems of individual species. Frank Herbert's "The Tactful Saboteur" (1964) and his other stories and novels of the ConSentiency are notable for their direct dealings with this point. Herbert presents not only multiple systems of law within a galactic federation but also, in the novel *The Dosadi Experiment* (1978), detailed exploration of the Gowachin legal system—a system simultaneously alien to humans and yet comprehensible and even to some degree compatible, since the human protagonist, McKie, is a licensed *legum* in the Gowachin system. "The Tactful Saboteur" itself, however, introduces the question of personal identity in multisystem courts, in the form of the shifting ego of the Pan-Spechi, and how this affects the legal responsibilities of the ego-holder and the court's ability to recognize and hold jurisdiction over a particular entity. Both *The Dosadi Experiment* and "The Tactful Saboteur" take pains to demonstrate, in addition, a consistency between the biological evolution of the aliens Herbert has created and the evolution of their legal systems.

More recently, the concept known as *metalaw* has been introduced into the consensus. As I have pointed out in a previous chapter in my discussion of compatibility, Robert J. Freitas Jr., in "The Legal Rights of Extraterrestrials" (1977), and G. Harry Stine, in "How to Get Along with an Extraterrestrial . . . or Your Neighbor" (1980), have dealt with this idea in the pages of *Analog*. But clearly, metalaw, as set out either by Freitas (citing Fasan and Haley) or Stine (citing Haley), offers no solution to the problems raised by Niven, Tenn, Brand, and Herbert in the stories I have discussed. If it does nothing else, in fact, the enunciation of the principle of metalaw, when introduced into the situation in most of the "legal" stories, illustrates on a grand scale the discrepancy between law and justice. Reader Lois Tilton in a letter in *Analog*, July 1980, in response to Stine's article, argues that "the system of principles he calls 'metalalaw' provokes mainly confusion" (174). If everybody obeys the codes of law that apply to them (local, provincial, state, federal, international, and in due course interspecies law—and follow the principles of metalaw as well), there is no problem—but, if decisions have to be made and the sanctions provided for under the law have to be applied to settle what happens when the same codes are not obeyed, then problems will arise in which metalaw is simply irrelevant and justice inaccessible except through some form of fudging the results.

Other than in the form of metalaw, however, law was not presented to magazine readers as a discipline with detailed and rigorous rules, analogous to the rules of the hard or physical sciences, until 1999, when an article by Joseph H. Delaney, "So, You Want to Write a Law Story?" appeared in the July–August issue of *Analog*. As articles that mediated the hard sciences to readers had done earlier, Delaney's article focuses on the need to get things right: It explains the complexity of legal systems within the geopolitical entity known as the United States and provides appropriate references to law research URLs. By including discussion of its hierarchical structure, however, Delaney implies a commonality underlying all the local divergences. But he does not offer very much guidance to writers wanting to explore or exploit conflicts of jurisdiction, concept, or procedure that arise in and between parts of the system, even though the nature of the system is such that such conflicts must occur, and even though this is precisely the area in which writers involved in the nature of aliens are likely to be interested. Moreover, Delaney implies that a wider commonality of law can exist, which can make the practice of law across international boundaries easier: "Most people are astonished (but shouldn't be) how much of the western world bases its jurisprudence on the English Common Law which the British Empire imposed upon its colonies. (English barristers are quite at home in courtrooms as widely separated as Israel and Australia)" (96). But in spite of this commonality, if the writer of alien stories wants to set them in alien courts he is more likely to have to place his lawyers in a completely opposite situation to that of the English barristers mentioned by Delaney: They are more likely to be lost and confused even where basics are concerned. The concept of human rights, for example, is accepted in principle if not always in practice by national governments around the world. But as Marianne Garre's book *Human Rights in Translation: Legal Concepts in Different Languages* (1999) demonstrates clearly, even lawyers working in the legal systems of those governments who have accepted the practice as well as the principle of human rights by signing international treaties such as the European Convention on Human Rights (ECHR) find that concepts, procedures, and terms cross national and linguistic borders only with immense difficulty.

Law is omnipresent as a system, therefore, in the multispecies galaxies of the science-fictional consensus. Delaney in his article suggests law is one of the oldest of human social systems, which might explain this almost unquestioned omnipresence. Ironically, however, in individual stories the problems raised by this omnipresence are foregrounded, not whatever benefits might be imagined to emerge from it. But perhaps the problems of law are as old as the system itself, and science fiction sees no reason for this irony not to continue into the sphere of interspecies relations.

War

Although by the end of the twentieth century humanity had become accustomed to the idea that only when law fails and negotiations break down (which they do with distressing frequency), does war (in all its forms from bush wars to global wars) take over, the consensus hypothesis postulates war as a commonality of immediate rather than delayed resort. In earlier magazine fiction, the human motivation for and fascinations with war carry over into the overall consensus that any sapient species will understand war as a method of defending their autonomy as a species and of defending and extending their territory and economy and that this will extend from the intraspecies to the interspecies level of interaction. In this respect, an important contribution to the formation of the consensus in its later stages is undoubtedly an *Analog* editorial by John Campbell entitled "The Nature of Intelligent Aliens," which appeared in October 1967. Its importance lies in the fact that in it Campbell links war to evolution: "When the evolving Intelligent Alien's race reaches that level of evolution where his strength, growing intelligence, competence and agility make him able to defeat any would-be predator species—when he is the unchallengeable most-dangerous-animal on the planet—he has no predator culling his species" (177). If a species is to evolve beyond this point, it must become predatory on itself: "Man had to be the predator that drove Man to further evolution" (177–78). Therefore, like humanity, "[a]ny Intelligent Alien will have in his history the long, long ages of war, covering the evolutionary stages between the time he first achieved absolute immunity to competing species, and the time he learned the evolutionary function of war, and developed a better substitute" (178). Having established his view that war is an evolutionary necessity, Campbell nevertheless carefully goes on to point out that although even war will outlive its usefulness as an evolutionary trigger, "[u]ntil we do get an adequate *and workable* substitute—War will inescapably continue to serve its ancient and valid evolutionary function" (178; original emphasis). Campbell's argument, although problematic in itself, should not to be taken as a glorification or even an approval of war and of the characteristics that contribute in humans to its continuation. It is, however, very clearly an endorsement of any theory which proposes that the capacity for war is a commonality among all sapient species.

Given Campbell's influence as editor of *Analog*, many writers may have been influenced by his views, either when directly communicated to his own stable of writers or when expressed in his editorials. Isaac Asimov, for example, appears to echo Campbell in his comment that

> [t]he possibility that man will be the ancestor of the multiorganismic society is strengthened by the fact that he represents, for the first time in evolutionary history, an organism which is consciously aware of the competition of other organisms and will surely make a special effort to wipe out any new group which threatens his own overall superiority. ("Beyond the Phyla" 1960, 102)

But stories involving war or the prospect of war between humans and aliens were common before this article appeared, and there is no substantial increase afterward.[5] But despite the number and variety of stories available, both before and after Campbell, interspecies war does not seem to be an overwhelming preoccupation among science fiction writers dealing with aliens.[6]

Moreover, when war is introduced, it is not usually for purposes of celebration or glorification. In Clifford Simak's "Honorable Opponent" (1956), for example, a war has been in progress, and Earth has been forced to surrender because its ships simply vanish when the enemy (the Fivers) engages: At the surrender ceremony it is revealed to the confused Earth commander that what was being fought was not an actual war but a war game, Earth's vanished ships and men are returned unharmed, and the commander is slapped on the wrist for playing rough and killing people. Finally, he is given a "taker" (215)—a weapon that will remove ships from combat without harming either the ship or its crew. The aliens and humans then settle down to planning further war games. But as the story closes, the Earth commander is, ironically, already planning to use the "taker" to do more than play war games with it: "What little war was left would be ended once for all. No longer would an enemy need to be defeated; he could simply be taken. No longer would there be years of guerrilla fighting on newly settled planets; the aborigines could be picked up and deposited in cultural reservations and the dangerous fauna shunted into zoos" (216). War is more, suggests the story with a certain condemnatory tone, than simple combat, and humans will continue to express the underlying aggressive impulses of war in other kinds of behavior when war as we know it is no longer necessary. Simak seems to be taking a rather more pessimistic attitude than Campbell toward the possibility of finding a substitute for war. More recently, in a Viewpoint column in *IASFM*, Joe Haldeman, a veteran of the Vietnam War, writes: "When my stories are about war, they don't celebrate it, but rather try to demonstrate its futility and insanity" ("Science Fiction and War" 1986, 36). Haldeman takes considerable care to distinguish between the presentation of war in serious science fiction with its "unique power to engage the reader's imagination" (38) and its presentation as a "convenient setting for manufactured entertainments" (38).

The actual details—causes, logistics, and so forth—of interstellar war are not often addressed directly in the short fiction of the magazines, in which the forms of war are more often seen simply as extensions of contemporary versions of it. A writer who has dealt with interstellar and interspecies hostilities extensively in her novels is C. J. Cherryh. She has also written short stories— "Pots" (1985), "The Scapegoat" (1985), and "Cassandra" (1978)—which touch on the topic but which deal not with combat and other common scenarios of war but rather with the effect of that combat on the survival of the species, the combatants' minds, and innocent civilians, respectively. In an essay titled "Goodbye Star Wars, Hello Alley-Oop" (1985), introduced by the editor of the collection of essays in which it occurs as "explaining scientifically how future wars will be fought, if at all" (Jarvis, *Inside Outer Space* 1985, vii), however, Cherryh argues cogently that war in space is probably less likely than other forms of interspecies activity, although not impossible, because it will be so difficult and expensive: "Interspecies war might be the most expensive of all, and very possibly without sensible or understandable issues. In such a war, humankind might never know why it had been fought, or even, at the conclusion, which side had won" (25). Cherryh's argument depends, however, on a subtle understanding of the causes and nature of war derived from a reading of classical and later history not always available to earlier writers. Nor was war as a subject always easily available for public fictional questioning in times of actual war through which many earlier practitioners of science fiction were writing.

In general, however, science fiction short stories do not appear to be en-
thusiastic about the possibilities of future wars. In most of the wars portrayed,
the aggressors, human or alien, are presented as committing an immoral act,
although defensive warfare remains morally acceptable. It is possible to argue,
consequently, that in the consensus, although war may well be a commonality
among sapient species (although even that is not an absolute), it is not either
necessary or desirable.

Game-Playing

Game-playing is also hypothesized as a commonality. A sapient species will
play games—both physical and intellectual, including war games as in the
Simak story—and always competitively. Games can appear in ways that suggest they may be related to war in their competitiveness.

Physical sports, in particular, offer considerable parallels with combat.
Sometimes the playing of physical sports is explicitly presented as a channel-
ing of competitiveness. In George R. R. Martin's "Run to Starlight" (1974), for
example, a crisis in interspecies relations requires interspecies games of American football (a contact sport) to defuse the situation. The situation in George
Alec Effinger's "From Downtown at the Buzzer" (1977), however, merely requires allowing the aliens to play basketball against humans. In the initial
stages of acquaintance between two species, therefore, sport may provide at
least partial understanding. The superior aliens in John Phillifent's "The Rites
of Man" (1968; previously discussed) challenge humans at the Olympic sports
of track and field, and the challenge there is plausible because they are not
only superior but humanoid. Other forms of human competitiveness related
to sport are also shown to be commonalities. In James Tiptree Jr.'s "Faithful to
Thee, Terra, in Our Fashion" (1968) the possibilities of new versions of horse-
racing are appreciated.

Among the mind games that appear in science fiction, chess predominates.
In Jack McDevitt's "Black to Move" (1982), for example, the clue to the danger from the alien race missing from the planet that the humans have found
is a picture of a group of them poised over a board game with "the joy of battle" in their eyes (110). The board game here is carefully presented as an analogue of chess to amplify the point: "But the position in that game: Black is
playing the Benko Gambit! It's different in detail, of course; the game is different. . . . And White, after the next move or two . . . will be desperately ex-

posed" (110). The established link between chess and war is probably one clue to its popularity in science fiction stories. H. J. R. Murray, the English chess historian, opens his monumental study, *A History of Chess* (1913), with a bold description of the parallel:

> Historically, chess must be classed as a game of war. Two players direct a conflict between two armies of equal strength upon a field of battle, circumscribed in extent, and offering no advantage of ground to either side. The players have no assistance other than that afforded by their own reasoning faculties, and the victory usually falls to the one whose strategical imagination is the greater, whose direction of his forces is the more skilful, whose ability to foresee positions is the more developed. (25)

But it should be pointed out, perhaps, that there is also an implicit parallel between the qualities necessary for playing chess and the qualities necessary for the pursuit of scientific research and that the identification of extrapolation and speculation in science fiction with the practice of scientific research permeates the genre from the beginning. The popularity of chess in science fiction, consequently, is not necessarily merely as a disguised version of the activities of the Killer Ape.

Trade

Trade is another commonality. Given the basic sapience factor of number and a social culture of whatever sort, a species will know how to trade to keep an economy going by building up from simple barter. Cherryh points out, in the course of discussing interspecies war, that trade is an alternative to war: "Trade is really humanity's favorite occupation, offering as it does the freedom to come and go in interesting places, and deal with new things—and still come back to some kind of stranger-free home base, be it ship, station and world, or just a thoroughly familiar region of space that humanity calls its own" ("Goodbye Star Wars" 1985, 25–26). The reasons offered for trade's preferred status as an occupation among humans suggest why trade might be considered to be the favorite interspecies interaction of other species as well as our own in a multispecies galaxy—such desiderata need not be species specific. Poul Anderson's group of stories about Nicholas Van Rijn, including "Hiding Place" (1961), and H. B. Fyfe's series of stories beginning with "Bureau of Slick Tricks" (1948) postulate not only that trade will be a universal commonality of sapience but also that the interspecies hegemony will be a trading guild, not a political or quasi-military organization. Many of the stories that explore the theme of trading emphasize the potential for interspecies hazard, as in James Tiptree Jr.'s "Birth of a Salesman" (1968); for mutual misunderstanding, as in Robert R. Chase's "Date Night" (1989); and for mutual trickery, as in H. B. Fyfe's "In Value Deceived" (1950) and Lee Killough's "Caveat Emptor" (1970). On the darker side and in different ways, both Nancy Kress's "People Like Us" (1989) and Frederik Pohl's "Children of Night" (1964) emphasize that a psychological bond of common purpose between traders of different species may well override intraspecies bonding and moral scruples. More often than not, however, trade goes on implicitly and unnoticed in stories dealing with almost every other kind of interspecies interaction.

Religion

Another commonality will be religion. According to the consensus, a sapient species will have the concept of religion, although in its evolved technological stage, it will not always practice religion involving a supernatural deity. Science fiction writers are by and large tackling theologies that are the symptoms of a belief in a god, and alien theologies are less of a problem than alien gods—which are outside the purview of science fiction. In his article, "SF: The Game-Playing Literature" (1971), Frederik Pohl, however, makes the point that

> [t]heologians are just now beginning to catch up with science-fiction writers in thinking about the religious implications of possible non-human life on other planets. Few if any of them have yet faced the problem of wholly *alien* theologies. . . . Nor has any theologian that I know of approached the question raised in Brian Aldiss's *The Dark Light-Years*. Most humans, Aldiss argues, attach sacramental importance to such biological functions as sex (ritual marriage) and eating (saying grace at meals, ingestion of bread and wine at mass, etc). But why should some other race not attach equal sacramental importance to such other biological function as, for instance, excretion? (192)

Pohl's illustration of his argument is straightforward. He goes on to say:

> Nearly every human society stipulates One True God, a Heavenly Father who rewards and punishes. Clearly this is biology-related; humans have two sexes and a helplessly dependent infancy requiring a family structure for survival. But

> what would be the theology of a sexless race, or one hatched from eggs laid and
> abandoned like the sea turtle's? (192)

Two things should, however, be pointed out. First, "most" religions are not
monotheistic in the "One True God" pattern; monotheism is found in some
world religions (e.g., Christianity, Judaism, and Islam) but not others (e.g.,
Buddhism, Hinduism, and Shinto). Second, it is the *extended* dependency of
helpless human infants that requires a family structure, and many female animals of species in which the period of helpless infancy is short or comparatively so—most felines, for example, from the tiger to the domestic cat, do not
require the presence of the male (and may even require his absence so that the
infants may be protected from him). The idea that religious forms develop
from the consecration of biological functions is problematic. Excretion-secrecy
and food-sharing could certainly derive from prehuman behaviors (the former
as a form of protection against predators practiced particularly by females with
young; the latter as a form of bonding behavior within family units) carried
over as learned behavior (mother cats teach their kittens to hide their excre-
ment; contemporary family counselors point to the importance of the family
meal). But the importance of marriage to humanity was not "sacramental" because it consecrated sex but because it enabled the men of a patriarchal society
to exercise control over offspring and property rights by making the rules clear,
even to the nonliterate members of the community, about which men owned
which women and their offspring and what political links were implied in that
ownership. Pohl is writing in 1971 (the article, reprinted in *In the Problem Pit*,
1976, was originally given at a Clarion workshop and first published in *Clarion*, 1971), but he gives the impression of writing in sociobiological terms as a
result of applying what I have identified as the principle of consistency. As explained by Pohl, the example from Aldiss's novel seems problematic. Nevertheless, Pohl is right in his claim that science fiction is not paying sufficient
attention to this aspect of species and interspecies behavior.

Even in those science fiction stories that attempt to deal with alien theologies, however, what is usually seen is the clash of human theology (or lack of
it) and alien theology (or lack of it). In "Science Fiction and the World of Religion," his introduction to his anthology *Other Worlds, Other Gods* (1971),
possibly the only anthology published with an announced purpose of collecting stories on extraterrestrial religion, Mayo Mohs outlines the relationships of

science fiction writers to religion, starting in the nineteenth century. Of writers contemporary with the anthology's publication he says: "More recently, science-fiction novelists who like to dwell on mankind's nature and future have been extrapolating destinies for the race that seem to owe more to humanistic or oriental philosophies" (14). In actuality, however, a conspectus of the range of stories in the anthology itself reveals that the writers here do not concern themselves with the "extrapolating destinies" in alien religious terms so much as with the echoing of human religious ideas in alien contexts. Even the possible exception of Winston Sanders in "The Word to Space" (1960), in which the Jesuit protagonist runs remote interference (by radio signals) with the religion of an alien species in order to facilitate contact between humans and this species, postulates the alien religion as, ironically, very much parallel to the Christian background of the protagonist. Although it may be true, as Mohs concludes, that "repetition of themes hardly dulls them, for the possible religious permutations seem endless" (15), the stories in this anthology do not speculate for us about the nature of alien religion. There are no gods in *Other Worlds, Other Gods* who are truly Other.

There are a few stories that do deal with alien gods—or more accurately, with alien theology. For example, although Mohs mentions Poul Anderson's "Kyrie" (1968) as an example of "the encounter theme . . . loaded with theological implications" (15–16), he overlooks one of the few true discussions of alien religion, also by Anderson, in "The Problem of Pain" (1973). The story, which begins with the words "Maybe only a Christian can understand this story" (26) examines how the winged, fiercely carnivorous Ythrians approach death. Peter Berg's wife has died in agony as a result of accidental poisoning on Yythri, denied painkillers in her last hours by Enherrian, the Ythrian who at the time is the only person with her and who withholds them so that according to his religious beliefs (the Ythrian "New Faith") she is not denied her "deathpride" but remains able "to give God a battle" (46). As Berg explains it to the narrator,

> They're hunters, or were until lately. They see God like that, as the Hunter. Not the Torturer—you absolutely must understand this point—no, He rejoices in our happiness the way we might rejoice to see a game animal gamboling. Yet at the last He comes after us. Our noblest moment is when we, knowing He is irresistible, give Him a good chase, a good fight.

> Then He wins honor. And some infinite end is furthered. . . . We're dead,
> struck down, lingering at most a few years in the memories of those who es-
> caped this time. And that's what we're here for. That's why God created the uni-
> verse. (47–48)

For Berg, portrayed as a devout Catholic who is confused by what has happened
to his wife and what he has subsequently learned, this belief seems to provide a
better answer to the problem of pain (announced in the story's title) than the
answer provided by his own church. Nevertheless, the Ythrian answer to the
problem of evil seems to him not as good as that of his own faith: "But it turned
out that the New Faith has no satisfactory answer to the problem of *evil*. It says
God allows wickedness so we may win honor by fighting for the right. Really,
when you stop to think, that's weak, especially in carnivore Ythrian terms" (47;
original emphasis). In a complex narrative, with its first-person inner narrative
(as Berg relates the events that have created his dilemma) set within a first-
person frame narrative (in which the narrator records and comments on Berg's
narrative), Berg is presented, in his own words and through the eyes of a narrator who has no faith of his own, as a man torn between two faiths. But the effect of seeing the Ythrian theology through the two human theological lenses
(Christianity and agnosticism/atheism) is not, as might be expected, to enhance
the parallelism between human and alien, but to enhance the otherness of the
alien. This enhancement is furthered in the discussion between Berg and the
narrator when Berg explains that among the Ythrians he encountered

> you could call Enherrian religious. . . . The rest varied, just like humans. Some
> were also devout, some less, some agnostics or atheists; two were pagans fol-
> lowing the bloody rites of what was called the Old Faith. . . . The New Faith in-
> terested me more. It was new only by comparison—at least half as ancient as
> mine. . . . I really knew nothing about it except that it was monotheistic, had
> sacraments and a theology though no official priesthood, upheld a high ethical
> and moral standard. (32)

The details of the Old and the New Faiths are sketched in lightly, but their impact is immense. Both are compatible and/or consistent with the biology Anderson gives them. Even the apparently casual introduction of the multiplicity
of attitudes to their faith among Ythrians and the implications of religious differences (especially between the Old Faith and the New) contribute to the
complex portrait of a cultural commonality.

Art

Art is also a commonality. It is almost always assumed that a sapient species will have art, and given the usually high-tech background of science fiction, the arts might be thought to play an unusually prominent role in fiction about aliens, particularly recently. Alien art, in the forms of music, painting, theater, stage magic, fiction, and poetry, is prominently featured in magazine science fiction. But if art may be considered as a reified or an externally represented epiphenomenon of the self or of some portion of it, and self-representation in this sense is not restricted to representational modes of art, then, given the "typically exotic" principle, members of any sapient species will therefore represent their own Selfs in analogous and appropriate external reification or representation.

Stories about alien arts, however, are not about a shared and comprehensible aesthetic sense—for alien art may not be immediately (if ever) comprehensible or attractive to humans—but about a response brought about in viewers or listeners by self-representation in ways that may transcend species boundaries. In Timothy Perper and Martha Cornog's "Guz's Place" (1988), for example, when a young human artist eating at a restaurant owned (unknown to her) by an alien (Guz) sees that "the light's inside the glass" when she looks at her wine glass and expresses her delight, she is told that the making of such glass is "a great art" (20), and she is offered the possibility of learning that art herself. On the other hand, in Ray Brown's "Getting Even" (1982) the protagonist (not himself an artist) responds unfavorably to a piece of art by the alien Cleph, on whose planet he is investigating possible attempted genocide:

> It was a carved box, in the shape of a human being who was bent over backwards, its stylized face and body distorted with the strain of trying to push its way out of another, invisible box around it. It *was* striking. It was powerful. It touched some nerve I didn't know I had and made me sick when I looked at it, sicker when I touched it. The human's mashed face was the lid. (9; original emphasis)

The protagonist does not understand why he responds as negatively as he does. Nevertheless, his response is plausibly and powerfully presented, and the reader can identify with it. In both these stories, the crossing of the boundary is from alien to human. In "Translations from the Colosian" (1984), however, Jack McDevitt implies that art's transcendence of species boundaries goes the other way—from human to alien. The narrator begins:

> During the years when the first starships were crawling out from Earth, I sat one night in an open-air theater under strange constellations, watching a performance of *Antigone*. The title was different, of course. And the characters had different names. I didn't understand the language, the playwright was somebody named Tyr, and Creon had fangs. For that matter, so did Antigone, and the guy sitting immediately to my right. But you can't miss the stark cadence of that desperate drama. (46)

This narrator is watching a version of *Antigone* plagiarized from Earth and translated into an alien civilization on a planet half-way across the galaxy. He reveals his own profound human response to *Antigone* and makes clear that the alien audience is responding in exactly the way that humans respond to the original, even as he reemphasizes their difference: "The spectators held their breath in the right places, and gasped and trembled on cue. When it was over, they filed out thoroughly subdued, some surreptitiously wiping their eyes. They had been a damned good audience, and I admired them, fangs, fur, snouts and all" (46). In both George, the narrator here, and Patti, the artist in "Guz's Place," the response evoked is positive (in the former it is the pleasure of appropriate catharsis and in the latter it is the simple aesthetic pleasure of visual beauty). In "Getting Even," the narrator, a private investigator named Pantara, responds negatively: The specific nature of negativity evoked by the artifact, which Pantara says "touched some nerve I didn't know I had and made me sick when I looked at it" (9) is unresolved in the story, but it is involved with the intricate themes of the only partial comprehensibility of the alien Cleph and the nature of heinous crime and just punishment. It may simply suggest that the response is an unconscious fear or horror on his part that is not comprehensible at the conscious level, or that the response is to something in the look or feel of the artifact that does not translate accurately across species boundaries and produces the neurological equivalent of a burst of static. Nevertheless, regardless of the difference between the positivity of the first two stories and the negativity in the last, a response of some sort is produced in all three, and also in all three it is clear that similar *forms* or *modes* of art (glass-making, drama, carving) also cross species boundaries.

The notion of the recognizability of modes of art across species boundaries is the most usual presentation of the topic of art in the magazines. Comprehensibility of specific modes across species boundaries is less frequent—it is sometimes implied that a particular form or mode of art may not, or perhaps cannot, exist in a particular species. The Garotha of Johnathan MacKenzie's "Overproof" (1965), for example, have no concept of fiction, regarding human fiction merely as lies. But the concept of art in some form is implied in the creativity required for sapience, and responses to forms of art will occur in different species as a commonality of the multispecies galaxy.

Within the science-fictional consensus, these commonalities emerge as necessary to the existence of sapience within a species. All of them are bonding processes (microbonds) between the individuals of the species. Severally, their functions are developmental (education, medicine), stabilizing (religion, art), ordering (government, law), competitive (war, game-playing, trade), and expressive (art, religion). Together, they operate synergistically to stabilize the species *as a species* in a dynamic equilibrium and to preserve it (just as on a microscale they preserved the tribe, community, nation) from dissolution into social chaos. Moreover, the microbonding process between individuals developed within the species will enable the macrobonding beyond the species in the form of the multispecies galaxy.

THE GALAXY AS CONTEXT

The speculative or extrapolative vision of the multispecies galaxy as the context for interspecies encounter is one of the clearest examples of the science-fictional consensual hypothesis at work. On the basis of the evidence in the SF magazine stories, there is a widely established (although not rigidly enforced) convention that such encounters between human and alien will take place within the context of the local galaxy.[7] In addition, just as the specifics of the participants are variable but regulated within the limits of the known laws of biology (or xenobiology), it is also established that the specifics of the galaxy as a context for multispecies habitation are variable but appropriately regulated within the limits of established astronomical knowledge. Likewise, it is widely assumed that different species coexisting in the multispecies galaxy will inevitably form some kind of political organization.

How many species it takes to constitute a multispecies galaxy has some bearing on the nature of the political context but has never been determined precisely. From the beginning, the ratio between human and alien in the stories vary. There may be only a single alien species interacting with humans (Stribling, "The Green Splotches" 1927) or many. All may interact simultaneously and directly with humans and each other, as in de Camp's Viagens Interplanetarius stories, which begin with "The Animal Cracker Plot" (1949) and were subsequently collected in *The Continent Makers and Other Tales of the Viagens* (1971). Or multiple other species may be merely implied in a particular encounter between humans and single alien species (Brin, "Shhhh" 1989). In hypothesized-contact stories, such as Bentley's "The Dip Stick" (1954), it may be left unclear whether or not there is more than one alien species behind the artifact or the traces the humans are investigating. Although, therefore, some distinction could theoretically be made between a galaxy inhabited by humans and one other species (*bispecies*, using *bi-*, two), one inhabited by several species (*plurispecies*, using *pluri-*, several), and one inhabited by many species (*multispecies*, using *multi-*, many), in practice no distinction has ever been made, and *multispecies* is conventionally used to describe any galaxy in which humans are not alone.

Although serious statistical analysis of the balance between the types of galactic context in magazine stories is not available, the impression given in the magazines is that encounters with a single alien species are in the majority in stories in the twenties and thirties, whereas there is a slow increase in multispecies encounters toward the end of the thirties and into the forties. Nevertheless, at least two major writers of novel-length fiction, Edmond Hamilton and E. E. "Doc" Smith, established their vision of the multispecies galaxy in serials beginning in the magazines as early as 1928. In *The Visual Encyclopedia* (1977), Ash notes that "Crashing Suns," the first story in Hamilton's Interstellar Patrol series, appeared as a two-part serial in *Weird Tales* in 1928, and *The Skylark of Space* (1946), the first story in Smith's Skylark series, appeared in *Amazing* in the same year, also in serial form. Isaac Asimov, however, moves the date of Smith's composition back further, in his response to Scott Jarrett's letter in *IASFM* about Robert Coles's *The Struggle for Empire* (1900) and the all-human-galaxy question, asserting that Smith's story was written by 1919 and waited nine years for publication. If Asimov is here correct, it appears that the idea of the multispecies galaxy preceded the readiness of the science fiction readers (or editors and publishers, at least) to accept it, whether in novel or short-story form. Moreover, in his discussion of his own approach to aliens in the galaxy, in "The All-Human Galaxy" (1983), Asimov specifically attributes the initiation of the multispecies galaxy to Smith and its popularity to the influence of John W. Campbell:

> Smith . . . introduced interstellar travel as a commonplace thing and placed his heroes and villains within a space-frame that included the entire Galaxy. . . . Smith and Campbell viewed the Galaxy as including many, many intelligent species. Almost every planet possessed them and Smith, in particular, was most inventive in drawing up unEarthly shapes and characteristics for his alien beings. (6)

But among the writers of short stories, Sewell Peaslee Wright, in "The Death-Traps of FX-31" (1933) and his other stories about Commander John Hanson of the Special Patrol Service, was the first to offer a multispecies galaxy to the readers of *Astounding*. Although at this time the popular writer Nat Schachner was contributing stories about encounters with single alien species to *Astounding*, including "Slaves of Mercury" (1932) and "The Saprophyte Men of Venus" (1936), only later did he too begin to present multispecies galaxies, notably in "The Eternal Wanderer" (1936) and "Crystallized Thought" (1937). In the years immediately following World War II, however, beginning with such efforts as John MacDougal's "Chaos Coordinated" (1946), the magazines offer a considerable increase in this type of story, and in the fifties and sixties the multispecies-galaxy stories of such major names as de Camp, Herbert, Anderson, Anvil, Clement, and H. B. Fyfe begin to dominate the magazine fiction about aliens. Writing in 1983, Asimov suggests in retrospect that this increase may have been a temporary one: "This 'many-intelligence Galaxy' is not as prominent in science fiction as it once was" ("The All-Human Galaxy" 1983, 6). Yet even a cursory examination of magazine fiction in the seventies and eighties reveals that, although the encounters within individual stories tend increasingly to focus on a single alien species, the galaxy within which most of them are set is actually a multispecies galaxy, and this pattern continues in the early nineties.

If the galaxy a writer has created is literally multispecies, he or she is faced with implying or explicitly discussing an appropriate organizational context for interspecies relationships. In most of these multispecies galaxies, the different worlds and species are members of an interworld or interspecies organization of some sort. The influence of, first, the short-lived League of Nations and, then, its successor, the United Nations Organization—especially with the increasing visibility of the latter in an age of global communications—has undoubtedly contributed to the consolidation of this concept within science fiction. Such organizations exist in stories from the earliest days of the magazines. At the end of Smith's *Skylark of Valeron* (1949; the third of the Skylark series, appearing in serial form in 1934–1935), for example, the mopping-up operations at the end of the main action of the narrative include "planning the perfect government—planetary, systemic, galactic, universal—for all intelligent races, wherever situated" (199) and the handing over to the "Galactic Council" of the dangerous artifact known as the "Brain" (205). On a slightly less sweeping scale is the "Galactic Federation" introduced as the organizing structure in Isaac Asimov's "Homo Sol" (1940), "The Imaginary" (1942), and "The Hazing" (1942), which is governed by the "Galactic Congress" ("Homo Sol" 1940, 199). In his editorial "The All-Human Galaxy" (*IASFM* 1983), discussing what he presents in these stories, Asimov writes that

> I naturally tried my hand at the "many-intelligence" Galaxy myself. . . . "Homo Sol" . . . dealt with a Galactic Empire consisting of the civilized beings from many, many planetary systems—each planetary system containing a different type of intelligent being. Each bore the name of the native star in the species name, so that they would be "Homo Arcturus," "Homo Canopus" and so on. (8)

That the "Federation" of the stories themselves has become the "Empire" of this discussion is probably a slip of the pen attributable to the influence of the Empire from the much more extensive Foundation series of short stories and novels intervening in Asimov's memory. But in his initial use of a federation, he is closer to the norm in the magazines. More often than not writers seem to prefer the implied structure of a loose association of autonomous or semi-autonomous worlds or planetary systems or groups of systems—something like an interplanetary version of its United Nations Organization prototype, and usually equally without teeth (i.e., legislative authority over its members)—which functions through its executive body (council or congress) consultatively or cooperatively only, for which *federation* becomes a sort of blanket or shorthand term. Galactic federations of the looser type, therefore, still constitute the most popular science-fictional form of government above the planetary level.

Occasionally, a more tightly controlled structure is implied. Phyllis Gotlieb's "Mother Lode" (1973) and other short stories and novels about the heavily bureaucratized "GalFed," for example, imply a structure that is authoritarian if not actually totalitarian. In such closed structures as GalFed, the executive body is superordinant—it legislates decisions binding on all its members—and the structure could be considered comparable to that of the later years of the Roman Republic. There is no obvious contemporary equivalent to structures such as GalFed above the national level, although the federal-provincial structure in Canada and the federal-state structure in the United States and in Australia provide suitable models for extrapolation. Both types of federation, and even such empires as exist, usually allow for nonmembers of the structure. Consequently, in most multispecies galaxies there can be species which have not yet been discovered, or which have refused to join, or which have not qualified to join, or which are members of other (often competing) organizations.

Other types of organization are occasionally suggested. In Christopher Anvil's story, "Mission of Ignorance" (1968), an organization—the "great Galactic organization" (50)—is introduced. It is called simply "the Greater Galactic Community" (43) and reports to an equally simply titled "Central Executive" (47), and although the capitalization suggests that these are indeed titles, they do not commit Anvil to any particular form of organization. Their extreme banality may be accidental, but it is much more likely to be, in keeping with the ironic stance of the story as a whole, deliberate. In practice, the Community consists of what appears to be nothing more than a loose coalition of species predatory toward Earth. Similarly, in Anvil's much later story, "The Underhandler" (1990), a galactic organization is again trying to annex Earth: "'Yes,' said Selouel, 'and now we offer you the chance to voluntarily join our Coequality.'" (46). In this later story much more about the attacker organization is revealed, and it is apparent that the somewhat disingenuously named "Coequality" is actually a heavily bureaucratized military junta. Moreover, in its intentions at least, it is no less predatory than the earlier Greater Galactic Community. Even Anvil, therefore, appears to subscribe in his own fashion to the principle of the galactic organization, extending the range of the concept even further.

From time to time, forms of interspecies galactic governmental organization are suggested that are more difficult to assess. "I Tell You Three Times" by
Raymond F. Jones (1951), in fact, is both more difficult to assess and more
problematic in its theorizing. It offers a galactic federation based on "Life
Unity" (10), in which a political theory of galactic organization is discussed at
length. In particular, the theory introduces a new and speculative idea to the
topic of political theory: The "Life Unity" concerned seems to be an innate
quality found in nearly all species (it is species-wide in those species in which
it is found)—the individual's ability to trust other sapient beings, whether of
his or her or its own or another species. Without it, interspecies government
cannot exist:

> Only among those creatures strong in interspecies Unity was any kind of inter-
> galactic government possible.
>
>   For there were strange species that seemed to Earthmen like something
> dredged from the bottom of the seas, ghastly apparitions whose visage was the
> stuff of nightmare—these were the companions with whom men sat in the
> sanctuary of the Galactic Council. These were the fellow Computermen with
> whom they worked to establish a community of law within the Universe. (11)

Species that do not have (or at least do not appear to have) this trait are not
truly sapient and cannot be members of the federation, although continuing
efforts are made to expand the understanding of Life Unity in species where it
appears to be missing. Within the federation, the organization seems to be the
familiar form of a standard democracy. This idea, although promising, is also
problematic (as the writer indicates within it, since it seems to discriminate on
the basis of innate behavior) and does not seem to have been taken up for further discussion elsewhere.

More recently, writers sometimes take a direct approach to the topic. The
cooperative fictions of the 1980s and 1990s (collections of short stories by
different writers set in a shared megatext or ficton)[8] usually lay out the organization of the galaxy (whether all human or multispecies) explicitly in
introductory or editorial material accompanying the stories. The editorial
blurb provided on the back cover for Dickson's *The Harriers: Of War and
Honor* (1991), for example, provides information about the galactic organization of his all-human galaxy as background for the existence of the military force whose adventures form the primary motivation for the fiction in

the collection, and the prominence of its display illustrates the importance of the concept:

> Earth is but a memory . . . the real action these days is in The Magnicate, a league of all the human worlds in the galaxy. At the center of the Magnicate is the Hub, a huge artificial world from which control of Human Space flows. The Hub government is in the main an instrument for progress and social good, but even so *control* sometimes requires *force*—enter *The Harriers*. (back cover)

Given such approaches, which relieve the writer or writers of further responsibility for discussion of interspecies structures, it could be said that the science-fictional galaxy almost always has some implicit if not explicit organizational structure, and the galaxy deliberately described as without any structure at all is a rarity. The apparent lack of such structure in a given story, therefore, might be more frequently assumed to result from the absence of any attention to organization than from actual intention to present it as existing without organization.

Any conceptualization of a form of galactic organization within the multispecies galaxy produces a requirement for the further conceptualization of "law and order" on a galaxy-wide scale. Much science fiction postulates that whatever form galactic governmental organization takes, it will necessarily include an interspecies or interworld suborganization to function as an enforcement agency for its laws. Under all its names (the Galactic Patrol of E. E. "Doc" Smith, the Interstellar Patrol of Edmond Hamilton, the Interplanetary Guard of J. M. Walsh, etc.), it remains essentially a military force (analogies with prespaceflight navies including a marine corps are most common) acting additionally as a combination of peacekeeping and police force. The duties of the protagonist in Frederick Kummer's "The Foreign Legion of Mars" (1939), for example, show that this Foreign Legion fulfils the military, peacekeeping, and police roles of the enforcement agency, while the story itself as a whole offers an obvious tribute to a well-known icon of military culture. In Gordon Dickson's *The Harriers*, however, the Harriers are described unequivocally as having been created as a military force in the service of the "Magnicate":

> *The Grand Harriers*: An elite military force created to guard the Hub and the diplomats who travel there—and to ensure their own position as the one unassailable force in Human Space.

The Petit Harriers: A motley band of hard-case adventurers created to do the planet-side jobs the Grand Harriers wouldn't soil their white gloves on. No mission is too tough, dirty or dangerous. No method unthinkable. And yet the Petit Harriers do have their own kind of honor . . . and a hell of a lot more fun! (back-cover blurb)

Nevertheless, the "planet-side jobs" of the *Petit Harriers*, as presented in the two stories included in this volume, seem to include more than pure combat. Peacekeeping and police functions are, however, much diminished if not entirely absent. Moreover, perhaps indirectly, the ironically romantic phrasing of this blurb describing them as "a motley band of hard-case adventurers" pays its own indirect tribute to the same icon of military culture as Kummer, and it implies the same versatility.

Not all such forces are created as military forces. In James White's stories of the interspecies Sector General Hospital, and in some of his nonrelated stories, such a force appears under the nonmilitary name of the Monitor Corps and with an explicitly nonmilitary ethos. This ethos was the result of a deliberate choice by White, as he explains in "The Secret History of Sector General" (1979), a prefatory essay to *Ambulance Ship*:

Essentially, the Monitor Corps was a police force on an interstellar scale, but I did not want them to be the usually ruthless, routine-indoctrinated, basically stupid organization that is so handy to have around when an idealistic principal character needs a bit of ethical conflict. . . . I wanted them to be good guys too, but with different ideas as to the kind of activity that produces the greater good.

Their duties included interstellar survey and first-contact work as well as maintaining the Federation's peace—a job that could, if they were unable to discourage the warmongers, give rise to a police action that was indistinguishable from an act of war. But the Corps much preferred to wage psychological warfare aimed at discouraging planetary and interplanetary violence and when, despite their efforts, a war broke out, then they very closely monitored the beings who were waging it. (xi)

Nevertheless, although the Monitor Corps is intended primarily as a peace-keeping, police, and diplomatic body, its organization, discipline, and rank structure are military, and its functions, although they are not restricted to it, do include combat in defense of the federation. In the second part of *Star Surgeon* (1963; originally entitled "Field Hospital"), in which Sector General Hospital is under attack from a ruthless multispecies alien empire, the Monitor Corps is shown in an almost entirely military action. Moreover, in the latest novels in the series, *Final Diagnosis* (1997), *Mind Changer* (1998), *Double Contact* (1999), White often inserts references that indicate his own and his characters' understanding of the problematic nature of the Corps' nature and activities. Even with the best intentions, therefore, and possibly partly as a result of the consensus opinion that war will be common to sapient species, the interworld enforcement agency seems never quite to escape from the influence of its military prototype or from all that that influence implies.

The interaction of cultures within the multispecies galaxy has produced the well-known problem of cultural interference. Although culture shock on the individual level can be dealt with in terms of individual psychology, when one culture encounters another in a different state of social and technological development, it is postulated that the shock gives rise to the phenomenon known as "cultural interference"—in which the more advanced culture damages and possibly destroys the development of the less advanced. As Mark Twain said: "Soap and water are less sudden than a massacre but just as effective." The roots of the concept of cultural interference are the patterns of history—as Brian Ash points out in *Faces of the Future: The Lessons of Science Fiction* (1975): "The consequences of interfering with unfamiliar societies and cultures has bothered 'civilized' Man little in the past, probably because the victims have been, after all, only 'less developed' branches of his own species on earth. He will do well to exercise some caution when it comes to imposing the joys of his company upon extra-terrestrials" (178). The classic science fiction story of cultural interference in action is Poul Anderson's "The Helping Hand" (1950), which I have discussed in detail in a previous chapter. The issue of the propriety of intervention, however, appears as early as Hugo Gernsback himself. In "The Struggle for Neptune" by Henrik Dahl Juve, published in the Fall 1930 issue of *Wonder Stories Quarterly*, Juve shows his human intruders exploiting a peaceful albeit monstrous alien society. One difference between the two stories is in the method of the interference: Juve's characters employ brutal force and their "hired gun" is a convict on parole who waves the "stick tipped with red crystal," which the Neptunians fear, "for the sheer joy of watching them fall back in terror" (95), whereas Anderson's protagonists peaceably offer the benefits of trade and tourism. Neither group of intruders, however, questions their own right to do what they do. In Anderson's story, the doctrine is articulated directly through the voice of one of the characters of a second alien culture that has refused the benefits offered by the humans; Juve may suggest the issue of right or wrong, but he does not do it with the same directness. In introducing the story, however, Gernsback himself questions the activities of the characters:

> [A]s Mr. Juve suggests, a question of morals arises here. Were our explorers justified in precipitating these peaceful Neptunians into civil war and carnage, destroying great numbers of them in order that we should extract their great deposits of radium? The question is not easy to answer for the Neptunians have apparently little use for the precious stuff and earthlings have. (95)

The result of these and other discussions of cultural interference was the emergence of the potential for a "noninterference" rule or directive, for which John J. Pierce, in *Foundations of Science Fiction: A Study in Imagination and Evolution* (1987), discussing the Viagens series and singling out "Finished" (1949) as a good example, suggests that "L. Sprague de Camp deserves credit" (120). Stanley Schmidt, too, comments in 1987 that "[c]ultural interference is, for very good reasons, one of the grand old themes of science fiction" ("In Times to Come" 1953, 122), and the steady popularity of stories which address the topic continues to bear him out.

The consensus in the fiction of the magazines about the commensality of the multispecies galaxy, therefore, is that it will not always be a safe or even a comfortable place, but it will be a place with some kind of recognizable order and organization. In some ways, this galactic commensality may seem remarkably similar—even unimaginatively identical—to the global commensality of Earth, the writers' home planet, which also offers a range of possible interactivity within the frame of a more or less constant order. In the galactic commensality, however, it will be different species, not merely different subgroups of a single species, who will meet and interact, and the forms of their interaction will be as diverse as are their physical forms. Consequently, the value of the familiarity of the framework of order within the commensality lies in its support for the presentation of the otherness of the aliens the writers wish to introduce.

CONCLUSION

In general, there is in the consensual hypothesis about the commonalities of sociocultural patterning that might exist in other sapient species a much heavier reliance on analogous patterning than there is in the consensus with regard to questions of form. Analogy, however, as I pointed out in discussing the design of analogous aliens, is a limited structural process, at its best where covert, and even at its best achieves otherness rather than alterity. In multiplying the commonalities, therefore, much of the thrust of the attempt to achieve alterity is blunted. Analogy allows for the presence of otherness in the commonalities, but even in the most skilled hands it does not encourage alterity. Moments of dislocation of the reader's understanding into a fleeting recognition of the alterity in the encounter with aliens do occur—the presence of another Self that is an OtherSelf is registered. Too often, however, it is a false recognition: After the moment passes, the alien is revealed as somewhat familiar as well as somewhat other.

Given some degree of otherness in form and psychology, however, in the portrayal of the aliens concerned, the general effect of the commonalities is to enhance the comprehensibility of aliens. The presence of analogously patterned commonalities within the constitution of a sapient society will extend the examination of factors involved in sapience and its recognizability across species boundaries. Moreover, because, as the consensus implies, all species do analogous kinds of things as a result of their sapience, regardless of their desirability or necessity, the possibility of meaningful interspecies interaction—and hence of conflict—in these particular areas is also enhanced. Furthermore, once established the consensus also provides not only for an examination of the differences between different species' versions of any or all of these common constituents but also for an extended approach to aspects of the nature of sapience by opening up the possibilities of exploring in different species behavioral patterns that are anomalous in terms of the consensus.

NOTES

1. Not until 1995, in *Aliens and Alien Societies*, was Stanley Schmidt's "basic plan" available to aspiring writers to guide them on how to develop alien societies for the aliens they designed. The plan specifically requires them to "survey some of the elements that have developed in human cultures, and then to think about how they

might develop differently—or be replaced by others—in beings with different evolutionary roots" (104), and Schmidt further suggests the pursuit of studies in anthropology and ethology.

2. Even alternative human systems of government in the future are fairly unimaginative. The humans of Earth have more than one form of government in Anvil's "Mission of Ignorance" (1968), for example, for the Burdeenites have seceded from the world government and "government in the Burdeenite territories rests largely with the House of Mogg. As nearly as the outsider can comprehend, the House is a nonheredit[ar]y monarchy and aristocracy, with a minimum of laws" (46). A nonhereditary monarchy sounds, at least faintly, a note simultaneously progressive and conservative, but Anvil does not get beyond this level of ingenuity in any of his alien governmental systems, and he does not explain in detail how it works.

3. No doubt Asimov would have been intrigued to learn in this context of the discovery of a mammalian eusociety (a cooperative society like that of bees or ants), described by Rodney L. Honeycutt as characterizing "the naked mole rat (*Heterocephalus glaber*)" (Honeycutt 1992, 43).

4. To the best of my knowledge, only one writer, W. R. Thompson, in "Second Contact" (1988), has postulated an alien species that has risen to sapience and to a higher-than-human level of technology (including space travel) without the concept of law.

5. They include, for example, such diverse examples as T. S. Stribling's "The Green Splotches" (1927), Henrik Dahl Juve's "The Monsters of Neptune" (1930) and "The Struggle for Neptune" (1930), R. H. Romans's "The Moon Conquerors" (1930) and "The War of the Planets" (1930), Murray Leinster's "Proxima Centauri" (1935), Donald Wolheim's "The Embassy" (1942), Fredric Brown's "Arena" (1944), Cyril Kornbluth's "Silly Season" (1950), and Marc Stiegler's "The Bully and the Crazy Boy" (1980). Later stories include Gordon Dickson's "Jackal's Meal" (1969), Michael Stall's "The Five Doors" (1973), Kevin O'Donnell's "Low Grade Ore" (1977), Jack Chalker's "In the Wilderness" (1978), and Joseph Green's "And Be Lost Like Me" (1983).

6. An important exception to this absence of preoccupation is the specific preoccupation with the Vietnam War (see H. Bruce Franklin's "The Vietnam War as American SF and Fantasy" 1990). Within the last decade or so, war has become an important topic in science fiction novels, but even where it is the focus, as in David Weber's Honor Harrington series, beginning with *On Basilisk Station* (1993), it is not in any sense of the word a glorification or a mere entertainment of the sort Haldeman objects to.

7. The term *universe* is frequently used, but *galaxy* makes more sense in my discussion, since I am excluding alien-encounter stories that are set in other times and in other dimensions that are equally called universes in the fiction.

8. For a detailed discussion of these cooperative fictions see Monk, "'The Shared Universe Thing'" (1990).

III

READING THE ALIEN

Figuring It Out:
The Literary Modeling
of the Alien

In spite of the difficulty of accommodating science fiction about aliens in any theoretical framework and in spite of the fact that aliens in science fiction tend to fall into recognizable and frequently recycled types, when the Other that has previously informed folklore, fairytale, myth, theology, and psychology is summoned to inform science fiction as the Alien and becomes subject not only to the constraints of conforming to current scientific knowledge (as discussed previously) but also to the constraints of a highly conventionalized genre, then the normal processes of literary modeling that produce characters in mainstream fiction begin to operate on them. These processes can, in the hands of skilled science fiction writers, produce characters who transcend the perceived limitations of the conventions. Too few in number, in fact, to be generally recognized as a type, these are actually the potentiated aliens of science among whom alterity rather than mere otherness will be found. As such they offer a foundation for the consideration of alterity as both a literary trope (which I shall discuss here in terms of E. M. Forster's theory of "round" characters in *Aspects of the Novel* 1927) and a psychological substrate (which I shall discuss in the next chapter in terms of Jung's theory of archetypes). To a very large extent the theory of characterization applied to a practical typology of the magazine stories isolates and refines what is necessary to the representation of alterity in the alien.

Whereas the structural principles of design (analogy, homology, heterology, and exoticism) distinguish alien forms, the literary principle of characterization distinguishes them according to their function. Although aliens—especially those within the multispecies galaxy—are apparently, when considered overall, as various as the minds of their creators, for purposes of discussion most of them actually fall into four functional types: the *bug-eyed monster* (*bem*—or BEM, or B.E.M.), the *humanoid,* the *little green man* (LGM), and the *potentiated alien.* Critical argument about precisely which type the alien of any given fiction might fall into is, of course, always possible. Nevertheless, the schema of the types holds good for almost one hundred years of stories selected from the major magazines. Each type exhibits some degree of otherness and can be used for various science-fictional purposes and effects. Because failures are sometimes as instructive as successes, I discuss the *bem* and the *humanoid* here, although these are not sufficiently sophisticated concepts of the alien for their otherness to demonstrate potential for alterity. The LGM, however, is at least sometimes sophisticated enough to demonstrate potential for rotundity in Forster's sense, although this may be dependent on the writer's initial ability to create round human characters, and hence potential for alterity. Finally, there are the potentiated aliens among whom individuality, conceptual sophistication, and Forster's rotundity may be found. All of these last, I shall suggest, constitute examples of varying levels of success in creating a literary trope of alterity and an archetypal figuring of the OtherSelf.

THE BEM

The *bem*—as the bug-eyed monster is familiarly known—is probably the most obvious type of the Alien in science fiction, and one of the most enduring (if not one of the most endearing) of science-fictional tropes. It is also one that has spread beyond the limits of the genre that spawned it, and its most frequent appearances now occur not as previously in written science fiction (particularly the short stories of the pulp era) but in the newer media of television and film aided by special effects technology as advanced as any imagined in the pages of *Astounding.* Whatever may be said about the *bem*'s effect in these media, in written science fiction its effect is limited.

The term *bem* itself was originally an acronym for "bug-eyed monster" but subsequently became a word in its own right. In the glossary entry on the term in *The World of Science Fiction* (1980), *bug-eyed* is taken by Lester del Rey to have originally referred to eyes like those of a "bug" (insect) as portrayed in the illustrations to the fiction itself: "[B]ug-eyed monster . . . refers to any alien creature, monstrous in form, used in science-fiction art. It need not have the faceted eyes of insects and rarely does" (325). J. J. Pierce, however, in *Great Themes of Science Fiction* (1987) suggests a different reference—that the eyes are *bugged* or protruding: "[W]hether a particular story inspired the epithet is uncertain, but Charles Willard Diffin's novelette 'Dark Moon' [1931], which features monstrous creatures with eyes on stalks, has been suggested" (2). The illustration that accompanies this story and shows the monster concerned is not clear about its eyes, but the description Diffin provides in the text certainly is: "Basilisk eyes in a hairy head [of] gray, stringy hairs; and the fearful head ended in narrow, outthrust jaws, where more of the gray hairs hung like moss from lips that writhed and curled and sucked at the air with a whistling shrillness. . . . The eyes shot forward on protruding antennae" (181–82). This memorable image was followed by subsequent writers and probably received the most reinforcement from Ray Cummings in "Wandl the Invader" (1932), in which one group of the invading creatures of Wandl are described as having eyes set, like those of Diffin's monster, at the end of stalks: "The head and face were most of all a personal mocking of mankind. . . . A nose orifice, with two protruding brown eyes above it, set outward on stems, and an up-ended slit of a mouth" (93). The artist for the serial publication in *Astounding* (1932) followed Cummings's description in the illustrations, and the eyes and their stalks are clearly visible. Unlike the illustrator for Diffin's story, however, Cummings's illustrator managed to produce an effect that was grotesque rather than terrifying, and the horror of the story lies more in the writer's invocation of it in the text than in the illustration itself. Moreover, not all early attempts at the stalk-eyed *bem* were creatures of horror either by intention or by ineptitude of execution. The Martians of Theodore Sturgeon's "Artnan Process" (1941) have these stalk-eyes to rather charmingly humorous effect in both illustration and text: "[The Martians] were lined up in front of a the air lock, their spare bodies quivering with the palpitation peculiar to their race, and with their eye-stalks pointing rigidly toward the approaching Earthmen, points together, in the well-known Martian cross-eyed stare" (58).[1] The design of unknown creatures, both aliens and monsters, was becoming more scientifically oriented as a result of the increasing pressure toward scientific accuracy in science fiction as a whole, and this pressure was probably responsible for the abandonment of the stalked eye as a possibility. In his important two-part article about the design of sapient aliens, "Design for Life" (1939), L. Sprague de Camp does not discuss eye design in detail, although he points out that "an extensible lens, to use like a telescope . . . hardly seems necessary" (2:113). Later, however, the question was taken up by Freitas:

> What about eyes on stalks? Most xenobiologists regard this as a rather unlikely adaptation for thinking animals. Eyestalks require a hydraulic support system inefficient except in small animals. Eyes are vital senses for large organisms, yet stalks could be lopped off by predators with a single stroke of claw or pincer, permanently depriving the owner of sight. Periscoping eyes unprotected by bone are also more prone to common injury—in an accident, stalks could be bumped, slammed or squashed all too easily. ("Extraterrestrial Zoology" 1981, 60)

In response, reader David King pointed out in a letter that

> [e]ye-stalks could probably make up for their hazardous construction through their flexibility—they allow the creature to look over any shoulder it might have and run away from its predators in time. A disadvantage you overlooked is the need to keep the optic link from the eye to the brain as short as possible to avoid neural distortion and inefficiency. (172)

But the stalk-eyed appearance of the *bem* is a minor consideration—a shorthand form, a glyph to indicate that it is indeed a *bem*.

The historical antecedents of the *bem* in terrestrial monsters are clearly extensive and, if we confine ourselves to British literature, perhaps might be said to begin with Grendel. In "Victorian 'Extraterrestrials'" (1975), Mark Hillegas argues convincingly that "[t]he nineteenth-century story of life on other worlds . . . culminates in Wells's Martians and Selenites, and from them are descended the horrible, often crudely portrayed creatures of a great deal of science fiction in the twentieth century, the beings lovingly called Bug Eyed Monsters by the 'fans'" (413). Neither Wells's Martians and nor his Selenites, however, are bug-eyed in either sense of the word. They are, however, sapient, whereas in many if not all of the earliest magazine stories the *bem* is often a nonsapient creature, such as the amoeba-like menace in Captain S. P. Meek's "Beyond the Heaviside Layer" (1930). Even at this level, therefore, the science-fictional Alien as *bem* is beginning to be differentiated from the natural or supernatural monster of folklore.

This particular example of the Alien as a sapient *bem* is typical, nevertheless, of what was to follow, for to a considerable extent *bems* have been predictable within the limits of analogy with known terrestrial forms. As I have indicated in my discussion of the principle of analogy in alien physical design, in Meek's "The Attack from Space" (1930), which describes itself as the sequel to "Beyond the Heaviside Layer," the attack is from different but also analogous species of aliens—"a race of giant beetles" (390), who originate on Mercury. Similarly, in Morrison Colladay's "The Blattids" (1931) the alien invaders resemble "giant roaches" (845), and in Charles Tanner's "Tumithak of the Corridors" (1932) and "Tumithak in Shawm" (1933) they appear as huge blood-drinking spiders. The otherness involved in such *bems* was minimal, but it was not long before more imaginative forms of *bem* began to appear. Two years after the appearance of Tanner's "Tumithak in Shawm" (1933), in "Proxima Centauri" (1935) Murray Leinster introduces an innovative version of the *bem* in the form of large, mobile, and carnivorous plants. Another of these more innovative *bems* is the Martian in Polton Cross's "The Martian Avenger" (1939), which is a creature of "pure cellulose" that looks, in its original form, "repulsively like a large blood red worm, its substance shot through with veins of a darker hue . . . palpitating steadily" (78), with "Martian intelligence of terrific power" (86). It can, however, take on human form and turn into "a perfect imitation" of the hero (86), who after its destruction points out to the heroine that "[b]eyond question, the Martian only spared your life with ideas of later matehood" (97). It is not clear, however, that this remarkable statement by Polton Cross's hero can be entirely responsible for the proliferation of the notion that alien invaders were driven by lust for human women, an idea that crops up in early stories and even on the covers of some magazines and that also attached itself to the idea of science fiction among those who did not actually read it.

Nevertheless, in spite of the ingenuity with which the analogies are introduced, the alterity involved in analogous *bems* is clearly still not much more than minimal, and it was left to John W. Campbell to make a breakthrough when he created the engulfing, shapechanging, enigmatic (it may or may not be sapient) creature of "Who Goes There?" (1938), a creature whose original and powerful menace rendered most subsequent science-fictional attempts at the *bem* inept by comparison. Nevertheless, all the early *bems* of the magazine stories, including Campbell's, have in common that they pose an overwhelming, apparently unstoppable, and gruesomely destructive threat to human life by an alien in a form that is itself terrifying and disgusting and draws heavily on atavistic fears of large carnivorous animals, bloodsucking and/or stinging insects, multitentacled slimy creatures, and other terrors handed down to modern readers from the prehistoric "generalized vegetarian prohominid hairy ape" (Morgan, *The Descent of Woman* 1973, 16) who was a human ancestor.

The *bem* did eventually, at least in its more obvious versions, lose its place in science fiction magazine stories. But it did not disappear because it lost its power, or even because Campbell had perfected it, for as Kingsley Amis points out in *New Maps of Hell* (1960), "menace is in itself a legitimate effect" (37). The critical, vocal, and increasingly sophisticated fans had some part in its disappearance (or its banishment to the "fantasy, occult, and horror" shelves of the bookstores where there are some remarkably similar manifestations every year, or to movie and television productions).[2] But the most important share of the responsibility for the disappearance of the *bem* lay with the writers themselves. For even among the earliest writers about aliens there were those who were more than capable of rising, sometimes inadvertently perhaps, above the simplistic concept of alien menace provided by the *bem*. Raymond Z. Gallun, for example, tries to capture the menace of the alien conference delegates in his story "Hotel Cosmos" (1938) in his description of the purpose for which the hotel exists: "The fact that it . . . was meant for beings far from human, even in an intellectual sense, made one think of the vast gulfs between the stars; of dark steamy worlds, where slimy horrors sported and thought and toiled; of great, stark, un-Earthly mountains and deserts; and of a thousand other fearful and near unimaginable things" (142). Gallun clearly intends to produce an impression of truly monstrous creatures. Nevertheless, an example of the type of writing that eventually eliminated the *bem* from serious science fiction is visible in his phrase "slimy horrors sported and thought and toiled," in which the apparently casual juxtaposition of the stereotypical phrase "slimy horrors" with the verbs "sported" (in the sense, one presumes, of *play*, with its overtones of innocence), "thought" (with its reminder of human rationality) and "toiled" (with its introduction of all-too-familiar, all-too-human image of hard work) creates an immense plausibility in the notion of the sapience of the alien as well as its alterity. Equally subtle is the effect of the phrase "near unimaginable" for which most writers of this period would have substituted simply "unimaginable" and lost thereby half the effect that

Gallun's understatement manages to create. Even lightly sketched in, however, Gallun's conference delegates, although dangerous, are dangerous aliens—plausibly realized, knowable, recognizably sapient, and comprehensible.

The place of the *bem* in magazine stories of alien menace was gradually taken over by what might be called the neo-*bem*, which is sapient but unwittingly (and more subtly and variously) destructive. The mere physical presence of one of these neo-*bems* may disrupt human neurological function, hormonal balance, reality orientation, or emotional stability to such an extent as to render the human involved unable to survive normally, either physically or psychologically. The neo-*bem* may also destroy the human by being parasitic or addictive (physically or psychologically). Another form of threat is posed by the neo-*bem* that destroys the human in the course of its own normal activity by creating some form of hazard, or the one that sees humans as vermin, or the one that wants to incorporate humans into a group organism. In at least two stories, Eric Frank Russell's "The Waitabits" (1955) and Theodore L. Thomas's "Ceramic Incident" (1956), the implied hazard arises from the fact that the neo-*bems*' metabolic rates are so different (too slow and too fast, respectively) that they would probably be unable to see humans as creatures with whom they could communicate. Occasionally, the threat from a neo-*bem* results from it being unrecognized, particularly in the case of the shapeshifter. The subtlety of the neo-*bem* is sometimes sufficient to obscure its actual nature as a form of *bem*.[3]

Regardless of the attitude that readers, writers, and critics take toward the *bem* and the neo-*bem*, it remains undeniably true that it produces engaging science fiction, in both its earlier and more recent manifestations. As I have pointed out, the range of images that it can reflect, however, is extremely limited. For so much emphasis must be placed on its menace that it can rarely be developed in other aspects (even where it is intelligent to any degree it is never individualized), and even its menace is usually unmotivated in order to increase its intensity. It offers too little room for either serious exploitation of otherness (where it has any at all) or complex development of narrative interest. Consequently, to put it simply, the original *bem* disappeared from science fiction because it was too simplistic to attract and engage the increasing level of skill among science fiction writers who were interested in dealing with concepts of otherness and sapience in literary form, since for these particular purposes the *bem* is simply inadequate.

THE HUMANOID

The humanoid or anthropomorphic form of some aliens is the result of their roots in human culture. The earliest form of the Other was the stranger, who had (in actuality if not in rumor) human form, and supernatural Others and monsters were also often partly or wholly human in form. Science-fictional aliens are extraterrestrial, but at least some extraterrestrial aliens are nevertheless still conceived in human form and can therefore be characterized as *humanoid*. The humanoid is a very simplistic concept of the Alien, minimally differentiated (if at all) from the human in form and behavior, and offering only minimal opportunity to develop otherness. Consequently, although in terms of literary modeling it requires the least skill, imagination, and effort and therefore offers certain dangers to the unwary writer, it nevertheless provides excellent opportunities in the hands of skilled and careful writers for certain types of science fiction story.

In science fiction itself, *humanoid* is the single most common descriptive term for the extraterrestrial alien who shares our human form. Like so many other terms used in science fiction and the discussion of science fiction, however, it is highly ambiguous and interchangeable with several other terms for the same concept, of which *humaniform* or *humanlike* are the most usual—none of them clearly defined—and *anthropomorphic* is least usual. *Humanoid* describes aliens who conform almost perfectly to the human design, although its precise signification varies from writer to writer. Joseph Green in "Robustus Revisited" (1973) uses *humanoid* to describe his aliens who are deliberately and with didactic intent versions of early forms of humanity.[4] Isaac Asimov is another who uses the term, but it is far from clear what he means by it. In the editorial "The All-Human Galaxy" in *IASFM* for March 1983, he writes:

> I naturally tried my hand at the "many-intelligence" Galaxy myself. . . . "Homo Sol" [1940] . . . dealt with a Galactic Empire consisting of the civilized beings from many, many planetary systems . . . each planetary system containing a different type of intelligent being. Each bore the name of the native star in the species name, so that they would be "Homo Arcturus," "Homo Canopus" and so on. (8)

His description of the delegates to the Galactic Congress as they welcome "Earthmen" into the "Galactic Empire" at the beginning of "Homo Sol" (1940), however, seems to rule out humanoid aliens:

Beings of every manlike type and shape were there. Some were tall and polelike, some broad and burly, some short and stumpy. There were those with long, wiry hair, those with scanty grey fuzz covering head and face, others with thick blond curls piled high, and still others entirely bald. Some possessed long, hair-covered trumpets of ears, others had tympanum membranes flush with their temples. There were those present with large gazellelike eyes of a deep-purple luminosity, others with tiny optics of a beady black. There was a delegate with a green skin, one with an eight-inch proboscis and one with a vestigial tail. Internally, variation was almost infinite.

But all were alike in two things.

They were all Humanoid. They all possessed intelligence. (199–200)

His "many intelligences" are both "manlike" and "Humanoid," but neither of these terms in his usage can be considered a synonym for *anthropomorphic*, since only some of the delegates could be considered truly anthropomorphic in form. At the same time, however, neither of them can be considered to be considered the marker of intelligence, since this is referred to as the second separate factor in the two common qualities of all the delegates. Further on in "The All-Human Galaxy," discussing why his stories under Campbell's influence did not deal with aliens, Asimov explains that Campbell's resistance to the superior aliens in "Homo Sol" led him to write about a multispecies galaxy that had no human beings in it at all in "The Imaginary" (1942) and that he eventually decided that "[i]nstead of having an Empire with no human beings ... I would have an Empire with nothing but human beings in it.... Thus was born the 'all-human galaxy'" (10). This later paragraph clearly shows him making a distinction between *human* and *humanoid*, but one that does not seem to match his earlier descriptions.

Nevertheless, in spite of the ambiguity of the term *humanoid* (whether this is created by different writers using *humanoid* in different senses or by one writer using it in different senses), I have used it for convenience in my discussion, rather than the more accurate *anthropomorphic*. Humanoid aliens appear over and over again in the short stories in the science fiction magazines. Indeed, in one of the earliest, "Vandals of the Stars" (1930), a straightforward early alien invasion story, T. A. Locke explicitly describes the alien Lodoreans as "erect, piercing-eyed beings, who had all the characteristics of humans" (402) and even refers to them as "the men of Lodore" (403). Even where some differentiation is introduced, it is often minimal: The aliens are distinguished only by their size in Clifford Simak's "Immigrant" (1954).[5] In the stories in which they occur, *humanoid* aliens, being usually only superficially different in form, introduce only a minimal otherness into the stories. This minimality of the otherness of humanoid aliens results in their offering least scope for the study of alterity and alien sapience. In fact, even mere otherness sometimes disappears from the humanoid alien. On the evidence, moreover, writers who might be prepared to undertake the amount of deliberate, careful work involved in successfully creating minimal otherness in humanoid aliens seem to find it more challenging to attempt to produce alterity in nonhumanoid aliens and sometimes do so with great success.

The humanoid resembles the *bem* in that it has a history before the advent of modern magazine science fiction. The humanoid alien is clearly linked to the humanoid supernatural Other of earlier centuries, whether of religious or folkloric tradition. The Judeo-Christian tradition of Western civilization, for example, asserts emphatically that "man" was made in God's image: "And God said, Let us make man in our image, after our likeness. . . . So God created man in his own image, in the image of God created he him; male and female created he them" (Genesis 1:26–27, King James Bible). Angels and devils (who were fallen angels) were therefore also imagined in humanoid forms—the former extremely beautiful, the latter grotesquely deformed, to represent iconographically their moral nature. When nonsupernatural extraterrestrial aliens were posited, writers coming from this tradition were most probably influenced to think that the form of the Other must be ugly but humanoid (if the writer sees the alien as bad or hostile) or beautiful but humanoid (if the writer sees the alien as good or benevolent). Outside this particular religious tradition, however, there were also other humanoid pantheons. The gods and goddesses of the pantheon of classical Greece (with the notable exception of Pan, who had goat legs and horns) were humanoid and beautiful. Even the gods and goddesses of the ancient (pre-Islamic) Egyptian pantheon were represented in hybrid forms—human bodies with animal heads. Similarly, the magic Others of folklore were also traditionally imagined as humanoid. They were assigned either exceptionally beautiful (elves, fairies) or exceptionally ugly (goblins, trolls) versions of the human form, and what was represented iconographically here was not their moral status but their relationship (friend or foe) to human beings. The humanoid form dominated religious and folkloric tradition about the supernatural Others because it could claim cultural justification for the preeminence of the human form.

The advance of scientific thinking and the acceptance of evolutionary theory to account for human development in a way that excludes the possibility of the supernatural also cut off, for the most part, this kind of religious and/or cultural justification of the human form in human theorizing about the Other. Yet the uniqueness of the human form is not completely eliminated by evolutionary theory, only the causes of its uniqueness. The innate desire to assign some kind of preeminence to the human form—to make clear that it is special even if it is not divinely authorized or "best"—is evident from the remarkable persistence of humanoid aliens in science fiction from the beginnings to the present day.[6]

Surprisingly, even after *The War of the Worlds* (1898) introduced the ugly Martian to such great effect, the humanoid persisted in much of the science fiction around the turn of the century. In Robert Cole's *The Struggle for Empire* (1901), for example, when the humans of the Earth Empire meet the Sirians, the form of the aliens must be assumed to be indistinguishable from the human, since no difference is mentioned—or even implied. The initial mention of the Sirians makes no reference to form, and the behavioral qualities noted are undifferentiated from the human (in fact, are pointedly identical):

> They came to the fixed star Sirius, and found that his planetary system was inhabited by a race of men who had attained to the same degree of civilization as themselves—a people who were hardy and bold, and whom they had to treat as equals.
>
> These people, who were all subject to the Sirian planet Kairet were extremely numerous and powerful, and were bound together by a close bond of union. (13)

Later in the novel, Sirians are mistaken for humans, and in the final chapter the hero marries a Sirian woman. In George Griffith's *A Honeymoon in Space* (1901), although toward the end of the novel the Venusians are described as "[h]alf bird, half human" (185), the Martians of the earlier chapters are still considered in entirely humanoid terms, except for the fact that the women are of equal size with the men (151). Consequently, when the earliest magazines began to present aliens in their stories, the tradition of the humanoid was close to hand and was incorporated alongside the *bem*.

The discussion of the design of alien sapients for science fiction addressed the humanoid only in a limited fashion. In the introduction to the first part of "Design for Life" (1939), for example, when de Camp offers a catalog of the aliens he has found in magazine stories by "comparing the ideas of the writers on the form that intelligent extra-terrestrials might have," he includes the humanoid at the beginning of the list when he introduces "e.-t.s in the form of men, even as you and I" (1:103). In issuing a warning against the most exotic forms of alien, however, de Camp may have inadvertently leaned too far in the opposite direction: "But, if intelligent life did develop on another planet, it is very unlikely that it would look like a chrysanthemum, or a starfish, or a fire hydrant. There are good reasons for thinking that it would probably look *something* like a man, at least at a sufficient distance" (103; original emphasis). His phrase "*something* like a man" might well have encouraged the creation of humanoid aliens by writers who failed to read attentively or simply failed to understand the rest of what de Camp had to say in the two parts of his article, nothing of which supports such an interpretation. Typical of such "e.-t.s in the form of men" are the humanoids in the stories written under the pen name of René Lafayette by Ron L. Hubbard, beginning with "Old Doc Methusaleh" in the October 1947 issue of *Astounding*. The stories recount the adventures of an itinerant medical-service ship with its doctor-pilot. A similar premise (the itinerant doctor in space) forms the basis of Murray Leinster's stories collected in *The Med Series* (1983),[7] which also involves humanoid aliens. Although an argument for the use of humanoids in these two series of stories might be justified on the grounds that human doctors could not otherwise practice medicine, James White was soon to begin a series of stories that would refute such an argument in no uncertain terms. In recent years, however, "e.-t.s in the form of men" have almost entirely disappeared from the fiction of the magazines.

Minimal otherness, however, is not necessarily detrimental to the story as a story if the focus is elsewhere than on the alien itself. In Roger Zelazny's "A Rose for Ecclesiastes" (1963), for example, the story requires both otherness in the aliens (Martians) *and* similarity, for the point on which the story turns is interfertility—human sperm is required to refertilize a sterile race—and for the story to work the Martians have to be close enough for interfertility. But this story is not primarily about aliens—it is about the rite of passage to maturity of a brilliant but emotionally stunted human being. The story employs, therefore, what might be called nominal otherness, the minimum necessary and sufficient for the storyteller's purpose.

Moreover, although the humanoid does not provide opportunity for more than minimal otherness, it does provide the opportunity for more than one variety of literary modeling. Many of the early examples of humanoid alien apparently resulted from simple indifference to the potential of alterity of form and behavior for effective storytelling, but some of them and some later stories use the humanoid alien deliberately as a matter of narrative strategy to make a humorous, allegorical, didactic, or satiric point. An early example is I. F. Stone's "Rape of the Solar System" (1934), where the fate of ancient non-human civilizations of the solar system is in danger of being repeated by humanity. Here the point is reinforced by the fact that the aliens are not only humanoid but aesthetically pleasing specimens, in a way very similar to the aesthetically pleasing Martians and others of the Victorian extraterrestrials discussed by Hillegas. In this example, the question of individualization of the alien is irrelevant, and this appears to be typical of all humanoid-alien stories. If such aliens were to be individualized, they could only be individualized in ways that would increase their humanity.

Occasionally, the humanoid alien is required to avoid distraction from the point of the story. In H. Beam Piper's "Omnilingual" (1957), the focus of the story is the way in which the knowledge of science (in particular, the periodic table of the elements) will enable the decipherment of the written archaeological treasures of the dead Martian civilization (and by implication, enable humans to communicate with any living aliens whom they may subsequently encounter). The form of the aliens is not important (at least in Piper's terms) to the point about a community of scientific knowledge, and might even be a distraction from it. Hence, it is mentioned only in passing and deliberately selected to be minimally distracting.

The use of humanoid aliens has dangers, however, even when used to avoid distraction from the point at hand or even when necessary for the point of the plot. On the evidence of Donald Wolheim's story "Storm Warning" (1942), where the aliens are appropriately differentiated and not humanoids, he clearly seems to have been in agreement with de Camp when designing them. Yet in "Embassy" (1942), written under the name Martin Pearson, Wolheim presents Martians and Venusians who are entirely humanoid and indistinguishable from humans among whom they live on Earth for purposes of political influence. The point of the story seems to be that sapients will not need differences in form to hate each other. But here the humanoid quality of the alien destroys the story as science fiction: These Martians and Venusians might just as well be the British and the French, for all the difference their extraterrestrial origin makes to the story.

As a result of its minimal otherness, the humanoid alien is too easily comprehensible and therefore becomes less attractive to the discriminating readers of science fiction—a group always on the increase. The gradual disappearance of the humanoid from science fiction in recent decades, except from texts directed to satiric or didactic ends, is therefore determined by reader response.

THE LITTLE GREEN MAN

The Little Green Man (LGM) is an alien whose form and psychology may be considerably differentiated from the human and whose creation demonstrates more skill, imagination, and effort in terms of literary modeling than either the humanoid or the *bem*. Its numbers came eventually to far exceed those of either of the other types over the full span of magazine fiction to the present. Ironically, moreover, although the term *little green man* is not indigenous to science fiction, it is an LGM that is usually produced (both inside and outside science fiction circles) as an example of a science-fictional alien when one is called for in the course of everyday events.

The term itself is of mysterious origin. The first occurrence of the phrase, according to the *Compact Oxford English Dictionary*, is in Kipling's *Puck of Pook's Hill* (1906). It therefore occurs in a fantasy context rather than in anything that might be considered science-fictional and with rather different meaning from the later popular sense. According to the text, "The little green man orated like a—like Cicero" (Kipling 1906, 185), but the "little green man" is a Pict named Allo, who is "painted blue, green, and red from his forehead to his ankles" (178). There does not, as the dictionary suggests, seem to be any way of connecting that earlier isolated instance and the later widespread use of the phrase. Partridge's 1962 supplement to his *Dictionary of Slang* defines *little green men* as "[m]ysterious beings alleged to have been seen emerging from flying saucers; often associated with *bug-eyed monsters*... since mid-1950s" (689). He offers as a derivation only the guess that it has been "prob[ably] adopted ex US, where the illustration of pulp 'sci-fi' has always been greater than in UK" (689), and this definition is itself the second recorded instance of the phrase, according to the *COED2*. The same suggestion is put forward in *Brewer's Dictionary of Twentieth-Century Phrase and Fable*: "The phrase 'little green men' . . . was probably the result of illustrations in early science-fiction magazines" (Pickering, Isaacs, and Martin 1992, 353). But in spite of these references to possible U.S. origins, both the *Random House Dictionary of the English Language* (1983) and Chapman's *Dictionary of American Slang* (1986) ignore the term. Lester del Rey's *The World of Science Fiction* (1980), although it includes, as previously noted, *bug-eyed monster*, omits *little green man*.

There is, however, despite these suggestions, no early evidence of the phrase in science fiction. The earliest graphic examples of little green men I have been able to discover are two magazine covers by Emsh, one for the December 1951 issue of *Galaxy* and the other for the July 1953 issue, and both of these are not only late in the history of science fiction but also clearly intended ironically. Certainly, there were green aliens before this. A fan by the name of Arthur Carrington refers to a "silver green gentleman" from the theater around the turn of the century in his letter to *Astounding* (1931), but unfortunately he does not identify the play. Eric Rabkin has pointed out (in a letter to the author) that Edgar Rice Burroughs's Martians were green, and there might be some influence from this widely known writer. But the phrase itself does not appear in Burroughs, and his green Martians were of normal stature. The earliest science-fictional use of the phrase *little green men* in a story seems to be Fredric Brown's "Martians, Go Home!" (1954), but he is already playing with it as a cliché apparently well-known both inside and outside the genre.

It was nevertheless a science fiction writer who was able to direct attention to the origins of the phrase, although not in his science fiction. In an article entitled "Little Green Men from Afar" (1976), L. Sprague de Camp describes a special lecture that took place in the University of Denver in 1950, designed by an instructor "to test his students' judgment of evidence," at which the invited speaker, Silas Newton, said that he had "learned from governmental officials that three unidentified flying objects, containing a total of thirty-four extra-terrestrials, had crashed, killing all their occupants. These were little blond, beardless men, around three and a half feet tall" (191). The popular book about the alleged flying-saucer crash, Frank Scully's *Behind the Flying Saucers* (1950), written and published in the same year and based on discussions with Newton, agrees that the supposed occupants were, as originally described by Newton, "of fair complexion" and "of small stature" (41). But, as de Camp points out, "They became green only in later versions of the story" (191), and the change in color is still mysterious. Certainly, the actual point at which it changed and the particular color it changed to (green, rather than blue or orange or any other color) are still mysterious. *Why* the color changed is not—quite obviously, little *blond* men were not sufficiently strange. During the late forties and early fifties, these and other alleged flying saucers and their alleged occupants were being discussed in many of the leading newspapers across the United States from coast to coast.

From this point in time, therefore, the term seems to have developed into a convenient stock phrase for those outside science fiction to describe aliens in general, both in science fiction and outside it. In 1968, the phrase was "originally applied to pulsars by their discoverer the English astronomer Antony Hewish . . . [and] so called from the popularized characterizations of extraterrestrial beings found in early science fiction" (Barnhart, *The Second Dictionary of New English* 1980, 282). American scientist George Gaylord Simpson, in his contribution to the contact debate, mentions "flying saucers and little green men, which belong only in science fiction" ("The Nonprevalence of Humanoids" 1964, 774), both of which as I have already noted most science fiction writers would reject out of hand as having nothing to do with science fiction. It might be assumed from this reference that his reading of science fiction was, at the time he wrote this passage, some distance behind the leading edge of the art. But these two occurrences clearly establish the phrase as having wide circulation—as a cultural commonplace—on both sides of the Atlantic. Consequently, having acquired the authority of a cultural commonplace, the phrase serendipitously offers itself as a useful identification for a particular concept of the Alien within science fiction.

Within the genre, moreover, LGM effectively identifies one of the most common of the alien types: the alien who is more or less a humanoid in behavior although often greatly differentiated in form. Most LGMs fall into a category de Camp identifies in "Design for Life" (1939) as "near-men, or men with a difference: tall men, short men, fat men, skinny men, men with oversized ears, men with scales, men with extra arms, *etc*" (1:103). If we set Asimov's galactic inhabitants from "Homo Sol" up against de Camp's category of "near men," it is possible to argue, pace Asimov himself with his insistence on his creation of an "all-human galaxy," that his humanoids are no other than LGMs in form, although not in behavior. In de Camp's own Viagens Interplanetarius series of stories from the forties and early fifties, one of the most important sources of influence in the multispecies galaxy stories of its period, the Krishnans are such "near-men" and are among the crowds celebrating at the "festival of Ànerik" (6) at the beginning of *The Tower of Zanid* (1958; one of the novels of the Viagens series). Here de Camp describes the Krishnans obliquely:

> Here and there you could see an Earthman who had gone Krishnan. . . . A few decades before, they would all have disguised themselves by dyeing their hair blue-green, wearing large pointed artificial ears, and gluing to their foreheads a pair of feathery antennae, in imitation of the Krishnans' external organs of smell. These organs were something like extra eyebrows rising from the inner ends of the true eyebrows. (6)

That mere cosmetic changes can enable a human to pass for a Krishnan reveals, in this instance, the often humanoid underpinning of the LGM. Some LGMs, however, are more humanoid than others, and in designing the Viagens aliens, de Camp also includes some less humanoid species. Among the celebrants at this same festival in *The Tower of Zanid*, therefore, he also presents as a counterbalance a sprinkling of aliens from other worlds: "A pair of Osirians, like small bipedal dinosaurs with their scaly bodies painted in intricate patterns . . . a trio of furry, beady-eyed Thothians, half the height of the Krishnans . . . a centaur-like Vishnuvan . . . a sober Ormazdian couple, near-human and crested, their carmine skins bare" (7). This second group corresponds to another of the categories of extraterrestrial beings in his articles "Design for Life," aliens "in the form of gorillas, lizards, turtles, and crickets" (1939, 1:103)—that is, in some way analogous to terrestrial forms of fauna. But neither group in the Viagens series is differentiated in its behavior from humans. Members of the crowd here are occupied in racing "shomals and ayas—either riding the beasts or driving them"—marching, jousting, sightseeing, gambling, and playing or watching games: "On the ball-field the crowd screamed as Zanid's team of minasht-players beat the diapers off the visiting team" (*The Tower of Zanid* 1958, 6–7). Among his own creations here, however, there are no aliens that "look like sow-bugs, marine worms, sea anemones," which make up the final group of examples from his research ("Design for Life" 1939, 1:103), suggesting that de Camp is, by his own standards, a conservative.

In the early years of the magazines, the LGM appears alongside the *bem* and the humanoid, although in lesser numbers. Each year, however, produced some stories involving LGMs and continues to do so.[8] In recent years, moreover, examples appear with increasing frequency, and an overview of the very large number of stories where the alien can be considered as falling into this category is suggestive not only of the variety of ways in which the LGM can function within a story but also to some extent of the nature of science fiction stories in general.

In stories of satiric or didactic intent, particularly where these are humorously presented, the LGM has specific artistic uses and functions. But whereas the story that involves the deliberate and skilled use of the humanoid with such intent selects its models from literary modes (that is, modes that, since their original inception as oral modes, have undergone a long incarnation as literary modes), the story that involves the use of the LGM is often a reflection of much nearer and later popular models. Early science fiction stories, as I have argued elsewhere, use models derived from story types in the popular magazines of the nineteenth century and the very early years of the twentieth century. They are subsequently influenced by contemporary mainstream models, although by the time this influence is established the ghettoization of science fiction tends to cut writers off from current mainstream writing and limit the effect of continuing mainstream developments in narrative technique. Consequently, the strengths and limitations of these earliest models have widespread, long-lasting, and not always beneficial effects on their successors.

As I have pointed out, the popularity of the LGM does not reduce it to a single function or status within the narrative. It is in fact the versatility with which its otherness may function in the story that accounts for the popularity, for its otherness may be nominal, implied, figurative, or essential. The nominal/pseudo/notional alien is the alien whose specific otherness is peripheral to the story, usually described as an alien but who in all respects other than name functions as a human character would function.[9] The implied alien is often the alien behind the Big Dumb Object (BDO) of the hypothesized contact stories but may appear in other types of hypothesized contact.[10] The figurative alien is the alien whose otherness is metaphoric in some way.[11] The essential alien is the alien whose otherness is integral to the story. Because of this versatility, and because the type of story and the status of the LGM within it can be completely independent, the LGM therefore becomes the workhorse version of the alien when writers choose to use these story models to focus on alien encounters. The versatility of function of the LGM is also a key to its independence from the storytelling (literary) values of the narrative. Lee Kil-lough's "Caveat Emptor" (1970) and H. B. Fyfe's "In Value Deceived" (1950) are explorations of the same theme: mutual trickery by human and alien. Both stories illustrate the importance of knowing what you are doing (or getting) in trading with strangers. In both stories the trading is between human and alien—the latter being in each story an LGM—and what makes the difference between the stories is not the treatment of the alien but the storytelling or lit-erary qualities of the stories.

Titles signal the nature of the story to follow, and the difference between "Caveat Emptor" and "In Value Deceived" begins with the titles. Both titles are "twist-in-the-tail" titles, or titles that are not fully appreciated until the end of the story, playing with words in the traditional science-fictional way. But their choice of words to play with is very different. On the one hand, Fyfe chooses to juggle with "in value received" ("words that may appear on a bill of exchange indicat-ing either that value has been received by the drawer from the payee or by the ac-ceptor from the drawer"; Martin, *A Concise Dictionary of Law* 1990, 233) and its similarity in sound to "in value deceived." The switch of one consonant to almost exactly reverse the meaning and to produce the resultant congruence with the outcome of the story is ingenious, but it lacks essential seriousness, as does the story itself. On the other hand, Killough plays on the Latin phrase *caveat emptor* (usually translated as "buyer beware"), which in England is "a common-law maxim warning a purchaser that he could not claim that his purchases were de-fective unless he protected himself by obtaining express guarantees from the ven-dor" (Martin 1990, 58). Since this responsibility still exists as a legal responsibility within the story's future, the phrase can still be introduced to refer to a mean-ingful and serious concept. The implication for the story is that it will also be meaningful and serious, and the historical derivation and longevity of the phrase add to the implications of weight inherent in it and hence also to its invitation to more serious involvement on the part of the reader. Consequently, it is possible to argue that whereas Fyfe with his title signals a humorous story, Killough with hers initiates a more serious one and signals its relative seriousness to the reader.

Relative seriousness is also discernible in the contextual density—the qual-ity which reflects how deeply the author's imaginative construct is extended through and beyond the immediate events of the story—of the two stories. In Fyfe's story, the context described is limited to what bears directly on the ac-tion. The setting is given as a planet barren of everything except "creepers and moss" on "shallow hills" under a "dim light"; Rylat and Akyro, the Olittran (alien) protagonists, are in their ship in a control room with a "plastic deck," where there are lockers, a "bank of detector instruments," and a "telescreen," which are described with minimal visual detail and only because they are necessary to the action. When, however, the Olittrans visit the "Solarian" (human) ship they have encountered on this barren planet, where the Olittrans are searching for plants to restock their devastated home planet and the humans are searching for minerals to resupply their exhausted one, the lack of visuality contributes significantly to the effect of the story. Rylat, the viewpoint character, is here seeing unfamiliar things in an unfamiliar setting with little time to absorb detail, so that the lack of detail maintains the cross-cultural estrangement. There is, however, no indication of conscious literary manipulation of contextual density on Fyfe's part either here or elsewhere in the story—he supplies merely what is necessary to involve the reader.

In Killough's story, on the other hand, contextual density is manipulated to maximum effect throughout. In the control room of Killough's ship, for example, the setting is economically yet vividly detailed, as well as elegantly shown as appropriate to the characteristics of the aliens who inhabit it:

> [H]e pivoted on his hindquarters for a sweeping survey of the controls. The tall, upright panels alternated with deck-to-overhead viewscreens around the circumference of the circular bridge. Aside from the column with the command controls, the center was empty. Necessarily. The centaurian bodies of the Andvarians needed maneuvering room. ("Caveat Emptor" 1970, 107)

Detailed context is also manipulated for other reasons: When the human traders and their interpreter visit the Andvarian ship's hold to conduct the trade that is at the center of the action,

> a broad doorway . . . slid open, admitting them to a cavernous room stacked to the overhead light panels with bales, barrels, and plastic crates. A space had been cleared in the center and lamps set around the edge, making it a bright pool against which the rest of the hold seemed dim and shadowed by comparison. The air hung heavy with an exotic mixture of scents . . . to the four bipeds, alien scents, emanating from sources they could only guess at. ("Caveat Emptor" 1970, 113)

The total effect implies a very seductive atmosphere, which is important to the denouement of the story. But elsewhere in the story we also are given visualizable small details: The human Danae must sit "cross-legged on a table" to play "Sei-tau with the ship's little grey supercargo" (108) since there are no chairs (108), which not only makes the point that the aliens are, like humans, players of competitive mind games, but also makes a point about the analogy of the horse in the creation of the centauroid, since centauroids would have no more use for chairs than horses—this latter point being further emphasized by the use of "grey" (a horse color) in the description of the supercargo. But excessive detail—what *sort* of a game Sei-tau is—is left to the imagination, although we are allowed to know that it uses "pieces," one of which, a "heavy pyramid," is subsequently thrown at an Andvarian troublemaker by his captain (109), so that we might assume an analogue of chess or some other board game. We are also given a picture through the Andvarian viewscreen of the human ship in space, so that its weaponry can evoke the Andvarian captain's appreciation, an incident introduced apparently casually for its own sake but that in fact supplies the covert implication that the Andvarians are not necessarily merely a naïve and peaceful people (111) and that foreshadows the twist-in-the-tail denouement (the *tail-hook*). The contextual density of the story is enhanced by the use of extremely visual detail, and together it all acts on the reader the way the atmosphere of the hold is set to act on those who take part in the trade there: He or she is seduced into a deeper involvement with the story. Every instance of it, moreover, increases the evidence for Killough's more consciously literary approach to her story.

The extent of the literary skill deployed in the approach, in the end, distinguishes the two kinds of LGMs present in the stories. On the one hand, Fyfe's LGMs are described with some differences but not in detail: Anatomically the Olittrans are differentiated—an Olittran has a tapering dull-blue body," with "eight walking legs, and two pairs of "tiny eating legs" ("In Value Deceived" 1950, 39). But psychologically, apart from a form of telepathy—"'You look it over,' he thought to Rylat. 'I'm hungry'" (165)—we see them behaving in a way that exactly mirrors the way the humans in the story behave. They are greedy to get their "hands" on something they find valuable that the people who own it do not, and in this they seem quite undifferentiated from the human. On the other hand, Killough's Andvarians are much more complexly presented. Anatomically, the differentiation from human is both more vivid and visualizable and less exotic. They are centauroids—a blend of equine and human

form familiar to readers from mythology (particularly Greek and Roman)—
yet the captain is described in detail:

> The captain's dark eyes skimmed the row of glowing lights and metered dials.
> Close-coupled but extremely limber, he stood just short of two meters in height,
> copper-colored hair covering all his body but face and hands. His copper mane,
> clipped in a neat fringe along his torso, fell somewhat longer in front of his large
> ears and across his wide forehead. A broad, flattened nose with flaring nostrils
> gave him a somewhat pugnacious look." ("Caveat Emptor" 1970, 107–8)

The mixture of equine descriptive terms ("close-coupled," "stood just short of
two meters," and "mane") with human ones ("limber," "face and hands," and
"pugnacious look") both clarify the reader's mental picture of the Andvarians
in general and increase (by the juxtaposition of normally mutual exclusive
terms) the alterity of the Andvarians. Moreover, this description of Jevan in
specific detail, as a human captain would be described, helps to focus the
reader's understanding of the notion not merely of an individual *alien* but
also of an individual *Andvarian*. Furthermore, it is a deliberate strategy and
conclusive evidence of literary skill on Killough's part. In the end, therefore, it
is this storytelling skill in the *presentation* of the LGMs in her story that distinguishes them from the generic and merely ingenious LGMs of Fyfe.

The LGM's versatility also permits the use of a much wider range of authorial intimacy, often involving direct authorial address to the reader, as in de
Camp, or using a first-person narrator, as in Edward Shaver's "The Sport of
Kings" (1985). Consequently, since it requires a high degree of skill and con-
fidence to manage authorial intimacy effectively enough to bring the story off,
the LGM story involves, consciously or unconsciously and one way or another,
a higher level of commitment to the story idea. Often, moreover, the LGM
makes repeated appearances within the framework of a galactic community,
such as, for example, the community that is the context of Fyfe's aliens in the
Bureau of Slick Tricks series. Since the construction of such a galactic context
requires skill, imagination, and effort, the writer is already committed to these
when modeling the inhabitants, and the LGM is open to an increased level of
otherness.

In addition, the LGM's versatility, which allows the alien to be presented
from its own point of view, facilitates another increase in otherness. In "Blind
Lightning" (1956), previously discussed, Harlan Ellison uses alternate view-

points to narrate the story of an unexpected first contact on a desolate planet. The alien's telepathy is used to project its thoughts into the mind of the human ecologist whom it has captured and whose essence it proposes to consume, and for the reader these brief glimpses into the alien mind imply enough of its viewpoint to establish it as a fully modeled character. Although Ellison's story offered neither the first nor the only use of even partial alien point-of-view narration, it was the first to do so without satire or didacticism and hence offers the more fully realized otherness.

The multifaceted and multifunctional otherness of the LGM make it a unique and valuable tool among those available to writers of science fiction. Where, moreover, like many examples of the humanoid, the LGM does not result from the author's simple indifference to the potential of alterity of form and behavior for effective storytelling, it may similarly accompany a deliberate subordination of questions of otherness to other storytelling purposes. Furthermore, even where the otherness is only minimal or no more than ingenious, the LGM always requires more imagination and more skill to invent and portray successfully than even the carefully drawn humanoid. Its effective functions range from furnishing stories with an exotic element to offering intermittent fragmentary glimpses into the depths of otherness. The LGM, moreover, can be seen, in some writers, to be pushing the envelope of its general use—its type—and advancing toward the status of potentiated alien. But although they advance toward it, they do not reach it, and why they do not do so is more than anything else a matter of characterization.

THEORIZING THE CHARACTER OF THE ALIEN

Although science fiction is still notorious for its lack of credible characters, it is not because the problem has not been acknowledged. Over the years there has been extensive discussion of characterization by both writers and critics of the genre. Until recently, however, the discussion seemed fairly consistently to privilege the theory of characterization initially articulated by Virginia Woolf—contemporaneously with the beginnings of science fiction's emergence as a genre—in "Mr Bennett and Mrs Brown" (1923) and "Character in Fiction" (1924), and subsequently developed in theories of the novel by other writers and critics. Much criticism of mainstream fiction appears to operate on the premise that the telos of fiction is to create an imaginary—virtual—version of the actual world in the reader's mind and therefore that the telos of characterization within the same fiction is to create an imaginary virtual person who, for the duration of the reader's engagement with the text, is sufficiently fully realized to be present to the reader in the same way and to the same extent as a actual person is present to him or her in the actual world. These virtual people will be individualized, fully realized, and nuanced, and will be created as such through their words, through their actions, through comment by other characters, and through direct authorial comment. In Woolf's view, such characters were not merely the foundation but the essence and raison d'être of the great novels that constitute the historical canon of fiction. For the most part, Woolf's theory has been used to berate science fiction for not measuring up to the standards of characterization in mainstream fiction. Current theories are more varied in their approach but also seem concerned to explain away or deny the problem.

In science fiction, however, a genre that according to Kingsley Amis began by privileging "the idea as hero" (*New Maps of Hell* 1960, 120), discussion was slow to provoke actual change. Certainly, characterization in science fiction is problematic if judged by Woolf's standards: Full characters, human or alien, are very difficult to find in the stories published in the magazines. In the earliest stories, in particular, the human characters are minimally characterized: They are stiff and undeveloped figures, moved through the action like crash-test dummies, and provided with unrealistic dialogue and stereotyped behaviors. Even Weinbaum, the inspired creator of the alien Tweel, is not exempt from this problematic treatment of human characters. His narrator Dick in "A Martian Odyssey" (1934) is minimally characterized and his human companions are pure cardboard—stiff, stereotyped, and implausible. The first signs of dissatisfaction with characterization appeared within the genre in the early postwar period, and reviewers in science fiction magazines did not always pull their punches. Of Hal Clement's juvenile *The Ranger Boys in Space* (1957), for example, F. G. Gale, reviewing it for *Galaxy*, said: "Some will say that Clement has reached his true audience with this, his first juvenile. Consensus has it that his youngsters and aliens emerge as humans, while his adult humans emerge as alien" (117). But Clement was no less adequate in his characterization than the majority of his contemporaries (and considerably more than adequate in his other storytelling skills). But once an initial complaint about characterization in science fiction was raised, it was enough to start debate, particularly about whether or not the science fiction writer is, with regard to characterization, accountable for producing characters of the same standard as writers of mainstream fiction.

For those who care about characterization in science fiction, Virginia Woolf's theory is difficult but tantalizingly attractive. Using the celebrated example of Mrs. Brown, Woolf argues that the telos of the novel is character. Mrs. Brown is introduced first, casually and in highly problematic terms (for purposes of practical application), in "Mr. Bennett and Mrs. Brown":

> When [the novelist] finds himself hopelessly at variance with Mr. Wells, Mr. Galsworthy, and Mr. Bennett about the character—shall we say?—of Mrs Brown. . . . [h]e must set about to remake the woman after his own idea. And that, in the circumstances, is a very perilous pursuit. For what, after all, is character—the way that Mrs. Brown, for instance, reacts to her surroundings—when we cease to believe what we are told about her, and begin to search out her real meaning for ourselves? . . . She becomes a will-o'-the-wisp, a dancing light, an illumination gliding up the wall and out of the window. . . . [I]t is from the gleams and flashes of this flying spirit that he must create solid, living, flesh-and-blood Mrs. Brown. (1923, 388)

More elaborately developed in "Character in Fiction" as the protagonist of an allegedly true anecdote about a woman encountered on a train from Richmond to Waterloo, Mrs. Brown becomes the focal point of Woolf's artistic credo: "I believe that all novels begin with an old lady in the corner opposite. I believe that all novels, that is to say, deal with character, and that it is to express character—not to preach doctrines, sing songs, or celebrate the glories of the British Empire, that the form of the novel, so clumsy, verbose, and undramatic, so rich, elastic, and alive, has been evolved" (425). She goes on to argue that "great novelists have brought us to see whatever they wish us to see through some character" (426), that Mrs. Brown "is, of course, the spirit we live by, life itself" (436), and that the novel should give "a complete and satisfactory presentment of her" (436). In the course of this discussion, Woolf lays down three conditions of characterization. She privileges the novel as *the* form of fiction for the presentation of character. She constrains fiction as mimetic (character in the novel can only refer to human behavior and human behavior can only be understood by observation),[12] although confusingly, character does not necessarily have to be (as might be assumed) "lifelike"—a point she makes only in passing: "some character who has seemed to you so real (I do not by that mean so lifelike) that it has the power to make you think not merely of it itself, but of all sorts of things through its eyes" (426). She privileges an essentialist view of humanity: The "spirit we live by, life itself" (436) is a simple rephrasing of "human nature." Some elaboration of these conditions was possible and subsequently emerged, but the whole was not easily or soon challenged.

Given the authority of Woolf's theory in mainstream literature and its attractiveness, therefore, its application to science fiction was inevitable. The most prominent figure to address the topic of characterization in science fiction is Ursula Le Guin. In "Science Fiction and Mrs. Brown" (1975), Le Guin quotes Woolf's credo from "Character in Fiction"—"I believe that all novels begin with an old lady in the corner opposite. I believe that all novels, that is to say, deal with character, and that it is to express character ... that the form of the novel, so clumsy, verbose, and undramatic, so rich, elastic, and alive, has been evolved" (425)—and, as it were, throws down the gauntlet to other science fiction writers: "I accept this definition. I don't know if it is a critically fashionable one at the moment, and really don't care. . . . [T]o a novelist—this novelist, at any rate—it is simply, and profoundly, and in one syllable, true" (102). She goes on to argue that for the most part science fiction has failed to achieve the standards in characterization required to produce a novel:

> But in none of the spaceships, on none of the planets, in none of the delightful, frightening, imaginative, crazy, clever stories are there any people. . . . There are captains and troopers, and aliens and maidens and scientists, and emperors and robots and monsters—all signs, all symbols, statements, effigies, allegories, everything between the Stereotype and the Archetype. But not Mrs. Brown.
> (106)

There are, that is, no characters as Woolf has laid down the requirements for them, and those science fiction writers who have failed to reach these requirements have thereby failed to achieve novels. Le Guin is, however, willing to concede that, even as she writes in 1975, a few characters are beginning to appear in science fiction novels and that this is, since Le Guin like Woolf privileges the novel, beneficial.[13]

But Woolf, and consequently Le Guin also, unhesitatingly privileges a particular version of the novel and of character. To counter the argument of

Woolf and Le Guin and to deproblematize the characterization in science fiction subsequently seemed to require critics to assert either the exemption of science fiction from normal standards of characterization, or the disappearance of the character altogether, or the detachment of science fiction from the tradition of the European novel. This kind of privileging, as Kingsley Amis had already noted in *New Maps of Hell*, reveals "a scale of priorities which operates throughout the medium and which, of course, is open to objection, though this is not often based on much more than an expectation that science fiction should treat the future as fiction of the main stream treats the present, an expectation bound to be defeated" (111). Certainly, there were enough subsequent arguments about human characters in science fiction to attest to the accuracy of this observation.

Many of the arguments about the problem are based on the sociocultural context of science fiction. Scott Sanders, for example, in "Invisible Men and Women: The Disappearance of Character in Fiction" (1977), argues forcefully that the nature of science fiction, like other forms of fiction in the twentieth century, mirrors the loss of the individual (who can be characterized) and the rise of the masses (who cannot): "[I]n the 20th century *science fiction as a genre is centrally about this disappearance of character*, in the same sense in which the 18th- and 19th-century bourgeois novel is about the emergence of character" (14; original emphasis). Victoria Maule, on the other hand, in "On the Subversion of Character in the Literature of Identity Anxiety" (1996), argues not for the disappearance of the individual and hence of the individual character but for the subversion of character to mimic the subversion of human identity in the real world:

> But character in speculative fiction is not simply disregarded; on the contrary, it is subverted. In the visions of conformity, homogeneity, and uniformity; in the guise of aliens, androids, robots and monsters; in the semblance of social machines and totalitarian governments; and in the metamorphoses of humans into something horribly "other" than themselves, we are presented with a distortion *ad infinitum* of our own fictional representatives. (108)

Both arguments rebuke Woolf's (and Le Guin's) claim that character is essential to the novel, reject "Mrs Brown," and privilege instead the "captains and troopers, and aliens and maidens and scientists, and emperors and robots and monsters" on which Le Guin focused her complaint ("Science Fiction and Mrs Brown" 1975, 106).

The arguments of Sanders and Maule run parallel to the argument about characterization in utopian fiction put forward by Frank Dietz. In "Everyperson in Nowhereland: Characters in Contemporary American Utopias" (1990), citing Woolf's statement that "it is to express character . . . that the form of the novel . . . has been evolved," Dietz goes on to argue that

> [i]f one wishes to sum up traditional critiques of characterization in literary utopias, one could say just the opposite—it is not to express character, but to preach doctrines or celebrate the glories of social systems that the clumsy, verbose and undramatic form of utopia has been evolved. Critics have often bewailed the absence of memorable characters in utopian fiction or, at most, grudgingly admitted that dystopias such as *1984* might produce an occasional Winston Smith. I maintain that this negative judgment not only ignores the different function of characters in utopian fiction but also refuses to recognize historical changes in the genre. While traditional utopias indeed concentrated on social and legal structures to the detriment of characterization, recent American utopias have shifted the focus of the utopian imagination from the social system to the individual. (1)

In addition to challenging the Woolf/Le Guin axis, Dietz identifies two specific types of character: "a utopian traveler . . . [and] average inhabitants of the utopian society, so-called 'cluster characters' (I borrow the term from Rachel Blau Du Plessis)" (3). The concept of the "cluster character" can be usefully applied to the discussion of character in science fiction, human and alien, as well as utopian fiction. In particular, I suggest, considering the LGM as a cluster character illuminates many of the problems of its appearances. Although Dietz's discussion is restricted to utopian fiction, what he argues can be argued to a great extent about science fiction. But Dietz and other modern critics often do not choose to address the problem of the alien character as distinct from the human character in science fiction.

One critic who does address the problem of alien character, doing so specifically in response to Le Guin, is Patrick Parrinder. In "The Alien Encounter: Or, Ms Brown and Mrs Le Guin" (1979), Parrinder claims that "[t]his judgment [by Le Guin], though it may be valid as the statement of a personal aesthetic, seems to burden SF with a quite unnecessary stigma" (49), and he

goes on to argue that mainstream fiction and science fiction are quite different cases when characterization is at issue:

> But individual characterization is usually a secondary concern in SF, in a way that
> it is not likely to be in novels which take personal relationships as their principal
> subject-matter. This is because SF describes a world transformed by some new
> element. . . . In SF it is the new element, and not the need for subtle and rounded
> characterization, which determines the basic rules of the genre. (49)

Parrinder's position seems to be that the science fiction writer who is dealing
with aliens may choose to pursue or not to pursue telos of characterization
with human and alien characters alike, that characterization in general is less
important to the quality of science fiction, and that he or she may achieve acceptable science fiction without the aid of subtle and rounded characters. He
does not deny that human characters can be given "a complete and satisfactory presentment" (Woolf, "Character in Fiction" 1988, 436) by science fiction
writers as by other writers. He is forced to admit, nevertheless, that even if this
allowance of metaphoric dimension is made for characterization in science
fiction, the characterization of aliens poses certain problems to which this rel-
egation of characterization to secondary status is no solution: "Yet, if the new
element is an alien life-form, the problem of the characterization is re-intro-
duced in a somewhat unfamiliar sense. It may even be that Virginia Woolf's
paradigm for the novelist's situation still holds" (Parrinder 1979, 49–50). Nevertheless, he continues, because the alien is always different "the choice of
alien features is always meaningful, whether or not it carries an openly satirical, ironic or didactic reference to human life; aliens in literature must always
be constructed on some principle of analogy or contrast with the human
world. . . . It follows from this that aliens in SF invariably possess a metaphorical *dimension*" (52; original emphasis).

For Parrinder, this metaphorical dimension is, in effect, the only thing
about the alien that really matters. They offer nothing meaningful in and of
themselves, he suggests, once their metaphoric import is apparent to the
reader, although this metaphoric import is often the key to a greater
metaphoric dimension of the story a whole: "Often there is little to be said
about the aliens themselves (especially in a short story) once their metaphorical purpose has been grasped. At the same time, the metaphorical *implications* of SF stories appear to go beyond their authors' "conscious intentions"

(52; original emphasis). He explains the structure of the metaphor as follows: "The tenor of the metaphor consists of some aspect of human behavior or human culture which the author intends to defamiliarize, or to reveal as an artificial and, it may be, an ideological construct rather than a natural necessity. The vehicle consists of a recognizable deviation from the human norm" (52). The implication of Parrinder's point about metaphor is that alien characters, being always metaphoric, need not be fully realized, since this would interfere with their metaphoric import and hence with the import of the whole story. Parrinder's solution, in these terms, however, becomes problematic with regard to a number of well-known science fiction stories. If Williamson's Mother in "The Moon Era" (1932), for example, has a metaphorical dimension deriving from her form, it is remarkably well concealed, and Knight's Aza-Kra in "Rule Golden" (1954), too, lacks a demonstrable metaphorical dimension, although he may be said to maintain the symbolic role of the hero, which has nothing to do with form. In Herbert's "The Tactful Saboteur" (1964), moreover, Panthor Bolin, who is Pan-Spechi, has (except for his faceted eyes) a "humanoid" form from which no metaphoric implications may be derived about humanity (and which exemplifies the rare constructive use of the humanoid form in the characterization of the alien). If Parrinder's argument is accepted, the science fiction writer seems to be exempt from the demands of characterization in a way that the writers of mainstream are not, especially where alien characters are concerned. I have already argued in chapter 2, however, that the reduction of the alien to metaphoric function disables any discussion of its alterity, and I would now add that exempting it from the general "rules" of characterization merely confirms this disabling.

Where such characters are concerned, some critics, rather than defend or explain away the characterization of aliens in the same terms as humans within the fiction, seek to remove all the characters from their status as characters and give them standing only as functions according to a nonmimetic theory of fiction, as distinct from the mimetic theory that is, of course, essential to Woolf. One such theory is the *actant* theory of A. J. Greimas. In Christian Vandendorpe's standard definition,

> *actant* (literally, "that which accomplishes or undergoes the action") refers, in
> semiotics, to the great functions or roles occupied by the various characters of
> a narrative, be they humans, animals, or simple objects. . . . One should be care-

ful not to confuse the *actant*, which is a narrative function based in the deep
structure, with the *actor*. The actor is the name given to the concrete manifestation of an actant in a given narrative. (*Encyclopedia of Literary Theory* 505)

In *Worlds Apart: Narratology of Science Fiction*, Carl Malmgren presents the
Alien as *actant*. He argues:

> Alien encounter SF involves the introduction of sentient alien beings into the
> actantial system of the fictional universe; one or more of the actants are non-
> human or superhuman or subhuman. The encounter with the alien necessarily
> broaches the question of Self and Other. In general, the reader recuperates this
> type of fiction by comparing human and alien entities. (54)

Although Malmgren's argument for the Alien as *actant* considerably illuminates the function of individual aliens in particular narratives of science fiction, it does not produce any significant information about their nature since
their difference—their alienness—is not a factor of their function but of their
nature. Difference is an *actorial* attribute, not an *actantial* function. Nevertheless, the Alien as archetype, as I shall develop it in the next chapter, may be said
to inform the individual alien as the *actant* informs the actor. This informing
process means that the characterization of the individual alien must always be
somewhat problematic, since a degree of incongruence must always exist between the archetype and its manifestation as *an* alien. Even the most skilled
literary characterization will not obliterate this incongruence, although it may
filter it with varying degrees of opacity.

The problematic status of the alien character is also affected by the shifted
or displaced mode of discourse in science fiction. In *Strategies of Fantasy*
(1992), Brian Attebery argues, using Greimas's terminology, that in the novel
a reportorial mode is engaged and the characters are actors, whereas in fantasy, the romance mode is engaged and the characters are *actants* (73). He explains:

> To avoid confusion with psychological theories or value judgments, I will not
> call these character formulations *realistic* or *archetypal*. A. J. Greimas has pro-
> vided a less loaded terminology: as an element in the construction of a story,
> a character may be called an *actant*—the French participial ending conveys
> the sense of *doing* that is essential to such characters. A character who is more

interesting for his individual qualities than for his place in a shaped narrative is an *acteur* (Scholes, *Structural Fabulation* 1975, 103), or, substituting the English form, an *actor*. (73)

Occasionally, Attebery concedes, mixed forms occur: "But modern fantasy is not simply a revival of the fairy tale, and its characters can combine the two forms of discourse, just as the genre of fantasy combines the mimetic and fantastic modes" (72). Although I agree with Attebery as far as fantasy is concerned, I would argue that the discourse of fantasy and the discourse of science fiction is effectively distinct and that, except in texts of satire and fable, this distinction removes the Alien from consideration as *actant*. In the fantasy text, the invented ficton are displaced (disjuncted) from the actual in the direction of the irrational, supernatural, and magic so that its viability is not in question and the reader is undistracted by the shift or blending of the characters between *actant* or *actor*. But in science fiction, the invented ficton is only shifted (not completely disjuncted), and reportorial and romance mode are simultaneously engaged throughout because the direction of the shift is toward the rational and scientific—that is, toward Robinson's "imaginary but viable ficton" (*Melancholy Elephants* 1984, xiii)—in deference to the requirement for the nonviolation of scientific knowledge. Here, therefore, the characters necessarily exist only in reportorial mode. Alien characters who appear to be no more than "elements of construction" certainly appear, but these are usually examples of a failed *actor* not an examples of an *actant*. In general, however, the theory of the Alien as *actant* simply revisits the theory of Alien as metaphor and returns with somewhat similar results.

A more promising approach to deproblematizing characterization in science fiction could perhaps have been achieved by returning not to Virginia Woolf but to E. M. Forster. In *Aspects of the Novel* (1927), Forster offers a very prescient view of the science fiction writer's problem in writing alien characters:

> Since the actors in a story are usually human, it seemed convenient to entitle this aspect People. Other animals have been introduced [into the novel], but with limited success, for we know too little so far about their psychology. There may be . . . an alteration here in the future . . . and we shall have animals who are neither symbolic, nor little men disguised, nor as four-legged tables moving, nor as painted scraps of paper that fly. It is one of the ways where science may enlarge the novel, by giving it fresh subject matter. (43)

The parallel between Forster's insight into the problem of animal characters and the science fiction writer's problem with alien characters is striking.[14] Forster's discussion of character is offered in two parts: The first part is the discussion of the difference between people outside fiction and people inside it—*Homo sapiens* and *Homo fictus* as he calls them—and the second part is his more celebrated distinction between "flat" and "round" characters.

He begins by conducting an interesting and extensive discussion of the difference between real (life-world) people and fictional people (characters).[15] What separates real people and characters, according to his theory, is the accessibility of their inner life: "We know each other approximately, by external signs, and these serve well enough. . . . But people in a novel can be understood completely by the reader, if the novelist wishes; their inner as well as their outer life can be exposed" (46–47). Consequently, the essential difference between characters and real people is that characters "are people whose secret lives are visible; we are people whose secret lives are invisible" (62). Fictional people, he argues, imitate real people. They will share their creator's humanity and "our make-up as human beings" (47), and Forster offers a conspectus of what he calls "[t]he main facts in human life . . . birth, food, sleep, love and death" (47). Novels will be populated in this way, and "[o]ne cannot generalize about [characters in] them, because they have nothing in common in the scientific sense. . . . Nevertheless, though incapable of strict definition, they tend to behave along the same lines" (50–51). Of a fictional character, he says: "[M]ost important—we can know more about him than we can know about any of our fellow creatures, because his creator and narrator are one" (54–55). Forster's final point about the difference between *Homo fictus* and *Homo sapiens* is that people in fiction may be, or appear to be, more real than real people, and although this may or may not happen with human characters in science fiction, it is not appropriately an issue for consideration in discussing alien characters.

Beyond the problem of general human makeup in character, Forster identifies problems of differentiation of the individual characters. His initial claim is that "[w]e may divide characters into flat and round" (65), and he goes on to assert that "[t]he really flat character can be expressed in one sentence" (65). He argues that flat characters have two advantages: first, "that they are easily recognized whenever they come in—recognized by the reader's emotional eye," and second, "that they are easily remembered" (66). Nevertheless, he concedes, "flat people are not in themselves as big achievements as round ones [and] . . . are best when they are comic" (70). Forster does not offer an extended definition of "round characters" at this point, arguing that "round characters proper . . . have already been defined by implication" (74), but he does offer a way of identifying them: "The test of a round character is whether it is capable of surprising in a convincing way. If it never surprises, it is flat. If it does not convince, it is a flat pretending to be round. It has the incalculability of life about it—life within the pages of a book" (75). In his discussion of the "reality" of fictional characters, with Moll in *Moll Flanders* (1722) as his example, however, he points out that "she seems absolutely real from every point of view, we must ask ourselves whether we should recognize her if we met her in daily life. . . . And the odd thing is, that even though we take a character as natural and untheoretical as Moll, who would coincide with life in every detail, we should not find her [in life] as a whole" (60). He answers the implied question as to why we cannot find Moll as a whole in life by saying,

> [S]he cannot be here because she belongs to a world where the secret life is visible, to a world that is not and cannot be ours, to a world where the narrator and the creator are one. And now we can get a definition as to when a character in a book is real: it is real when the novelist knows everything about it. He may not choose to tell us all he knows—many of the facts, even of the kind we call obvious, may be hidden. But he will give us the feeling that though the character has not been explained, it is explicable, and we get from this a reality of a kind we can never get in daily life. (61)

Although Forster's point here is reality, not rotundity, it is not unreasonable to assume that the definition of reality of a character will effectively operate as a definition of rotundity. Consequently, it is possible to apply this definition in the discussion of characters both inside and outside science fiction, although some qualifications may have to be made.

But it is in the interstices between flat and round, in the "transition to the round" (71), that Forster offers the effective key to the deproblematization of science-fictional characters both human and alien. In his discussion of Jane Austen he argues that "she is never two-dimensional. All her characters are round, or *capable of rotundity*" (72; my emphasis). He bases his argument on the subtle way in which Austen in *Mansfield Park* (1814) takes Lady Bertram, a flat character, "whose formula is 'I am kindly, but must not be fatigued,' and

[who] functions out of it" (71), and in one sentence "modulates from her formula into an area where the formula does not work" (73). The "one sentence" Forster points to is "Lady Bertram did not think deeply, but, guided by Sir Thomas, she thought justly on all important points, and she saw therefore in all its enormity, what had happened, and neither endeavoured herself, nor required Fanny to advise her, to think little of guilt and infamy." His analysis of it is as follows:

> See how subtly it modulates from her formula into an area where the formula does not work. "Lady Bertram did not think deeply." Exactly: as per formula. "But guided by Sir Thomas she thought justly on all important points." Sir Thomas' guidance, which is part of the formula, remains, but it pushes her ladyship towards an independent and undesired morality. "She saw therefore in all its enormity what had happened." This is the moral fortissimo—very strong but carefully introduced. And then follows a most artful decrescendo, by means of negatives. "She neither endeavoured herself, nor required Fanny to advise her, to think little of guilt or infamy." The formula is reappearing, because as a rule she does try to minimize trouble, and does require Fanny to advise her how to do this. . . . The words, though they are negatived, remind us of this, her normal state is again in view, and she has in a single sentence been inflated into a round character and collapsed back into a flat one. (73)

Having made his point in this extended analysis of one example, however, Forster also includes in the context of his discussion of Austen some apparent hallmarks of characters "capable of rotundity." They will be, he argues, like hers, "highly organized. They function all round, and even if her plot made greater demands upon them than it does, they would still be adequate" (72). They are "ready for an extended life, for a life which the scheme of her books seldom requires them to lead, and that is why they lead their actual lives so satisfactorily" (73). They may be "apparently so simple and flat, never needing reintroduction and yet never out of their depth. . . . [Austen] may label her characters "Sense," "Pride," "Sensibility," "Prejudice," but they are not tethered to those qualities" (74).

Taken as a whole, moreover, Forster's discussion allows us to infer that the human characters of science fiction may be more difficult to create because it is more difficult for the creator to allow the created character to share her or his human makeup because human makeup is no longer fully common to novelist and character. This separation is inevitable given that the writer of science fiction does not live in the same time-frame (future) as her/his character, so that "narrator and creator" cannot be "one" (61). But this is not therefore an excuse for the lack of effective characterization in science fiction, although it is a reason why ineffectiveness may be present, if the fundamental difficulty remains unarticulated or unresolved in the mind of the writer.

The utility of Forster's theory in dealing with alien characterization depends upon the writer's ability to stimulate the reader's imaginative participation in the text. Both in the strictly literary (Barthean) sense and in agreement with the more general sense indicated by Niven in his claim that in good science fiction "[s]omething should be left behind at the end of the story. There are characters unkilled and actors who never reached the stage" ("Playgrounds for the Mind" 1990, 26), imaginative participation in the text is the key that allows the reader to access and expand the characters that are "capable of rotundity" to fuller status as Austen does with Lady Bertram. Despite the constant allegations that science fiction is populated by stock characters and types—both human and alien, especially where the short stories of the early magazines are concerned—human characters "capable of rotundity" populate science fiction magazine stories if not exclusively at least in substantial numbers. Properly understood in terms of Forster's theory, the same potential for rotundity can be found in alien characters. To the best of the author's ability they are equally at least "capable of rotundity" (Forster 1927, 72) where rotundity is understood to mean individualized, fully realized, nuanced, and created through their words, through their actions, through comment by other characters, and through authorial comment. Implicitly, also, they defy any requirement for the intrinsic metaphoric implications of their nonhuman form or status. If an alien character in science fiction fulfills the same requirement as the human characters for being "capable of rotundity" and does defy any requirement for intrinsic metaphoricity, then his/her/its potential rotundity can also be accessed and expanded with sufficient imaginative participation on the part of the reader.

Aliens who are intended to appear as fully realized characters, however, present a multilayered problem to their creators. To begin with, whereas any character, human or alien, is created as a member of its species, the alien must be doubly created—a created member of a species which is also created. The creator of the human as character, even within science fiction, has the human species ready at hand to provide the matrix from which a particular character may be differentiated and hence individualized—the "human makeup" as Forster terms it. The most basic problems of the alien as a fully realized and "present" character, therefore, are those that arise from the need to differentiate the individual alien from the matrix of his/her/its already differentiated (from the human) species while simultaneously establishing the alien as an appropriately individualized member of that species.

One of these problems is the resistance of aliens to differentiation—resistance that requires all the skill and attention of the writer to the problem. Where this is minimal, the resulting figure is the alien who remains totally unindividualized: "the alien" or "an alien" (sometimes literally so). The alien who is distinguished only by name and/or activity remains partially differentiated—remains Alien A or Alien B only, rather than a true individual or a true "round" character—and these are in Forster's terminology "flat" characters, and the "really flat character can be expressed in one sentence" (65). But Forster's argument appears to distinguish between two versions of "flat" characters. On the one hand are those like Caleb Balderstone in Sir Walter Scott's *The Bride of Lammermoor* (1819), who "has no existence outside his formula" (66).[16] On the other hand, there are those like the flat characters of Dickens of whom "[n]early every one can be summed up in a sentence, and yet there is this wonderful feeling of human depth" (68). Similarly, it is quite obvious from even a casual inspection of many alien characters that they are not all equally "flat." A similar distinction could be made between the aliens of Christopher Anvil's "Mission of Ignorance" (1968), who have no existence outside their formula (there is one whose formula is merely a "horrified shriek"), and those who, although formulaic, nevertheless give the impression of depth, if not of "human depth" (Forster 1927, 68)—for example, the military analyst Selouel in the same writer's "The Underhandler" (1990), whose formula is "I am a genius who is being bothered by idiot subordinates and they will be sorry." It is the latter group who are "capable of rotundity," and it may be argued therefore that, in general terms, the LGM begins as a "flat" character but is "capable of rotundity" (72).

Beyond A and B, however, is Alien C. She has her name and her activity too, but she is in addition at once herself and a member of her species, and she may be a fully "round" character if, in addition to her differentiated alien nature, she is "capable of surprising in a convincing way" (Forster 1927, 75), or if, like Becky Sharp in *Vanity Fair* (1847–1848), she "cannot be summed up in a single phrase ... [and] we do not remember her so easily because she waxes and wanes and has facets like a human being" (Forster 1927, 67). At the same time, C is someone whose alien nature we never lose sight of, however much of an individual she may become, so that we find ourselves as readers directly faced with an OtherSelf.

Any discussion of individualization of alien characters, however, presupposes that the species of the alien allows for individualization. Separate members of Frank Herbert's Pan-Spechi —a species in which group-entities of five bodies have a single ego shifting from body to body—are not individuals in the usual sense of the term. They therefore have to be considered in some alternative way. But they will be at best resistant to this even if such an alternative way can be found. Only the overcoming of the alien resistance to differentiation and individualization results in the alien who becomes a personality in his/her/its own right and whose successful realization as an alien individual results in the foundation of the alterity of the potentiated alien.

Not all the resistance of the alien to individualization, however, can be attributed to failure of the intention or skill of the writer. In *The Brighter Side of Human Nature: Altruism and Empathy in Everyday Life* (1990), in the course of a discussion about "what Marx might have called animal fetishism" (140), Alfie Kohn points out that "[p]erhaps when we cannot be of help, when we feel overwhelmed by dehumanizing forces, we displace our responsiveness to other species" (139). Kohn's examples, one of them the pronounced emotional response to the death of a rabbit used to test the gas chamber in a documentary about a condemned criminal and the other of a similar response to the death of a dog thrown into a river in a feature film, suggest that an animal does not have to be characterized as an individual in art to evoke a response of empathy, as a person does (in both contexts cited the human deaths also shown did not evoke any response). A point raised by Isaac Asimov in his afterword to "The Talking Stone" (1955), reprinted in *Asimov's Mysteries* (1968), indicates how this might be at work in some science fiction stories about aliens. He describes the response he received to the story about the Silicony, a mysterious rocklike alien:

> After this story appeared, I received quite a bit of mail expressing interest in the Silicony and, in some cases, finding fault with me for allowing it to die in so cold-blooded a fashion.
>
>   As I reread this story now, I must admit the readers are right. I showed a lack of sensitivity to the Silicony's rather pathetic death because I was concentrating

on his mysterious last words. If I had to do it over again, I would certainly be warmer in my treatment of the poor thing.

    I apologize. (53–54)

The Silicony is an extremely passive alien—almost inert—totally without individualization ("personality") and labeled rather than named. But it does have antennae that resemble the ears of a rabbit. It is possible, therefore, that the displaced response to animals is for some reason triggered here by the alien Silicony. Asimov's comment makes it clear that this response to the Silicony was totally unexpected. Consequently, it may be assumed that part of the resistance of the science-fictional alien to individualization may lie in this widespread displaced human response to other species if the writer does not evade it deliberately and is therefore caught off-guard.[17]

   The other problem of alien characterization—one that, ironically, only comes into play as full individualization is approached with a particular alien—is the extremely difficult question of how far the individualization of the alien can proceed before it becomes "individualization as a human." In stories other than the small but significant number where all the characters are aliens (for example, Tiptree's "Love Is the Plan, the Plan Is Death" 1973), the alien is usually shown in the context of an encounter between an individual human and an alien (for example, Weinbaum's "A Martian Odyssey" 1934; Williamson's "The Moon Era" 1932). Given the compression effect of the short story or novella form, writers may choose—or at least go ahead without worrying about the effect—to individualize the alien in more-or-less human terms because (as a factor of its individual relationship with a human) we see it entirely (or in a greater part) only from the human viewpoint. Even where the author chooses to acknowledge the problem by mentioning it, the issue may or may not be resolved in the story. Examples of this tactic usually amount to no more than utterances by the narrator such as, "I was never sure I was always addressing the same alien twice" (Brown, "Getting Even" 1982, 31). More sophisticated discussions are reserved for novels. The human character (first-person or limited third-person or omniscient narrator) is appropriately allowed only to recognize the alien's individuality by recognizing it as an individual in the same terms (whether or not he/she is unconsciously thinking of it or consciously comparing it to humans in general) as his/her own human individuality. Where a number of aliens are presented, and each is individualized but not humanized, the writer's success must be more strenuously won.

THE POTENTIATED ALIEN

Fewest in number, possibly, among the aliens of the magazine fiction, but by far the most satisfying for the reader, are those aliens who go beyond the type and appear as potentiated aliens—nonhuman individuals. Unlike the *bem*, the *humanoid*, or the LGM, the potentiated alien represents a deliberate engagement with the problem of the Alien in a way that attempts to produce the self of the Alien, transmuting it into a representation of OtherSelfness or alterity. In my argument, alterity marks the presence of the OtherSelf. For an alien to possess alterity, therefore, it must demonstrably be an OtherSelf, demonstrating among its attributes OtherSelfness. If the demonstration of the existence of a Self (selfness) in human characters requires, in Forster's terms, a "round" character,[18] the OtherSelfness (alterity) of the alien requires therefore a character both truly other and truly "round." Although, as I have already pointed out, such a requirement is difficult to fulfill, it is not impossible. There are a considerable number of aliens in the short fiction of the magazines who can offer both otherness and rotundity.

The task of simultaneously creating the *otherness* that derives from membership of a successfully created alien species and the *selfhood* that derives from full "rotundity" challenges even the strongest of writers. In his story "The Tactful Saboteur," Frank Herbert sets a story of alterity within a multispecies galaxy framed as the ConSentiency, a developed and deliberate construct whose genesis he describes in an article, "The ConSentiency—And How it Got That Way" (1977). The protagonist is human—the BuSab agent, Jorj X. Mckie, who was also to be the protagonist of Herbert's two novels of the ConSentiency, *Whipping Star* (1970) and *The Dosadi Experiment* (1977)—and his antagonist, whose alterity he must cope with in terms of the safety of the ConSentiency itself, is the Pan-Spechi whom we meet as Panthor Bolin ("humanoid but with Pan-Spechi multifaceted eyes"; "The Tactful Saboteur" 1987, 188). Herbert proceeds in the presentation of the alterity of the PanSpechi more indirectly than previous writers: The story's course is punctuated by oblique and sinister hints about PanSpechi. While waiting to meet Panthor Bolin, currently the chief officer of the Tax Watchers Organization, for example, McKie remembers that he has seen "a fifth gender Pan-Spechi here in company with the fourth-gender ego-holder. That could only mean that the creche with its three dormants was nearby. But by all accounts, this was a dangerous place for someone not protected by bonds of friendship and community" (188). During the meeting, McKie remains fully cognizant of danger: "Each Pan-Spechi group maintained a supremely jealous attitude of and about its wandering ego. The ego imbued the holder of it with a touchy sense of honor" (188). But at the same time as Herbert is presenting the Pan-Spechi Panthor Bolin as a member of a species whose otherness is strange, dangerous, and characterized by "unspeakable practices" (210), he is also developing Panthor Bolin as a character who in spite of his otherness engages the reader's empathy as he suffers through the public discussion about Pan-Spechi nature that McKie's trial—on a charge of attempting an act of sabotage in his "attempt to sway the chief officer of the Tax Watchers from his duties" (196)—produces in open court. It is nevertheless an act that McKie has designed and Panthor Bolin understands as a necessary preliminary to installing Panthor Bolin as the new Secretary of Sabotage for the InterGalactic government of the ConSentiency. The more emphatic and enigmatic the hints about the "unspeakable practices" and hence the otherness of the Pan-Spechi become, the more Panthor Bolin is revealed as an individual whose dignity and selfhood transcend his differences from the human. Moreover, Herbert never gives in to the nonwriterly solution of explaining the actuality of the "unspeakable" practices. At the end of the story, however, he draws an analogy between Pan-Spechi "creche shame" and human shame about sexuality—but it remains an analogy both with regard to what is actually practiced and with regard to how Panthor Bolin feels about it. *How* he feels it is unmistakably as deep and as painful as any normal human male might feel about, as Panthor Bolin hints to the judge, having someone "witness the tenderest intimacies between you and your wife" (190). But *what* he feels is nontranslatable across the species barrier. In creating empathy with someone feeling an unsharable emotion, Herbert creates in Panthor Bolin a potentiated alien with full alterity.

The substantial alterity of the potentiated alien is always further intensified by increasing the sophistication of symbolic underpinning in its presentation while maintaining its essential Selfhood as a person. In Octavia Butler's "Bloodchild" (1984), for example, alterity is directly addressed in Butler's attempt to present what might be seen as one of the most extreme examples of what will be necessary to accommodate the alterity of aliens in the context of human lives. The aliens here, the Tlic, are a species in whom only the females are truly sapient and whose children hatch as "long, thick grubs" from eggs laid in the flesh of human hosts. When refugee humans are stranded on the Tlic planet, they are taken at first for "convenient big warm-blooded animals" (41) for egg-hosting and then recognized as sapients who could be induced to host eggs cooperatively and more safely than actual animals, and in this fashion they have become symbiotic partners with the Tlic, in family-to-family "adoptions." The narrative of the story is presented very straightforwardly as Gan, the fourteen-year-old narrator, attempts to face up to beginning the duty that pays for the aliens' preservation of humans. Through Gan, Butler introduces T'Gatoi, the alien to whom his duty is owed, to the reader. T'Gatoi is an adult female Tlic whose next clutch of eggs is imminent,[19] and the duty, which Gan has been brought up knowing is his duty, is to have those eggs deposited in his flesh and carry them there, nurturing them until the moment of their hatching. In this story, the alterity of the alien is presented not in straight description but in the form of multiple descriptive hints in support of a psychologically triggered response. T'Gatoi is never directly described (she seems sometimes like an otter or cat and sometimes like a lizard), and much of the key to the reader's understanding of T'Gatoi's people is linked to the typical human response to the word *worms*, which implies not only earthworms and the parasitic worms that infect humans (tapeworms, pin worms, round worms) as do in fact the young of T'Gatoi's people, and which brings with it a natural feeling of disgust, but which also, through its older form *wyrm*, indicates a form of life (snake or serpent) with accompanying connotations of danger, treachery, and evil. Yet after the psychological resonances of T'Gatoi's suggested heterologous form have been taken into account, some of the effect of her alterity can still be seen to be created by the shifting, sliding way in which her strangeness of form is half-seen and half-hidden throughout the story. In this design, however, although Butler uses symbolism of terrestrial animals to suggest alterity, the alterity itself is real not symbolic. T'Gatoi's psychological alterity is also presented in this half-seen and half-hidden technique. The half-seen aspect of her mind is presented and familiar: We see the alien female primarily in terms of her "motherhood," for the imminence of her new eggs increases the need to find a host. The strangeness that underlies this familiarity of behavior is, however, the completely nonhuman strategy of parking the incubating eggs in another (and in this case, sapient) being who may well be eaten by them in order to survive if they hatch when their mother is not there to remove them immediately and supply them with other food. We also see her relationships to Gan's mother and to the narrator. Neither of these relationships is completely explicable in human terms. Gan's mother and T'Gatoi are, in Gan's human vocabulary, "friends" (36), but T'Gatoi is in charge of allotting N'Tlic (a human who serves a female Tlic as host for her eggs) to the community, and her own family (in which she is the only fertile female) is partnered with Gan's family as their protector in return for Gan's service as a N'Tlic for her own eggs. Given the exchange of services involved, *friend* camouflages a relationship that is not human friendship (although it maybe as close as a Tlic and human can approach), although it is clear from the hints about the problematic nature of the family-adoption system that Butler slips into the narrative that T'Gatoi is unusual, if not unique, in her concern for her adopted humans. Similarly, in what we see of T'Gatoi's relationship to Gan, she seems to be acting as mentor to Gan—discussing the nature of her people and the nature of human-Tlic relationships since the arrival of the humans on her planet. We see her explaining to Gan, for example, that "[b]ecause your people arrived, we are relearning what it means to be a healthy, thriving people. And your ancestors, fleeing from their homeworld, from their own kind who would have killed them—they survived because of us. We saw them as people and gave them the Preserve when they still tried to kill us as worms" (51).[20] In this explanation there is a locus of the secret life revealed, in that behind "we are relearning" is T'Gatoi's feeling about an experience of "lost learning," and although a human might share a parallel experience, a feeling about lost learning, the exact nature of that feeling is not duplicated across species barriers. A more subtle example of parallel or analogous but nonidentical mental activity is T'Gatoi's experience or understanding of motherhood. She is characterized as a good mother, who wants a good host for her fertile eggs to be implanted into, one whom she will monitor very carefully so that there will be no accident that may kill him. She takes care, therefore, of Gan and his family, and her care includes extra food beyond their "ration" as hosts to ensure that Gan is not only healthy but happy. But the extra food consists of her own infertile eggs. In this particular instance, therefore, the excellent quality of her motherhood in terms of her own species is completely other than human.

Butler's real achievement in this story is to make T'Gatoi a "round" alien character. She is a being who can be understood fully only in terms of her own strangeness. The writer partially reveals and partially conceals her "hidden" life, and she is not only lifelike (to whatever extent this may be necessary in a round character) but also actually likeable. T'Gatoi is as fully realized as any potentiated alien may be.

Such full realization may be enabled by additional literary tropes. The immediate presentation of the potentiated alien, for example, can be enhanced by the use of first-person narration in the same way this trope is customarily used as a method of enhancing human character development in narratives focusing on character. James Tiptree Jr. (a pseudonym of Alice Sheldon) experiments with first-person narration from the alien's point of view to enhance the presentation of otherness in that character. In "Love Is the Plan, the Plan Is Death," she presents a sapient, albeit pretechnological, alien narrator, Moggadeet. Moggadeet speaks from an otherness that derives from his membership in a successfully created alien species, and he speaks as a fully rounded Self with a secret life that is partly revealed to the reader. His alterity grips the reader relentlessly from the opening words:

> Remembering—
> Do you hear, my little red? Hold me softly. The cold grows.
> I remember:
> I am hugely black and hopeful, I bounce on six legs along the mountains in the new warm! . . . *Sing the changer, Sing the stranger! Will the changes change forever!* . . . All my hums have words now. Another change! (173)

Moggadeet's species is implied to be one in which the larger black males first compete for, then win, then protect the females, which increase massively in size under this care; then in turn the males are expelled from the nest or are captured and eaten by the females in the act of mating. In the course of his life, however, Moggadeet not only learns the nature of time by observing change, but is able to take advantage of his knowledge by binding up "fat climbers" (189) for food in foodless times and therefore helping his mate to grow to a fuller maturity than ever before they mate. The implication is not merely that the knowledge of change, but the knowledge of how to use it, which is Moggadeet's personal contribution to the development of his species, may be passed on by the unusual female his care has produced, in addition to the more general knowledge that has been passed down to him by his "Father" whether that knowledge is specific to Moggadeet's father or common to other fathers to be passed on to other sons. Ironically, part of what he has done leads to his death (he speaks at the moment of his death) as he is devoured by his more than usually powerful mate. A strong impetus to potentiated alien status is created by the first-person narration and the skill with which the idiom of this alien is enabled. Moggadeet's secret life is demonstrated in the attribution to him of memory—he remembers many events of his life and he remembers change—so that he must be capable of remembering in general; thus, although further memories may not be revealed, nevertheless they are implicitly there. Moreover, he is characterized by his own mother as being odd like his father. And we see him developing his own ideas, for example, in the conversation with the dying Black. Moggadeet, like his alleged "Father," is a visionary among his people, capable of seeing beyond their immediate cycle of love and death to a greater thing, whose dying words to his mate are "Tell them of the cold, Leelyloo. Tell them of our love. Tell them . . . the winters grow" (193). Moggadeet is truly other, truly a Self, and truly round. Because he is all of these his anticipated imminent death is the death of a person.[21]

In each of these examples, the individual Self of a potentiated alien is presented. The potentiated alien is not merely Other—being fully differentiated in form (significant, substantial physical otherness) and in behavior (significant, substantial psychological otherness)—but *an* Other in whom an individual Self (Forster's "round" character) that is not a human Self is clearly discoverable. Consistently, moreover, it is presented by means of the now controversial technique of characterization as this might be understood in discussion of mainstream fiction.

CONCLUSION

The literary modeling of the Alien when imposed upon scientifically competent biological and psychological modeling produces the potentiated alien—the Other who is fully realized as a "round" character, with its secret life at least partially revealed, an individual who is present, nuanced, plausible, internally consistent, consistent with its species, and with its own point of view. It is the OtherSelf. OtherSelfness (alterity) as a trope is strictly a product of literary modeling and requires full otherness and full rotundity to emerge from the multitudinous presentations of aliens in science fiction. Yet, for all the creations of the Other or the OtherSelf, regardless of the quality of their conception or literary modeling, the question of why such creations should be presented must still be answered.

The answer, I contend, lies in the status of the trope as an artifact of the human mind. As I have already made clear, I believe that this status can best be clarified by approaching the mind responsible for the trope's creation according Jung's archetypal theory of personality. In my next chapter, therefore, I shall move into a discussion of the nature of the archetype of the OtherSelf by relating it to the identified trope and by locating it within Jung's general theory of archetypes. It is, moreover, the complexity of the relationship between trope and archetype that must be questioned for answers as to why images of the Other in science fiction are so inordinately impressive, so constantly produced by writers, and so urgently demanded by readers.

NOTES

1. An interesting point about Sturgeon's Martians, although unrelated to their eyes, is that he also introduces the notion that humans and Martians are (however distantly), related: "Laidlaw said that the inhabitants of any Solar System have a mutual ancestor, parallel evolutions, and similar metabolism. You know yourself that Martians, Earthmen, Venusians and the extinct Jovians are all bipeds composed mainly of hydrocarbons" (57). Although this theory may have been derived from Arrhenius's theory of *panspermia*—the idea that all life has been spread through the universe by space-traveling spores—a theory that does crop up from time to time in science fiction, Sturgeon's postulated theory that all life within a solar system (but not apparently beyond it) is related, is not one that, as far as I can determine, crops up anywhere else in the magazines.

2. Its very popularity, too, had a part in its disappearance, for repetition made it a cliché, and the focus of science-fictional in-jokes, as in Russ Winterbotham's "Lonesome Hearts" (1954), where the alien first-person narrator concludes: "I do not die. For I crept away into a hole in the ground, where I will live forever. I do not starve, for roots reach me here. But . . . I can never be a mother or a sister. I will always be me, a lonesome old bem" (94).

3. See, for example, the neo-*bems* in Knight, "Stranger Station" (1956); Tiptree, "And I Awoke . . ." (1971); Kapp, "Ambassador to Verdammt" (1967); Stiegler, "Petals of Rose" (1981); Thurston, "She/Her" (1973); Coney, "Symbiote" (1969); Lindholm, "A Touch of Lavender" (1989); Schmitz, "Pork-Chop Tree" (1965); Jablokov, "Place of No

Shadows" (1990); Green, "Raccoon Reaction" (1983); Asimov, "Breeds There a Man . . ." (1951); and Asimov, "Green Patches" (1950).

4. The story takes place on a planet occupied by two species of closely related alien sapients: the *Thumesin*, who are large, herbivorous, and peaceable; and the *Cardi*, who are small, carnivorous, and aggressive. The relationship of the two peoples is said by one of the visiting humans to resemble "the two most important subhuman species, *Australopithecus africanus* and *robustus*. . . . They lived in the same part of Africa and became contemporaries. . . . They weren't contemporary too long; the carnivore wiped out the herbivore. We eventually descended from *africanus* as the all-purpose unspecialized animal, the omnivore. . . . Here we have a re-creation of that old battle, and it's going to have the same ending unless we do something" (100). The point of the story, however, is the humans' discovery, that although the situation resembles the hypothesized relationship between the two protohumans on Earth, it is different and that the *Thumesin* are on the way to solving it without learning to become humanly aggressive. The didactic point is clear, and, to add emphasis, both the *Cardi* and the *Thumesin* are portrayed as almost totally humanoid, although with furry pelts (97, 103).

5. "Immigrant" is the story of Earth's most intelligent man, who is selected by an advanced species known as the Kimonians to go to their homeworld where he finds that the only job he is qualified for is, essentially, that of babysitter to the Kimonian children, although he does not realize this at first because they are approximately his own size. Typical humanoids appearing later are Frederick Arnold Kummer's Martians in "The Forgiveness of Tenchu Taen" (1938), Murray Leinster's Masans in "Propagandist" (1947), and Jerry Craven's Salomites in "A Matter of Etiquette" (1980), all of whom are practically indistinguishable from human beings—and in Kummer's story, in fact, might even actually be human beings who have mutated, since the writer gives so little direct information. Minimal differentiation is also present in Algis Budrys's "Lower Than Angels" (1956), where aliens are differentiated by skin color. Myrtle Benedict's "Sit By the Fire" (1958) differentiates them by skin type and by differing internal organs (discovered only in an autopsy). In the latter, nevertheless, it is implied—very discreetly—that the similarity is close enough for sexual intercourse, although the degree of discretion is such that the question of interfertility is neither raised nor answered.

6. Moreover, the natural humanoid of magazine science fiction is even to some extent identifiable in nineteenth-century speculative and utopian fiction. In discussing the "dozen or more Martian romances [that] appeared in the 1880s and 1890s" and led up to Wells's *The War of the Worlds* (1898), for example, Mark Hillegas considers four works whose Martians may be considered leading influences among the nineteenth-century precursors of the twentieth-century magazine humanoid: Percy Greg's *Across*

the Zodiac (1880), Robert Cromie's *A Plunge into Space* (1890), Gustavus Pope's *Journey to Mars* (1894), and Kurd Lasswitz's *Auf Zwei Planeten* (1897; translated as *Two Planets* 1971). Typically in these romances, the Martians are not only an older race (for which tendency Hillegas provides a rationale from nineteenth-century astronomical theory about Mars) but also a more beautiful one in human form. When Cromie, therefore, quite frankly announces the sameness of his Martians' form by saying at the first meeting of his travelers with the inhabitants of Mars: "I may call them men at once, for they were almost identical in physical organization to human beings, with only some characteristic differences of which more anon" (110), he suggests for the "characteristic differences" only that

> [i]n stature the Martians were smaller than a man of medium height, but their figures were so admirably proportioned that this was not apparent unless an actual comparison was made by placing a man close beside one of them. Their heads were larger than what we would consider to be in keeping with perfect symmetry, but their bearing was so graceful no ungainly effect was observable. The only very striking characteristic which they possessed was the expression of their faces. One look at a Martian's face would convince the most obstinate sceptic that in them the *animal* had been suppressed and supplanted by the *intellect.* (111–12; original emphasis)

Hillegas notes, for example, that "the Martians of *Auf Zwei Planeten* are physically identical to us except for their brighter eyes, which flash moral and intellectual superiority" ("Victorian 'Extraterrestrials'" 1975, 408). It might be reasonable to suppose, in the Victorian religious and aesthetic culture common to Cromie and Lasswitz, that moral superiority might be reflected in increased physical beauty, given that the human being is supposed to reflect the image of a divine creator. Neither Cromie nor Lasswitz, however, raises this point.

7. The collection incorporates "The Mutant Weapon" (1959), "Plague on Kryder II" (1948), "Ribbon in the Sky" (1957), "Quarantine World" (1966), and "This World Is Taboo" (1961).

8. See, for example, Stanton A. Coblentz, "Missionaries from the Sky" (1930); A. R. Holmes, "The Slave Ship from Space" (1931); Warren B. Sanders, "Sheridan Becomes Ambassador" (1932); Henry Kostkos, "The Meteor-Men of Plaa" (1933); Jack Williamson, "Born of the Sun" (1934); Raymond Z. Gallun, "Blue Haze on Pluto" (1935); Eric G. Iverson, "The Road Not Taken" (1985); W. T. Quick, "Gentrification Blues" (1986); Michael P. Kube-McDowell, "Nanny" (1987); Gail Schnirch, "A Cat for Katie" (1988); Brad Ferguson, "To Tell the Troof" (1989); Michael Flynn, "The Common Goal of Nature" (1990); F. A. Brejcha. "I'll Show You Mine If . . ." (1991); Janet Kagan, "The Nutcracker Coup" (1992); Rob Chilson, "The Worting's Testament"

(1993); G. D. Nordley, "Network" (1994); Paula Robinson, "The Maze" (1950); Joanna Russ, "Invasion" (1996); David Bischoff, "The Xaxrkling of J. Arnold Boysenberry" (1997); W. R. Thompson, "Roundup" (1998); Miriam Landau, "Allies" (1999); Kristine K. Rusch, "Retrieval Artist" (2000); Elisabeth Malartre, "A Windy Prospect"(2001); and Eleanor Arnason, "Knapsack Poems" (2002).

9. In Jayge Carr's "The Walls That Bind" (2001), for example, humans have been snatched from earth by unknown aliens and placed in an environment that mimics Earth except that it contains other aliens (not their captors). The story follows the activities of the protagonist as she befriends one of these other aliens and eventually brings about the reconciliation of her own and the other species, so that their complementary skills may be used for the maximum good of both species. The otherness of all the aliens involved is minimal.

10. In Edward M. Lerner's "Hostile Takeover" (2001), the alien appears only as an intelligence contacted by long-range computer activity.

11. Karen Traviss, in "A Slice at a Time" (2002), presents a narrative of a human "social worker" on an alien planet who is thrust into a psychotic episode by his inability to change the conditions that are responsible for the breakdown of the alien society and the death of individuals within it. The metaphoric parallel in the novel is signaled by the human protagonist's knowledge that this breakdown with its deadly results mirrors the same breakdown on Earth (and hence, by implication, on today's Earth). The specific nature of the alien, although not without its own interest, is not significant in the story.

12. "My first assertion is one that I think you will grant—that every one in this room is a judge of character," Woolf writes. "Indeed it would be impossible to live for a year without disaster unless one practiced character-reading and had some skill in the art. . . . [N]ovelists differ from the rest of the world because they do not cease to be interested in character when they have learnt enough about it for practical purposes. They go a step further; they feel that there is something permanently interesting in character itself. . . . The study of character becomes to them an absorbing pursuit; to impart character an obsession" (422).

13. Le Guin phrases this privileging in extremely strong terms: "[My second question] was . . . Should a book of science fiction be a novel. If it is possible, all the same is it advisable or desirable that the science fiction be also a novelist of character? . . . I have already said yes. I have already admitted that this, to me, is the whole point. That no other form of prose, to me, is a patch on the novel. That if we can't catch Mrs. Brown, if only for a moment, then all the beautiful faster-than-light ships, all the irony and

imagination and knowledge and invention are in vain" (112–13). In her introduction to *A Fisherman of the Inland Sea* (1994), however, Le Guin revisits this question of the centrality of character in science fiction and reassesses the situation in science fiction again:

> The cardboard-character syndrome was largely true of early science fiction, but for decades writers have been using the form to explore character and human relationships. I'm one of them. An imagined setting may be the most appropriate in which to work out certain traits and destinies. But it's also true that a great deal of contemporary fiction isn't a fiction of character. This end of the century isn't an age of individuality as the Elizabethan and the Victorian ages were. Our stories, realistic or otherwise, with their unreliable narrators, dissolving points of view, multiple perceptions and perspectives, often don't have depth of character as their central value. Science fiction, with its tremendous freedom of metaphor, has sent many writers far ahead in this exploration beyond the confines of individuality—Sherpas on the slopes of the postmodern. (3–4)

14. Forster adds, however, "But that help has not been given yet, and until it comes we may say that the actors in a story are, or pretend to be, human beings" (43).

15. In the course of this discussion, Forster acknowledges the standard "aesthetic reply" to the question of the difference, that "a novel is a work of art, with its own laws, which are not those of daily life, and that a character in a novel is real when it lives in accordance with such laws" and goes on to say that "the barrier of art divides [characters] from us. They are real not because they are like ourselves (though they may be like us) but because they are convincing" (61). But this aesthetically defined point is largely peripheral to his argument, which he makes on the grounds of psychology.

16. Forster tells us that Caleb's formula can be expressed in the sentence "I must conceal, even by subterfuges, the poverty of my master's house." He goes on to say that "he does not use the actual phrase, but it completely describes him; he has no existence outside it. . . . It is not his *idée fixe* because there is nothing in him into which the idea can be fixed. He is the idea, and such life as he possesses radiates from its edges and from the scintillations it strikes when other elements in the novel impinge" (65–66).

17. The metaphorical dimension of aliens, on which Parrinder seems to insist, is also, except where the writer has been able to avoid it, a contributory factor to resistance to differentiation and individualization. Similarly, this same metaphoric dimension may interfere when alien characters, with or without the presence of human characters, must be placed in a situation in which the difference between individuals has the potential to create conflict (in the strictly literary sense of the term) and tension that can be resolved in the development of the narrative.

18. Even though these round characters are examples not even of *Homo fictus* but of, if I may extend Forster's wordplay slightly, *Homo scientia fictionalis.*

19. A minor side effect of the otherness that is part of the success of Butler's creation of a potentiated alien in T'Gatoi is the fact that *clutch* (the familiar and correct term for several; eggs laid by a reptile or bird in the human context) does not seem appropriate as a collective noun for T'Gatoi's eggs, and, deliberately or not, Butler does not supply the reader with an alternative.

20. Moreover, from the foreshadowing of his future activities (beyond the end of the story) that Butler slips into Gan's narration, T'Gatoi is capable of forward thinking. It appears that T'Gatoi is grooming Gan to be an intermediary between the two species, as well as her own N'tlic, so that her revealed "hidden" life includes a hidden agenda, which is not entirely self-centered.

21. Although Moggadeet retains both rotundity and strangeness throughout, the end of the story evades Niven's criterion that "[s]omething should be left behind at the end of the story" ("Playgrounds for the Mind" 1990, 26). Paradoxically, it is the strength of the literary modeling of the protagonist that cuts the reader off from speculative play at the end of the story. To attempt to play beyond the end of this story would be futile, if not impertinent.

7

Necessary Alterity: The Why of the Alien

Why aliens in science fiction are so inordinately impressive, so constantly produced by writers, and so urgently demanded by readers are the questions with which I began this study, and I return to them here, having in my previous chapter, I hope, provided at least half the answer. The Alien, the trope of the OtherSelf (alterity), is a literary trope of extraordinary flexibility, capacity, and range, capable of furnishing stories of widely differing types from complex psychological studies to simple entertainments, at the writer's discretion. But the OtherSelf's existence as a literary trope is only half its existence—and hence only half an answer. The other half of the answer lies in the nature of the human mind that calls the trope into existence in the first place.

No literary trope comes into existence ex nihilo. It is always the product of a human mind, and the human mind is a complicated and not completely understood phenomenon. As I have previously indicated, the philosophical and psychological theory of *embodiment* asserts, however, that—borrowing once again from Poole (1988)—"perception and understanding of the world are partly a function of the fact that consciousness is not 'pure', but exists within a membrane of flesh and blood" (265). One of the extended benefits of this theory, according to Poole, is that "[l]iterary theory has . . . profited from the insight, allowing a new recognition of the importance of a writer's embodiment in the textual displacements of his or her own literary constructions. . . . [N]o text is innocent of its embodied origins" (265). It is not necessary to invoke and discuss the whole of the theory of embodiment to examine the effects in science fiction texts of the notion that human bodies affect the minds "contained in" or "attached to" them and so affect the products of those minds, especially since embodiment has not yet been precisely defined.[1] "Embodied origins" may be taken as a given in the texts of science fiction as easily as in any other texts.

Given the fact of embodiment, the point at issue for my argument here is that the consciousness that exists in the "membrane of flesh and blood" is neither the whole nor necessarily even the larger part of the human mind. There is a large terra incognita in each mind called the "subconscious" (typically by Freudians) or "unconscious" (typically by Jungians), which operates as a substrate of consciousness. There is no evidence that this unconscious is innocent of "embodied origins" any more than consciousness is innocent. The properties of our bodies affect our unconscious makeup as much as our conscious makeup, and the "embodied origins" of unconscious contents and processes therefore affect the texts equally. The effect of filtration of "embodied origins" material through the substrate of unconscious content on its way to consciousness and to the text is significant and not simple. For, as I have previously suggested, according to C. G. Jung, the contents of the unconscious include the powerful libidinal energies known as archetypes, and these energies manifest in characteristic forms that exert powerful shaping forces on anything that they touch—which is effectively everything in the unconscious—and hence on everything from the unconscious that reaches consciousness.

The trope of alterity as a simple trope, a literary trope consciously organized and practiced as a matter of writerly skill, entails as much of the "embodied origins" in the writer's embodiment as any other part of the texts that emerge from the human mind to be written down and disseminated. My argument, however, is that the trope of alterity is not only a literary trope and not at all simple. It has a specific substrate in the unconscious mind, a unique constellation of libidinal energy—an archetype. Alterity therefore exists both as trope and archetype. Each alien is an example of the trope, which is constantly and complexly modified by the archetype, and the archetype is only accessible through the individual examples of the trope. The relationship of trope and archetype may be metaphorically illustrated. In *Mindkiller* (1982), Spider Robinson writes: "If you take a hologram of the word 'love' and try to read a page of print through it, you will see only a blur. But if the word 'love' is printed anywhere on that page, in any typeface, you will see a very bright light at that spot on the page" (208). Similarly, if you consider to be a hologram any alien that serves as an example of the literary trope of alterity, and you look through that alien at the originating unconscious of such tropes, you will see "a very bright light" that signals the presence of the archetype of alterity. It is often but by no means always the writer who is most skilled in the presentation of human characters who writes the alien that reveals the archetype of the OtherSelf most brightly. But at the same time, it has to be emphasized that the trope and the archetype can never merge in any single example of the Alien in science fiction. The trope and the archetype are ontologically distinct, albeit complexly interrelated.

Out of the concatenation in science fiction of trope and archetype, alien and Alien, distinct but interrelated, emerges the principle of *necessary alterity*. Behind the many individual alien figures of the magazines, all suggesting the existence of OtherSelfs, lies the single archetype (in the Jungian sense of the term) of OtherSelfness (with all the concomitant implications of Jungian archetypal nature), which is necessary to the understanding of humanity's nature as sapient beings (human Selfs) as well as to the proleptic conceptualization of other nonhuman sapient beings (alien Selfs). In my previous chapter, I have discussed the nature of the trope, a familiar element of literary criticism, as it is involved in the figure of the Alien. In this chapter, I turn to a consideration of the complex and much less familiar—and hence less well understood— nature of the archetype. The power of the archetype, I contend, is what compels writers to return again and again to creating multifarious, strange, and fascinating aliens, and what compels readers to require them again and again in what they read. These compulsions are what I term the "why" of the Alien— *necessary alterity*.

The answer to this question, however, begins with more than the presence of a single archetype, for the identification and ordering of the archetypes themselves is part of a larger framework of ideas within the mind. Humans appear always to have imposed a structure of order (a cosmology) on the universe in which they exist.[2] Different human communities produce different cosmologies, but no community seems to be without any cosmology all: Only by defining a structure for the universe and designating a place within it for themselves, apparently, can humans render it properly habitable. In *The Discarded Image* (1964), C. S. Lewis discusses this desire for order as he finds it manifest among the people of the Middle Ages, in whose "most sublime achievements . . . we see the tranquil, indefatigable, exultant energy of passionately systematic minds bringing huge masses of heterogeneous material into unity" (10); included among those achievements is "the medieval synthesis itself, the whole organization of their theology, science, and history into a single, complex, harmonious mental Model of the Universe" (11). As Lewis indicates, models of the universe (cosmologies) change as human minds change their thinking to include different sets of the observed phenomena that are available to them (*Discarded Image* 1967, 221).

In the cosmology of the Western world in the nineteenth century, when science fiction was gestating, humans saw themselves existing in an order in many ways similar to the order enjoined by the medieval model from which it was descended. The new cosmology, in fact, continued to incorporate some features of the older model, in spite of what Lovejoy in *The Great Chain of Being* (1948; as I have already mentioned in chapter 1) describes as its increasing temporalization (269). In particular, the nineteenth-century cosmology still largely continued to assume, if not to actually assert, that the order it discerned had been divinely ordained by God (its Creator) as a hierarchy—the Great Chain of Being—with God at the top and inanimate objects at the bottom. In the medieval model, according to Lewis, humans occupy a key position in the total vertical length of this chain, for they provide the link between the upper and the lower portions of it: "Man is a rational animal, and therefore a composite being, partly akin to the angels who are rational but . . . not animal, and partly akin to the beasts which are animal but not rational" (*The Discarded Image* 1967, 152). As hybrids between spirits and beasts, humans not only enjoy a unique status, they also have a unique function, for they rule—have "dominion" over, to borrow the biblical term—their inferiors, the beasts of the physical world (Genesis 1:26, King James Bible). Moreover, "[i]n every age," says Lewis, "the human mind is deeply influenced by the accepted Model of the universe," but there can be "a change of Models" because "the Model is also influenced by the prevailing temper of mind" (*The Discarded Image* 1967, 222). This process of cosmological change, therefore, continues into the present century, but does not continue unchanged, and does not have to continue unchanged in the future.

The cosmology of the twentieth century still shares the increased temporalization of its predecessor, but more importantly it is characterized by a continued increase of scientific rationalization. It incorporates contemporary scientific knowledge—the knowledge provided by the physical sciences, such as physics, chemistry, biochemistry, and biology, and the social sciences, such as psychology, sociology, and anthropology. Science fiction, as a product of the twentieth century, shares the values of twentieth-century cosmology. Insofar as it is a literary form, however, it inherits and incorporates fictionalized or poeticized versions of many elements from previous models, which temper the otherwise purely scientific rationalization of the cosmology as viewed by the scientists. Science fiction interprets the ambient cosmology with particular emphasis on the interaction of humans with the new elements of science and its derived technology, and, in this way, it offers a new version of the human position within that cosmology. One of its most important offerings is exploration of the possible status of human beings in relation to other nonhuman, but equally sapient beings, which cosmology now seriously postulates in scientific terms, or as scientifically possible, for the first time: the Alien. Consequently, understanding the possible OtherSelfs of science fiction, beings not of this world but sapient like ourselves, becomes somewhat more urgent, and for this purpose the analytical psychology of C. G. Jung, in which the actual human Self is central, is, as I have previously argued, the peculiarly appropriate guide.

THE ALIEN AS THE ARCHETYPE OF ALTERITY (OTHERSELFNESS)

In his theory of analytical psychology, C. G. Jung identifies particular elements of human nature and behavior that offer a clear understanding of the science-fictional Alien. Analytical psychology is directed toward harmonizing and understanding the internal universe of the individual and that individual's relationships to others. Among the elements associated with this process, one of the most important—and certainly the most important for the study of literature—is the archetype. Properly understood, the Jungian archetype goes far toward accounting for the dominance of the figure of the Alien in science fiction by suggesting the inner sources of its multifariousness (multiplicity and variety), persistence, fascination, and strangeness, and by identifying these as the hallmarks of its origin as an archetype—the archetype of alterity or OtherSelfness—in the unconscious psyche.

The Jungian theory of the archetype reveals the profound roots of the concept of the Other—and hence the science-fictional Alien—in the life of the individual through its accounts of the individual's development of consciousness and of the understanding of the unconscious. As I have noted already in my introduction, beginning at birth, a sense of separate identity is fundamental to the individual, and one of the first things that happens in a baby is the development of its consciousness of the difference between itself and its environment—between "the I and the Not-I." In her Jungian study of the differentiation of the Self and the Other that takes this phrase as its title, M. Esther Harding (1974) discusses "the stages by which consciousness develops in the human being, so that, from being merely an integer in a continuum, he gradually becomes a person in his own right" (8–9). The newborn infant, she says, "is not even aware of its own body limits; there is no differentiation whatever between the 'I' and the 'Not-I'" (9), but "usually, sometime after his second birthday, an important change occurs in the child. . . . [H]e discovers that to himself he is no longer just like other objects or other people. He becomes self-aware, and so speaks of himself in the first person" (11). At this point, therefore, the individual has reached the stage of understanding otherness at the most basic level. But, according to Harding, it is not sufficient for the infant only to recognize him or herself as "I" to achieve true adulthood. In order to develop appropriately, it must acquire clearer awareness of itself: "[A]nother definitive moment may be experienced, usually around puberty, when the sense of 'I'-ness becomes suddenly clearer. It is not until this step in awareness has been taken that it can dawn on an individual that others, too, may have a similar sense of being 'I'" (14–15). But even as the developing human continues to undertake the successive clarifications of itself leading toward self-determination and autonomy in its own psyche, it is also making similar discriminations about what it finds in the environment from which it is discriminating itself. In the opinion of Colwyn Trevarthen and Katerina Logotheti, the potential for "intersubjectivity" (which I take to include the recognition of the Other as a Self) exists at birth: "Now we possess evidence that the newborn can imitate expressions of persons and enter into an exchange of feelings" ("Child in Society and Society in Children" 1989, 167). Trevarthen and Logotheti do not, however, specifically include the psychological development of the sense of "I" in their discussion. But given such early capacity, the child steadily discriminates itself from the things, animals, and people which it finds itself among (but separate from) and which it can then in turn discriminate from each other. If "Not-I" is the Other, then Silverberg, in placing the origin of the fascination with the Other as the encounter between the child and the strangers "who do not fit into the family circle [and] who cannot be recognized, whose existence is an uncomfortable mystery" (*Earthmen and Strangers* 1968, 7), suggests too simple an origin for the concept of the Alien. Paradoxically, even family members are, in Jungian terms, strangers (*Not-I*) to begin with; they must be recognized and become familiar to the child as it understands more and more about its environment, and they will probably be among the first whose *alterity* is recognized. Moreover, in separating itself from them, and them from each other, and understanding the "real existence of others" (Harding 1974, 15), the growing child learns not only the concept of the Other and the concept of the *different kinds* of Other, but the actual concept of OtherSelf-ness (*alterity*).

Even more paradoxically, as the child matures he or she must discover and deal with the strangers within. Jung called these inner strangers *archetypes*. He did not invent the term, which had been used, as he acknowledges, by earlier writers and philosophers of whom Plato seems to have been the first. He borrowed it from them and then redefined it to use in sense different from and more personal than any of his predecessors. In 1929, in a letter to Dr. J. Allen Gilbert, a psychologist friend, he explained his use of the archetypes as follows:

> Science is the art of creating suitable illusions which the fool believes or argues against, but the wise man enjoys their beauty or their ingenuity, without being blind to the fact that they are human veils and curtains concealing the abysmal Darkness of the Unknowable. . . . All things are *as if* they were. *Real* things are *effects* of something unknown. The same is true of anima, ego, etc, and moreover, there are no real things that are not *relatively real*. We have no idea of absolute reality, because "reality" is always something "observed." (Jung, *Letters* I:56–57; original emphasis)

Here he clearly indicates that these archetypes and archetypal processes are interpretative tropes to assist in the exploration of the unconscious. Given the problem of knowability in dealing with aliens in science fiction, the notion that the archetypes are "human veils and curtains concealing the abysmal Darkness of the Unknowable" provides a particularly appropriate authority for discussing aliens as archetypes.

That part of the theory of the archetype most relevant to the concept of the Alien begins with Jung's point that an archetype is part of the unconscious mind. According to Jung, an archetype "represents or personifies certain instinctive data of the dark, primitive psyche, the real but invisible roots of consciousness" ("The

Psychology of the Child Archetype" CW 9(i):*271*:160). It is not "an inherited *idea*," as is so often assumed, "but an inherited mode of psychic functioning, corresponding to the inborn way in which the chick emerges from the egg, the bird builds its nest, a certain kind of wasp stings the motor ganglion of the caterpillar, and eels find their way to the Bermudas. In other words, it is a 'pattern of behavior'" (Foreword to Harding: *Woman's Mysteries* CW 18:*1228*:518; original emphasis). Jung's use of the words *inherited* and *inborn* (and, elsewhere, *organic* and *phylogenetic*) in describing the point of origin of the archetypes may be noted. In a note to "Answer to Job," Jung says, "I have often been asked where the archetype comes from and whether it is acquired or not. This question cannot be answered directly. . . . They exist preconsciously, and presumably they form the structural dominants of the psyche in general" ("Answer to Job" CW 11:*556*:362). In asserting the organic, inherited, and phylogenetic roots of the archetypes— which he did on numerous occasions prior to his death in 1961—Jung appears to anticipate some of what was included in Wilson's discussion of the origins of human behavior in *Sociobiology: The New Synthesis* (1975), as Anthony Stevens points out in his book *Archetype Revisited: An Updated Natural History of the Self* (2003).[3] But in his discussion of the concept of the Shadow in Jungian theory, Stevens makes clear the outstanding difference between Jung and the sociobiologists when he points out that the aim of recognizing the archetypes is to deal with their influence by asserting an ethical control of behavior:

> What matters, after all, is not that we *are* aggressive, xenophobic, sexual, hierarchical and territorial, but what *attitude* we adopt to these fundamental *a priori* aspects of our nature—how we live them, and how we mediate them to the group. It is the ethical orientation that counts.
>
> However, in order to be ethical one must be conscious, and consciousness means awareness of things as they really are. We *have* to abandon the romantic dream that evil, conflict, and aggression can be banished from human affairs, because it is when we *deny* our own capacity for evil that we project or displace it onto others. (240; original emphasis)

Jung further asserts, in discussing the Shadow, that "[i]f you imagine someone who is brave enough to withdraw all these projections, then you get an individual who is conscious of a pretty thick shadow. . . . Such a man knows that whatever is wrong in the world is in himself, and if he only learns how to deal with his own shadow he has done something real for the world" ("Psychology and Religion" CW 11:*140*:83).

Elsewhere, Jung distinguishes between the unactualized archetype of the unconscious and its actualization in the conscious mind. The unactualized archetype is "the archetype *an sich*," and "is an 'irrepresentable' factor, 'disposition' which starts functioning at a given moment in the development of the human mind and arranges the material of consciousness into definite patterns" ("Answer to Job" CW 11:*556*:362). This unactualized archetype *an sich* actualizes or manifests itself in consciousness by appropriating material from the conscious content that is congruent with the specific nature of the underlying "disposition": "The unconscious supplies as it were the archetypal form, which itself is empty and irrepresentable. Consciousness immediately fills it with related or similar representational material so that it can be perceived. For this reason, archetypal ideas are locally, temporally, and individually conditioned" ("The Philosophical Tree" CW 13:*476*:346). Jung does not explain the process of actualization directly at this point. In "Answer to Job," however, he suggests, changing the metaphor of the "empty" archetypal form that has be filled to something more apt, that the unactualized archetypes "may be compared to the invisible presence of the crystal lattice in a saturated solution" ("Answer to Job" CW 11:*556*:362), implying that the process of actualizing the latent archetype is a process like the precipitation of the crystals in the solution by some outside catalyst, corresponding in the psychological process perhaps to some kind of change or shock in the individual's developmental life. The precipitated representation of the archetype *an sich* is the actualized archetype or *archetypal symbol*.

Jung also points out, moreover, that the effect of the individualization of this precipitation of the symbols is to multiply them. Because they are "locally, temporally, and individually conditioned," he asserts, the archetypes manifest themselves in "multitudinous forms . . . as images and groups of images" ("On the Nature of the Psyche" CW 8:*414*:212). According to Jolande Jacobi, Jung's associate and fellow analyst, in *Complex/Archetype/Symbol in the Psychology of C. G. Jung* (1959), furthermore, this multiplicity of symbolic manifestations is directly related to the depth at which the unrealized archetype is rooted in the unconscious mind: "The deeper the unconscious stratum from which the archetype stems, the scantier will be its basic design, but the more possibilities

of development will be contained in it, and the richer it will be in meanings"
(56). Jacobi indicates the almost limitless range of this representational material in the contents of the conscious mind upon which the archetype typically
draws in the process of actualization:

> [E]ven the most abstract relationships, situations, or ideas of archetypal nature
> are visualized by the psyche as specific forms, figures, images, objects, etc.
> (which may be concrete, as in the case of human, animal, or plant forms, or ab-
> stract, as in the case of the circle, the cube, the cross, the sphere, etc.), or at least
> translated into events susceptible of being represented in images or pictorial se-
> quences. (76)

In addition, she links these representations or images directly with fiction: "It
was this image-making power of the human psyche which . . . in general created the boundless realm of myths, fairy tales, fables, epics, ballads, dramas . .
. as from the inexhaustible treasure house of the archetypes of the collective
unconscious it untiringly produces new and ever new symbols" (76–77). Jacobi's implication is not, however, that art is no more than the manifestation
of archetypal symbols, but that art, like all aspects of human life, has roots in
the underlying activity of the archetypal processes of the unconscious.

The most prominent characteristic of the archetype *an sich* is its *numinosity*—its share of the *numinosum*.[4] Numinosity may be understood metaphorically as a charge of energy or affect (like a psychic version of electricity) that
is present in the archetype. The power of the charge varies, but its presence is
unmistakable and indicates that an archetype has been "activated" (Jung, "A
Psychological Approach to the Dogma of the Trinity" CW 11:*223*:151). Each
actualization of the original archetype, moreover, retains the full numinosity
or "compelling force which it derives from the unconscious" (Jung, "A Psychological Approach to Dogma of the Trinity" CW 11:*222*:149). Like an electrical charge, too, the numinosity discharges on contact and "shocks" the
individual who touches upon the archetype in its actualized form.

Such numinously charged actualized archetypes and archetypal processes
are regularly encountered in the lives and dreams of individuals and in the
myths and literature of groups. Foremost among them are Jung's archetypes
of the personal unconscious, of which the most important are the Shadow
(the dark twin), the Anima/Animus (the contrasexual element), the Old Wise
Man, the Old Wise Woman, and the Self (the total integrated personality,

comprising both the conscious and the unconscious psyche). The most important archetypal process is the process of maturation or development into the autonomous Self—a process which Jung came to call *individuation*. The individual's ability to recognize the *nature* of his or her Self arises as part of this process, during which the individual's Self (and other psychic components) may be projected onto other people and must be retrieved and reintegrated for individuation to proceed. These personal archetypes and the archetypal process of individuation in its typical manifestation as a journey or quest, although they by no means constitute the whole or even the greater part of Jung's psychological theory, are the most well-known elements of it because they are the most accessible to general understanding. They form, for example, the subject of Kenneth Golden's *Science Fiction, Myth, and Jungian Psychology* (1995), previously mentioned. Golden's study, integrating (as he suggests in his preface) "two interrelated radical points of view . . . Jungian depth psychology and . . . the comparative approach to myth," develops "the validity of both viewpoints to the study of science fiction" (i). In various chapters, Golden deals with the appearance of the Anima, the Shadow, and the Self, and discusses various aspects of the quest myth as an image of "psychic evolution" (individuation), treating them as tropes. Although at various points in his argument he discusses aliens, Golden does not select them out for any special treatment. His argument is pursued through a number of classical science fiction novels (Hoyle's *The Black Cloud*, 1957, and Clarke's *Rendezvous with Rama*, 1973, for example) and through various movies and Star Trek episodes from the original series. The approach Golden takes in treating individual archetypes and processes in individual texts clarifies their presence and produces original and fascinating readings of the various texts and media items. Lying in the personal unconscious, these archetypes are relatively accessible.

Beyond the archetypes of the personal unconscious, however, exist many more archetypes that lie in the *transpersonal* unconscious. These are what Jung referred to as the "*symbols of transformation*" ("Archetypes of the Collective Unconscious" CW 9(i):*80*:38; original emphasis). Like the personal archetypes, these transpersonal archetypes are actualized in the form of archetypal symbols. For most individuals, the encounter takes place in dreams, but for writers and other artists, the imagination provides enhanced access.

Jung's use of the term *symbol*, like his use of the term *archetype*, is highly specialized. In its simplest definition, removed from all theoretical systems, a symbol is a *marker* that designates something else,[5] and it consists of the *marker* itself and the *marked*. In general use, the marker may be called either a sign or a symbol. But for Jung, *sign* and *symbol* were entirely different in nature, and he insisted on an absolute distinction between them on the grounds that "symbolic and semiotic meaning are entirely different things" ("Definitions. 51. Symbol" CW 6:*814*:473). He offers examples that indicate that semiotic meaning is "bound" meaning, overtly and completely represented by or bound to the sign (marker), whereas symbolic meaning is "free" and not bound to a particular signs. It is the nature of what is marked, moreover, that governs his distinction of sign from symbol: "[E]very view which interprets the symbolic expression [the *marker*] as an analogue or an abbreviated designation for a *known* thing is *semiotic*," whereas "a view which interprets the symbolic expression [the *marker*] as the best possible formulation of a relatively *unknown* thing, which for that reason cannot be more clearly or characteristically represented, is *symbolic*" ("Definitions. 51. Symbol" CW 6:*814*:473; original emphasis).[6] This distinction was crucial to Jung's complex theory of archetypal symbols in which a sign points semiotically to a known and a symbol points enigmatically to an unknown. The unknown indicated by a symbol is "something that cannot be characterized in any other or better way" ("Definitions. 51. Symbol" CW 6:*816*:474), and for Jung, the use of the term *symbol* "presupposes that the chosen expression is the best possible description or formulation of a relatively unknown fact, which is none the less known to exist or is postulated as existing" ("Definitions. 51. Symbol" CW 6:*814*:474). The specific importance of this point derives from Jung's already established theory that the archetypes (*archetypes an sich*) are fundamentally unknowable in themselves, but knowable (at least partially) in mediated versions only:

> Like the personalities [personal archetypes], these [transpersonal] archetypes are true and genuine symbols that cannot be exhaustively interpreted, either as signs or as allegories. They are genuine symbols precisely because they are ambiguous, full of half-glimpsed meanings, and in the last resort inexhaustible. The ground principles . . . of the unconscious are indescribable because of their wealth of reference, although in themselves recognizable. The discriminating intellect naturally keeps on trying to establish their singleness of meaning and thus misses the essential point; for what we can above all establish as the one thing consistent with their nature is their *manifold meaning*, their almost limit-

less wealth of reference, which makes any unilateral formulation impossible. Besides this, they are in principle paradoxical. ("Archetypes of the Collective Unconscious" CW 9(i):*80*:38; original emphasis)

Symbols, *archetypal* symbols in Jung's usage, bridge the gap between the archetypes in the unconscious and the conscious mind, representing them idiomorphically and rendering the unknowable knowable. The fact that the archetype is unknowable and yet perceptible through archetypal symbols has some bearing on the knowability issue with regard to the presentation of aliens. The unknowable archetypes, according to Jung, exist within us, and although they are unknowable, they are (to use my earlier terminology) perceptible through the medium of the archetypal symbols thrown up in dreams, in analysis, and in literature. If it is possible to accept simultaneously that the "irreducibly unknowable" exists within us and also that we can "know" it in some indirect sense by examining (for those who care to do so) the symbols it presents us with, then in the same way we can reconcile the irreducible unknowability of aliens with their constant presence in science fiction.

The function of these archetypal symbols is for Jung as complex as their nature. The function of the specific archetype *an sich* that underlies a particular symbol when it is activated in the individual psyche is to produce order: "Archetypes are . . . factors and motifs that arrange the psychic elements into certain images, characterized as archetypal" ("A Psychological Approach to the Trinity" CW 11:*556*:362). Jacobi also provides a commentary and gloss on Jung's theory of the archetype. On the point of the archetype's function as an arranging mechanism in the psyche, she glosses "arrange" as *order*: "[T]he archetypes, as the voice of the human species, are the great ordering factors, disregard or violation of which brings with it confusion and destruction. . . . [T]hey have an *ordering* effect on the psychic process and also on the contents of consciousness, leading them by labyrinthine ways toward a possible totality" (Jacobi 1959, 72; original emphasis). Jung explains this function at the level of the actualized archetype (or archetypal symbol) by calling the symbols *transformers of energy*, converting libido "from a 'lower' to a 'higher' form" (*Symbols of Transformation* CW 5:*344*:231–32). Jacobi glosses this remark as the "healing" character of the Jungian symbol and says that it "helps to restore wholeness as well as [psychic] health" by shifting libido from unproductive regression into the unconscious to "meaningful activity" (Jacobi 1959, 100). In this process, says Jung, "[t]he symbol works by suggestion; that is to say, it carries conviction and at the same time expresses the content of that conviction. It is able to do this because of the numen, the specific energy stored up in the archetype" (*Symbols of Transformation* CW 5:*344*:231–32). When an archetype is actualized, the effect on the conscious mind is extremely powerful: "Whenever it clothes itself in suitable symbols . . . it seizes hold of the individual in a startling way, creating a condition amounting almost to possession, the consequences of which may be incalculable" (Foreword to Harding: *Woman's Mysteries* CW 18:*1229*:518–19). Elsewhere, Jung uses even stronger terms to describe this compelling force: "[W]hen . . . a complex of the collective unconscious [a transpersonal archetype] becomes associated with the ego, *i.e.* becomes conscious, it is felt as strange, uncanny, and at the same time fascinating. . . . [T]he conscious mind falls under its spell" ("The Psychological Foundations of Belief in Spirits" CW 8:589:311). In part, at least, the compelling nature of the archetypes arises from the fact that the compulsion is associated with what seems to be a personality: "Nothing that is autonomous in the psyche is impersonal or neutral. Impersonality is a category pertaining to consciousness. All autonomous psychic factors have the character of personality, from the 'voices' of the insane to the control-spirits of mediums and the visions of the mystics" ("Mind and Earth" CW 10:*83*:42). A "specific archetype," according to Jung, actualizes from the unconscious "with all the specific marks of its autonomy and authority" (*Symbols of Transformation* CW 5:*617*:397). Unfortunately, this autonomy and authority is associated, particularly in the personal archetypes, with ambivalence: "[I]t turns out that all archetypes spontaneously develop favourable and unfavourable, light and dark, good and bad effects. In the end we have to acknowledge that the self is a *complexio oppositorum* precisely because there can be no reality without polarity" (*Aion* CW 9(ii):*423*:267; original emphasis). The same ambivalence is obviously also, however, true of the transpersonal archetypes. Moreover, just as the actualized symbols share the numinosity of the unactualized archetype from which they derive, so they also share its ambiguity.

Considered in light of Jungian theory of the archetypes and archetypal symbols, therefore, the Alien as OtherSelf is unmistakably and undeniably a specific unactualized transpersonal archetype *an sich*, whereas the individual aliens of different texts are actualizations of that underlying archetype—archetypal symbols. By defining individual aliens as archetypal symbols (symbols derived from the archetype), we can begin also to account not only for the strangeness and fascination as similar to the strangeness and fascination that have characterized other symbols of this type in other modes of literature (the dark wood of Dante's *Divina Commedia*, the sea in English poetry from Anglo-Saxon times onwards, and the White Whale in *Moby Dick*, for example), but also for their multifariousness and variety. As an archetypal symbol, defined in this special sense rather than in the more usual sense of the word, each example of the Alien partakes of the nature of and retains the numinosity of the underlying archetype of the Alien. In her article "Myth and Archetype in Science Fiction" (1976), Ursula Le Guin accuses English professors of teaching students that "[y]ou just ain't no good unless you can see a symbol hiding, like a scared gerbil, under every page" (77), and she goes on to distinguish between the true and the false symbol: "The real mystery is not destroyed by reason. The fake one is. You look at it and it vanishes. You look at the Blond Hero—really look—and he turns into a gerbil. But you look at Apollo, and he looks back at you" (75). The "real mystery" of the Alien depends on the writer's experience of the underlying archetype. If the writer's experience is genuine, the symbolic manifestation will be genuine. From the work of a writer whose experience of the archetype is genuine, therefore, like Le Guin's Apollo, the alien, strange and numinous, "looks back at you."

The numinosity and strangeness of the archetypal symbol, moreover, prevent the Alien from becoming, as simple metaphor often does, truly a didactic trope. A metaphoric equation can often be established between an alien and some aspect of human nature, behavior, activity, or environment: Wells's Martians, to take an example, can be seen, according to Mark Rose, as a metaphor for human intellect stripped of its normal accompaniment of human passion (*Alien Encounters* 1981, 78). Yet this metaphoric signification, although it may be one element of the effect of the Martians, fails to account for the impact of the narrator's first encounter with the invaders:

A big greyish, rounded bulk, the size perhaps, of a bear was rising slowly and painfully out of the cylinder. As it bulged up and caught the light, it glistened like wet leather. Two large dark-coloured eyes were regarding me steadfastly. It was rounded, and had, one might say, a face. There was a mouth under the eyes, the brim of which quivered and panted, and dropped saliva. . . . Those who have never seen a living Martian can scarcely imagine the strange horror of their appearance. (24)

Although Wells's description continues to detail the appearance of the Martians,[7] the essential impact of the alien presence has already been made—like Apollo in Le Guin's example, the Martian is looking back, and, although it is not human, it nevertheless has "a face" (as animals do not). That impact is both far beyond the effect of even the most effective metaphor and completely without clear and direct reference to either intellect or passion or any imbalance between them. Similar problems arise with many attempts, although not all, to limit the alien in a text to metaphoric function. The total effect of any alien, if it is artistically effective and psychically (archetypally) genuine, always overbalances the neat equation of metaphor into a symbolic relationship in which what is signified by the Alien continually evades definition.

When the archetype manifests as a specific archetypal symbol, the specifications of the symbol are derived from the acquired contents of the writer's mind operating at a no more than semiconscious level. As a symbol, therefore, the alien in a given text not only retains the numinosity and fascination of the underlying archetype, but controls a stock of potential images limited only by the volume of the conscious contents of the writer concerned. In theory, since all writers have a stock of potential images in their conscious mind contributed to by a unique individual experience of life, literature, art, the media, and the world, the stock of suitable symbols within the genre is limited only by the number of writers engaged in the creation of stories about aliens and the extent of their experience. In practice, however, the symbols tend to be somewhat constrained in a given writer by cultural determinants acquired at the conscious level and by the constraint of scientific plausibility current in the genre. Nevertheless, even within these constraints, the multiplicity and variety of the images of the Alien are enormous.

The sheer number of the aliens in science fiction is, in fact, the first and obvious sign of their status or nature as archetypal symbols. As I have pointed out in my introduction, the greatest number of stories on a single topic in the magazines are on the topic of alien contact. *Astounding*, for example, regularly printed "interplanetary stories"—"interplanetary" being the accepted shorthand for stories of alien beings. Moreover, the appearance of such stories on a regular basis has continued, through several changes of editor and the change of the magazine's title to *Analog*, right up to the present. *Amazing*, which also printed stories of this type (although relatively fewer), also used the term *interplanetary* to describe them. The great and continued popularity of stories of the Alien in science fiction is, consequently, identifiable as a response entirely consistent with the effect of the awakened archetypal energy deep in the unconscious psyche of both writer and reader.

The second signal of the archetypal nature of science-fictional representations of aliens is their variety. Stimulated by the energy of the unconscious archetype's impulse to realization, the process of translating it into images is carried out by the imagination, which is fed by the variety of conscious experience. According to Jung, moreover, such experience includes not only factors peculiar to the individual but factors deriving from the individual's belonging to humanity in general: "All those factors, therefore, that were essential to our near and remote ancestors will also be essential to us, for they are embedded in the inherited system. They are even necessities which make themselves felt as needs" ("Analytical Psychology and *Weltanschauung*" CW 8:717:371–72). Artistic imagination therefore produces literary forms, using new symbols like those supplied to the individual in dreams. In Jacobi's words, "[T]he nocturnal world of dreams, as from the inexhaustible treasure house of the archetypes of the collective unconscious, untiringly produces new and ever new symbols" (*Complex/Archetype/ Symbol in the Psychology of C. G. Jung* 1959, 76–77). The "multitudinous forms" (Jung, "On the Nature of the Psyche" CW 8:*414*:212) that an archetype takes on in the process of actualization are unmistakably paralleled by the "multitudinous" aliens that appeared from the beginning in the science fiction magazines. Whether they are humanoids, *bems*, LGMs, potentiated aliens, or analogous, heterologous, or exotic aliens, together they demonstrate that the manifestations of the archetype tend to be as various as their authors' imaginations can manage. Consequently, given that variety is a function of the archetype realizing itself in symbols provided by the imagination and stimulated by energy from the unconscious, such an archetype is unmistakably and powerfully at work in the huge variety of aliens that emerge in the pages of the early magazines.

The strangeness that attaches to these multitudinous aliens is, however, the most important sign of their archetypal nature. The "sense of wonder" is often used to characterize the attraction of the genre as a whole, but it is of particular relevance to the response created by aliens. The reader feels the sense of wonder about an alien character because it is strange—not in the sense in which a hitherto unknown human is strange, but in a new and indefinable way. For this indefinable strangeness, the numinosity that the archetype "always possesses" is, in Jungian terms, entirely responsible (Foreword to R. J.

Zwi Werblowsky's *Lucifer and Prometheus* 1952, CW 11:*472*:315). Individual manifestations—the "appropriate symbols"—of the alien share the numinous charge of the underlying archetype, evoking to different degrees the feeling of strangeness. It is important to note that the numinosity of the archetype of the alien is felt, rather than understood intellectually: "At the same time they have a 'specific charge' and develop numinous effects which express themselves as affects" ("Synchronicity: An Acausal Connecting Principle" CW 8:*841*:436). In the discussion of aliens in the letter columns of *Astounding*, the "felt" quality of the strangeness of the aliens accounts for the lack of analysis of their appeal. The appeal of stories involving other topics, on the other hand, could be analyzed rationally, especially by invoking their plausibility and their congruence or otherwise with known scientific fact. Moreover, although "archetypal forms . . . have a numinous quality that sometimes arouses fear" ("The Undiscovered Self," CW10:*530*:272), fear is not the only affect that may be aroused. Because of this, numinosity can account for the different labels attached to the image of the alien. It is, in fact, the trigger for the images of the provider, the guardian or protector, and the companion identified by some psychologists and critics, as well as for the "icon of the monster" (including sapient aliens) identified by Wolfe in *The Known and the Unknown* (1979; 184ff.). Here too, however, is the explanation of the diverse responses of the early readers of *Astounding*. Although there was clearly some satisfaction with the numerous stories about alien invasions (successful or otherwise), reader Gertrude Hemken complained in a letter to the editor after only one year of *Asotunding*'s existence (March 1931) about the frequency with which such hostile aliens appeared: "Here's one point that I don't like: Why are all those invaders from other planets hostile? Why can't they go on an exploring expedition to our Earth?" (424). In fact, the activity of aliens in *Astounding* stories did become much more diverse soon after her letter appeared. Nevertheless, her complaint clearly illustrates the fact that from the beginning there was more than the appeal to the single response of fear at work in the creation and appreciation of aliens.

Finally, the fascination of the Alien is again a sign of its archetypal nature. The strangeness and numinosity of the individual aliens account for the largest part of their fascination. But in part the fascination is also due to the mystery that inevitably surrounds the products of the unconscious, which can never be properly explained: "[T]he archetype represents a profound riddle surpassing our rational comprehension . . . there is some part of its meaning that always remains unknown and defies formulation" (Jacobi 1959, 31). Its mysteriousness arouses our curiosity and keeps our attention focused on it. Moreover, particular manifestations, which may be on a very small scale, undoubtedly represent a source of "concentrated psychic energy" (Jacobi 1959, 75). Readers of science fiction consistently hungered for more stories about aliens: The letter columns of *Astounding/Analog* included repeated expressions of preference for this kind of story and requests for more. Stephen Takacs, in a letter to the editor published in the April 1930 issue of *Astounding*, for example, wrote: "My favorite type of story is the interplanetary one" (130). His letter was one of two in this issue expressing a preference for interplanetary stories. In the next issue (May 1930), Forrest Ackerman, even then a well-known and in some ways an influential member of the science fiction community, exercising the absolute right of every science fiction fan to tell writers and editors what to do, offered in his letter to the editor "some suggestions which I think would improve the magazine. . . . I. Try and have an interplanetary story in each issue" (278). There were occasional expressions of dissent, but letters expressing the preference for interplanetary stories continued to be published fairly frequently throughout the early years. In keeping with the "unconscious" power of the archetype, no reason for preferences was supplied. In spite of the expressed like for such stories and the requests for more, the precise nature of the attraction of the "interplanetary story" was simply not discussed in the early readers' letters, in the way that, for example, the science of so-called interdimensional stories was. For example, although Ackerman, in his previously cited letter, places the need for more "interplanetary stories" first on his list of requirements for improving *Astounding*, he does not explain why it would be more of an improvement than any of the other things he suggests (May 1930, 278). One letter to the editor of *Astounding* does draw attention to the attraction of mystery in connection with science fiction in general: Dale Mullen in his letter to the editor published in the July 1931 issue, after expressing disappointment about a story, requests the writer "to forget all about time and probe the mysteries of the infinitely large and small, of interplanetary space, of future civilization and future warfare" (131). If "the mysteries . . . of interplanetary space" refers to "interplanetary stories" about aliens, this letter could be construed as a reference to part of the fascination of the Alien, but it is not very clear or convincing evidence of it. Overwhelmingly, however, the evidence demonstrates that early readers did not attempt to understand their fascination with the multiple figures of the aliens created by different writers.

The multiplicity, variety, strangeness, and fascination of the Alien in science fiction are clearly accounted for by considering it as an archetype, actualizing itself in symbols. Clearly, too, just as the archetypes of the personal unconscious—the strangers within—are required to order the individual's experience of internal energies, events, and processes which make up the complete Self, so an equal energy is required to order what is experienced by the ego as not part of the Self. Like other archetypes, the Alien as the archetype of OtherSelfness (alterity) has a specific function of ordering human experience. Just as the archetypes of the personal unconscious order the individual's experience of the Self, the archetype of OtherSelfness orders the individual's experience of the OtherSelf. In this way, consequently, it offers a powerful contribution to the ordering of the universe.

THE DYNAMICS OF THE ARCHETYPAL IMPULSE

In Jungian theory, the archetypes of the personal unconscious do not just exist—they require response from the individual whose personal unconscious they inhabit. This is reflected in the interspecies relationships that characterize stories of aliens, for just as they hypothesize that each species in a multispecies galaxy will constitute an autonomous society, science fiction writers also postulate that relationships between the species will be possible. The naming and characterization of the different types of relationships is significant in connection to the archetypal nature of the aliens involved, since the clustering of the images reflects the clustering of responses to the underlying archetype with its characteristic numinosity and ambivalence.

From the beginnings of magazine science fiction, relationships between species have been portrayed as offering a wide range of possibilities, and this range has been commented on by writers and editors on different occasions. As early as 1941, for example, in a letter to John W. Campbell Jr. about one of his own alien stories, Robert Heinlein identifies several kinds of relationship and seeks to increase the range by adding one of his own:

"Creation Took Eight Days" ["Goldfish Bowl"] . . . was intended to give an entirely fresh angle on the invasion-by-alien-intelligence theme. So far as I know, every such story has alien intelligences which treat humans as approximate equals, either as friends or as foes. It is assumed that A[lien]-I[ntelligence] will either be friends, anxious to communicate and trade, or enemies who will fight and kill, or possibly enslave, the human race. There is another and much more humiliating possibility—alien intelligences so superior to us and so indifferent to us as to be almost unaware of us. . . . [T]hey are no threat to us, except that their "engineering" might occasionally disturb our habitat. . . . Some few of them might study us casually—or might not. Some odd duck among them might keep a few of us as pets. (17)

Later, in his 1980 introduction to *Aliens!*, Gardner Dozois says that the variety and multiplicity of aliens in science fiction illustrate that "humans and aliens can interact with one another over a wide spectrum" in which "[s]ometimes they are benevolent space brothers, sometimes sinister monsters. . . . The contact can . . . instruct and uplift us or cast us disastrously down, but it must always affect us, change us, alter our perceptions of ourselves and the universe" (x). Dozois's assessment suffers from the same assumption as Heinlein's that the agents in such interactions are necessarily the aliens: He does not really address the fact that humans may be the sinister alien monsters or that humans may affect and change the aliens, or alter their perceptions of themselves and their universe, even though at least one of the stories he has selected for the anthology demonstrates this point. Nevertheless, he does spell out at least some of the kinds of relationships that may exist. Ursula Le Guin, in the course of her previously mentioned essay "American SF and the Other" (1975, 97), lists the categories as "the sexual Alien, and the social Alien, and the cultural Alien, and finally the racial Alien," but she is not concerned with extraterrestrial aliens as such—her "sexual Alien" is woman seen by man as the Other. Generally speaking, interspecies relationships in the commensality of the galaxy, such as those suggested here, given some degree of knowability with respect to the alien concerned, are derived imaginatively on an ad hoc basis from the observed intraspecies relationships of human beings as groups and as individuals, with some additional material drawn from observation of human-animal and animal-animal relationships. Such relationships across species boundaries cluster according to the general role of the alien in the story and in a given example may be acted out (so to speak) by groups or by individuals. Consequently, just as these observed relationships are influenced by the shifting balance of archetypal processes in the individual observer, so interspecies relationships shift according to the aspect of the archetype that is dominant.

More specifically, however, potential interaction with the alien can, with only two exceptions, be characterized according to two criteria—whether the relationship is amical or inimical and whether it is hierarchical or nonhierarchical. The application of these criteria to aliens creates four clusters of relationships, each relationship casting the alien in a specific role. Within each cluster, the various roles are, however, not determined with taxonomical exactitude, and in some cases they may not be mutually exclusive. Moreover, each such role cluster entails particular kinds of narrative structures or scenarios, some of which have developed what might be called mythic or vested status, and all of which are subject to ironic reversal.

The two exceptions to the criteria for the groups are *investigator* and *examiner (tester)*, which, although hierarchical, can only be determined to be amical or inimical within the context of an individual story. The *investigator* or *examiner* is a key figure in stories of the multispecies galaxy. Implicitly or explicitly in those stories, as I have pointed out, there is a galactic organization, and if there is a galactic organization, there may well logically be something analogous to an entrance exam or initiation rite. Most, if not all, stories deal with the testing of individuals with a view to selection either for their personal advancement or as representatives of humanity. In particular, Clifford D. Simak attacks the question of testing directly. In "Kindergarten" (1953), a mysterious artifact offers gifts to people based on what it "sees" in their minds as they look at or touch it—but only those whose minds reveal peacefulness receive gifts with a particular symbol on it, and these gifts allow the recipients, beginning with the protagonist and the woman he loves, to enter the mysterious alien building associated with the artifact, where, at the end of the story, "side by side, they sat down, waiting for the Teacher" (49); in "Courtesy" (1951), only the young member of the exploration team who has treated the natives with courtesy escapes death when disease strikes the encampment; and in "Immigrant" (1954), the protagonist has to learn humility by becoming a babysitter for alien children before he can begin his education by the adults. Similarly, James White's "Something of Value" (1985) and "Sanctuary" (1988) both show human conduct being tested for a sense of values by or in the presence of aliens. In "Something of Value," an alien visitor walks through the ward of a children's hospital, observing the attitude and conduct of the young doctor in charge toward his incurably physically and mentally challenged patients. In "Sanctuary," an alien who crashes near an isolated convent evaluates humanity's readiness for entry into the galactic community on the basis of the humane and sensible care he receives from the nuns who find him in their basement. The alien presence in these and other stories enables humanity to be evaluated and, depending upon the particular context of a story, either pass magna cum laude or fail miserably.

Within the amical-hierarchical cluster, the Alien manifests in the figures of the *creator*, the *savior*, the *guardian/protector*, the *provider*, the *tutor*, and the *mentor*. Here the alien is superior (in varying degrees, sometimes simply by being more advanced technologically) and benevolent, although whether the actual outcome of the encounter may be considered good for humanity or not may vary considerably—sometimes benevolence means doing nothing at all. The relationship between the figures in this cluster is relatively clear, and their individual presentation relatively unambiguous.

The amical-hierarchical Alien as *creator* is rare. One memorable direct treatment of the Alien as creator of humanity is featured in Eric Frank Russell's "Hobbyist" (1947), where the human protagonist, "tossed into uncharted regions" of the galaxy (110), lands on a planet which appears to be the workshop of the creator of uncountable species of creatures and catches a glimpse of what/who (we are led to believe) that creator is: "a great column of golden haze . . . except that small, intense gleams of silver sparkled within it" (120), which he sees from a closer approach as flaming "like the rising sun or like something drawn from the heart of a sun" (136). As the protagonist, having stolen the fuel he needs from the workshop, leaves in haste, "something nearer the gods" (144) annotates its file on the human species with the comment "moderately successful" (145). In contrast to the somewhat romantic irony of "Hobbyist" is the deprecatingly ironic treatment of human origins in Wallace's "Big Ancestor" (1954), in which the human protagonist's long search for the origin of all the varieties of humanity in the galaxy results in the discovery that they all sprang from a small verminous creature accidentally spread around the galaxy by the ships of a long-dead race unable to exterminate them and who therefore became in a twisted fashion their inadvertent creators. David Brin's "Fortitude" (1996), in contrast to Russell's and Wallace's merely ironic treatment, takes the notion to extremes in a strongly sardonic version in which human beings have evolved through millions of years from the excreted "intestinal flora" (101) of passing aliens. The story of the Alien as *creator*, even with the strongly technological approach and the careful limitation of such a creator to the natural sphere, appears to be almost impossible without irony given science fiction's commitment to scientific understanding of the universe and hence to the principle of evolution.

The amical-hierarchical Alien as *savior* offers more room for variation than the Alien as *creator*. On the one hand, in Damon Knight's "Rule Golden" (1954) the alien Aza-Kra enacts a truly self-sacrificial role as savior by undertaking a dangerous and unpleasant visit to Earth in order to spread a cure for human violence and cruelty around the world, thus saving human beings from themselves and civilizing them to a point where they may be fit to join galactic society.(The cure seeds the population of Earth, beginning in large cities widely separated around the planet, with a virus that re-creates in any aggressor the pain and damage he or she creates in his or her victim.) Knight plays on the literary and cinematic cliché of ill-assorted fugitives on the run and employs highly developed techniques of characterization for human characters and for presenting the extrapolated setting. But the focus of his attention, and the point of interest to which the literary modeling of the story is directed to support, is on his alien protagonist: Aza-Kra. Like Williamson's Mother in "The Moon Era" (1932), Aza-Kra is presented, through the simple descriptive technique of flooding, at the point where the human first-person narrator first encounters him: "The top was about four feet off the floor, a small truncated cone about the size and shape of one of those cones of string that some merchants keep to tie packages. Under that came the eyes, three of them . . . set into a flattened bulb of flesh that just fitted under the base of the cone; there was no nose, no ears, no mouth, and no room for any. The cone was black; the rest of the thing was a very dark, shiny blue-gray" (233–34). Further differentiation from the human is emphasized by the placement of the limbs—"spaced evenly round the body so that you couldn't tell front from back" (234). Aza-Kra's specific otherness of form does not imply in any way the role that he is carrying out in the story, but it is essential to the story that he should be as other as he is. He must be completely alien because only someone completely alien can make humanity completely human. His alterity is not only literal rather than metaphorical, but real, and at the end of the story, when the human first-person narrator is released from the pressure of his own hostility and suspicion caused by the anxiety that he has been unconsciously picking up from Aza-Kra, the full individuality of Aza-Kra is revealed. In the same process as saving humanity, Aza-Kra saves the peaceful and nonviolent galaxy from being overrun by violent and warlike humanity as soon as it achieves space flight, but this consequence does not really detract from his moral and physical heroism as a superior alien. In Eric Frank Russell's "Dear Devil" (1950), on the other hand, although the Martian protagonist sacrifices only his chance to return to his own planet with his visiting shipmates, by staying on as the only adult on Earth (since a plague has wiped out all adult humans) able to guide the few surviving human children to adulthood, he is able to ensure something equally great in terms of the story's future—the survival of the whole human species. In general, the notion of the natural being, even a being of another species, as savior is given greater amplitude and acceptability by historical and mythic instances of such heroic and savior-like behavior within the human species itself. It is a vested scenario that benefits from the numinosity of the Alien.

Like the figure of the *savior*, the amical-hierarchical Alien as *guardian/protector* is also a fairly varied figure, and although sometimes found in nonironic treatments is more often subject to ironic treatments. The *guardian/protector* is also a somewhat more controversial version of the Alien than the savior. Debate on the protector appeared in the letter columns of *Analog* when reader Margaret Howes, in a letter printed in the October 1986 issue, responded to another reader's question about whether "Contact Optimists are driven to their optimism by a need to avoid belief in God" by pointing out that the two are not mutually exclusive: "The answer is no, sorry—at least in a good many cases. I happen to be a Catholic, and a pretty conservative one at that; I have friends who are also religious believers and we, too, will continue to hope that there are other intelligent beings in the universe, unless or until it is proven otherwise" (185–86). Both the suggestion by Plank that the Alien as *protector* is psychologically related to the theological supernatural Other as *protector* and the indication by Howes that the two are distinct (she does not in her letter of October 1986 to *Analog* conflate alien visitors, protectors, or providers with the supernatural beings of the theological system in which she is a believer) are relevant to discussions of the amical-hierarchical Alien. Nevertheless, neither explanation is sufficient to explain it in its entirety, since it is not true of all aliens (not all aliens appear as protector figures), and the attitude of mind which seeks such a protector is not universal among all those who, as writers or readers, find the aliens fascinating. That the classic example of straight treatment of this figure, however, occurs in a novel—Arthur C. Clarke's *Childhood's End* (1953)—underscores the attractiveness of the theory. Almost the whole point of the Overlords' existence is their role as guardian and protector of humanity and of other races in their movement toward the next stage of their evolution: joining with the Overmind. But this blend of mysticism and hard science fiction, although typical of this writer in many of his longer fictions, is not typical of science fiction in general, especially in the magazines. Isaac Asimov's treatment of the Alien as protector in "The Gentle Vultures" (1957), previously discussed, illustrates the ambivalence of science fiction's usual treatment of the Alien in this role. Although it is possible that the relative infrequency of this role in short science fiction results from the limitation on the length of shorter forms of fiction, it is more probable that the line between guardian and owner is too thin for science fiction not to be resistant to the concept of Alien as guardian, given the overwhelming optimism of science fiction in general: Humanity, it is postulated, should be left to look after itself, regardless of potential dangers.

Moreover, if *guardian* and *protector* are linked with *mentor*, then this resistance becomes even more marked, since an increasing sophistication of dealing with "superior" alien mentors can be traced almost chronologically. In an early pair of stories on this theme, Lilith Lorraine's "Jovian Jest" (1930) and Nat Schachner's "He from Procyon" (1934), the authorial stance of both writers toward the concept of vastly superior alien visitors is respectful and uncompromised by irony. By contrast, in a much later pair, Laurence Janifer's "Worldwreckers" (1987) and David Brin's "Shhhh!" (1989), this respect is replaced by an entirely skeptical and pragmatic irony. In Janifer's tale, the human protagonist, on his way to troubleshoot a species-wide infertility problem of another alien race, discusses the superior race with an engaging mixture of respect and scepticism:

> [T]he Kelans being, as I may have been caught saying before, pretty good stand-ins for Wise Beings of the Universe, until and unless some Wiser Beings pop up out of everywhere and into the news. . . . I did not get any good advice from the Kelans on this one. I haven't seen a Kelan in some time, and neither has anybody else. They've gotten snarled up in one of their Passn tournaments, and a little thing like the end of the universe, or universes, wouldn't attract their attention any. (132)

In Brin's story, the main character narrates a series of events that seem to suggest, in his reflection upon them, the possibility that upon the arrival of the alien mentors, which took place at the first contact of humanity with the galactic organization of alien races, a human conspiracy was set up to thwart the inevitable traumatic depression of humanity at being faced with such overwhelming superiority. The conspiracy hints to the aliens that humanity has destroyed all evidence of something specifically human that might prove to these superior aliens that they are not quite so superior after all (which might traumatize *them*, something which humanity is too civilized to do). Humanity, feeling that it has scored a vital point in interspecies relationships with this strategy, can therefore feel quite equal to the rest of the galaxy and can continue to develop without feelings of inferiority. Both the later stories are told in first-person narration, thus closing the writer/narrator distance, and in Brin's story at least, the narrator, although a participant in the events he narrates, is not the major character but merely an observer. Brin's aliens are superior, but this superiority is never immediately felt by the readers since it is always filtered through the narrator who is himself distanced and supported psychologically by the ploy he describes. Consequently, the more sophisticated storytelling ploys of Janifer and Brin act to mute the numinosity of the archetype that underlies the superior alien, but at the same time act to increase the power of the story to affect the reader.

The amical-hierarchical Alien as *provider* is closely related to its appearance as *guardian/protector* and *mentor*. In the same letter as her discussion of the *protector*, and referring to the contact debate, Howes draws attention to the figure of the *provider* when she expresses a concern about the psychological underpinnings of the SETI program: "SETI does remind me far too much of the cargo cults of the South Pacific islanders. An essentially passive program, hoping some Superior Intelligence will contact us and shower us with new ideas and answers for our problems" (186). In addition to doing a probable serious injustice at least to the scientists of SETI if not necessarily also to all their supporters, the image of the provider and the attitude which welcomes it have no solid foundation in science fiction. A survey of stories up to the date of her letter does not support any similar conclusion. The most typical appearance of the alien as *provider* is the alien who figures in the many cautionary fables of which science fiction as a whole is well supplied. In Damon Knight's "Stranger Station" (1956), for example, the alien stranger itself is a figure of the provider, bringing the golden elixir of rejuvenation, but in the process the human intermediary is mentally destroyed. The Monks in Larry Niven's "The Fourth Profession" (1971), bringing a magnificent offering in the form of pills that can instill alien abilities—"starship commander," "alien teleport," "translator for Monks," and "trained assassin" are mentioned (181)—are also provider figures. In both stories, however, the provider provides his offering for a price—and whereas in the former story that price is the sanity and eventually the life of one human for each installment, in the latter it is the requirement that the providers been given a boost on the next leg of their trip, with the destruction of Earth the penalty for failure. Often the apparent provider in magazine stories is the *tutor*, and the lesson he/she/it brings is explicitly spelled out, as in William Morrison's "The Sack" (1950) and Jerry Oltion's "No Strangers Meet on Trails" (1983): Humanity will not be provided for. In the consensus, humanity, as often as not, is shown or told that it must obtain its own knowledge in order to enter the galactic club not as a poor relation existing on handouts but as an equal partner bringing its own endowment for equal exchange.

Within the inimical-hierarchical cluster, the Alien appears in the roles of the *predator*, the *owner*, the *parasite*, and the *jailor/keeper*. In this cluster, however, unlike those in the amical-hierarchical cluster, the figures are peculiarly interdependent and therefore difficult to discuss separately. The most evolutionarily simple of the group is, perhaps, the *predator*. Predation as a metaphor for the relation of one species to another occurs explicitly at the end of Anvil's "Mission of Ignorance" (1968). But in its literal meaning, defined as the taking of another species for food, it is illustrated in Charles R. Tanner's "Tumithak" stories, "Tumithak of the Corridors" (1932) and "Tumithak in Shawm" (1933), in which the alien Shelk, having successfully conquered Earth, collect and keep humans as a form of food animal, whose blood they drink to survive, while the humans become progressively weaker and finally die from repeated blood loss. If early hierarchical aliens retain in their conception vestiges of the supernatural Other, a connection between the entirely natural Shelk and the supernatural figure of the vampire becomes apparent. Tanner's Shelk, however, are merely bloodthirsty natural beings, sapient only by implication in the possession of the technology for their conquest but without any ethical inhibitions about the use of force on other sapient beings—without any consideration of their sapience at all, in fact. Specifically,

Tanner never addresses the issue of sapient food animals in relation to the Shelk draining of human blood. Alien predation on humans also features in Murray Leinster's "Proxima Centauri" (1935) among earlier stories, as well as among later stories such as Mary Kittredge's "Renascence" (1982) and Fergusson and Robson's "Hunting Rights" (1988), but in all of them the concept is raised for its threat-value rather than for any extended discussion of its moral/ ethical implications.

Equally complex is the Alien as *owner*. In Gordon Dickson's story "Enter a Pilgrim" (1974), the conquering alien Aalaag consider conquered humanity as animals to be owned and tamed not as food animals but as animal slaves. They are, moreover, enslaved according to a specific theory of slavery, explicitly spelled out in the story's early pages by one of the Aalaag:

> To conquer is nothing. . . . Anyone with power can conquer. We rule—which is a greater art. We rule because eventually we change the very nature of our cattle. . . . Over their generations we teach them to love us. We tame them into good kine. Beasts still, but broken to obedience. To this end we leave them their own laws, their religions, their customs. Only one thing we do not tolerate—the concept of defiance against our will. And in time they tame to this. . . . Only we know that it is the heart of the beast that must at last be broken. So we teach them first the superiority of our weapons, then of our bodies and minds; finally, that of our law. At last, with nothing of their own left to cling to, their beast-hearts crack; and they follow us unthinkingly, blindly loving and trusting like newborn pups behind their dam, no longer able to dream of opposition to our will. (19–20)

Such ownership might well be considered only a more sophisticated form of predation. What distinguishes the two concepts, however, even more than Dickson's careful establishment of the aliens' intellect (demonstrated in their elaborated theory of conquest *versus* rule) is their moral and ethical characterization of the alien conqueror. Unlike Tanner's Shelk, Dickson's Aalaag are conceived and presented as immensely civilized beings in many ways, and their theory of rule can be understood as a justification of slavery imposed according to a strictly observed code of ethics, however inexcusable or unjustifiable by human standards any form of slavery can be. Like that of Tanner's stories, the scenario of Dickson's story—and of the novel into which it was subsequently developed, *Way of the Pilgrim* (1987)—is that of semisuccessful resistance to the oppressor, which, given the history of the twentieth century over which science fiction has been evolving, is not surprising.

The Alien as *parasite* is sometimes difficult to distinguish from the Alien as *predator* or *owner*. Fortuitously, the scientific nature of parasitism defined in terms suitable for science fiction is explicitly presented in Charles Sheffield's science fiction short story "The Subtle Serpent" (1980) in a discussion among the characters:

> "I wasn't precise enough," said Parker. "You see, I was using the word parasite as a general expression, for anything that lives inside another animal. Most of the things inside the natives are true parasites—they harm the host they live in. But biologically there are really three different situations. There's *parasitism*, the one we usually think about. But there's also *commensalism*, where the host provides a habitat for another animal but isn't harmed by it. We have protozoa in our own alimentary canals that fall into that category—they neither harm nor help us. And finally there's *mutualism*, where the host and the animal that live inside it are something dependent on each other, with a relationship that benefits both of them. . . . Most people mean mutualism when they talk about symbiosis." (229; original emphasis)

Ironically, however, in Sheffield's story it is not clear (at least, not to his human protagonists) if the alien is truly sapient. In many other stories, such as Roger Dee's "Unwelcome Tenant" (1950), Frederik Pohl's "We Purchased People" (1974), and Spider Robinson's "User Friendly" (1986), matters are complicated in a number of ways because the owner-occupier is nonmaterial. In addition, although Pohl's aliens own their hosts, having "purchased" them, their original owners (so to speak) are other humans (i.e., humans other than the hosts themselves):

> After concluding the planned series of experimental procedures, which were duly recorded, the purchased person known as Carolyn Schoerner was no longer salvageable. Appropriate entries were made. The Probation and Out-Service department of the Meadville Women's Reformatory was notified that she had ceased to be alive. A purchasing requisition was initiated for a replacement, and her account was terminated. (157)

Pohl clearly expects a response to the fact that, regardless of the outcome of a particular instance of use, use always involves a violation of the civil rights of the hosts, and human as well as alien ethics are clearly an issue. His aliens, however, are true parasites—destructive of their hosts to a greater or lesser degree. Robinson's aliens, on the other hand, merely borrow humans temporarily for longer or shorter periods, without the intervention of civil authorities or bureaucrats, and the effect of his parasites on their hosts as revealed in the story itself is inconvenient but not necessarily destructive. The aliens in both these stories are, although present only nonmaterially, genuinely alien. Greg Bear's "Blood Music" (1983) complicates the matter even further, since the aliens inhabiting the protagonist's body as parasites are his own gengineered cells, evolved to sapience as a new species as a result of his own experiments, but eventually destroying their host after copying his mind into their own bioware. The genuine parasite resembles the blood-sucking alien. Just as the early hierarchical aliens retain vestiges of the supernatural other through such resemblances as that between the blood-feeding alien and the vampire, so there is also a resemblance between various forms of parasitic/symbiotic invasion and the concept of the vampire. In "The Pork Chop Tree" (1965), however, James Schmitz offers a reversal of the common pattern of parasitism in interspecies relationships: The tree turns the humans who invade its planet into blind helpless creatures crawling about in its branches unable to leave and so unable to injure it. Characteristically, in these stories of parasitic aliens the scenario is that of hopeless resistance, where there can be any resistance at all—there is no overthrow of the alien, whether actual or foreshadowed, at the end.[8]

The strength of the revulsion against the Alien as *parasite/owner* is highlighted by the fact that whereas the parasitic alien is quite common, the symbiont, its amical and nonhierarchical equivalent, is hard to find in short stories. The classic story of the alien symbiont is, like the classic story of the alien protector, a novel: Hal Clement's *Needle* (1950), although like many novels of this vintage it first appeared as a two-part serial in *Astounding* (May and June 1949). There are also other more recent examples, including Clement's much later sequel to *Needle*, entitled *Through the Eye of a Needle* (1978), and Warren Norwood and Ralph Myliu's *The Seren Cenacles* (1983). Among the short stories involving symbiosis, according to Sheffield's definitions, however, the aliens and humans in Michael Coney's "Symbiote" (1969) exist in a true state of mutualism, for although the aliens certainly have the upper hand in the relationship and are externally parasitic, they cannot exist at all easily without their hosts, and both (at least initially) benefit from the association. In this particular story the scenario includes more or less successful resistance to the oppressor, although this is not true of all stories of the Alien as parasite and owner, and it might be inferred from the story that even symbiosis resembles ownership too closely for humans to find it acceptable. Even in what might be considered the classic short story about the symbiont, Octavia Butler's "Bloodchild" (1984), the alien symbiont is perilously close to parasitism, although the physical invasion by the symbiont is only intermittent. Moreover, the single example of a relationship in which the result is destructive of the host does not affect the protagonist personally and is explicitly presented as an accident—and the ongoing relationship between the alien and the human protagonist is clearly deep, warm, and abiding in spite of such accidents. The late appearance of this more ambivalent, less clear-cut concept is perhaps indicative of continuing human ambivalence toward anything invasive of the body—an ambivalence similar to that which largely characterizes the thinking of the characters in the story itself.

The Alien as *keeper* is a variant of the Alien as *owner* that is less charged and ambivalent than the Alien as *parasite* or even *symbiont*. In Bertram Chandler's "The Cage" (1957), for example, human survivors of a crashed spaceship are mistakenly collected like animals and put in a zoo, their sapience only revealed to their captors by their own capture and caging of a small animal that enters their cage, for "only rational beings . . . put other beings in cages" (535). In Reginald Bretnor's "Without (General) Issue" (1981), too, the aliens, having mistakenly captured an all-male human crew as specimens, release them out of pity because they fail to breed in captivity and must therefore—as the aliens mistakenly see it—be unhappy. In Robert Silverberg's "Collecting Team" (1957), however, there is no error and no release: The human team of animal specimen collectors is itself collected by an alien species that, it is implied, enjoys collecting sapients. Chandler and Bretnor both present their stories with a certain amount of humor, and Silverberg employs a fairly ironic tone so that the humor serves to distance the threat. Stories where humor is not used in presenting the alien in what might appear as a keeper's role relegate the alien to the role of owner.

In hierarchical relationships, whether amical or inimical, the sapience of the aliens is not usually explored in detail or made an issue of. Their activities, for good or ill, are usually obvious (even painfully obvious), but their nature is at the very least enigmatic—if not actually completely incomprehensible. Ironically, therefore, although their superiority might be assumed to produce a clarification or a demonstration of the nature of sapience in an enhanced form, what their depiction actually tells us about is often disappointingly minimal.

Within the amical-nonhierarchical cluster, the Alien manifests in the figures of the *companion* and the *cohabitant*. The figures in this cluster, however, unlike those in the hierarchical clusters, are independent. Although they too raise a series of morally and ethically problematic issues, they do so on a story-by-story basis, not as a group. The scenarios in which they appear are scenarios of encounters between autonomous species, although there may be technological and other developmental differences.

The figure of the *cohabitant* (an awkward term, although no better seems to be available, for species existing side by side in the galaxy without any qualification of the relationship or in a neutral relationship) appears in stories of generalized interspecies relationships, especially in multispecies galaxies. The member species of the ConSentiency as portrayed in Herbert's "The Tactful Saboteur" (1964) and of Jack Chalker's "In the Wilderness" (1978) illustrate the nature of cohabitation. Typically the Alien as cohabitant is characteristic of the type of science fiction described as "space opera" (see Monk, "Not Just 'Cosmic Skulduggery'"), and, although there are exceptions such as Herbert's PanSpechi Panthor Bolin, most cohabitants appear as LGMs (little green men). Cohabitation among species describes a relationship of more or less equals— cohabitants appear as allies in war; trade partners in peace; and collaborators in science, technology, and exploration; as well as appearing in many other political and social relationships that parallel those of intraspecies group and individual relationships.

The figure of the Alien as *companion* might be considered a special case of the Alien as *cohabitant*, in that the *companion* often appears in a story in which there is a multispecies galaxy in the background. The figure of the *companion*, however, is a consideration of a personal and individual relationship between members and encompasses variants as diverse as those of the protagonist and the Mother in Jack Williamson's "Moon Era" (1932), the protagonist and Tweel in Stanley Weinbaum's "Martian Odyssey" (1934), and the protagonist and Bunundig in Robert Chilson's "The Hand of Friendship" (1983), although in the last of these, as previously noted, the concept of companion is considerably shifted by the alien nature of Bunundig's species. The precedence in the creation of individualized and plausible individual aliens belongs to Jack Williamson for the alien story "The Moon Era." Of this story, Isaac Asimov said, in introducing it in his anthology *Before the Golden Age* (1974), "Once in those early years, however, I recall being really moved by the relationship between a man and a woman as pictured in a science fiction story. It is perhaps inevitable that the woman involved wasn't really a woman. . . . I fell in love with the Moon woman whom Williamson called the 'Mother'" (320–21). Other than the fact that she has no name (which is entirely explicable within the terms of the story, since she is the only surviving member of her people and the mother of all those who will come after), the Mother could well be the first potentiated alien. She is not a physical clone: The precise nature of her form is not integral to the needs of the story, but it is both alien and beautiful, as I have previously argued, as well as feminine. Psychologically, too, Williamson offers us someone who is not a clone: Although she is "the Mother," her motherhood is alien in nature, for her children are to be the myriad members of the next generation of neuter workers of her hive civilization. Yet the barrier between the human and the alien is breached by recognizable behavior—she cares for the injured human and she cooperates and associates with him as he attempts to care for her and returns her cooperation. At the end of the story, the reader, like the human protagonist, must grieve for the loss of a companion. Williamson's writerly approach here goes beyond simple otherness to achieve a genuine albeit otherness that closely approaches alterity. The concept of the Alien as companion is sometimes interpreted by those outside the genre as a sign of human weakness, but within the genre it is highly regarded and very frequent. There is a fine distinction in concept, moreover, between the companion and the mentor or guardian, a distinction that is often blurred in practice by either writer or reader.

Within the *inimical-nonhierarchical* cluster, the Alien manifests in the figures of the *enemy* and the *rival*. The figures in this cluster, however, like those in the amical-nonhierarchical cluster, are independent of each other and raise issues on a similar story-by-story basis. They differ, however, in that both the enemy and the rival can offer either sociopolitical relationships or personal relationships. The figure of the Alien as *enemy* is the focus of alien invasion stories from the earliest days of the magazines, as in Ray Cummings's "Wandl the Invader" (1932), but it persists in such later stories as Kevin O'Donnell's "Low

Grade Ore" (1977), in which hostile aliens raid Earth to steal human children to incorporate them as intelligent ship systems in their spaceships. The Alien as *rival* figures to considerable effect in Gordon Dickson's "3-Part Puzzle" (1962), in which humans, newly emerged into a galaxy divided between numerous Submissive and Conqueror species (with other species known as Invulnerables sitting on the sidelines), come into competition with a Conqueror species known as the Mologhese but refuse to acknowledge the "gentlemen's agreement" about the relationships between different Conqueror species; this refusal casts doubt on the humans' status as Conquerors, but when the Mologhese consider treating them as Submissives and conquering them, the Invulnerables intervene for the first time in known history and forbid it.

In these nonhierarchical relationships, whether amical or inimical, the sapience of the aliens is often explored in detail or made an issue. The nature of sapience itself may be foregrounded—even discussed explicitly. By contrast with the presentation of sapience in hierarchical relationships, moreover, the presentation of it in nonhierarchical relationships can be, although is not always, a significant contribution to the consensus hypothesis on alien sapience.

In the relationships that are postulated between species, since the archetypes are "living" figures with which the conscious mind of the individual can and should interact, the archetypal nature of the Alien is also unmistakably reflected. On the one hand, the amical-inimical dichotomy reflects the ambivalence of the underlying archetype with its "positive, favourable, bright" and "negative and unfavourable, partly chthonic" sides (Jung, "The Phenomenology of the Spirit in Fairytales" CW 9(i):*413*:226). The Alien resembles, in this duality, the archetypes of the personal unconscious, of whom P. W. Martin writes in *Experiment in Depth*:

> The nature of these beings is one of manifold ambivalence. They are infantile, undeveloped, semi-animal, semi-reptile even, and at the same time, semi-divine. They are completely indispensable and an insufferable nuisance. They have immense energy, extraordinary insight; and (so long as no adequate relationship is made with them) they will endeavour to use this energy and insight to run the man their own way—which will not be his way. They are immensely wise and can give the worst possible advice. They can be the truest guides and the most arrant deceivers. They are the light and the darkness, inspiration and madness, the new life and a perpetual distraction. Only as and when they take

their proper place in relationship to consciousness do they carry out their true function as part of the whole. (72–73)

On the other hand, the hierarchical-nonhierarchical dichotomy reflects, although less obviously, the numinosity of the archetype. The more "superior" or powerful the alien is, the less differentiated is the actualized archetypal symbol from the underlying unactualized archetype, and hence the greater portion it retains of the archetype's numinous charge, so that they are "felt as strange, uncanny, and at the same time fascinating" and "seem alien, as if they came from outside" (Jung, "The Psychological Foundation of Belief in Spirits" CW 8:591:311–12). It is therefore easy to identify in each of the relationships a particular actualized aspect of the underlying unactualized archetype. In hierarchical relationships, the symbols of the benevolent alien (creators, guardians, mentors) actualize the light side of the underlying archetype; the symbols of the malevolent alien (predators, owners, parasites) actualize its chthonic dark side. In both types, the greater numinosity makes a response more difficult for the writer. Typically, therefore, the numinosity of the former group is distanced and filtered through irony, whereas the numinosity of the latter shapes narratives of hopelessness and fear. By contrast, the nonhierarchical alien is more differentiated from the underlying archetype and partakes of relatively less of its numinosity: The figures of the companion, the cohabitant, the rival, and the enemy are nearer the personal—they still feel strange, but not overwhelmingly so, and they allow a much greater range of response.

The archetype of alterity and of the OtherSelf is, however, a new archetype. It is different qualitatively from our understanding of the natural Other (human strangers) and the supernatural Other. Its appearance in science fiction, moreover, is peculiarly appropriate: Science fiction is the literature that most closely resonates with science, and it is science that has produced the circumstances which make the emergence of the new archetype both necessary and possible.

CONCLUSION

Behind the multiplicity and variety of the aliens who have trooped through science fiction since the earliest days stands the archetype of the Alien—the OtherSelf—with all its numinous power and fascination. Fueled by the unconscious energies of the deepest reaches of the human mind, shaped by the powerful drive for order and meaning which characterizes all human activity—and in particular scientific and artistic activity—the Alien of science fiction, examined in both its worst and its best examples and properly understood, offers an unparalleled opportunity for examining what humans think about what it means to be human and, equally importantly, whether whatever it is that makes us human might be manifest in other nonhuman forms elsewhere. The psychological need for a representative "Not-I" for the "I" of humanity to measure itself against is, once defined by science, ultimately what drives the creation of the science fiction Alien. For in the visionary creation of the Alien, writers of science fiction, as writers of all fiction, poetry, and drama have always done, envision human potential, and envisioning human potential in the context of the universe as the new millennium approached required that humanity be envisioned not merely as an evolved being but also as, just possibly, one among many species of evolved beings.

NOTES

1. Jung himself does touch on the mind-body topic in an early paper, although he is careful to point out that the relationship is not yet clear:

> I consider the idea of reciprocal action tenable, and can see no reason to prejudice its credibility with the hypothesis of psychophysical parallelism. To the psychotherapist, whose special field lies just in this crucial sphere of the interaction of mind and body, it seems highly probable that the psychic and the physical are not two independent parallel processes, but are essentially connected through reciprocal action, although the actual nature of this relationship is still completely outside our experience. (Jung, "On Psychic Energy" CW 8:13:17–18)

2. I use this rather old-fashioned term instead of the more recent and common *metanarrative*, since the latter seems not yet to have achieved a settled level of application, so that science and history are both referred to as *metanarratives* independently, whereas *cosmology* includes both science and history.

3. I have discussed the relevance of Wilson's work to the construction of the alien mind and the subsequent discussion about it in chapter 4.

4. *Numinosum* is the term used by Jung in *Psychology and Religion*, where he defines it as "a dynamic agency or effect not caused by an arbitrary act of will. On the contrary, it seizes and controls the human subject, who is always rather its victim than its creator. The *numinosum* . . . is an experience of the subject, independent of his will . . . either a

quality belonging to a visible object or the influence of an invisible presence that causes a peculiar alteration of consciousness" (CW 11:6:7).

5. "Something that stands for, represents, or denotes something else (not by exact resemblance, but by vague suggestion, or by some accidental or conventional relation); *esp.* a material object representing or taken to represent something immaterial or abstract, as a being, idea, quality, or condition; a representative or typical figure, sign, or token" (*OED2*).

6. He also insists that "a view which interprets the symbolic expression as an intentional paraphrase or transmogrification of a known thing is *allegoric*" (CW 6:*814*:474).

7. Wells's description continues: "There was something fungoid in the oily brown skin, something in the clumsy deliberation of their tedious movements unspeakably terrible. Even at this first encounter, this first glimpse, I was overcome with disgust and dread" (24–25). The phrases "unspeakably terrible" and "overcome with disgust and dread" suggest an early occurrence of Shaw's "arachnid reaction."

8. A striking exception to this is Robert Heinlein's *The Puppet Masters*, which first appeared in serial form in *Galaxy* (September, October, and November 1951).

Conclusion:
The Archetype, the Alien,
and the Human

"Thing about aliens is, they're alien," reflects Killeen in Greg Benford's *Great Sky River* (1987, 318). Yet, paradoxically, it is precisely because aliens are alien that they are present here and now in science fiction. As archetype and as trope, the Alien carries implications for human nature in general and for the genre of which it is a major concept. Through the archetype we—*we* here meaning humanity[1]—can hypothesize our place in the universe in the form of a "humanity myth," and speculation about sapient aliens therefore becomes more than merely a scientifically imaginative exercise in literary form. Through the trope, science fiction presses its claim to be a uniquely transgressive literary form, for here science fiction transgresses the ultimate boundary—the boundary between the known and the unknown—since the creation of any alien, however well or badly done, is a transgression of the limits of the knowledge of the human Self as a sapient being—a trespass into the unknown OtherSelf.

As archetype, the Alien (the archetype of alterity—the OtherSelf) in the narratives of science fiction focuses speculation on the nature of sapient beings. Given the parallel between biological and psychological narrativization of the life of the individual and the life of the species, or "how the microhistory of the individual is grafted on to the macrohistory of our species" (Stevens, *Archetype Revisited* 2003, x), the science-fictional Alien therefore also offers, for those who will take account of it, a new humanity myth. In this humanity myth is incorporated a necessary prosecution of the process of human species entelechy, a necessary validation of the human species as a uniquely sapient species, a key to the implications of a changed understanding of the nature of humanity, and a necessary *mythologem* of human status in the universe. The science-fictional Alien, is, consequently, what makes possible the next stage of evolutionary thinking—a new kind of self-awareness in human beings of humanity as a species.

The humanity myth's necessary prosecution of the process of human species entelechy derives from the principle of evolution. In order to understand the full value of the science-fictional Alien in human experience, therefore, it is necessary to look at the parallel that exists between the individual (a unitary organism) and the species (a collective organism) as the biological life (process of existence through time) of each is described. Misia Landau's definition of *narrative* in her preface to *Narratives of Human Evolution* (1991) is that "[a]ny account of a sequence of events—so that it manifests 'a deeper kind of belonging'—is a form of narrative" (ix).[2] Since the life-processes of both individual and species consist of sequences of events, in description they inevitably form narratives. Once narrativized, the analogies between the events in both sequences become more obvious, and casual metaphoric references become susceptible of more legitimate application.

As early as Aristotle, however, it was noticed that the end result of growth in unitary biological organisms was not random but identifiable as the way in which the potential of the organism in its initial state became actual in the final state of the same organism. Aristotle's term for the final state of the organism was *entelecheia* (entelechy): The *entelecheia* of the caterpillar is the butterfly. In subsequent use, the application of the term seems to have shifted from the final changed state to the process of change by which that final state comes about—"that which gives perfection to anything; the informing spirit" (*COED2*)—so that *entelechy* becomes the process by which the potential in a living organism becomes actual.

It is in this dynamic sense that Jung selects the term to express the development of the Self within the psyche of the individual, at the same time extending its original application in the biology (*soma*) of all organisms to a new one in the psychology (*psyche*) of the human organism. The Self, as he explains it in "The Psychology of the Child Archetype," is his term for the transcendent psyche of the individual: "I have called this wholeness that transcends consciousness the 'self'" (CW 9(i):*278*:164). In another paper, "The

Holy Men of India," the complex process by which the individual achieves wholeness is defined as the "entelechy of the self" (CW 11:960:583), which "with few exceptions . . . consists in a succession of endless compromises, ego and self labouriously keeping the scales balanced if all is to go well" (CW 11:960:583), and to which all archetypes (personal and transpersonal) and all archetypal images contribute, each fulfilling a specific function. Significantly, moreover, in his discussion of the "entelechy of the Self" at this point, Jung also speaks of the "evolving Self" ("The Holy Men of India" CW 11:960:583), evoking a parallel between entelechy and evolution. Consequently, if the analogy between the species and the individual holds, it is possible to speak of evolution as the entelechy of the species.

The prosecution or forwarding of this entelechy of the human species in the humanity myth is the function of the archetype of alterity in the form of the science-fictional Alien. If we are evolving, rather than evolved, then this new "psychological"evolution must continue until the process is complete. In the magazine stories of alien contact, humans are nearly always presented as an evolved species—not significantly different from what they are now (there are a few notable exceptions, such as Arthur C. Clarke's *Childhood's End*, 1953, in which the future evolution of humanity is the direct thematic focus of the novel, whose title is itself a striking illustration of the metaphorical analogy, previously noted, between the life of the individual and the existence of the species). Similarly, aliens are usually considered as evolved, rather than evolving, species. It has been suggested in science fiction more than once, moreover, that once humanity stopped eliminating the weakest individuals from the species by allowing them to die or even by killing them off, evolution in the sense of "survival of the fittest" halted. Nevertheless, humans in general, at some point in the physical and psychological evolution of the species, stopped eliminating the weakest individuals because they began to think and feel that such behavior was "wrong" in a way that it had not seemed previously, as if a hitherto latent factor had actualized—or evolved. Evolution had switched lanes, so to speak, from the merely physical (which is now, in a very real sense—with the advent of such things as genetic engineering and reproduction technology—on the verge of becoming almost a matter of choice) to the psychological, which is still largely involuntary. The entelechy of the species continues psychologically, and, for those who are living through it and feeling its effect in the increasing multiplicity of psychological problems and ethical dilemmas, it is probably just as painful as the process of physical evolution was for our earlier forebears.

The humanity myth's second use is to offer necessary validation of the human species as sapient—uniquely sapient as far as terrestrial species are concerned—by showing us what sapience looks like by manifesting the archetype of alterity as science-fictional aliens. When we look at an alien we do not look at our own Self—we look at someone who is not our Self. It will have to be like us in those things we know as essentials of our Self in order for us to be able to recognize it as a Self, but sufficiently different to provide us with the necessary experience of at least acknowledging the existence and the nature of a Self that is not our own. This experience is necessary because, just as a child needs the validation of others (particularly parents) in order to develop fully as a unique individual and the adult needs the validation of other adults to remain fully functional as an individual, humanity as a species needs validation provided by the concept of the Alien to develop fully as a sapient species in the absence of actual other sapient species. But what precisely *sapient* means with reference to human beings (and hence to the aliens that humans imagine) is still very much in doubt.

When Darwin proclaimed evolution as the ordering principle of cosmology, the old hierarchical order as the majority of humans understood it, which had depended upon the presence of a divine creator, was interrupted. If the publication of *On the Origin of Species by Natural Selection* in 1858 created a storm of protest, the subsequent publication of *The Descent of Man and Selection in Relation to Sex* (1859), with its claim that humans were derived from apelike stock, raised the disturbance to hurricane level. At whatever level of consciousness people understood it, the old system of cosmology had installed human beings in a unique position, the image and representative of God on earth, superior to all other created beings and qualitatively different from them in kind. The new system erased human uniqueness and superiority. Since Darwin's announcement, therefore, humanity has been subject to a process of repeated self-examination, which has had the effect of sorting through human characteristics in an effort to identify the single element that would be *the* critical factor in accounting for the difference between human and nonhuman: something that could be described as *the Sapience Factor*.

In the century and a half since Darwin, the Sapience Factor has been a moving target for searchers. As popularly understood, it was initially thought of in terms of the cumulative results of physical mutation, singly or in combination (e.g., larger cranial capacity *and* opposable thumbs *and* upright stance). This concept did not remain satisfactory for very long: Physical development was clearly necessary to the evolution of sapience, but by itself it was not sufficient to make the critical difference. The search soon switched to differences in behavioral activities (e.g., tool-making and using fire), but subsequent observation showed that other animals can make and use tools although in a less-sophisticated way. The greater sophistication of human as opposed to animal tool use and tool-making is clearly indicative of the existence of a difference between human and nonhuman, but because some form of it exists in other species, it could not be considered to constitute the critical difference. The emphasis then shifted to more abstract capacities such as the use of symbols, and specifically to the uniqueness or otherwise of the human use of language. The search slackened, without coming to a standstill, and a new possibility emerged late in the process. Merlin Donald set out to "reflect upon the most likely scenario of human cognitive emergence":

> I consider data from many disciplines, and on this evidential base I propose a specific hypothesis on the origins of the modern human mind. Although archaeological and anthropological data provide crucial insights, the main event is on the level of cognitive evolution; cognition is the mediator between brain and culture and therefore must have been the engine, as well as the locus, of change. (*Origins of the Modern Mind* 1991, 2)

In his scenario, he bypasses language as the critical factor and asserts that

> if we compare the complex representational architecture of the modern mind with that of the ape, we must conclude that the Darwinian universe is too small to contain humanity. We are a different order.... Our genes may be largely identical to those of a chimp or gorilla, but our cognitive architecture is not. And having reached a critical point in our cognitive evolution, we are symbol-using, networked creatures, unlike any that went before us. Regardless of whether our current chronological framework is verified or radically changed by future research, this much is not speculation: humans are utterly different. (382)

Through the powerful arguments set out in this book, Donald clearly seeks to reinstate the unique and superior status of humanity but without giving up Darwin completely. For Donald, humans are a different order from even the highest order previously included in the Darwinian schema ("the order of Pri-mates"), but this new order is an order of which humans are the only mem-bers, and the differentiation between this new order and that older "order of Primates" is qualitative not quantitative. New and different "complex repre-sentational architecture" is a new and different—and fascinating—version of the Sapience Factor.

The distinction between animal and human as Donald defines it has im-plications for the science-fictional Alien. The adoption of some combination of the early criteria by science fiction writers into the rules-of-thumb test for sapience referred to previously is a tribute to the successful spread of scientific thinking into at least part of the general population. But even in the short sto-ries of the magazines, additional twists are often introduced, whether ironi-cally (for example, in the form of Larry Niven's suggestion, in "The Fourth Profession," 1971, that humans might not be considered truly sapient unless they could build a laser cannon to launch a spaceship) or more seriously (for example, in the form of Damon Knight's suggestion of a requirement for greater empathy, in "Rule Golden" 1954): The rules of thumb are, as I have ar-gued, necessary but not sufficient. Since science fiction writers, with few sig-nificant exceptions, continue to reference established scientific thinking about human sapience in order to shape the sapient alien, what Donald argues may well prove of importance in the development of science-fictional theories of the sapient alien, not by complete abandonment of the old rules of thumb but by bringing into play the entirely new concept of "cognitive architecture" or "complex representational architecture" in a science-fictional guise. As a re-sult, the assimilation into science fiction of advanced theory of human sapi-ence sophisticates the science-fictional Alien, because the more we learn about our own sapience, the more we can imagine about how the sapience of the alien might work. For if there is a Sapience Factor, it will necessarily, until proven otherwise, characterize the OtherSelf as well as the Self.

The archetype of the OtherSelf, which has come into existence cotermi-nously with the principle of evolution and the theories of the Sapience Factor, offers us a key to the implications of a changed understanding of the nature of humanity. The emergence of a new archetype is acceptable in Jung's theory: New archetypes can and do arise, although the reason for their emergence is not fully identified. Jung says that "[it] is very probable that the activation of an archetype depends on an alteration of the conscious situation, which requires a new form of compensation" ("A Psychological Approach to the Dogma of the Trinity" CW 11:*223*:68). If the change in mind-model that took place following the introduction of the evolutionary principle—as generally understood—constitutes such an alteration in the conscious situation, particularly in the present circumstances of the astrophysical search for ETI (extraterrestrial intelligence), then the Alien may well have come into consciousness from the unconscious as an image actualizing unconscious archetypal compensation. The ongoing choice to construct the Alien imaginatively in fiction is one means to stabilize and deal with the uncertainty of change.

The needs and responses invoked in compensation for change in the human situation can best be explained through an understanding of the concept of "complementarity"—a key concept in the psychiatric theory of R. D. Laing, himself an admirer of Jung. In Laing's discussion of complementarity in *Self and Others* (1970), the acknowledgment of "you"—that is, of the other independent self—is as important to the individual's mental equilibrium as understanding the inner unconscious Self is to him or her in the psychology of Jung. What Laing says about the self in relation to others, therefore, has considerable implications for any consideration of the science-fictional Alien. Complementarity, the essential function of the other according to Laing, defines "that function of personal relations whereby the other fulfils or completes self" (*Self and Others* 1970, 66–67). Being complemented by the other reinforces individual boundaries: "Every relationship implies a definition of self by other and other by self" (69). Interactions between human beings confirm the identities of those concerned: "Any human interaction implies some measure of confirmation. . . . The slightest sign of recognition from another at least confirms one's presence in *his* world" (82; original emphasis). If the individual may stand synecdochically for the species, what applies in the case of the human individual can be held to be true for the human species, even though the boundary between the human species and the other species is as yet purely a hypothesis. Laing himself implies that this hypothetical nature need not be an obstacle when, at the outset of his discussion of the Self and the Other, he writes: "In accounts of experience and action in imagination, dream, and phantasy, it is always necessary to extend our account explicitly or by implication to a whole 'nexus' of others, imaginary, dreamed, phantasied, or real" (65). Real or hypothetical, therefore, the OtherSelf, in Laing's view, complements, confirms, and defines the boundaries between Self and Other, and it is possible to extend this mutual confirmation of existence and identity beyond the individual. Moreover, the reciprocity of relationship in Laing—between Self and OtherSelf—implies an equality of relationship in which selfness may be considered a psychological analogue of sapience. The science-fictional Alien, in all its multifariousness, strangeness, and fascination, can be seen in Laingian terms as a manifestation that predicts the possibility of species definition by boundaries between human and nonhuman people, and at the same time allows for the confirmation of human-people identity by nonhuman people. Paradoxically, *alien* gives *human* meaning.

Conversely, *human* gives *alien* meaning—or at least new meaning. For much of human history, the other has been defined by being different—strange—a stranger. Traditionally, the response followed a primitive pattern: *see the stranger, fear the stranger, hate the stranger, kill the stranger.* Sometimes, however, as Ursula Le Guin points out in "American SF and the Other" (1975), the process has been begun and continued by actively creating difference where no difference exists: "If you deny any affinity with another person or kind of person, if you declare it to be wholly different from yourself—as men have done to women, and class has done to class, and nation has done to nation—you may hate it, or deify it; but in either case you have denied its spiritual equality, and its human reality. You have made it into a thing" (99).[3] By postulating, understanding, and acknowledging the selfness of the Alien and by then comparing it across species boundaries to our own selfness, we transcend the superficialities of difference in form and culture by understanding that the selfness of the Alien, like the selfness of the human, constitutes the measure of sapience shared by human and alien. We cannot deny the selfness/sapience of the Other without denying our own selfness/sapience.

Our knowledge of our selfness/sapience and of our nature as a species are now a part of our cosmology—the ordered accumulation of our information about the universe. That knowledge is, possibly, the most important single factor in that cosmology, although the fact that it has come into being in the years leading up to the recent chronological transition we call the millennium is, of course, merely a coincidence. What was important about the millennium and particularly about its accompanying "millennial anxiety" was not what it was but what it revealed about the presence of the irrational in the everyday life and thinking of human beings.[4] I use the word *irrational* here without prejudice and nonpejoratively in the sense that Jung himself uses it: "not as

denoting something contrary to reason, but something beyond reason, something, therefore, not grounded on reason" ("Definitions. 36. Irrational" cw
6:774:454). It is in terms of the irrational in human makeup that the significance of OtherSelf, the archetype of alterity, in human cosmology must be examined.

The idea that the irrational, however carefully defined, is a normal part of
humanity's psychological makeup may not be particularly welcome within the
rational confines of science fiction. Nevertheless, as I argued in the first chapter, the science-fictional Alien has antecedents in the supernatural and magic
Other of tradition. Moreover, the unconscious impulses that gave rise to the
supernatural and magic Other do not disappear with the development of scientific rationalism, and, indeed, they should not. As Jung points out: "[O]ur
modern attitude looks back arrogantly upon the mists of superstition or
primitive credulity, entirely forgetting that we carry the whole living past in
the lower storeys of the skyscraper of rational consciousness. Without the
lower storeys our mind is suspended in mid air. No wonder it gets nervous"
("Psychology and Religion" cw 11:56:35). The irrationality that allowed the
expression of the instinct for numinous otherness in the supernatural and
magic Other was not replaced, but intensified and redirected by the actualization of the OtherSelf—its emergence as a trope in science fiction.

The narratives of science fiction, in which the trope of the OtherSelf figures
so prominently and powerfully, emerged as a genre and, as readers today generally understand the term science fiction, almost entirely in the popular magazines in the earliest decades of the twentieth century and later expanded to
include the novel form. From this beginning, over the almost century of the
existence of the magazines, the brief and often one-shot notional concepts of
the sapient alien—a sketchy version of another kind of sapient being in an illustrative situation of some sort, but modeled according to roughly agreed
physical parameters and shaped by the application of understood rules of
thumb—begin to pull together into what I have described as *the consensual
hypothesis of alterity*. As isolated and scattered suggestions, the particular assumptions and theories of numerous writers in individual short stories or
groups of texts of whatever length remain relatively uninformative; if assem-
bled, ordered, and examined as a coherent body of information, however, they
offer insight into the nature of sapience as well as the nature of science fiction.
This insight represents a substantial proposition not merely about human

sapience in particular (although this is an important part of it) but also about the nature of sapience universally.

Narrative is the mode by which we interpret data and explain things to ourselves and to each other. Stephen Jay Gould says:

> We are storytelling animals and cannot bear to acknowledge the ordinariness of our daily lives (and even of most events that, in retrospect seem crucial to our fortunes or our history). We therefore retell actual events as stories with moral messages, embodying a few limited themes, that narrators through the ages have cultivated for their power to interest and to instruct. (*Wonderful Life* 1989, 70)

The events of inner life are actual events, and when we interpret the non-physical, nonobjective elements of human nature and inner life, we employ not the rational narratives of science but the irrational narratives of mythology and their associated and derived forms such as fiction (which is a manifestation of the irrational unconscious and autonomous creative impulse shaped by the rational discipline of the conscious mind). Although he uses a more restricted definition of the content of mythology than mine, in the course of arguing for the use of *mythology* rather than *myth* in his *Prolegomena* to Jung and Kerenyi's *Essays on a Science of Mythology* (1949), Carl Kerenyi introduces the term *mythologem* as "the best Greek word for . . . tales already well known but not unamenable to further reshaping" (3). In the sense that the actualization of the archetype of alterity is a tale already (at this time) well-known, and recognizing that it has been and is still being subject to further reshaping, it is possible therefore to consider the multiple stories about the archetype of alterity in the forms of the science-fictional Alien as *mythologomena* that together constitute a coherent mythology.

We are, however, dealing with a new extension of the mythology we have previously known, one that accommodates more responsively the stage of evolution that the human species has reached in its ongoing entelechy. This stage is characterized by the need to integrate the irrational elements of the psyche more closely with the rational—to remake the figure of the Other we have always known as a counterpart of our Self into a new and more valid counterpart of our new understanding of our Self as a sapient being. This understanding of the Self must remain psychologically active and maintain, according to Jung, a "spiritual vitality" that "depends on the continuity of myth, and this can be preserved only if each age translates the myth into its own language and makes it an essential content of its view of the world" (*Mysterium Coniunctionis* CW 14:474n:336). The myth—or *mythologomenon*—of the sapient Other as a counterpart of the sapient Self can easily be seen to offer such a translation. In particular, these new *mythologomena* of the Alien as Other-Self are of particular significance because this archetype appears to have a proleptic function in relation to humanity's entelechy as a species.

It is clear however, that the *mythologomena* of the archetype of alterity in the short stories of the science fiction magazines do not provide a complete mythology. With few exceptions they are, as I have already suggested, merely notional—a sketched-in version of another kind of sapient being in an illustrative situation of some sort. The alien of the short story was not, however, notional because of any inadequacy of the medium but because in the early years the medium (magazine short fiction) encouraged the introduction of the *idea* of the Alien—the notional Alien. It did not then require prolonged theoretical exploration or sustained psychologically informed narrative structures, largely because readers demanded action. It might even be more accurate to say that the medium allowed the intrusion of the *idea* of the Alien as a consequence of the power of the archetype behind it, and wrapped the required action around it. For when what is found in short science fiction texts is the notional Alien, it is nevertheless disproportionately compelling. Although the shorter forms of science fiction about aliens are therefore arguably important in themselves in their attempt to reify the power and nature of the archetype of alterity, the mythology they constitute may be a mythology still in the process of articulation.

The nature of the authorial stance in magazine stories about aliens, moreover, seems to have begun to change. The stories in *The Ultimate Alien* (1995), for example, demonstrate this new stance, revealing a shift away from the focus on the nature of the alien and the nature of sapience and toward a self-conscious revisiting of central older themes. (Karen Haber and Carol Carr's "First Contact—Sort Of" (1995) reveals even in its title some of the characteristics of this new stance.) When human and alien meet in the science fiction short stories of the nineties, the results increasingly seem to be metaphysical encounters rather than encounters between natural beings. I am not suggesting that this shift is either universal or a bad thing for science fiction. It is not likely that the natural alien and the actual encounter will disappear altogether from short fiction (in *Analog,* to name but one example among the magazines,

the natural alien is still the primary topic of alien stories), for the two approaches can coexist comfortably. Certainly, too, the science-fictional Alien as
a natural being rather than a metaphysical entity remains prominent in longer
fiction as well as in other media.

The obvious shift toward completion of the mythology comes with the advent of the science fiction novel—and even more obviously with the advent of
the science fiction trilogy, or the series of novels. When the extended medium
of the mass-market paperback became more readily available for the publication of science fiction,[5] writers were provided with an alternative to presenting notional concepts and given a medium for presenting sustained, detailed,
and philosophically worked-out representations of aliens. Admittedly, many
of the earlier science fiction "novels" were simply cut-and-paste collages of
previously published short-story series, or novellas and novelettes expanded
and published as novels. But the advent of novel-length fiction as the first
publication mode for science fiction (the "paperback original" noted on many
copyright pages until the more recent advent of first publication in hard-
cover) initiated more extended treatment of the Alien, springing from the
same psychological impulse and employing the same theories of the physical,
psychological, and sociological nature of the Alien. In those novels that are seriously concerned with aliens, for example, the rules of thumb for the examination of sapience are replaced by deeper inquiry, and it is in them, too, that
the notional exploration of the Alien of the short stories can be supplanted by
deeper insights into the power and nature of the archetype of alterity, set in an
extended context of other-species culture or interspecies coexistence.

It is more than a question of mere length and increased detail. In the more
extensive context of a novel, the limited and scattered inquiries into the possibilities for individual aspects of sapience, such as language, technology, religion, art, game-playing, and so on, may be supplanted (or supplemented) by
examination of the larger patterns that integrate them—*linguality*, *hability*, *sociality*, and *justiciability*. So, for example, a novel or group of novels might focus not on *language*, but on *linguality*, for although you (the individual) have
to be able to communicate with your conspecifics, and although language in
some form is the way this is achieved, language is only a part of linguality. In
the pluralistic universe offered in Rebecca Ore's three novels (*Becoming Alien*,
1988; *Being Alien*, 1989; and *Human to Human*, 1990), the mere possession of
language is insufficient for true sapience; what is required is that the psycho-

logical capacity underlying a species' linguality (demonstrated by producing their own intraspecies language) is able to extend its capacity to also provide for interspecies communication and interaction. Similarly, because you must not merely possess tools but also be able to manipulate things in your environment in a more complex way to produce "goods," *hability* (from the Latin *habilis* as in *Homo habilis* [Leakey] and *Australopithecus habilis* [others]) is explored for what it reveals of the patterns of mentation within the species that manifest in the technician (the creator of technic—to borrow Mumford's term—or technology in its widest sense of anything from a stone axe to a spaceship), in the artisan (the creator of useful arts), and in the artist (the creator of art) and for how it therefore provides potential for interspecies coexistence and cooperation through trade. In C. J. Cherryh's novels of the Compact (*The Pride of Chanur*, 1982; *Chanur's Venture*, 1985; *The Kif Strike Back*, 1985; *Chanur's Homecoming*, 1986; and *Chanur's Legacy*, 1992), the organizational structure of interspecies relationships—"the Compact"—in a multispecies galaxy is trade because all sapient species have goods (the products of hability) to trade with, and the ramifications of the process of trade have an effect on the life of the individual as well as the life or continuation of the species.

Similarly, because you have to interact with your conspecifics with patterns of social behavior, custom, and personal relationships for the continuation of the species, *sociality* is explored for what it reveals of intraspecies mentation patterns that produce both macrosocial relationships (for example, government, educational systems, work organizations) and microsocial relationships (for example, mating and friendship), which provide a basis for extension into interspecies interaction or macrobonding. In the novels of David Brin that constitute the Uplift series (*Sundiver*, 1980; *Startide Rising*, 1983; *The Uplift War*, 1987; *Brightness Reef*, 1995; and *Infinity's Shore*, 1996), the organizational principle is similar to that of the medieval European guild system raised to the level of interaction between species. Finally, because you have to have appropriate standing among your conspecifics to produce law and government to regulate the continued life of the species, *justiciability* ("liable to legal consideration" [*COED2*]) is explored for what it reveals of the mentation patterns that produce intraspecies responsibility, whether in the sense of legal responsibility or ethical/moral responsibility—for example, the treatment of rights for the individual and the group, the definitions of normal behavior, the possibility and definition of crime or deviant behavior, systems for dealing with the violation of rights and with deviant behavior—on which a system of interspecies responsibility might be constructed. One approach to *justiciability* is already available in Frank Herbert's novels of the ConSentiency: *Whipping Star* (1969) and *The Dosadi Experiment* (1978). Response to the archetype, however, drives the dealings with the Alien in science-fiction novels no less than it drives the dealings with the Alien in short stories. Consequently, despite the shift in format, the archetype of alterity in the science-fictional Alien continues in its expanded form to extend our knowledge of OtherSelfness in "ever new" symbols and with broader and deeper effect on the knowledge of our selfness as a species.

The use of magazine publication of short fiction—whether short story, novelette, or novella—to offer specimens of the trope and the archetype of alterity and of the nature of sapience in the universe may well have been overtaken by the shift in science fiction in general toward the novel as the preferred format. But their existence has been a valuable contribution to the nature of the genre. In all their persistent, multifarious fascination, they have provided what amounts to a matrix-full—or a cyberspace-full—or even a virtual reality of relevant *exempla* to inspire the continuing reexamination of the topic in the novel. Good, bad, or indifferent, they have all contributed in some fashion, direct or indirect, to the novelist's understanding of his or her topic when he or she takes on the alien.

But their contributory function to the genre is not their only value. As their vast and still-growing number makes abundantly clear, science fiction short stories own a vitality that repeatedly engages the reader, and a substantial part of that vitality in stories of the Alien derives from the engagement with the archetype that has been concurrently going on in the novel. For, ironically, having been overtaken by the Alien of the science fiction novel to which they have substantially contributed, as I have pointed out, they have also reaped substantial benefits from its existence. Their briefly delineated specimens of aliens are more thoughtfully conceived and more skillfully presented, more frequently bought by modern editors, and more eagerly read by modern readers. In spite of the emergence of the science fiction novel, consequently, the aliens of *The Ultimate Alien* are still distantly pre-antepenultimate, and short stories as a vehicle for science fiction, whether about aliens or on other themes, are not in danger of disappearing.

Finally, through the reciprocity of the relationship between our human Self and the archetypal OtherSelf that we carry within us, we also extend our hypothesis of our place in the universe. The archetype of alterity, emerging into human consciousness as a result of humanity's recognition of itself as a species, permits the speculative construction of such a nexus of imaginary Others in the ordering narratives of science fiction. Through the experience of the OtherSelfness in the science-fictional Alien, humanity has been enabled to send out into the universe a mind probe that turns its gaze back upon that same humanity, identifying it imaginatively from the outside on the same terms as we have rationally been able to identify it from the inside. This self-reflexive gaze changes our understanding of ourselves and our place in the universe as radically and irreversibly as the NASA photograph "Earthrise," taken from the surface of the moon, changed our perception of the world on which we live and its place in the universe. The shift of perspective in this picture was radical: Before we saw it, we on Earth were always observers "in here" of a universe "out there," but after we have seen it, there can be no more "in here" *or* "out there"—we and the universe together are both, to borrow a phrase from the vernacular, "where it's at." Science fiction with its many and various stories of alien beings enables us to wonder about others who may be with us "where it's at" by creating a new mythology of our place as sapient beings in the universe.

NOTES

1. I use the first-person plural personal pronoun deliberately as one of the indications of the status of science fiction narratives (particularly science fiction about the alien) as *documents humains*, not as an indication of any confessional mode of writing involved in this conclusion.

2. Specifically, Landau privileges scientific explanations: "Even physics addresses questions of the form 'how come . . . ?' by presenting repeatable sequences of events whose description and relation must obey stringent (though not unchanging) criteria of causal 'belonging'" (ix). She goes on to suggest that when we interpret any of the physical elements of our environment, therefore, we employ the rational narratives of science (ix).

3. The ethical or moral consequence of making a person into a thing is further extrapolated in John Brunner's *The Shockwave Rider* (1975) in which the protagonist

points out to another character that "[i]f there is such a thing as absolute evil, it consists in treating another human being as a thing" (236).

4. It was also occasionally referred to as "millennial panic." The millennium was a calendar event that had a considerable emotional impact on a large proportion of human beings. Realistically and scientifically considered, it was arbitrary event—a point on a chronological scale that has no properly fixed beginning. Popular perception, however, seemed to be that the world would change significantly at midnight between 31 December 1999 and the first day of the new millennium—1 January 2000 (or for some people, 1 January 2001). The perception was aided by the fact that humanity's icon of technological advance, the computer, was popularly expected to fail catastrophically on a global scale at this point in time. Precisely *what* the change would signify was left unspecified in discussion, although a reading of the supermarket tabloids, whose tone revealed anxiety verging on panic in North America, suggested that there was at least some conflation with biblical accounts of the apocalypse. For the mythologically literate, moreover, the fact that the world was reaching the end of the *second* millennium since the birth of Christ added significance, since according to traditional calculation, the current Platonic Great Year of two thousand ordinary years also ends at that time. Few people in the West were altogether immune to the effects of the millennium. It had little effect in countries using other calendars than the Christian. Under the Islamic Haj calendar, for example, the year was 1242. In the years immediately preceding the millennium, as it loomed over the horizon, it informed (as a useful trope, perhaps) predictions of the end of history (Francis Fukuyama), the end of science (John Horgan), and the end of humanity (the Carter Catastrophe Theory). The anxiety about the millennium was purely irrational—although ironically it also seemed to offer a form of closure to the past and the possibility of a new start.

5. The mass-market paperback arrived with Sir Allen Lane's Penguins in the 1930s but did not reach full modern proportions until after 1945.

Bibliography

**PRIMARY TEXTS: SCIENCE FICTION—
SHORT STORIES, NOVELLAS, SERIALS, AND NOVELS**

Anderson, Poul. *The Earthbook of Stormgate.* New York: Berkley, 1978.

———. "The Helping Hand." *Astounding* 45.3 (May 1950): 6–29.

———. "Hiding Place." *Analog* 67.1 (March 1961): 116–50.

———. "Kyrie." 1968. *The Best of Poul Anderson.* New York: Pocket Books, 1976. 119–31.

———. "The Master Key." *Analog* 73.5 (July 1964): 64–80.

———. *The People of the Wind.* New York: Signet, 1973.

———. "The Problem of Pain." 1973. *The Earthbook of Stormgate.* Anderson. New York: Berkley, 1978. 26–48.

———. *World without Stars.* 1967. New York: Ace, 1978.

Anvil, Christopher. "Experts in the Field." *Analog* 79.3 (May 1967): 49–66.

———. "Mission of Ignorance." *Analog* 82.2 (October 1968): 36–51.

———. "The Underhandler." *Analog* 110.12 (November 1990): 12–48.

Arnason, Eleanor. "Knapsack Poems." *Asimov's* 26.5 (May 2002): 36–42.

Asimov, Isaac. "Breeds There a Man . . . ?" 1951. *Nightfall and Other Stories.* Asimov. Greenwich, CT: Fawcett Crest, 1969. 100–34.

———. "The Gentle Vultures." 1957. *Earthmen and Strangers.* Ed. Robert Silverberg. New York: Dell, 1968. 97–112.

———. "Green Patches." [1950, as "Misbegotten Missionary"]. *Nightfall and Other Stories.* Asimov. Greenwich, CT: Fawcett Crest, 1969. 45–59.

———. "The Hazing." 1942. *The Early Asimov—Book Two.* Asimov. Greenwich, CT: Fawcett Crest, 1972. 37–52.

———. "Homo Sol." 1940. *The Early Asimov—Book One*. Asimov. Greenwich, CT: Fawcett Crest, 1972. 199–218.

———. "The Imaginary." 1942. *The Early Asimov—Book One*. Asimov. Greenwich, CT: Fawcett Crest, 1972. 246–62.

———. "The Talking Stone." 1955. *Asimov's Mysteries*. Asimov. New York: Dell, 1968.

Atwood, Margaret. *The Handmaid's Tale*. 1985. Toronto: McClelland-Bantam, 1986.

Baird, Wilhelmina. *Clipjoint*. New York: Ace, 1994.

———. *Crashcourse*. New York: Ace, 1993.

———. *Psykosis*. New York: Ace, 1995.

Bear, Greg. "Blood Music." *Analog* 113.6 (June 1983): 12–36.

Benedict, Myrtle. "Sit By the Fire. 1958. *Gentle Invaders*. Ed. Hans Stefan Santesson. New York: Belmont, 1969. 9–17.

Benford, Greg. *Great Sky River*. New York: Bantam, 1987.

———. *If the Stars Are Gods*. 1977. New York: Berkley, 1978.

Benford, Greg, and Gordon Eklund. *Find the Changeling*. New York: Dell, 1980.

Bentley, William E. "The Dip Stick." *Astounding* 54.3 (November 1954): 30–38.

Bischoff, David. "The Xaxrkling of J. Arnold Boysenberry." 1997. *First Contact*. Ed. Martin H. Greenberg and Larry Segriff. New York: Daw, 1997. 102–12.

Blish, James. "Common Time." 1953. *Galactic Cluster*. Blish. New York: Signet, 1959. 38–59.

———. "Skysign." *Analog* 81.3 (May 1968): 137–61.

Boucher, Anthony. "The Star Dummy." 1952. *Omnibus of Science Fiction*. Ed. Groff Conklin. New York: Crown, 1952. 178–89.

Boult, S. Kye. "The Habitat Manager." *Analog* 87.4 (June 1971): 67–102.

———. "The Safety Engineer." 1973. *The Alien Condition*. Ed. Stephen Goldin. New York: Ballantine, 1973. 121–81.

Bradbury, Ray. *The Martian Chronicles*. New York: Doubleday, 1960.

Brand, Jonathan. "Long Day in Court." *If* 13.5 (November 1963): 52–67.

Brejcha, F. A. "I'll Show You Mine If . . ." *Analog* 111.5 (April 1991): 76–96.

Bretnor, Reginald. "Without (General) Issue." *IASFM* 5.12 (November 1981): 80–85.

Brin, David. *Brightness Reef*. New York: Bantam, 1996.

———. "Fortitude." *Science Fiction Age* 4.2 (January 1996): 76–79, 100–101.

———. *Heaven's Reach*. New York: Bantam Spectra, 1998.

———. *Infinity's Shore*. New York: Bantam Spectra, 1996.

———. "Shhhh." *Amazing* 64.1 (May 1989): 12–21.

———. *Startide Rising*. New York: Bantam, 1983.

———. *Sundiver*. New York: Bantam, 1980.

———. *The Uplift War*. New York: Bantam Spectra, 1987.

Brown, Fredric. "Arena." *Astounding* 33.4 (June 1944): 70–94.

———. "Martians, Go Home!" *Astounding* 54.1 (September 1954): 9–55.

———. "Puppet Show." 1962. *The Year's Best S-F 8*. Ed. Judith Merril. New York: Dell, 1963. 251–61.

———. "The Waveries." 1945. *Angels and Spaceships*. Brown. New York: E. P. Dutton, 1952. 62–89.

Brown, Ray. "Getting Even." *Analog* 102.12 (November 1982): 16–41.

Brunner, John. *The Shockwave Rider*. 1975. New York: Ballantine, 1976.

———. *Total Eclipse*. 1974. New York: Daw, 1975.

Bryant, Edward. "Dancing Chickens." 1984. *Alien Sex*. Ed. Ellen Datlow. New York: Roc, 1992. 189–201.

Budrys, Algis. "Lower Than Angels." 1956. *Earthmen and Strangers*. Ed. Robert Silverberg. New York: Dell, 1968.

Burdick, Bruce Stanley. "Q.E.D." *Analog* 104.12 (December 1984): 96–112.

Busby, F. M. "The Learning of Eeshta." *If* 22.1 (September-October 1973): 119–30.

Butler, Octavia. "Bloodchild." *IASFM* 8.6 (June 1984): 34–54.

———. *Xenogenesis: Dawn, Adulthood Rites, Imago*. New York: Guild America Books, 1989.

Cadigan, Pat. "Roadside Rescue." 1984. *Alien Sex*. Ed. Ellen Datlow. New York: Roc, 1992. 202–11.

Campbell, John W., Jr. "Who Goes There?" 1938. *The Best of John W. Campbell*. Campbell. New York: Ballantine, 1976.

Caraker, Mary. "The Innocents." *Analog* 109.8 (August 1989): 91–92.

———. *Seven Worlds*. New York: Signet, 1986.

———. "Suffer the Children." *Analog* 115.6 (May 1995): 104–28.

———. "The Vampires Who Loved Beowulf." *Analog* 103.1 (January 1983): 68–83.

Carr, Jayge. "The Walls That Bind." *Analog* 1212.7 & 8 (July-August 2001): 138–47.

Carr, Terry. "The Dance of the Changer and the Three." 1968. *The Light at the End of the Universe*. Carr. New York: Pyramid, 1976. 20–38.

Cartmill, Cleve. "The Green Cat." *Worlds Beyond*. 1.2 (January 1951): 78–82.

Chalker, Jack. "In the Wilderness." *Analog* 98.7 (July 1978): 110–25.

Chandler, A. Bertram. "The Cage." 1957. *The Penguin Omnibus of Science Fiction*. Ed. Brian W. Aldiss. Harmondsworth, UK: Penguin, 1973. 523–35.

Chapdelaine, Perry A. "Initial Contact." *Analog* 83.3 (May 1969): 143–62.

Chase, Robert R. "Date Night." *Analog* 109.6 (June 1989): 112–23.

———. *The Game of Fox and Lion*. New York: Ballantine Del Rey, 1986.

———. *Shapers*. New York: Ballantine Del Rey, 1989.

Cherryh, C. J. "Cassandra." 1978. *The Collected Short Fiction of C. J. Cherryh*. New York: Daw, 2004. 199–206.

———. *Chanur's Homecoming*. 1986. New York: Daw, 1987.

———. *Chanur's Legacy.* 1992. New York: Daw, 1993.

———. *Chanur's Venture.* New York: Daw, 1985.

———. *The Kif Strike Back.* New York: Daw, 1985.

———. "Pots." 1985. *Afterwar.* Ed. Janet Morris. New York: Baen, 1985. 214–50.

———. *The Pride of Chanur.* New York: Daw, 1982.

———. "The Scapegoat." *Alien Stars.* Ed. Elizabeth Mitchell. New York: Baen, 1985. 7–72.

Chilson, Robert. "The Hand of Friendship." *Analog* 103.3 (March 1983): 134–59.

———. "The Worting's Testament." *Analog* 113.4 (March 1993): 8–98.

Chomsky, Noam. *Aspects of the Theory of Syntax.* Cambridge: M.I.T. Press, 1965.

———. *Current Issues in Linguistic Theory.* The Hague: Mouton, 1964.

———. *Syntactic Structures.* The Hague: Mouton, 1965.

———. *Topics in the Theory of Generative Grammar.* The Hague: Mouton, 1966.

Clarke, Arthur C. *Childhood's End.* New York: Harcourt, Brace and World, 1953.

———. *Rendezvous with Rama.* 1973. New York: Ballantine, 1973.

———. "Rescue Party." 1945. *Nine Billion Names of God.* Clarke. New York: Signet, 1974. 31–55.

Clement, Hal. *Mission of Gravity.* 1953. New York: Ballantine Del Rey, 1978.

———. *Needle.* 1950. New York: Lancer Books, 1969.

———. "Technical Error." 1943. *Natives of Space.* Clement. New York: Ballantine, 1965. 65–99.

———. *Through the Eye of a Needle.* New York: Ballantine Del Rey, 1978.

Coblentz, Stanton A. "Missionaries from the Sky." *Amazing* 5.8 (November 1930): 744–51.

Cole, Robert. *The Struggle for Empire: A Story of the Year 2236.* London: Elliott Stock, 1900.

Colladay, Morrison. "The Blattids." *Amazing* 6.9 (December 1931): 844–58.

Coney, Michael G. "Symbiote." 1969. *New Writings in SF9.* Ed. John Carnell. New York: Bantam, 1969. 33–51.

Conner, Mike. "Guide Dog." *F&SF* 80.5 (May 1991): 5–39.

Correy, Lee. *A Matter of Metalaw.* New York: Daw, 1986.

Craven, Jerry. "A Matter of Etiquette." *IASFM* 4.1 (January 1980): 100–7.

Cromie, Robert. *A Plunge into Space.* 1890. Reprint ed. Westport, CT: Hyperion Press, 1976.

Cross, Polton. "The Martian Avenger." *Amazing* 13.4 (April 1939): 76–87.

Cummings, Ray. "Wandl the Invader." Pt. 1. *Astounding* 9.2 (February 1932): 168–201; Pt. 2. *Astounding* 9.3 (March 1932): 376–401; Pt. 3. *Astounding* 10.1 (April 1932): 90–119; Pt. 4. *Astounding* 10.2 (May 1932): 234–55.

de Camp, L. Sprague. "The Animal Cracker Plot." *Astounding* 43.5 (July 1949): 67–84.

———. *The Continent Makers and Other Tales of the Viagens.* New York: NAL Signet, 1971.

———. "Finished." 1949. *The Continent Makers and Other Tales of the Viagens.* de Camp. New York: NAL Signet, 1971. 47–64.

———. *Tower of Zanid.* 1958. New York: Airmont, 1963.

Dee, Roger. "Unwelcome Tenant." 1950. *Short Science Fiction Tales.* Ed. Isaac Asimov and Groff Conklin. New York: Collier Books, 1963. 73–78.

de Ford, Miriam Allen. "The Margenes." *If* 6.2 (February 1956): 92–97.

Dick, Philip K. "Beyond Lies the Wub." 1952. *The Preserving Machine.* Dick. New York: Ace, 1969. 143–52.

Dickson, Gordon R. "3-Part Puzzle." 1962. *The Star Road.* Dickson. 1973. New York: Daw, 1974. 92–106.

———. "Enter a Pilgrim." *Analog* 93.6 (August 1974): 14–32.

———. *The Harriers: Book One: Of War and Honor.* New York: Baen, 1991

———. "Jackal's Meal." 1969. *The Star Road.* Dickson. New York: Daw, 1973. 172–92.

———. "Lulungomeena." *Galaxy* 7.5 (January 1954): 70–88.

———. "The Odd Ones." *If* 4.6 (February 1955): 6–21.

———. *Way of the Pilgrim.* 1987. New York: Ace, 1988.

Diffin, Charles Willard. "Dark Moon." *Astounding* 6.2 (May 1931): 148–97.

Dulski, Thomas R. "In Whose Name Do We Seek the Quark?" *Analog* 102.9 (September 1983): 14–52.

Easton, Thomas A. "Mood Wendigo." *Analog* 100.5 (May 1980): 76–86.

Effinger, George Alec. "From Downtown at the Buzzer." 1977. *Idle Pleasures.* Effinger. New York: Berkley, 1983. 31–51.

Ellison, Harlan. "Blind Lightning." 1956. *Earthmen and Strangers.* Ed. Robert Silverberg. New York: Dell, 1968. 169–83.

Farley, Ralph. "Liquid Life." *TWS* (October 1936): 60–74.

Farmer, Philip J. "Prometheus." 1961. *Other Worlds, Other Gods.* Ed. Mayo Mohs. New York: Avon, 1971. 87–136.

———. *Strange Relations.* New York: Ballantine, 1960.

Ferguson, Brad. "To Tell the Troof." *F&SF* 76.1 (January 1989): 88–111.

Fergusson, P. M., and G. L. Robson. "Hunting Rights." *Analog* 108.5 (May 1988): 12–37.

Flynn, Michael. "The Common Goal of Nature." *Analog* 110.5 (April 1990): 12–51.

Fyfe, H. B. "Bureau of Slick Tricks." *Astounding* 42.4 (December 1948): 70–90.

———. "In Value Deceived." *Astounding* 46.3 (November 1950): 38–47.

———. "Protected Species." *Astounding* 47.1 (March 1951): 110–19.

Gallun, Raymond Z. "Blue Haze on Pluto." *Astounding* 15.4 (June 1935): 90–97.

———. "Hotel Cosmos." *Astounding* 21.5 (July 1938): 140–52.

———. "Mad Robot." *Astounding* 17.1 (March 1936): 66–75.

Garrett, Randall [*as* David Gordon]. "The Asses of Balaam." *Analog* 66.2 (October 1961): 69–160.

———. "The Best Policy." 1957. *Earthmen and Strangers*. Ed. Robert Silverberg. New York: Dell, 1968. 46–63.

———. "Needler." *Astounding* 59.4 (June 1957): 66–111.

Gibson, William. *Neuromancer*. New York: Ace, 1984.

Gotlieb, Phyllis. "Mother Lode." 1973. *Mother Lode*. Gotlieb. Edmonton, AB: Tesseract Books, 1995. 59–85.

Green, Joseph. "And Be Lost Like Me." *Analog* 103.6 (June 1983): 78–90.

———. "Raccoon Reaction." *Analog* 103.9 (September 1983): 100–9.

———. "Robustus Revisited." *F&SF* 44.4 (April 1973): 96–111.

Greg, Percy. *Across the Zodiac: The Story of a Wrecked Record*. 1880. Westport, CT: Hyperion Press, 1974.

Griffith, George. *A Honeymoon in Space*. London: Pearson, 1901.

Haber, Karen, and Carol Carr. "First Contact—Sort Of." 1995. *The Ultimate Alien*. Eds. Byron Preiss, John Betancourt, and R. A. DeCandido. New York: Dell, 1995. 225–40.

Hambly, Barbara. *The Armies of Daylight*. The Darwath Trilogy 3. New York: Ballantine Del Rey, 1983.

———. *The Time of the Dark*. The Darwath Trilogy 1. New York: Ballantine Del Rey, 1982.

———. *The Walls of Air*. The Darwath Trilogy 2. New York: Ballantine Del Rey, 1983.

Hamilton, Edmond. "Crashing Suns." 1928. *Crashing Suns*. Hamilton. New York: Ace, 1965. 5–54.

———. "The Monsters of Mars." *Astounding* 6.1 (April 1931): 1–25.

———. "The Stars, My Brothers." 1962. *What's It Like out There? and Other Stories*. Hamilton. New York: Ace, 1974. 97–143.

———. "Within the Nebula." 1928. *Crashing Suns*. Hamilton. New York: Ace, 1965. 90–129.

Heinlein, Robert A. "Goldfish Bowl." [1942, *as* "Creation Took Eight Days"]. *First Contact*. Ed. Damon Knight. New York: Pinnacle Books, 1971. 128–63.

———. "The Puppet Masters." Pt. 1. *Galaxy* 2.6 (September 1951): 5–66. ; Pt. 2. *Galaxy* 3.1 (October 1951): 100ff. ; Pt. 3. *Galaxy* 3.2 (November 1951): 101ff.

———. *Starman Jones*. New York: Charles Scribner, 1953.

———. *Starship Troopers*. 1959. New York: Berkley, 1968.

Herbert, Frank. *The Dosadi Experiment*. New York: Berkley, 1977.

———. "The Tactful Saboteur." 1964. *Eye*. Herbert. New York: Ace, 1987. 159–90.

————. "Try to Remember." 1961. *Eye.* Herbert. New York: Ace, 1987. 119–57.

————. *Whipping Star.* New York: Berkley, 1970.

Hiller, Neil W. "Peace Feelers." *F&SF* 70.3 (March 1986): 65–70.

Hilton, James. *Lost Horizon.* 1933. New York: Pocket Books, 1939.

Holmes, A. R. "The Slave Ship from Space." *Astounding* 7.1 (July 1931): 68–87.

Hoyle, Fred. *The Black Cloud.* 1957. Harmondsworth, UK: Penguin, 1960.

Hyde, Gavin. "Sparkie's Fall." 1959. *Star Science Fiction Stories 5.* Ed. Frederik Pohl. New York: Ballantine, 1959. 86–89.

Iverson, Eric G. "The Road Not Taken." *Analog* 105.11 (November 1985): 14–38.

Jablokov, Alexander. "The Place of No Shadows." *IASFM* 14.11 & 12 (November 1990): 170–87.

James, D. L. "Philosophers of Stone." *Astounding* 21.4 (June 1938): 62–74.

Jameson, Malcolm. "Alien Envoy." *Astounding* 34.3 (November 1944): 116–35.

Janifer, Laurence M. "Worldwreckers." *Analog* 107.10 (October 1987): 130–43.

Jones, Gwyneth. *White Queen.* London: Gollancz VGSF, 1992.

Jones, Raymond F. "Discontinuity." *Astounding* 46.2 (October 1950): 76–109.

————. "I Tell You Three Times." *Astounding* 46.6 (February 1951): 6–44.

————. "Tools of the Trade." *Astounding* 46.3 (November 1950): 48–67.

Juve, Henrik Dahl. "The Monsters of Neptune." *Wonder Stories Quarterly* 1.4 (Summer 1930): 536–47.

————. "The Struggle for Neptune." *Wonder Stories Quarterly* 2.1 (Fall 1930): 94–105.

Kagan, Janet. *Hellspark.* New York: Tor, 1988.

————. "The Nutcracker Coup." *IASFM* 16.14 (December 1992): 136–68.

Kahn, Bernard I. "A Pinch of Culture." *Astounding* 45.6 (August 1950): 78–107.

Kapp, Colin. "Ambassador to Verdammt." *Analog* 79.2 (April 1967): 145–61.

————. *The Unorthodox Engineers.* London: Dennis Dobson, 1979.

Killough, Lee. "Caveat Emptor." *Analog* 85.3 (May 1970): 105–19.

————. *The Monitors, the Miners, and the Shree.* New York: Ballantine Del Rey, 1980.

————. "Sentience." *If* 22.1 (September-October 1973): 102–16.

Kipling, Rudyard. *Puck of Pook's Hill.* 1906. The Writings in Prose and Verse of Rudyard Kipling 23. New York: Charles Scribner's Sons, 1916.

Kittredge, Mary. "Renascence." *IASFM* 6.3 (March 1982): 140–65.

Knight, Damon. "Rule Golden." 1954. *Rule Golden and Other Stories.* Knight. New York: Avon, 1979. 5–85.

————. "Stranger Station." 1956. *Earthmen and Strangers.* Ed. Robert Silverberg. New York: Dell, 1968. 113–36.

Kornbluth, C. M. "The Silly Season." 1950. *First Contact.* Ed. Damon Knight. New York: Pinnacle Books, 1971. 111–27.

Kostkos, Henry. "The Meteor Men of Plaa." *Amazing* 8.4 (August-September 1933): 392–455.

Kress, Nancy. "People Like Us." *IASFM* 13.9 (September 1989): 92–99.

Kube-McDowell, Michael P. "Nanny." *Analog* 107.11 (November 1987): 14–52.

———. "Slac//." *IASFM* 5.8 (August 1981): 142–66.

Kummer, Frederic Arnold. "The Foreign Legion of Mars." *Amazing* 13.5 (May 1939): 98–108.

———. "The Forgiveness of Tenchu Taen." *Astounding* 22.3 (November 1938): 119–27.

Lafayette, René. "Old Doc Methuselah." *Astounding* 40.2 (October 1947): 6–38.

Lafferty, R. A. "The Primary Education of the Camiroi." 1966. *SF–12*. Ed. Judith Merril. New York: Dell, 1968. 161–74.

Lake, David J. *The Right Hand of Dextra*. New York: Daw, 1977.

Lamb, Jean. "Galley Slave." *Analog* 116.10 (August 1996): 80–97.

Landau, Miriam. "Allies." *Asimov's* 23.8 (March 1999): 84–95.

Lanier, Sterling E. "Join Our Gang?" *Analog* 67.3 (May 1961): 51–59.

Lasswitz, Kurd. *Two Planets*. [*Auf Zwei Planeten*.] 1897. Carbondale: Southern Illinois University Press, 1971.

Le Guin, Ursula K. *A Fisherman of the Inland Sea*. Le Guin. New York: HarperPrism, 1994.

———. *The Left Hand of Darkness*. 1969. New York: Ace, 1976.

Leinster, Murray. "First Contact." *Astounding* 35.3 (May 1945): 7–35.

———. *The Med Series*. New York: Ace, 1983.

———. "Propagandist." 1947. *Great Stories of Space Travel*. Ed. Groff Conklin. New York: Grosset and Dunlap Tempo, 1969. 112–36.

———. "Proxima Centauri." 1935. *Before the Golden Age*. Ed. Isaac Asimov. New York: Doubleday, 1974. 655–700.

Lem, Stanislaw. *Solaris*. 1961. New York: Berkley Medallion, 1970.

Lerner, Edward M. "Hostile Takeover." *Analog* 121.5 (May 2001): 111–31.

Lesser, Milton. "Tyrants of Time." *Imagination* 5.3 (March 1954): 6–69.

Lindholm, Megan. "A Touch of Lavender." *IASFM* 13.11 (November 1989): 18–63.

Locke, T. A. "Vandals of the Stars." *Astounding* 1.3 (March 1930): 390–418.

London, Jack. *The Scarlet Plague*. London: Mills and Boon, 1915.

Longyear, Barry. "Savage Planet." *Analog* 100.2 (February 1980): 14–38.

Lorraine, Lilith. "The Jovian Jest." *Astounding* 2.2 (May 1930): 228–33.

Lovecraft, H. P. "The Call of Cthulhu." 1928. *The Colour out of Space and Others*. Lovecraft. New York: Lancer, 1969. 45–75.

M'Intosh, J. T. "Mind Alone." *Galaxy* 6.5 (August 1953): 4–54.

MacDougal, John. "Chaos Coordinated." *Astounding* 38.2 (October 1946): 36–57.

Mackenzie, Johnathan Blake. "Overproof." 1965. *7 Trips Through Space and Time*. Ed. Groff Conklin. London: Coronet, 1969. 66–113.

MacLean, Katherine. "Pictures Don't Lie." 1951. *The Diploids*. New York: Avon, 1962. 173–92.

Malartre, Elisabeth. "A Windy Prospect." *Asimov's* 25.4 (April 2001): 58–81.

Marsh, Willard. "The Ethicators." *If* 5.5 (August 1955): 55–59.

Martin, Elizabeth A., ed. *A Concise Dictionary of Law*. 2nd ed. Oxford and New York: Oxford University Press, 1990.

Martin, George R. R. "Run to Starlight." *Amazing* 48.4 (December 1974): 26–49.

McCaffrey, Anne. "Velvet Fields." *If* 22.2 (November-December 1973): 91–98.

McDevitt, Jack. "Black to Move." *IASFM* 6.9 (September 1982): 104–11.

———. "Translations from the Colosian." *Asimov's* 8.9 (September 1984): 46–59.

Meek, Captain S. P. "Beyond the Heaviside Layer." *Astounding* 3.1 (July 1930): 5–17.

———. "The Attack from Space." *Astounding* 3.3 (September 1930): 390–407.

Merril, Judith. *The 7th Annual of the Year's Best SF*. New York: Dell, 1952.

Miller, P. Schuyler. "Tetrahedra of Space." 1931. *Before the Golden Age*. Ed. Isaac Asimov. New York: Doubleday, 1974. 156–93.

Miller, Walter M. "No Moon for Me." 1952. *Space Space Space*. Ed. William M. Sloane. New York: Franklin Watts, 1953. 15–41.

Morrison, William. "Bedside Manner." *Galaxy* 8.2 (May 1954): 143–60.

———. "The Sack." 1950. *Science Fiction: The Great Years*. Ed. Carol Pohl and Frederik Pohl. 2 vols. New York: Ace, 1976. 77–103.

Niven, Larry. "Cruel and Unusual." 1977. *Convergent Series*. Niven. New York: Ballantine Del Rey, 1979. 165–68.

———. "The Fourth Profession." 1971. *A Hole in Space*. Niven. New York: Ballantine, 1974. 147–96.

———. "The Meddler." 1968. *Convergent Series*. Niven. New York: Ballantine Del Rey, 1979. 61–86.

———. *Ringworld*. 1970. 2nd corrected ed. New York: Ballantine Del Rey, 1981.

Nordley, G. D. "Network." *Analog* 114.3 (February 1994): 44–93.

Norwood, Warren C., and Ralph Mylius. *The Seren Cenacles*. New York: Bantam, 1983.

O'Donnell, Kevin. "Information Station Sabbath." *Analog* 97.8 (August 1977): 82–99.

———. "Low Grade Ore." *IASFM* 1.2 (Summer 1977): 12–33.

———. *Mayflies*. New York: Berkley, 1979.

Oltion, Jerry. "No Strangers Meet on Trails." *Analog* 103.3 (March 1983): 122–33.

Ore, Rebecca. *Becoming Alien*. Becoming Alien 1. New York: Tor, 1988.

———. *Being Alien*. Becoming Alien 2. New York: Tor, 1989.

———. *Human to Human*. Becoming Alien 3. New York: Tor, 1990.

Orwell, George. *Animal Farm*. 1945. Harmondsworth, UK: Penguin, 1951.

Overstreet, Lee. "Angel of Destruction." *Galaxy* 37.1 (January 1976): 114–30.

Perkins, Lawrence. "Delivered with Feeling." *Analog* 75.5 (July 1965): 133–44.

Perper, Timothy, and Martha Cornog. "Guz's Place." *Analog* 108.13 (December 1988): 14–53.

Phillifent, John. "The Rites of Man." *Analog* 82.3 (November 1968): 86–120.

Piper, H. Beam. *Little Fuzzy*. New York: Ace, 1962.

———. "Omnilingual." 1957. *From Mind to Mind: Tales of Communication*. Ed. Stanley Schmidt. New York: Davis Publications, 1984. 109–39.

Pohl, Frederik. "The Children of Night." 1964. *The Best of Frederik Pohl*. Pohl. New York: Ballantine, 1975. 317–56.

———. *In the Problem Pit*. New York: Bantam, 1976.

———. "Sitting around the Pool, Soaking up the Rays." *IASFM* 8.8 (August 1984): 28–38.

———. "We Purchased People." 1974. *Pohlstars*. Pohl. New York: Ballantine, 1984. 140–58.

Pohl, Frederik, and C. M. Kornbluth. "The Gift of Garigolli." *Galaxy* 35.8 (August 1974): 96–118.

Pope, Gustavus. *Journey to Mars*. 1894. Ed. with a new introduction by Sam Moskowitz. Westport, CT: Hyperion Press, 1974.

Porges, Arthur. "Emergency Operation." 1956. *Great Science Fiction about Doctors*. Ed. Groff Conklin and Noah D. Fabricant. New York: Collier Macmillan, 1963. 333–41.

Quick, W. T. "Gentrification Blues." *Analog* 106.3 (March 1986): 62–75.

———. *Yesterday's Pawn*. New York: Signet, 1989.

Read, Herbert. *The Green Child*. London: William Heinemann, 1935.

Robins, Madeleine. "The Boarder." *IASFM* 6.7 (July 1982): 84–96.

Robinson, Frank M. "The Hunting Season." *Astounding* 48.3 (November 1951): 6.

———. "The Maze." *Astounding* 45.4 (June 1950): 69–84.

Robinson, Spider. *Mindkiller*. 1982. New York: Berkley, 1983.

———. "User Friendly." 1986. *Ark of Ice: Canadian Futurefiction*. Ed. Lesley Choyce. Lawrencetown Beach, NS: Pottersfield Press, 1992. 253–62.

Romans, R. H. "The Moon Conquerors." *Science Wonder Quarterly* 1.2 (Winter 1930): 150–233.

———. "The War of the Planets." *Wonder Stories Quarterly* 1.4 (Summer 1930): 438–67, 566.

Rosenberg, Joel. "Dutchman's Price." *Emile and the Dutchman*. Rosenberg. New York: Signet, 1985. 209–51.

Rusch, Kristine Kathryn. "Retrieval Artist." *Analog* 120.6 (June 2000): 8–44.

Russ, Joanna. "Invasion." *IASFM* 20.1 (January 1996): 44–52.

———. "Souls." 1981. *Extra(Ordinary) People.* London: Women's Press, 1985. 1–59.

Russell, Eric Frank. "Dear Devil." 1950. *Gentle Invaders.* Ed. Hans Stefan Santesson. New York: Belmont, 1969. 123–56.

———. "Hobbyist." *Astounding* 40.1 (September 1947): 33–61.

———. "Impulse." *Astounding* 22.1 (September 1938): 110–17.

———. "Now Inhale." 1959. *Aliens from Analog.* Ed. Stanley Schmidt. New York: Davis Publications, 1984. 118–38.

———. "The Waitabits." *Astounding* 55.5 (July 1955): 41–77.

Sagan, Carl. *Contact.* New York: Charles Scribner, 1986.

Sanders, Warren B. "Sheridan Becomes Ambassador." *Amazing* 7.4 (July 1932): 356–69.

Sanders, Winston P. "The Word to Space." 1960. *Other Worlds, Other Gods.* Ed. Mayo Mohs. New York: Avon, 1971. 69–85.

Sawyer, Robert J. *Far-Seer.* New York: Ace, 1992.

———. *Foreigner.* New York: Ace, 1994.

———. *Fossil Hunter.* New York: Ace, 1993.

Schachner, Nat. "Crystallized Thought." *Astounding* 19.6 (August 1937): 73–106.

———. "The Eternal Wanderer." *Astounding* 18.3 (November 1936): 14–37.

———. "He from Procyon." *Astounding* 13.2 (April 1934): 92–145.

———. "The Saprophyte Men of Venus." *Astounding* 18.2 (October 1936): 84–97.

———. "Slaves of Mercury." *Astounding* 11.1 (September 1932): 78–134.

Schmidt, Stanley. "His Loyal Opposition." *Analog* 96.7 (July 1976): 120–57.

Schmitz, James H. "Lion Loose." *Analog* 68.2 (October 1961): 6–58.

———. "The Pork Chop Tree." *Analog* 74.6 (February 1965): 42–45.

Schnirch, Gail. "A Cat for Katie." *Analog* 108.10 (October 1988): 126–37.

Scott, Sir Walter. *The Bride of Lammermoor: A Legend of Montrose.* Waverley Novels 4. Edinburgh: Cadell, 1852.

Serviss, Garrett Putnam. *A Columbus of Space.* 1894. Westport, CT: Hyperion Press, 1974.

Shaw, Robert. *Orbitsville.* London: Panther, 1975.

Shaver, Edward F. "Sport of Kings." *F&SF* 69.5 (November 1985): 76–94.

Sheffield, Charles. "The Subtle Serpent." 1980. *Stellar #5 Science Fiction Stories.* Ed. Judy-Lynn del Rey. New York: Ballantine Del Rey, 1980. 182–244.

Shelley, Mary. *Frankenstein or the Modern Prometheus.* 1818. London: Penguin, 1985.

Silverberg, Robert. "Alaree." 1958. *Earthmen and Strangers.* Ed. Robert Silverberg. New York: Dell, 1968. 64–76.

———. "Collecting Team." 1957. *The Science Fiction Bestiary.* Ed. Robert Silverberg. New York: Dell, 1974. 232–51.

Simak, Clifford D. "Courtesy." *Astounding* 47.6 (August 1951): 44–61.

———. "Honorable Opponent." 1956. *The Third Galaxy Reader.* Ed. H. L. Gold. 1958. New York: Permabooks, 1960. 202–17.

———. "Immigrant." 1954. *The Best Science Fiction Stories of Clifford Simak.* Simak. London: Faber & Faber, 1967. 26–84.

———. "Kindergarten." *Galaxy* 6.4 (July 1953): 4–49.

Smith, Cordwainer. "The Game of Rat and Dragon." *The Best of Cordwainer Smith.* Ed. J. J. Pierce. New York: Ballantine, 1975. 67–83.

Smith, Edward Elmer. "Doc." 1949. *Skylark of Valeron.* New York: Pyramid, 1963.

Smith, Edward Elmer, and Lee Hawkins Garby. *The Skylark of Space.* 1946. New York: Berkley, 1978.

Stall, Michael. "The Five Doors." 1973. *New Writings in SF–23.* Ed. Kenneth Bulmer. London: Corgi, 1975. 93–108.

Stewart, George R. *Earth Abides.* New York: Random, 1949.

Stiegler, Marc. "The Bully and the Crazy Boy." 1980. *War and Peace: Possible Futures from Analog.* Ed. Stanley Schmidt. New York, NY: Davis, 1983. 227–40.

———. "Petals of Rose." *Analog* 101.12 (November 1981): 12–47.

Stone, I. F. "The Rape of the Solar System." *Amazing* 9.8 (December 1934): 12–25.

Stribling, T. S. "The Green Splotches." *Amazing* 1.12 (March 1927): 1086–111.

Sturgeon, Theodore. "Artnan Process." *Astounding* 27.4 (June 1941): 50–68.

———. "The [Widget], the [Wadget], and Boff." 1955. *Aliens 4.* Sturgeon. New York: Avon, 1959. 143–224.

Szilard, Leo. "Grand Central Terminal." 1952. *Great Science Fiction by Scientists.* Ed. Groff Conklin. New York: Crowell-Collier, 1962. 289–96.

Tanner, Charles R. "Tumithak in Shawm." *Amazing* 8.8 (June 1933): 201–32.

———. "Tumithak of the Corridors." *Amazing* 6.10 (January 1932): 898–919, 950.

Tenn, William. "Firewater." *Astounding* 48.6 (February 1952): 7–36.

———. "Party of the Two Parts." 1954. *The Human Angle.* Tenn. New York: Ballantine, 1956. 75–98.

Thomas, Theodore L. "Ceramic Incident." *Astounding* 58.2 (October 1956): 135–39.

Thompson, W. R. "Roundup." *Analog* 118.9 (September 1998): 8–41.

———. "Second Contact." *Analog* 108.4 (April 1988): 10–59.

Thurston, Robert. "She/Her." 1973. *Infinity Five.* Ed. Robert Hoskins. New York: Lancer, 1973. 48–63.

Tiptree, James, Jr. "And I Awoke and Found Me Here on the Cold Hill's Side." 1971. *Ten Thousand Light-Years from Home.* Tiptree. New York: Ace, 1973. 1–13.

———. "Birth of a Salesman." 1968. *Ten Thousand Light-Years from Home.* Tiptree. New York: Ace, 1973. 293–314.

———. "Faithful to Thee, Terra, in Our Fashion." 1968. *Ten Thousand Light-Years from Home*. Tiptree. New York: Ace, 1973. 146–86.

———. "Love Is the Plan, the Plan Is Death." 1973. *Warm Worlds and Otherwise*. Tiptree. New York: Ballantine Del Rey, 1975. 173–93.

Traviss, Karin. "A Slice at a Time." *Asimov's* 26.7 (July 2002): 52–59.

Turtledove, Harry. *Earthgrip: Tales from the Traders' World*. New York: Ballantine Del Rey, 1991.

———. "The Foitani." 1991. *Earthgrip: Tales from the Traders' World*. New York: Ballantine Del Rey, 1991. 87–264.

Van Scyoc, Sydney J. "Skyveil." *Galaxy* 34.7 (April 1974): 75–93.

van Vogt, A. E. "Black Destroyer." *Astounding* 23.5 (July 1939): 9–31.

———. "Cooperate—Or Else!" *Astounding* 29.2 (April 1942): 78–92.

———. "Enchanted Village." 1950. *A. E. van Vogt's Science Fiction Monsters*. van Vogt. New York: Paperback Library, 1965. 67–79.

———. "The Rull." *Astounding* 41.26 (April 1948): 7–23.

———. *The Voyage of the Space Beagle*. 1963. New York: McFadden, 1968.

———. *The War against the Rull*. 1959. New York: Pocket Books Timescape, 1982.

Vance, Gerald. "Monsoons of Death." *Amazing* 16.12 (December 1942): 208–21, 241.

Vance, Jack. "Gift of Gab." 1955. *From Mind to Mind*. Ed. Stanley Schmidt. New York: Davis Publications, 1984. 53–93.

———. "The Potters of Firsk." *Astounding* 45.3 (May 1950): 88–106.

Verne, Jules. *A Journey to the Center of the Earth*. New York: Charles Scribner's Sons, n.d.

Vincent, Harl. "Parasite." *Amazing* 10.4 (July 1935): 71–107.

Wallace, Alfred Russel. *Is Mars Habitable?* London, Macmillan, 1907.

Wallace, F. L. "Big Ancestor." *Galaxy* 9.2 (November 1954): 134–59.

Weber, David. *On Basilisk Station*. New York: Baen, 1993.

Weinbaum, Stanley G. "A Martian Odyssey." 1934. *A Martian Odyssey and Other Stories*. Ed. Sam Moskowitz. Westport, CT: Hyperion Press, 1974. 1–27.

Wellen, Edward. "Tar Baby." *If* 22.4 (1974): 62–77.

Wells, H. G. *The War of the Worlds*. 1898. Harmondsworth, UK: Penguin, 1946.

Wells, Robert. *Right-Handed Wilderness*. New York: Ballantine, 1973.

White, James. *Ambulance Ship*. New York: Ballantine Del Rey, 1979.

———. *Code Blue—Emergency*. New York: Ballantine Del Rey, 1987.

———. "Combined Operation." 1983. *Sector General*. White. New York: Del Rey 1983. 117–96.

———. *Double Contact*. New York: Ballantine Del Rey, 1999.

———. *Final Diagnosis*. New York: Tor, 1997.

———. *The Genocidal Healer.* New York: Ballantine Del Rey, 1991.

———. *Mind Changer.* New York: Tor, 1998.

———. "Sanctuary." *Analog* 108.1 (December 1988): 10–41.

———. "Sector General." *Hospital Station.* New York: Ballantine, 1962. 39–83.

———. "Something of Value." *Analog* 105.2 (February 1985): 74–87.

———. *Star Surgeon.* New York: Ballantine, 1963.

Wightman, Wayne. "Do unto Others." *Amazing* 27.6 (February 1980): 60–68.

Williamson, Jack. "Born of the Sun." *Astounding* 13.1 (March 1934): 10–38.

———. "The Moon Era." 1932. *Before the Golden Age.* Ed. Isaac Asimov. New York: Doubleday, 1974. 286–336.

Wilson, Colin. *The Outsider.* London: Gollancz, 1956.

Wilson, Robin Scott. *Clarion.* New York: Signet, 1971.

Winterbotham, Russ. "Lonesome Hearts." *If* 3.5 (July 1954): 76–79, 94.

Wolheim, Donald A. "The Embassy." 1942. *Mars, We Love You.* Ed. Jane Hipolito and Willis E. McNelly. New York: Pyramid, 1973. 85–94.

———. "Storm Warning." 1942. *Invaders of Earth.* Ed. Groff Conklin. New York: Vanguard Press, 1952. 75–85.

Wright, Sewell Peaslee. "The Death-Traps of FX–31." *Astounding* 12.1 (March 1933): 82–98.

Wyndham, John. *The Midwich Cuckoos.* Harmondsworth, UK: Penguin, 1957.

Zelazny, Roger. "A Rose for Ecclesiastes." 1963. *The Science Fiction Hall of Fame I.* Ed. Robert Silverberg. New York: Avon, 1971. 636–72.

SECONDARY REFERENCES:
CRITICAL, SCIENTIFIC, AND MISCELLANEOUS

Absolon, L. F. Letter. *Astounding Stories* 9.2 (February 1932): 282.

Ackerman, Forrest. Letter. *Astounding Stories* 2.2 (May 1930): 278.

Alcubierre, Miguel. "The Alcubierre Warp Drive." *Classical and Quantum Gravity* 11 (1994): L72–L77.

"Alien Captured by U.S. Agents!" *Weekly World News.* 30 October 1990: 1.

Alvarez-Del Ray, Ramon. Letter. *Astounding Stories* 15.1 (March 1935): 158.

Amis, Kingsley. *New Maps of Hell: A Survey of Science Fiction.* 1960. London: New English Library Four Square, 1963.

Anderson, C. E. Letter. *Astounding Stories* 2.3 (June 1930): 422–23.

Anderson, Poul. "Alien Worlds." *The New Encyclopedia of Science Fiction.* Ed. James Gunn. New York: Viking, 1988. 6–9.

———. "The Asking of Questions." *Analog* 88.5 (January 1972): 5–7, 174–78.

———. "The Creation of Imaginary Worlds: The World Builder's Handbook and Pocket Companion." *Science Fiction, Today and Tomorrow.* Ed. Reginald Bretnor. New York: Harper and Row, 1974. 235–57.

———. *Is There Life on Other Worlds?* New York: Collier Books, 1968.

———. "Our Many Roads to the Stars." *Galaxy* 36.8 (September 1975): 73–87.

Andriano, Joseph. *Immortal Monster: The Mythological Evolution of the Fantastic Beast in Modern Fiction and Film.* Westport, CT: Greenwood Press, 1999.

Angenot, Marc. "The Absent Paradigm: An Introduction to the Semiotics of Science Fiction." *Science Fiction Studies* 6 (1979): 9–19.

An Interested Reader. Letter. *Astounding* 4.2 (November 1930): 42.

Antczak, Janice. *Science Fiction: The Mythos of a New Romance.* New York: Neal-Schuman, 1985.

Arbur, Rosemarie. "Teleology of Human Nature for Mentality?" *The Intersection of Science Fiction and Philosophy: Critical Studies.* Ed. Robert E. Myers. Westport, CT: Greenwood Press, 1983. 72–88.

Ardrey, Robert. *African Genesis: A Personal Investigation into the Animal Origins and Nature of Man.* 1961. New York: Dell, 1967.

———. *The Territorial Imperative: A Personal Inquiry into the Animal Origins of Property and Nations.* New York: Delta, 1966.

Aristotle. *The Basic Works of Aristotle.* Ed. Richard McKeon. New York: Random House, 1941.

Armitt, Lucie. "Re-Theorizing Textual Space: Feminist SF (and Some Critical Limitations)." *Impossibility Fiction: Alternativity—Extrapolation—Speculation.* Ed. Derek Littlewood and Peter Stockwell. Amsterdam: Rodopi, 1996. 37–44.

Armitt, Lucie, ed. *"Where No Man Has Gone Before": Essays on Women and Science Fiction.* London: Routledge, 1991.

Asch, Gale. Letter. *Analog* 79.5 (July 1967): 167–68.

Ash, Brian. "Biologies and Environments." *The Visual Encyclopedia of Science Fiction.* Ed. Ash. New York: Harmony Books, 1977. 94–99.

———. *Faces of the Future: The Lessons of Science Fiction.* London: Elek/Pemberton, 1975.

———. *Who's Who in Science Fiction.* 1976. London: Sphere, 1977.

———, ed. *The Visual Encyclopedia of Science Fiction.* New York: Harmony Books, 1977.

Asimov, Isaac. Afterword to "The Talking Stone." *Asimov's Mysteries.* Asimov. New York: Dell, 1968. 53–54.

———. "The All-Human Galaxy." *IASFM* 7.3 (March 1983): 6–12.

———. "Anatomy of a Martian." 1965. *Is Anyone There?* Asimov. London: Rapp and Whiting, 1968. 207–11.

———. *Asimov on Science Fiction*. 1981. New York: Avon Discus, 1982.

———. "Beyond the Phyla." *Astounding* 65.5 (July 1960): 83–105.

———. Introduction: "Robots and Aliens." *Changeling*. Stephen Leigh. Isaac Asimov's Robot City—Robots and Aliens 1. New York: Ace, 1989. ix–xiv.

———. *Is Anyone There?* London: Rapp and Whiting, 1968.

———. "The March of the Phyla." *Analog* 65.3 (May 1960): 83–104.

———. Response to Letter. *IASFM* 15.9 (August 1991): 12.

———. Response to Letter from John Barnes. *IASFM* 14.1 (January 1990): 10.

———. Response to Letter from Scott Jarrett. *IASFM* 13.7 (July 1989): 15.

———. "Standing Tall." *Magazine of Fantasy and Science Fiction* 74.1 (January 1988): 123–33.

———. *The Wellsprings of Life*. New York: Signet Science Library, 1960.

Attebery, Brian. *Strategies of Fantasy*. Bloomington: Indiana University Press, 1992.

Atwood, Margaret. Interview: "There's Nothing in the Book That Hasn't Already Happened. Interview." *Quill & Quire* 51.9 (September 1985): 66–67.

Austen, Jane. *Mansfield Park*. London: 1814.

Bacon, Camille. Letter. *Analog* 103.5 (May 1983): 170–71.

Baen, James. Blurb. *Galaxy* 37.3 (March 1978): 2.

———. "The Myth of the Light Barrier." *Galaxy* 36.7 (August 1975): 4.

Bagwell, Timothy J. "Science Fiction and the Semiotics of Realism: Alternatives." *Intersections: Fantasy and Science Fiction*. Ed. George E. Slusser and Eric Rabkin. Carbondale: Southern Illinois University Press, 1987.

Baier, Annette. "Knowing Our Place in the Animal World." *Postures of the Mind: Essays on Mind and Morals*. Anon. Minneapolis, MN: University of Minnesota Press, 1985. 139–56.

Bailey, J. O. *Pilgrims through Space and Time: Trends and Patterns in Scientific and Utopian Fiction*. New York: Argus, 1947.

Bailey, K. V. "Alien Gifties: The Reflexive Perspective." *Foundation* 49 (Summer 1990): 23–34.

Baird, James. "Jungian Psychology in Criticism: Theoretical Problems." *Literary Criticism in Psychology*. Ed. Joseph P. Strelka. New York: Spring Books, 1976. 3–30.

Baker, Robert A. "The Aliens among Us: Hypnotic Regression Revisited." *Skeptical Enquirer* 12.2 (Winter 1987): 147–62.

Baldick, Chris. *The Concise Oxford Dictionary of Literary Terms*. Oxford and New York: Oxford University Press, 1990.

Ball, John A. "Extraterrestrial Intelligence: Where Is Everybody?" *American Scientist* 68 (1980): 656–63.

———. "The Zoo Hypothesis." *Icarus* 19.3 (1973): 347–49.

Barlowe, Wayne Douglas. *Barlowe's Guide to Extraterrestrials.* 1979. 2nd ed. New York: Workman Publishing, 1987.

Barnes, John. Letter. *IASFM* 14.1 (January 1990): 10–12.

Barnes, Myra Edwards. *Linguistics and Languages in Science Fiction-Fantasy.* New York: Arno Press, 1974.

Barnhart, Clarence L., Sol Steinmetz, and Robert K. Barnhart, eds. *The Second Dictionary of New English.* Bronxville, NY: Barnhart, 1980.

Barr, Greg. "Contact in the Classroom." *Analog* 112.1 & 2 (January 1992): 223–37.

Barr, Marleen S. *Lost in Space: Probing Feminist Science Fiction and Beyond.* Chapel Hill: University of North Carolina Press, 1993.

———. *Alien to Feminity: Speculative Fiction and Feminist Theory.* Contributions to the Study of Science Fiction and Fantasy 27. Westport, CT: Greenwood Press, 1987.

Barron, Neil. *Anatomy of Wonder: A Critical Guide to Science Fiction.* 5th ed. Westport, CT: Libraries Unlimited, 2004.

Barrow, John D. "Anthropic Definitions." *Quarterly Journal of the Royal Astronomical Society* 24 (1983): 146–53.

Barrow, John D., and Frank J. Tipler. *The Anthropic Cosmological Principle.* Oxford: Oxford University Press, 1980.

Bates, F. Harry. Editorial Announcement. "Additions—Improvements." *Astounding* 11.3 (January 1933): 420–21.

Baxter, Stephen. "Stephen Baxter: Future Dilemmas." Interview. *Locus* 41.1 (July 1998): 4–5, 72–73.

Benedict, Ruth. *Patterns of Culture.* 1946. New York: Bantam, 1960.

Benford, Gregory. "Aliens." *The New Encyclopedia of Science Fiction.* Ed. James Gunn. New York: Viking, 1988. 9–11.

———. "Aliens and Knowability: A Scientist's Perspective." 1980. *Bridges to Science Fiction.* Ed. George E. Slusser, George R. Guffey, and Mark Rose. Carbondale: Southern Illinois University Press, 1980. 53–63.

———. "Effing the Ineffable." *Aliens: The Anthropology of Science Fiction.* Ed. George E. Slusser and Eric S. Rabkin. Carbondale: Southern Illinois University Press, 1987. 12–25.

———. "Imagining Other Minds." *F&SF* 95.3 (September 1998): 115–27.

———. "A Portrait of Humanity." *F&SF* 95.3 (October 1998): 170–81.

———. "Searching for Alien Artifacts." *Amazing* 64.6 (March 1990): 84–93.

Benison, Jonathan. "Science Fiction and Postmodernity." *Postmodernism and the Re-Reading of Modernity.* Ed. Francis Barker, Peter Hulme, and Margaret Iversen. Manchester, UK: Manchester University Press, 1992

Bernabeu, Ednita P. "Science Fiction: A New Mythos." *Psychoanalytic Quarterly* 26 (October 1957): 527–35.

Bertens, Johannes Willem. *The Idea of the Postmodern: A History.* London: Routledge, 1995.

Bhabha, Homi K. *The Location of Culture.* London: Routledge, 1994.

Biggle, Lloyd Jr. "The Morasses of Academe Revisited." *Analog* 98.9 (September 1978): 143–46.

———. "Science Fiction Goes to College: Groves and the Morasses of Academe." *Riverside Quarterly* 6.2 (April 1974): 100–9.

Blish, James. *The Issue at Hand: Studies in Contemporary Magazine Science Fiction by William Atheling Jr.* Chicago: Advent Press, 1964.

———. *More Issues at Hand: Critical Studies in Contemporary Science Fiction by William Atheling Jr.* 1964. Chicago: Advent Press, 1970.

Bonhoff, Maya Kaathryn. Letter. *Analog* 112.1 & 2 (January 1992): 316.

Bova, Ben. "The Alien Worlds." *Thrilling Science Fiction* (June 1974): 70–79, 125.

———. "Extraterrestrial Life: An Astronomer's Theory." *Thrilling Science Fiction* (October 1974): 53–63.

———. "Extraterrestrial Life: A New Era Begins." *Analog* 116.7 (June 1996): 60–67.

———. "Genetic Politics." *Analog* 96.8 (August 1976): 5–6, 8–9, 174.

———. "Ideas and Ideologies." *Analog* 96.10 (October 1976): 5–7, 168.

———. "The Inevitability of Life: Extra-Terrestrial Life Part 3." *Thrilling Science Fiction* (July 1975): 122–30.

———. "Intelligent Life in Space." *Thrilling Science Fiction* (February 1973): 99–109.

———. "Progress Report: Life Forms in Meteorites." *Thrilling Science Fiction* (April 1974): 100–12.

———. "Where Is Everybody?" *Thrilling Science Fiction* (April 1973): 121–29.

Bova, Ben, and Byron Preiss, eds. *First Contact: The Search for Extraterrestrial Intelligence.* 1990. New York: Penguin Plume, 1991.

Bracewell, Ronald N. *The Galactic Club: Intelligent Life in Outer Space.* San Francisco, CA: San Francisco Book, 1976.

Brecht, Bertolt. "Short Organon for the Theatre." *Brecht on Theatre.* Ed. and tr. John Willett. New York: Hill and Wang, 1964.

Bretnor, Reginald, ed. *The Craft of Science Fiction.* New York: Harper and Row, 1976.

———. "Memories of the Future." *Amazing* 63.2 (July 1988): 111–17.

————. *Modern Science Fiction: Its Meaning and Its Future.* 1953. 2nd ed. Chicago: Advent Publishers, 1979.

Brewster, David. *More Worlds than One.* 1854.

Brin, David. "The Dangers of First Contact." *Aboriginal Science Fiction* 5.2 (March-April 1991): 23–100.

————. "The Dogma of Otherness." *Analog* 106.4 (April 1986): 4–12, 189–91.

————. "The 'Great Silence': The Controversy Concerning Extraterrestrial Intelligent Life." *Quarterly Journal of the Royal Astronomical Society* 24 (Autumn 1983): 289–309.

————. "Just How Dangerous Is the Galaxy?" *Analog* 105.7 (July 1985): 80–95.

————. "Neoteny and Two-Way Sexual Selection in Human Evolution: Paleo-Anthropological Speculation on the Origins of Secondary-Sexual Traits, Male Nurturing, and the Child as Sexual Image." *Journal of Social and Evolutionary Systems* 18.3 (1995): 257–76.

————. "A Shaman's View." *The Profession of Science Fiction.* Ed. Maxim Jakubowski and Edward James. London: Macmillan, 1992. 161–68.

————. "Xenology: The New Science of Asking 'Who's Out There?'" *Analog* 103.5 (May 1983): 64–83.

Brin, David, with T. B. H. Kuiper. "Resource Letter ETC–1: Extraterrrestrial Civilization." *American Journal of Physics* 57.1 (January 1989): 12–18.

Broderick, Damien. *Reading by Starlight: Postmodern Science Fiction.* London: Routledge, 1995.

————. "SF and the Postmodern." *New York Review of Science Fiction* 30 (February 1991): 12–16.

————. *Theory and Its Discontents.* Geelong, Victoria, Australia: Deakin University Press, 1997.

Brooke-Rose, Christine. *A Rhetoric of the Unreal: Studies in Narrative and Structure, Especially of the Fantastic.* Cambridge: Cambridge University Press, 1981.

Brown, Andrew. *The Darwin Wars: How Stupid Genes Became Selfish Gods.* London: Simon and Schuster, 1999.

Brown, E. B. Letter. *Astounding* 14.2 (October 1934): 153–54.

Buchanan, Louis D. Letter. *Astounding* 4.1 (October 1930): 134–35.

Budrys, Algis. "Literatures of Milieux." *Missouri Review* 4.2 (1984): 499–563.

————. "Books." *F&SF* 74.4 (April 1988): 20–25.

————. "State of the Art." *Analog* 100.10 (October 1980): 107–14.

Bunyard, Peter, and Edward Goldsmith, eds. *Gaia: The Thesis, the Mechanisms and the Implications.* Camelford, Cornwall, UK: Wadebridge Ecological Centre, 1988.

Burwasser, David. Letter. *Analog* 66.2 (October 1960): 172–73.

Bushnik, C. S. "An Alien Viewpoint." *Analog* 107.4 (April 1987): 4–8, 186.

Butterworth, George. "Intelligence." *Harper Dictionary of Modern Thought.* Ed. Alan Bullock, Oliver Stalleybrass, and Stepen Trombley. Rev. ed. New York: Harper and Row, 1988. 428–29.

Campbell, Bernard. "The Evolution of Technological Species." *Life in the Universe.* Ed. John Billingham. Cambridge, MA: MIT Press, 1981. 277–85.

Campbell, John W., Jr. Blurb for Chapdelaine: "Initial Contact." *Analog* 84.3 (November 1969): 9.

———. Blurb for Perkins: "Delivered with Feeling." *Analog* 75.5 (July 1965): 133.

———. Blurb for Perkins: "Target: Language." *Analog/Astounding* 79.3 (May 1967): 81.

———. Editorial: "Arithmetic and Empire." *Astounding* 32.3 (November 1943): 3–4.

———. Editorial: "A Difference of Intelligence." *Analog* 84.2 (October 1969): 4–7, 177–78.

———. Editorial: "Flying Saucers." *Astounding* 46.2 (October 1950): 4–5, 138.

———. Editorial: "Flying Somethings." *Astounding* 40.2 (October 1947): 4–5, 103.

———. Editorial: "History to Come." *Astounding* 27.3 (May 1941): 5–6.

———. Editorial: "Interpreters May Still Be Needed." *Astounding* 27.4 (June 1941): 6.

———. Editorial: "Interstellar Communication." *Analog* 79.4 (June 1966): 6–7, 174–78.

———. Editorial: "Invention." *Astounding* 16.5 (January 1941): 5.

———. Editorial. "Learning Patterns." *Astounding* 60.1 (September 1957): 6.

———. Editorial: "Life as We Know It." *Astounding* 29.6 (August 1942): 6.

———. Editorial. "The Modern Black Arts." *Analog* 86.4 (December 1970): 4–7, 175–78.

———. Editorial: "The Nature of Intelligent Aliens." *Analog* 80.2 (October 1967): 5–7, 172–78.

———. Editorial: "New Order." *Astounding* 31.2 (April 1943): 6.

———. Editorial: "On the Selective Breeding of Human Beings." *Analog* 66.6 (February 1961): 4–7, 176–78.

———. Editorial: "Postulate an Alien Who—?" *Astounding* 50.5 (January 1953): 6–8.

———. Editorial: "Question . . ." *Astounding* 50.4 (December 1952): 6, 170.

———. Editorial: "We're Not All Human." *Astounding* 28.1 (September 1941): 123–27.

———. Editorial: "What Do You Mean . . . Human." *Astounding* 64.1 (September 1959): 5–7, 160–62.

———. Editorial Announcement: "In Times to Come." *Astounding* 31.5 (January 1953): 38.

———. "Science Fiction We Can Buy." *Writer* 81 (September 1968): 27–28.

Canfield, Matthew. Letter. *Analog* 107.6 (June 1987): 186.

Carr, Bernard, and Tony Rothman. "On Coincidences in Nature and the Hunt for the Anthropic Principle." *IASFM* 5.11 (October 1981): 32–46.

Carrington, Arthur H. Letter. *Astounding* 7.1 (July 1931): 131.

Carrithers, Michael. "Sociality, Not Aggression, Is the Key Human Trait." *Societies at Peace: Anthropological Perspectives.* Ed. Signe Howell and Roy Willis. London: Routledge, 1989. 187–209.

———. *Why Humans Have Cultures.* Oxford: Oxford University Press, 1992.

Carter, Paul A. *The Creation of Tomorrow: Fifty Years of Magazine Fiction.* New York: Columbia University Press, 1977.

Cartmill, Matt. Letter. *Analog* 83.4 (June 1969): 170–72.

Chan, Stafford. Letter. *Astounding Stories* 12.6 (February 1934): 139–40.

Chapdelaine, Perry A., Sr., Tony Chapedelaine, and George Hay. *The John W. Campbell Letters, Vol. 1.* 1985. Franklin, TN: AC Projects Inc., 1985.

Chapman Robert L., ed. *Dictionary of American Slang.* New York: Harper and Row, 1986.

Cheetham, Anthony. Introduction. "What is a Vug?" *Bug-Eyed Monsters: Ten SF Stories.* Ed. Anthony Cheetham. 1972. London: Panther, 1974. 7–8.

Cherryh, C. J. "Goodbye Star Wars, Hello Alley-Oop." *Inside Outer Space: Science Fiction Professionals Look at Their Craft.* Ed. Sharon Jarvis. New York: Frederick Ungar, 1985. 17–26.

———. Afterword: "Thoughts on the Future of Conflict." *The Game Beyond.* Ed. Melissa Scott. New York: Baen, 1984. 342–50.

Chomsky, Noah. *Language and Mind.* New York: Harcourt Brace Jovanovich, 1968.

Christian, James L., ed. *Extra-Terrestrial Intelligence: The First Encounter.* Buffalo, NY: Prometheus, 1976.

Church, Francis P. "Is There a Santa Claus?" *New York Sun.* 21 September 1897. Editorial Page. http://www.stormfax.com/virginia.htm (accessed 7 December 2005).

Cioffi, Frank. *Formula Fiction? An Anatomy of Science Fiction, 1930–1940.* Contributions to the Study of Science Fiction and Fantasy 3. Westport, CT: Greenwood Press, 1982.

Clareson, Thomas D., ed. *Many Futures, Many Worlds: Theme and Form in Science Fiction.* Kent, OH: Kent State University Press, 1977.

———. "Science Fiction: The New Mythology." *Extrapolation* 10 (1969): 69–115.

Clark, Stephen R. L. "Squirrels and Alien Life." *Foundation* 65 (Autumn 1995): 98.

Clarke, Arthur C. "In Defense of Science Fiction." *UNESCO Courier* 15 (November 1962): 14–17.

———. "When Earthman and Alien Meet." *Playboy* 15 (January 1968): 118.

Clayton, David. "Science Fiction: Going around in Generic Circles." 1987. *Intersections: Fantasy and Science Fiction.* Ed. George E. Slusser and Eric S. Rabkin. Carbondale: Southern Illinois University Press, 1987. 201–24.

Clear, Val, ed. *Marriage and the Family through Science Fiction*. New York: St. Martin's Press, 1976.

Clement, Hal. "The Creation of Imaginary Beings." *Science Fiction, Today and Tomorrow*. Ed. Reginald Bretnor. New York: Harper and Row, 1974. 259–75.

———. "Whirligig World." *Astounding* 54.1 (June 1953): 102–14.

———. "Uncommon Sense." *Astounding* 36:1 (September 1945): 47–62.

Clute, John, and Peter Nicholls, eds. *The Encyclopedia of Science Fiction*. London: Little, Brown (UK) Orbit Books, 1993.

Cohen, Jeffrey J. "Monster Culture." 1925. *Monster Theory: Reading Culture*. Ed. Jeffrey Jerome Cohen. Minneapolis: University of Minnesota Press, 1996.

———. *Monster Theory: Reading Culture*. Minneapolis: University of Minnesota Press, 1996.

Colladay, Morris. "Highly Civilized Animals." *Astounding* 26.3 (November 1940): 161–62.

Collender, Harold. Letter. *Astounding Stories* 12.5 (January 1934): 143.

Collings, Michael R. "Science Fiction and the Cliché: The Sociology of Meaning and Function." 1985. *Just the Other Day: Essays on the Suture of the Future*. Ed. Luk de Vos. Antwerp, Belgium: Uitgeverij EXA, 1985. 65–70.

Collins Dictionary of the English Language. London: Collins, 1979.

Conklin, Groff. Blurb for van Vogt: "Not Only Dead Men." *Invaders of Earth*. Ed. Conklin. New York: Vanguard Press, 1952. 160.

———. Introduction. *Invaders of Earth* . Ed. Conklin. New York: Vanguard Press, 1952. ix–xiii.

———. Comment on Robert Plank: "The Reproduction of Psychosis in Science Fiction." *Galaxy* 9.5 (February 1955): 106.

Conrad, Joseph. "The Brute." 1908. *A Set of Six*. Anon. London: J. M. Dent, 1954. 105–31.

Cook, Rick. "Life as We Don't Know It." *Analog* 86.3 (November 1970): 38–59.

———. "The Long Stern Chase: A Speculative Exercise." *Analog* 106.7 (July 1986): 32–43.

———. "Neural Nets." *Analog* 109.8 (August 1989): 86–99.

Coon, Carleton S. Foreword. *Apeman, Spaceman: Anthropological Science Fiction*. Ed. Harry Harrison and Leon E. Stover. London: Rapp and Whiting, 1968. 11–12.

Corballis, Michael. *The Lopsided Ape: Evolution of the Generative Mind*. New York: Oxford University Press, 1991.

Cornillon, Susan Koppelman, ed. *Images of Women in Fiction: Feminist Perspectives*. 1972. Bowling Green, OH: Bowling Green University Popular Press, 1973.

Coupling, J. J. "Science for Art's Sake." *Astounding* 46.3 (November 1950): 83–92.

Cox, Arthur J. "Varieties of Culture." *Astounding* 46.4 (December 1950): 87–97.

Cramer, John G. "The Alcubierre Warp Drive." *Analog* 116.13 (November 1996): 82–85.

———. "More about Wormholes—To the Stars in No Time." *Analog* 110.6 (May 1990): 99–103.

———. "Wormholes and Time Machines." *Analog* 109.6 (June 1989): 124–28.

Crick, F. H. C., and L. E. Orgel. "Directed Panspermia." *Icarus* 19.3 (1973): 341–46.

Croutch, Leslie A. Letter. *Amazing* 9.7 (November 1934): 135–36.

Crowe, Michael J. *The Extraterrestrial Life Debate, 1750–1900: The Idea of a Plurality of Worlds from Kant to Lowell.* Cambridge: Cambridge University Press, 1986.

Csicsery-Ronay, Istvan, Jr. Editorial Introduction: "Postmodernism's SF/SF's Postmodernism." *Science Fiction Studies* 18.3 (November 1991): 305–8.

Dalzell, Bonnie. "Hexapedia." *Galaxy* 37.4 (May 1976): 68–72.

Darrow, Jack. Letter. *Astounding* 3.3 (September 1930): 424–25.

Dart, Raymond A. "The Predatory Transition from Ape to Man." *International Anthropological and Linguistic Review* 1.4 (1953): 201–19.

Darwin, Charles Robert. *The Descent of Man.* London: Murray, 1871.

———. *On the Origin of Species by Means of Natural Selection.* 1858. London: John Murray, 1859.

Davenport, Basil. *Inquiry into Science Fiction.* New York: n.p., 1955.

Davis, B. G. Editorial Comment. *Amazing* 13.2 (February 1939): 137–38.

Davis, Hank. "Animal Cognition *Versus* Animal Thinking: The Anthropomorphic Error." 1997. *Anthropomorphism, Anecdotes, and Animals.* Ed. Robert W. Mitchell, Nicholas S. Thompson, and H. Lyn Miles. Albany: Statue University of New York Press, 1997. 335–47.

Dawkins, R. *The Selfish Gene.* 1976. New York: Oxford University Press Paperback, 1978.

de Camp, L. Sprague. "The Breeds of Man." *Analog* (April 1976): 11–42.

———. "Design for Life—1." *Astounding* 23.3 (May 1939): 103–16.

———. "Design for Life—2." *Astounding* 23.4 (June 1939): 103–15.

———. "How to Plan a Fauna." 1963. *The Fringe of the Unknown.* de Camp. Buffalo, NY: Prometheus Books, 1983. 109–18.

———. "Little Green Men from Afar." 1976. *The Fringe of the Unknown.* de Camp. Buffalo, NY: Prometheus Books, 1983. 191–202.

———. "Man's Biological Future." *Analog* 100.11 (November 1980): 55–66.

———. *Science-Fiction Handbook: The Writing of Imaginative Fiction.* 1st ed. New York: Hermitage House, 1953.

De Castillejo, Irene Claremont. *Knowing Woman: A Feminist Psychology.* 1967. New York: Putnam for the NY C. G. Jung Foundation, 1973.

"Declaration of Principles Concerning Activities Following the Detection of Extrater-restrial Intelligence." *Acta Astronautica* 21.2. London: Pergamon Press, 1990. 153–54. http://seticlassic.ssl.berkeley.edu/declaration.html (accessed 6 December 2005).

Defoe, Daniel. *The Fortunes and Misfortunes of the Famous Moll Flanders.* 2nd ed. London: printed for John Brotherton, 1722.

Delaney, Joseph H. "So You Want to Write a Law Story?" *Analog* 119.7 & 8 (July-August 1999): 90–97.

Delany, Samuel R. "Generic Protocols: Science Fiction and Mundane." *The Technological Imagination: Theories and Fictions.* Ed. Teresa deLauretis, Andreas Huyssen, and Kathleen Woodward. Madison, WI: Coda, 1980. 175–93.

———. "The Gestation of Genres: Literature, Fiction, Romance, Science Fiction, Fantasy . . ." *Intersections: Fantasy and Science Fiction.* Ed. George E. Slusser and Eric S. Rabkin. Carbondale: Southern Illinois University Press, 1987. 63–73.

———. "Modernism, Postmodernism, Science Fiction." *New York Review of Science Fiction* 1 (August 1990): 8–9.

———. "Neither the Beginning nor the End of Structuralism, Poststructuralism, Semiotics, or Deconstruction for SF Readers: An Introduction." Pt. 1. *New York Review of Science Fiction* 6 (February 1989): 1, 8–12; Pt. 2. *New York Review of Science Fiction* 7 (March 1989): 14–18; Pt. 3. *New York Review of Science Fiction* 8 (April 1989): 9–11.

del Rey, Lester. Review of George Bamber, *The Sea is Boiling Hot. If* 21.3 (January-February 1972): 154–60.

———. *The World of Science Fiction 1926–1976: The History of a Subculture.* New York: Garland, 1980.

Dennett, Daniel C. "Consciousness." *The Oxford Companion to Mind.* Ed. Richard L. Gregory. Oxford: Oxford University Press, 1987. 160–64.

Derleth, August. Introduction. *Far Boundaries.* New York: Pellegrini and Cudahy, 1951. viii–x.

de Vos, Luk. Introduction. *Just the Other Day: Essays on the Suture of the Future.* Ed. de Vos. Antwerp, Belgium: EXA, 1985.

Dewdney, Christopher. *Last Flesh: Life in the Transhuman Age.* New York: Harper Collins Canada, 1998.

Dietz, Frank. "Everyperson in Nowhereland: Characters in Contemporary American Utopias." *New York Review of Science Fiction* 2.8 (April 1990): 1–5.

Disch, Thomas M. *The Dreams Our Stuff Is Made of: How Science Fiction Conquered the World.* 1998. New York: Touchstone, 2000.

Doherty, G. H. "Use of Language in Science Fiction." *SF Horizons* 1 (1964): 43–53.

Dolan, James Francis. Letter. *Astounding* 14.4 (December 1934): 134.

Dole, Stephen. *Habitable Planets for Man.* 1964. 2nd ed. New York: American Elsevier, 1970.

Donald, Merlin. *Origins of the Modern Mind: Three Stages in the Evolution of Culture and Cognition.* Cambridge: Harvard University Press, 1991.

Donaldson, Thomas. "How to Go Faster Than Light." *Analog* 105.6 (June 1985): 77–91.

———. "Neuroscience and Other Intelligences." *Analog* 120.8 (September 2000): 40–49.

Downer, Warren E. Letter. *Analog* 80.1 (September 1967): 174.

Dozois, Gardner. Introduction. *Aliens!* Ed. Dozois and Jack M. Dann. New York: Pocket Books, 1980.

Ducommun, Pascal. "Alien Aliens." *Aliens: The Anthropology of Science Fiction.* Ed. George Slusser and Eric S. Rabkin. Carbondale: Southern Illinois University Press, 1987. 36–42.

Dunn, J. R. Letter. *Analog* 106.3 (March 1986): 186.

DuPlessis, Rachel Blau. "The Feminist Apologues of Lessing, Piercy, and Russ." *Frontiers* 4.1 (1979): 1–8.

Earley, George W. Editor's Preface. *Encounters with Aliens: UFOs and Alien Beings in Science Fiction* . Ed. Earley. Los Angeles: Sherbourne Press, 1968. 11–22.

Easton, Tom. Review of Susan Schwartz, *Hostile Takeover. Analog* 125.5 (May 2005): 134–36.

Easton, Thomas A. "Altruism, Evolution, and Society." *Analog* 96.10 (October 1976): 57–70.

———. "The Future of Biological Engineering." *Analog* 102.12 (November 1982): 42–49.

Elkins, Charles. "The Uses of Science Fiction." *Science Fiction Studies* 17.2 (July 1990): 269–72.

Emsh. "Season's Greetings to Our Readers." *Galaxy* 3.3 (December 1951): cover.

———. "A Settlement Out of Court." *Galaxy* 6.4 (July 1953): cover.

Eulach, V. A. "Those Impossible Autotrophic Men." *Astounding* 58.2 (October 1956): 98–103.

Evans, Bergen. *The Natural History of Nonsense.* 1947. London: Michael Joseph, 1953.

Evans, Richard I. *R. D. Laing: The Man and His Ideas.* New York: Dutton, 1976.

"The Extraterrestrial Exposure Law" [Text]. Title 14 Aeronautics and Space, Part 1211 Extra-terrestrial Exposure. www.zerotime.com/ufo/etexpos.htm (accessed 7 December 2005).

"The Extraterrestrial Exposure Law." *Open Line Newspaper* (Environmental Stewards) [Spokane, WA]. August 1992. www.qsl.net/w5www/etlaw.html (accessed 7 December 2005).

"Extraterrestrial Exposure Law Could Apply to UFO Experiencers." 6 March 2005. www.cninews.com/Search/CNI.0197.html (accessed 7 December 2005).

Fairman, Paul F. Blurb for Hamm, "The Last Supper." *If: Worlds of Science Fiction* 1.4 (September 1952): 105.

Fasan, Ernst. *Relations with Alien Intelligences.* Berlin-Verlag: Arno Spitz, 1970.

Feinberg, G., and R. Shapiro. *Life beyond Earth: The Intelligent Earthling's Guide to Life in the Universe.* New York: Morrow, 1980.

Finch, Sheila. "Berlitz in Outer Space: How Alien Communication Might Just Work." *Amazing Stories* 63.1 (May 1988): 50–56.

Finer, S. E. "Profile of Science Fiction." *Sociological Review* n.s. 2 (December 1965): 239–46.

Fitting, Peter. "'So We All Became Mothers': New Roles for Men in Recent Utopian Fiction." *Science Fiction Studies* 12 (1985): 156–57.

Forster, E. M. *Aspects of the Novel.* London: Edwin Arnold, 1927.

Forward, Robert L. "Interstellar Probes and Star Ships." *Galaxy* 38.1 (March 1977): 37–43.

Franklin, H. B. "The Vietnam War as American SF and Fantasy." *Science Fiction Studies* 17.52 (November 1990): 341–59.

Fredericks, S. C. "Revivals of Ancient Mythologies in Current Science Fiction and Fantasy." *Many Futures, Many Worlds: Theme and Form in Science Fiction.* Ed. Anon. Kent, OH: Kent State University Press, 1977. 50–65.

Freedman, Carl F. *Critical Theory and Science Fiction.* Hanover, NH: Wesleyan University Press, 2000.

Freitag, Betsy G. Letter. *Analog* 66.1 (September 1960): 159.

Freitas, Robert A. "Alien Sex." *Analog* 102.6 (June 1982): 46–53.

———. "Extraterrestrial Zoology." *Analog* 101.8 (July 1981): 53–67.

———. "Fermi's Paradox: A Real Howler." *IASFM* 9.9 (September 1984): 30–44.

———. "Interstellar Probes: A New Approach to SETI." *Journal of the British Interplanetary Society* 33 (1980): 95–100.

———. "The Legal Rights of Extraterrestrials." *Analog* 97.4 (April 1977): 54–67.

———. "Xenopsychology." *Analog* 104.4 (April 1984): 41–53.

Freud, Sigmund. "The Transformations of Puberty." 1905. *Three Essays on the Theory of Sexuality.* Freud. New York: Avon Library Book, 1965. 107–49.

———. "The 'Uncanny.'" [*Das Unheimliche*]. 1919. Standard Edition of the Works of Sigmund Freud. Tr. James Strachey. London: Hogarth Press, 1955. 17: 217–56.

Freudenthal, Hans. *Lincos: Design of a Language for Cosmic Intercourse.* Amsterdam: North-Holland, 1960.

Friedman, Norman. "Symbol." *The New Princeton Encyclopedia of Poetry and Poetics.* Ed. Alex Preminger and T. V. F. Brogan. Princeton, NJ: Princeton University Press, 1974. 833–36.

Friend, Tim. "Bird Shows Brains in Crafty Use of Tool." *USA Today,* 9 August 2002. www.arizonarepublic.com/new/articles/0809crow90.html (accessed 15 August 2002).

Fukuyama, Francis. "The End of History?" *National Interest* 16 (Summer 1989): 3–18.

Fulton, Sandra J. Letter. *Analog* 66.4 (December 1960): 173–77.

Gale, Floyd C. Review of Clement, *The Ranger Boys in Space. Galaxy* 14.4 (August 1957): 117.

Gamst, Frederick C., and Edward Norbeck. *Ideas of Culture: Sources and Uses.* New York: Holt, Rinehart and Winston, 1976.

Garre, Marianne. *Human Rights in Translation: Legal Concepts in Different Languages.* Copenhagen: Copenhagen Business School Press, 1999.

Gernsback, Hugo. "Science Fiction Vs. Science Faction." *Wonder Stories Quarterly* 2.1 (Fall 1930): 5.

Gernsback, Hugo, and David Lasser. "Results of Interplanetary Plot Contest." *Wonder Stories Quarterly* 2.4 (Summer 1931): 437.

Gervais, Edward F. Letter. *Astounding* 14.1 (September 1934): 158–59.

Gillett, Stephen L. "The Fermi Paradox." *IASFM* 8.8 (August 1984): 42–50.

———. "On Building an Earthlike Planet." *Analog* 107.78 (July 1989): 90–107.

———. "Those Halogen Breathers." *Analog* 104.10 (October 1984): 60–70.

———. *World-Building: A Writer's Guide to Constructing Star Systems and Life-Supporting Planets.* Science Fiction Writing Series. Cincinnati, OH: Writer's Digest Books, 1996.

Ginzberg, Louis. *The Legends of the Jews.* Vol. 1. Philadelphia, PA: Jewish Publication Society of America, n.d.

Golden, Kenneth L. *Science Fiction, Myth, and Jungian Psychology.* Lewiston, NY: Edwin Mellen Press, 1995.

Goldenberg, Naomi. "Archetypal Theory after Jung." *Spring* (1975): 199–220.

Goldin, Stephen. Introduction. *The Alien Condition.* New York: Ballantine, 1973. ix–xii.

Goldsmith, Donald, ed. *The Quest for Extraterrestrial Life: A Book of Readings.* Mill Valley, CA: University Science Books, 1980.

Goodall, Jane. Interview. "Quirks and Quarks." CBC Radio, 19 May 1990.

———. *Through a Window: My Thirty Years with the Chimpanzees of Gombe.* Boston: Houghton Mifflin, 1990.

Gordon, Michael. Letter. *IASFM* 9.2 (February 1985): 18.

Gould, Stephen Jay. *Wonderful Life: The Burgess Shale and the Nature of History.* New York: W. W. Norton, 1989.

Green, Roland J. "A World of Ideas." *Amazing* 62.6 (March 1988): 74–83.

Gregory, Richard L. "Empathy." *The Oxford Companion to the Mind.* Ed. Gregory. Oxford: Oxford University Press, 1987. 220–21.

———. Preface. *The Oxford Companion to the Mind.* Ed. Gregory. Oxford: Oxford University Press, 1987. v–viii.

Greimas, Algirdas J. "Actants, Actors, and Figures." *On Meaning: Selected Writings in Semiotic Theory.* Minneapolis: University of Minnesota Press, 1987. 106–20.

Grosse, Bruno. "5 Girls Give Birth to UFO Babies." *Sun* 8.17 (April 1990): 19.

Gruebner, R. J. Letter. *Fantastic Adventures* 5.10 (December 1943): 196–97.

Guirard, Pierre. *Semiology.* Tr. George Gross. London: Routledge and Kegan Paul, 1975.

Gunn, James, ed. *The New Encyclopedia of Science Fiction.* New York: Viking, 1989.

———. e-mail to author, 23 December 1997.

Gutin, Jo Ann C. "A Brain That Talks." *Discover* 17.6 (June 1996): 82–90.

Haldane, J. B. S. "Possible Worlds." *Possible Worlds and Other Papers.* New York: Harper Brothers, 1927. 272–99.

Haldeman, Joe. "Science Fiction and War." *IASFM* 10.4 (April 1986): 27–38.

Haley, Andrew G. "Space Law and Metalaw—A Synoptic View." *Proceedings of the Seventh International Astronautical Conference:* Rome: Associazione Italiana Razzi, 1956.

Hall, Edward T. *The Hidden Dimension.* 1966. New York: Doubleday Anchor, 1969.

Hammerton, M. Letter. *Foundation* 62 (Winter 1994-1995): 81.

Hampden-Turner, Charles. *Maps of the Mind: Charts and Concepts of the Mind and Its Labyrinths.* New York: Macmillan, 1981.

Hanna, Judith. "The Greenskins Are Here: Women, Men and Aliens." *Contrary Modes: Proceedings of the World Science Fiction Conference, Melbourne, Australia 1985.* Ed. Jenny Blackford. Melbourne: Ebony Books, 1985. 122–32.

Hanson, Pete. "Space Alien Meets with Ross Perot." *Weekly World News* (July 1992): 1, 4–5.

Haraway, Donna Jeanne. *Simians, Cyborgs, and Women: The Reinvention of Nature.* New York: Routledge, 1991.

Harding, Mary Esther. *The I and the Not-I: A Study of the Development of Consciousness.* Bollingen Series 307. Princeton, NJ: Princeton University Press, 1974.

Harrison, Harry, and Leon E. Stover. Introduction. *Apeman, Spaceman: Anthropological Science Fiction.* Ed. Harrison and Stover. London: Rapp and Whiting, 1968. 13–14.

Hart, Michael H. "An Explanation for the Absence of Extraterrestrials on Earth." *Extraterrestrials: Where Are They?* Ed. Michael H. Hart and Ben Zuckerman. 1975. New York: Pergamon, 1982. 1–8.

Harvard Working Group on New and Resurgent Diseases. "New and Resurgent Diseases: The Failure of Eradication." www.converge.org.nz/pirm/lurgi.htm (accessed 7 December 2005) ("published slightly abridged with the permission of Edward Goldsmith" from *Ecologist* 25.1, 1 January 1995: 21ff).

Heidkamp, Bernie. "Responses to the Alien Mother in Post-Maternal Cultures: C.J. Cherryh and Orson Scott Card." *Science Fiction Studies* 23.70 (November 1996): 339–54.

Heinberg, Richard. *Memories and Visions of Paradise: Exploring the Universal Myth of a Lost Golden Age.* Los Angeles: J. P. Tarcher, 1989.

Heinlein, Robert A. "The Discovery of the Future (Guest of Honor Speech at the Third World Science Fiction Convention, Denver 1941)." *Requiem.* Heinlein. New York: Tor, 1994. 203–23.

———. *Expanded Universe.* 1980. New York: Ace, 1982.

———. Future History Chart. *Astounding* 27.3 (May 1941): 124–25.

———. Letter to John Campbell about "Creation Took Eight Days." *Grumbles from the Grave.* Ed. Virginia Heinlein. New York: Ballantine Del Rey, 1990.

———. "On the Writing of Speculative Fiction." *Of Worlds beyond: The Science of Science Fiction.* Ed. Lloyd Arthur Eschbach. Chicago: Advent Press, 1964. 13–19.

———. "Science Fiction: Its Nature, Faults and Virtues." *Turning Points: Essays on the Art of Science Fiction.* Ed. Damon Knight. New York: Harper and Row, 1977. 3–28.

Hemken, Gertrude. Letter. *Astounding* 5.3 (March 1931): 424.

Herbert, Frank. Comment on "Missing Link." 1959. *Backdrop of Stars.* Ed. Harry Harrison. London: New English Library, 1975. 138–39.

———. "The ConSentiency—And How It Got That Way." *Galaxy* 38.3 (May 1977): 5–9.

———. "Listening to the Left Hand." *Harper's Magazine* 247 (December 1973): 92–100.

"Here's the Latest on Saucers." *Summerside Journal,* 27 March 1950, 21, 23.

Hickman, J. G. Letter. *If* 6.3 (April 1956): 118.

Hillegas, Mark R. "Victorian 'Extraterrestrials.'" *The Worlds of Victorian Fiction.* Ed. Jerome Buckley. Cambridge, MA: Harvard University Press, 1975. 391–414.

Hockett, Charles F. "How to Learn Martian." *Astounding* 55.3 (May 1955): 97–106.

Hollinger, Veronica. "Feminist Science Fiction: Breaking up the Subject." *Extrapolation* 31.3 (Fall 1990): 229–39.

———. "Feminist Science Fiction: Construction and Deconstruction." *Science Fiction Studies* 16.2 (July 1989): 223–27.

———. "(Re)Reading Queerly: Science Fiction, Feminism, and the Defamiliarization of Gender." *Science Fiction Studies* 26.1 (March 1999): 23–40.

Holman, C. Hugh, and William Harmon. *A Handbook to Literature*. 5th ed. New York: Macmillan and Collier Macmillan, 1986.

Honeycutt, Rodney L. "Naked Mole Rats." *American Scientist* 80 (January–February 1992): 43–53.

Horgan, John. *The End of Science: Facing the Limits of Knowledge in the Twilight of the Scientific Age*. New York: Harry N. Abrams, 1996.

Houston, Bud. Letter. *Galaxy* 37.2 (February 1976): 156–57.

Howes, Margaret. Letter. *Analog* 106.10 (October 1986): 185–86.

Huizinga, Johan. *Homo Ludens: A Study of the Play Element in Culture*. 1950. Boston, MA: Beacon Press, 1955.

Hunt, Gavin R. "Manufacture and Use of Hook-Tools by New Caledonian Crows." *Nature* 379 (18 January 1996): 249–51.

Huntington, John. *Rationalizing Genius: Ideological Strategies in the Classic American Science Fiction Short Story*. New Brunswick, NJ: Rutgers University Press, 1974.

Hutcheon, Linda. *A Poetics of Postmodernism: History, Theory, Fiction*. New York: Routledge, 1988.

Huygens, Christiaan. *Cosmotheoros*. The Hague: Adriaan Moetjens, 1698.

Irwin, W. R. *The Game of the Impossible: A Rhetoric of Fantasy*. Urbana, IL: University of Illinois Press, 1976.

Isaacs, Leonard. *Darwin to Double Helix: The Biological Theme in Science Fiction*. London: Butterworths, 1977.

Jacobi, Jolande. *Complex/Archetype/Symbol in the Psychology of C. G. Jung*. Tr. Ralph Manheim. London: Routledge and Kegan Paul, 1959.

Jacoby, Mario. "The Analytical Psychology of C. G. Jung and the Problem of Literary Evaluation." *Problems of Literary Evaluation*. Ed. Joseph Strelka. University Park: Pennsylvania State University Press, 1969. 99–128.

Jaeger, C. Harry. Letter. *Astounding* 2.2 (May 1930): 278.

Jarrett, Scott. Letter. *IASFM* 13.7 (July 1989): 14–15.

Jarvis, Sharon. Introduction. *Inside Outer Space: Science Fiction Professionals Look at Their Craft*. Ed. Jarvis. New York: Frederick Ungar, 1985. vii–viii.

Jonas, Doris, and David Jonas. *Other Senses, Other Worlds*. New York: Stein and Day, 1976.

Jones, H. Spencer. *Life on Other Worlds*. London: English Universities Press, 1940.

Joseph, Lawrence E. *Gaia: The Growth of an Idea*. New York: St Martin's Press, 1990.

Jung, Carl Gustav. *C. G. Jung Letters*. 2 vols. London: Routlege and Kegan Paul, 1973–1976.

———. *The Collected Works of C. G. Jung.* Tr. [except vol. 2]. R. F. C. Hull. Bollingen Series xx. 20 vols. Princeton, N.J.: Princeton University Press for the Bollingen Foundation, 1953–1979.

———. *Aion: Researches into the Phenomenology of the Self.* 1959. CW 9 (ii).

———. "Analytical Psychology and *Weltanschauung.*" *The Structure and Dynamics of the Psyche.* CW 8. 358–81.

———. "Answer to Job." *Psychology and Religion: West and East.* CW 11. 355–470.

———. "Archetypes of the Collective Unconscious." *Archetypes of the Collective Unconscious.* CW 9 (i):80:38. 3–41.

———. "Definitions. 36. Irrational." *Psychological Types.* CW 6. 454–56.

———. "Definitions. 51. Symbol." *Psychological Types.* CW 6. 473–81.

———. "Flying Saucers: A Modern Myth of Things Seen in the Skies." *Civilization in Transition.* CW 10. 307–433.

———. Foreword to Harding: *Woman's Mysteries. The Symbolic Life.* CW 18. 518–20.

———. Foreword to Werblowsky's *Lucifer and Prometheus. Psychology and Religion: West and East.* CW 11. 311–15.

———. "The Holy Men of India." *Psychology and Religion: West and East.* CW 11. 576–86.

———. "Mind and Earth." *Civilization in Transition.* CW 10. 307–433.

———. *Mysterium Coniunctionis: An Inquiry into the Separation and Synthesis of Psychic Opposites in Alchemy.* CW 14.

———. "On Flying Saucers." *The Symbolic Life.* CW 18. 626–33.

———. "On the Nature of the Psyche." *The Structure and Dynamics of the Psyche.* CW 8. 159–234.

———. "On Psychic Energy." *The Structure and Dynamics of the Psyche.* CW 8. 3–66.

———. "On the Psychology of the Unconscious." *Two Essays on Analytical Psychology.* CW 7. 9–119.

———. "On the Relation of Analytical Psychology to Poetry." *The Spirit in Man, Art, and Literature.* CW 15. 65–83.

———. "The Phenomenology of the Spirit in Fairytales." *The Archetypes and the Collective Unconscious.* CW 9 (i). 207–54.

———. "The Philosophical Tree." *Alchemical Studies.* CW 13. 251–341.

———. "A Psychological Approach to the Dogma of the Trinity." *Psychology and Religion: West and East.* CW 11. 109–200.

———. "The Psychological Foundation of Belief in Spirits." *The Structure and Dynamics of the Psyche.* CW 8. 301–18.

———. *Psychology and Alchemy.* 1953. CW 12.

———. "Psychology and Literature." *The Spirit in Man, Art, and Literature.* CW 15. 84–105.

———. "Psychology and Religion." *Psychology and Religion: West and East.* CW 11. 355–470.

———. "The Psychology of the Child Archetype." *The Archetypes and the Collective Unconscious.* CW 9 (i). 151–81.

———. "Synchronicity: An Acausal Connecting Principle." *The Structure and Dynamics of the Psyche.* CW 8. 417–519.

———. *Symbols of Transformation.* CW 5.

———. "Ulysses: A Monologue." *The Spirit in Man, Art, and Literature.* CW 15. 109–34.

———. "The Undiscovered Self." *Civilization in Transition.* CW 10. 245–345.

Jung, Carl Gustav, and C. Kerenyi. *Essays on a Science of Mythology: The Myth of the Divine Child and the Mysteries of Eleusis.* Tr. R. F. C. Hull. Bollingen Series 22. 1949. Rev. ed. Princeton, NJ: Princeton University Press, 1993.

Kafatos, M. "The Universal Diagrams and Life in the Universe." *The Search for Extraterrestrial Life: Recent Developments.* Ed. Michael D. Papagiannis. Dordrecht, Netherlands: Reidel, 1985. 245–49.

Kahn, Bernard I. Letter. *Astounding* 45.6 (August 1950): 160.

Kanes, Christy. Letter. *Galaxy* 36.6 (July 1975): 158.

Katz, Harvey, Martin H. Greenberg, and Patricia S. Warrick, eds. *Introductory Psychology through Science Fiction.* 2nd ed. Chicago: Rand McNally, 1977.

Keesing, Felix M. *Cultural Anthropology: The Science of Custom.* 1958. New York: Holt, Reinhart and Winston, 1962.

Kepler, Johannes. *Somnium seu Opus posthumum de astronomia lunari.* Osnabruck: Zeller, 1969.

Keyes, Noel. Introduction. *Contact.* Ed. Keyes. New York: Paperback Library, 1963. 7–10.

King, David. Letter. *Analog* 102.3 (March 1982): 172.

King, Patricia, and Thomas Hayden. "Dawn of a Solar System." *Newsweek* 133.17 (26 April 1999): 66–64.

Kingwell, Mark. *Dreams of Millennium: Report from a Culture on the Brink.* Toronto: Penguin Viking, 1996.

Knight, Damon Francis. *In Search of Wonder: Essays on Modern Science Fiction.* Rev. and enlarged 2nd ed. Chicago: Advent Publishers, 1967.

Knight, Damon Francis, ed. *Turning Points: Essays on the Art of Science Fiction.* New York: Harper and Row, 1977.

Kohn, Alfie. *The Brighter Side of Human Nature: Altruism and Empathy in Everyday Life.* New York: Basic Books, 1990.

Kristeva, Julia. *Étrangers à Nous-Mêmes.* Paris: Fayard, 1988.

———. *Strangers to Ourselves* [Etrangers à Nous Mêmes]. 1988. Tr. Leon S. Roudiez. New York: Columbia University Press, 1991.

Kroeber, A. L. *Anthropology*. New York: Harcourt Brace, 1948.

———. *Anthropology: Culture Patterns and Processes*. New York: Harbinger, 1963.

Kroeber, A. L., and Clyde Kluckhohn. *Culture: A Critical Review of Concepts and Definitions*. New York: Vintage, 1952.

Kroeber, Karl. *Romantic Fantasy and Science Fiction*. New Haven: Yale University Press, 1988.

Krueger, John R. "Language and Techniques of Communication as Theme or Tool in Science Fiction." *Linguistics* 39 (May 1963): 68–86.

———. "Names and Nomenclatures in Science Fiction." *Names: Journal of the American Name Society* 14 (1966): 203–14.

Kuiper, T. B. H., and [Glen] David Brin. "Resource Letter ETC–1: Extraterrrestrial Civilization." *American Journal of Physics* 57.1 (January 1989): 12–18.

Kuiper, T. B. H., and M. Morris. "Searching for Extraterrestrial Civilizations." *Science* 196 (1977): 616–21.

Laing, Ronald D. *The Divided Self: An Existential Study in Sanity and Madness*. New York: Penguin, 1979.

———. *Self and Others*. 2nd rev. ed. New York: Pantheon Books, 1970.

Lambe, Dean R. "Biological Ignorance." *Analog* 98.8 (August 1978): 5–13.

Landau, Misia. *Narratives of Human Evolution*. New Haven: Yale University Press, 1991.

Larson, Carl A. "Cracking the Code." *Analog* 72.4 (December 1963): 13–16, 81–84.

———. "Live Sensors." *Analog* 77.4 (June 1966): 86–105.

Latham, Arthur B. Letter. *Fantastic Adventures* 5.10 (December 1943): 195.

Laumer, Keith. "Alternatives to Intelligence." *Alien Minds*. Laumer. New York: Baen Books, 1991. 1–8.

———. "The Limiting Velocity of Orthodoxy." *Galaxy* 31.1 (December 1970): 187–90.

Le Guin, Ursula K. "American SF and the Other." 1975. *The Language of the Night: Essays on Fantasy and Science Fiction*. Ed. Susan Wood. New York: Putnam, 1979. 97–100.

———. "The Child and the Shadow." 1975. *The Language of the Night: Essays on Fantasy and Science Fiction*. Ed. Susan Wood. New York: Putnam, 1979. 59–71.

———. "Escape Routes." *Galaxy* 35.12 (December 1974): 40–44.

———. "Is Gender Necessary?" 1976. *The Language of the Night: Essays on Fantasy and Science Fiction*. Ed. Susan Wood. New York: Putnam, 1979. 161–69.

———. "Is Gender Necessary? Redux. 1976/1987." *Dancing at the Edge of the World: Thoughts on Words, Women, Places*. Le Guin. New York: Grove Press, 1989. 7–16.

———. "Ketterer on *The Left Hand of Darkness*." *Science Fiction Studies* 6 (July 1975): 137–39.

———. Introduction. "On Not Reading Science Fiction." *A Fisherman of the Inland Sea.* Le Guin. New York: HarperPrism, 1994. 1–11.

———. "Science Fiction and Mrs. Brown." *Science Fiction at Large.* Ed. Peter Nicholls. New York: Harper and Row, 1975. 15–33.

———. "Myth and Archetype in Science Fiction." 1976. *The Language of the Night: Essays on Fantasy and Science Fiction.* Ed. Susan Wood. New York: Putnam, 1979. 73–81.

Lefanu, Sarah. *Feminism and Science Fiction.* [also as, *In the Chinks of the World Machine.*] Bloomington: Indiana University Press, 1988.

Lem, Stanislaw. *Microworlds: Writings on Science Fiction and Fantasy.* San Diego: Harcourt Brace Jovanovich, 1984.

———. "On the Structural Analysis of Science Fiction." *Science Fiction Studies* 1 (Winter 1973-1974): 26–33.

Lenneberg, E. H. *Biological Foundations of Language.* New York: Wiley, 1967.

Levins, R. and Members of the Harvard Working Group on New and Resurgent Diseases. "The Emergence of New Diseases." *American Scientist* 82:52 (1994): B60.

Lévi-Strauss, Claude. *The Savage Mind.* Chicago: University of Chicago Press, 1966.

———. *Structural Anthropology.* Tr. Claire Jacobson and Brooke Schoepf. New York: Basic Books, 1963.

Lewin, Roger. *Bones of Contention: Controversies in the Search for Human Origins.* New York: Simon and Schuster, 1987.

Lewis, C. S. *The Discarded Image: An Introduction to Medieval and Renaissance Literature.* 1964. Cambridge: Cambridge University Press, 1967.

———. "On Science Fiction." *Turning Points: Essays on the Art of Science Fiction.* Ed. Damon Knight. New York: Harper and Row, 1977. 119–31.

———. "Psycho-Analysis and Literary Criticism." *Selected Literary Essays.* Lewis. London: Cambridge University Press, 1969. 286–300.

———. "Unreal Estates." *Of Other Worlds: Essays and Stories.* Lewis. New York: Harcourt Brace Jovanovich, 1966. 86–86.

Ley, Willy. "Let's Build an Extraterrestrial!" *Galaxy* 11.6 (April 1956): 43–55.

———. "Prelude to Engineering." *Astounding* 17.6 (August 1941): 110–19.

Lieberman, Philip. *Uniquely Human: The Evolution of Speech, Thought, and Selfless Behavior.* Cambridge, MA: Harvard University Press, 1991.

Lomax, William. "The 'Invisible Alien' in the Science Fiction of Clifford Simak." *Extrapolation* 30.2 (Summer 1989): 133–45.

Lovecraft, Howard P. "Some Notes on Interplanetary Fiction." *H. P. Lovecraft Marginalia.* Collected and edited by August Derleth and Donald Wandrei. Sauk City, WI: Arkham House, 1944. 140–47.

Lovejoy, A. O. *The Great Chain of Being: A Study of the History of an Idea.* Cambridge, MA: Harvard University Press, 1936.

Lovelock, James E. *The Ages of Gaia: A Biography of Our Living Planet.* 1988. Oxford: Oxford University Press, 1989.

Lowell, Percival. *The Evolution of Worlds.* New York: Macmillan, 1909.

———. *Mars.* 1895. London: Longmans, 1896.

———. *Mars as the Abode of Life.* New York: Macmillan, 1908.

Lunan, Duncan. "Fermi Paradox—The Final Solution?" *Analog* 106.5 (May 1986): 64–72.

Lyotard, Jean-François T. *The Postmodern Condition.* Tr. Geoff Bennington and Brian Massumi. Minneapolis: University of Minnesota Press, 1984.

Lyster, Karen. "Extraterrestrial Exposure Law Part One." www.karenlyster.com/law .html (accessed 27 February 2006).

Maccabee, Howard. "Nuclear Winter: How Much Do We Really Know?" *Reason* (May 1985): 26–35.

Macksey Richard, and Eugenio Donato, eds. *The Structuralist Controversy: The Languages of Criticism and the Sciences of Man.* Baltimore: Johns Hopkins University Press, 1970.

Malmgren, Carl D. "Self and Other in SF: Alien Encounters." *Science Fiction Studies* 20.59 (March 1993): 15–33.

———. *Worlds Apart: Narratology of Science Fiction.* Bloomington: Indiana University Press, 1991.

Mandeville, John, Sir. *Mandeville's Travels.* Oxford: Clarendon Press, 1967.

Manser, A. R. "Alien Sociology." *The Advancement of Science* 22.98 (1975): 204–7.

Margulis, Lynn, and Gregory Hinkle. "Biota and Gaia." *Abstracts of the Chapman Conference on GAIA Hypothesis.* Chapman Conference on GAIA Hypothesis, San Diego, California. 7–11 March 1988. 11.

Martin, P. W. *Experiment in Depth.* London: Routledge and Kegan Paul, 1955.

Mason, Carol, Martin H. Greenberg, and Patricia S. Warrick, eds. *Anthropology through Science Fiction.* New York: St. Martin's Press, [1974].

Mason, Robert Grant, ed. *Life in Space.* Alexandria, VA: Time-Life Books, 1983.

Mason, Vincent. Letter. *Astounding* 10.1 (April 1932): 137.

Mattis, Toni M. Letter. *Analog* 97.11 (November 1977): 176–77.

Maule, Victoria. "On the Subversion of Character in the Literature of Identity Anxiety." *Impossibility Fiction: Alternativity—Extrapolation—Speculation.* Ed. Derek Littlewood and Peter Stockwell. Amsterdam: Rodopi, 1996. 107–25.

May, Rollo. *The Cry for Myth.* New York: W. W. Norton, 1991.

Mayr, Ernest, and Carl Sagan. "The Search for Extraterrestrial Intelligence: Scientific Quest or Hopeful Folly?" *Planetary Report* 16.3 (May-June 1996): 4–13.

McClintock, Michael W. "Some Preliminaries to the Criticism of Science Fiction." *Extrapolation* 15.1 (December 1973): 17–24.

McCubbin, Chris W. *Gurps Aliens: Nonhuman Races for Interstellar Roleplaying.* New York: Steve Jackson Games, 1990.

———. *Gurps Space Bestiary: A Guide to Creatures of the Endless Frontier.* New York: Steve Jackson Games, 1990.

McHale, Brian. *Constructing Postmodernism.* London and New York: Routledge, 1992.

———. "Science Fiction." *International Postmodernism: Theory and Literary Practice.* Ed. Hans Bertens, Douwe Fokkema, and Mario J. Valdes. Amsterdam: Benjamins, 1997. 235–39.

McIntyre, Vonda. "Potential and Actuality in Science Fiction." *Nebula Award Stories Eleven.* Ed. Ursula K. Le Guin. New York: Bantam, 1978. 201–9.

McLuhan, Marshall. *War and Peace in the Global Village: An Inventory of Some of the Current Spastic Situations That Could Be Eliminated by More Feedforward.* New York: Bantam Books, 1968.

McNelly, Willis E. "Archetypal Patterns in Science Fiction." *CEA Critic* 35.4 (1973): 15–19.

McNelly, Willis E., and Leon E. Stover. Afterword. "Science Fiction as Culture Criticism." *Above the Human Landscape: A Social Science Fiction Anthology.* Ed. McNelly and Stover. Pacific Palisades, CA: Goodyear, 1972. 355–76.

Mendlesohn, Farah. "Gender, Power, and Conflict Resolution: 'Subcommittee' by Zenna Henderson." *Extrapolation* 35.2 (Summer 1994): 120–29.

Mercer, D. M. E. "Problems of Communication with Alien Intelligent Beings." *Advancement of Science* 22.98 (1965): 200–3.

Michaud, Michael A. G. "Organizing Ourselves for Contact." *Analog* 118.1 (January 1998): 51–63.

Miller, Fred D., Jr., and Nicholas D. Smith. *Thought Probes: Philosophy through Science Fiction Literature* . Englewood Cliffs, NJ: Prentice Hall, 1989.

Miller, P. Schuyler. The Reference Library: "Men of Many Worlds." *Analog* 93.2 (April 1974): 163–65.

———. The Reference Library: "Premature Funeral." *Analog* 66.4 (December 1960): 159–60.

Milstead, John W., Martin H. Greenberg, Joseph D. Olander, and Patricia S. Warrick. Introduction. *Sociology through Science Fiction.* New York: St Martin's Press, 1974. ix–xiii.

Minsky, Marvin. "Communication with Alien Intelligence." *Byte* 10.4 (April 1985): 127–38.

Mitchison, Naomi. "Wonderful Deathless Ditties." *The Profession of Science Fiction: SF Writers on Their Craft and Ideas.* Ed. Max Jakubowski and Edward James. London: Macmillan, 1992. 34–43.

Mohs, Mayo. Introduction. *Other Worlds, Other Gods: Science Fiction and the World of Religion*. Ed. Mayo Mohs. New York: Avon, 1971. 11–17.

Monk, Patricia. "Goddess on the Hearth: The Archetypal Significance of Cats in Modern Fantasy." *Journal of the Fantastic in the Arts* 12.1 (2001): 309–21.

———. "Not Just 'Cosmic Skulduggery': A Partial Reconsideration of Space Opera." *Extrapolation* 33.4 (1992): 295–316.

———. "'The Shared Universe Thing': An Experiment in Speculative Fiction." *Journal of the Fantastic in the Arts* 2.4 (1990): 7–46.

Morgan, Elaine. *The Descent of Woman*. New York: Bantam, 1973.

Morris, Desmond. *The Naked Ape*. 1967. Toronto: Bantam, 1969.

Moskowitz, Sam, ed. Introduction. "Dawn of Fame." *Martian Odyssey and Other Stories: The Collected Short Stories of Stanley G. Weinbaum*. Westport, CT: Hyperion Press, 1974. vii–xxiii.

Mosleh, Joseph M. Letter. *Astounding* 10.3 (June 1932): 428.

Mullen, Dale. Letter. *Astounding* 7.1 (July 1931): 131.

Münster, Sebastien. *Cosmographica*. 1544.

Murray, H. J. R. *A History of Chess*. 1913. 2nd ed. Oxford: Clarendon Press, 1962.

NAIC (National Astronomy and Ionosphere Center). "The Arecibo Message of November 1974." *Life in the Universe:* Ed. John Billingham. Cambridge, MA: Harvard University Press, 1982. 293–96.

Nicholls, Peter, ed. Introduction. *Science Fiction at Large*. Ed. Nicholls. New York: Harper and Row, 1976. 15–33.

———. *The Science Fiction Encyclopedia*. New York: Doubleday Dolphin Books, 1979.

Niven, Larry. "The Alien in Our Minds." *N–Space*. Niven. New York: Tor Books, 1990. 640–49.

———. Foreword: "Playgrounds for the Mind." *N-Space*. Niven. New York: Tor Books, 1990. 26–32.

———. "Galaxy Stars—J. E. Pournelle." *Galaxy* 36.6 (July 1975): 71–72.

———. "The Words in Science Fiction." *The Craft of Science Fiction: A Symposium on Writing SF*. Ed. Reginald Bretnor. New York: Harper and Row, 1976. 178–94.

Nordley, David G. "Fugue on a Sunken Continent." *Analog* 116.13 (November 1996): 12–59.

Olander, Joseph D., ed. *American Government through Science Fiction*. Chicago: Rand McNally College Publishing, 1974.

"On the Question of the Mars Meteorite." www.lpi.usra.edu/lpi/meteorites/The_Meteorite.html (accessed 6 March 2005).

Osmańczyk, Edmund Jan, ed. *Encyclopedia of the United Nations and International Agreements*. Philadelphia: Taylor and Francis, 1985.

The Oxford English Dictionary. 2nd ed. Oxford: Oxford University Press, 1989.

Papagiannis, Michael D. "The Fermi Paradox and Alternative Search Strategies." *The Search for Extraterrestrial Life: Recent Developments.* Ed. Papagiannis. Dordrecht, Netherlands: Reidel, 1985. 437–42.

———. "A Historical Introduction to the Search for Extraterrestrial Life." *The Search for Extraterrestrial Life: Recent Developments: Proceedings of the 112th Symposium of the International Astronomical Union:* Ed Michael D. Papagiannis. Dordrecht, Netherlands: Reidel/Kluwer Academic Publishers, 1984.

Park, Robert E., and Ernest W. Burgess. *Introduction to the Science of Sociology.* 1921. Ed. Morris Janowitz. 3rd rev. ed. Chicago: University of Chicago Press, 1969.

Parker, Helen N. *Biological Themes in Science Fiction.* Ann Arbor, MI: UMI Research Press, 1987.

Parrinder, Patrick. "The Alien Encounter: Or Mrs. Brown and Mrs. Le Guin." *Science Fiction Studies* 6.1 (March 1979): 46–58.

———. "Science Fiction as Truncated Epic." *Bridges to Science Fiction.* Ed. George E. Slusser, George R. Guffey, and Mark Rose. Carbondale: Southern Illinois University Press, 1980. 91–106.

Partridge, Eric. *A Dictionary of Slang and Unconventional English.* 1937. Ed. Paul Beale. Rev. ed. London: Routledge and Kegan Paul, 1984.

Pearsall, Judy, ed. *The Concise Oxford Dictionary.* 10th ed. Oxford: Oxford University Press, 1999.

Peppers, Cathy. "Dialogic Origins and Alien Identities in Butler's *Xenogenesis.*" *Science-Fiction Studies* 22.65 (March 1995): 47–62.

Perkins, Lawrence A. "Target: Language." *Analog* 79.3 (May 1967): 81–85.

Pesch, Hans. "A Myth Retold: Towards a Rhetoric of Science Fiction." *Just the Other Day: Essays on the Suture of the Future.* Ed. Luk de Vos. Antwerp, Belgium: Uitgeverij EXA, 1985. 17–24.

Philips, Michael, ed. *Philosophy and Science Fiction.* Buffalo, NY: Prometheus Books, 1984.

Pickering, David, Alan Isaacs, and Elizabeth Martin, eds. *Brewer's Dictionary of 20th-Century Phrase and Fable.* 1991. Boston: Houghton Mifflin, 1992.

Pielke, Robert G. "Humans and Aliens: A Unique Relationship." *Mosaic* 13 (1980): 19–40.

Pierce, John J. *Foundations of Science Fiction: A Study in Imagination and Education.* Contributions to the Study of Science Fiction and Fantasy 25. New York: Greenwood Press, 1987.

———. *Great Themes of Science Fiction: A Study in Imagination and Evolution.* Contributions to the Study of Science Fiction and Fantasy 29. Westport, CT: Greenwood Press, 1987.

Plank, Robert. *The Emotional Significance of Imaginary Beings: A Study of the Interaction Between Psychopathology, Literature, and Reality in the Modern World.* Springfield, IL: Charles C. Thomas, 1968.

———. "The Reproduction of Psychosis in Science Fiction." *International Record of Medicine and General Practice Clinics* 167.7 (July 1954): 407–21.

Pohl, Frederik. Editorial: "On Doing Better." *If* 18.1 (January 1968): 4–5.

———. "SF: The Game-Playing Literature." 1971. *In the Problem Pit.* Pohl. New York: Bantam, 1976. 190–93.

———. Interview: "What Science Fiction Should Do." *Grolier Encyclopedia of Science Fiction on CD-ROM.* Danbury, CT: Grolier Electronic Publishing, 1995.

Poole, Roger. "Embodiment." *The Harper Dictionary of Modern Thought.* Ed. Alan Bullock, Oliver Stalleybrass, and Stephen Trombley. Rev. ed. New York: Harper and Row, 1988. 264–65.

Pournelle, Jerry. "A Step Further Out: On *Cultures Beyond the Earth.*" *Galaxy* 37.2 (February 1976): 37–45.

Pournelle, Jerry, and Larry Niven. "Building *The Mote in God's Eye.*" *Galaxy* 37.1 (January 1976): 92–113.

Pringle, David William. "Aliens for Neighbours: A Reassessment of Clifford D. Simak." *Foundation* 11/12 (March 1977): 15–29.

Proctor, Richard A. "A New Theory of Life in Other Worlds." *Our Place among the Infinities: A Series of Essays Contrasting Our Little Abode in Space and Time with the Infinities around Us.* Proctor. New ed. London: Longman's Green, 1886. 45–69.

———. *Other Worlds Than Ours.* London: Longmans, 1870.

Propp, Vladimir. *Morphology of the Folktale.* Ed. and tr. Svatava Pirkova-Jakobson and Laurence Scott. Bloomington: Indiana University Research Center, 1958.

Puschman-Nalenz, Barbara. *Science Fiction and Postmodern Fiction: A Genre Study.* New York: Peter Lang, 1992.

Rabkin, Eric. "Fairy Tales and Science Fiction." *Bridges to Science Fiction.* Ed. George E. Slusser, George R. Guffey, and Mark Rose. Carbondale: Southern Illinois University Press, 1980. 79–90.

Rainbow, Tom. "Sentience and the Single Extraterrestrial." *IASFM* 8.2 (February 1984): 42–59.

Random House Dictionary of the English Language. Revised ed. New York: Random House, 1983.

Read, Wolf. "Epona." *Analog* 116.13 (November 1996): 60–81.

Reber, Arthur S. "Empathy." *The Penguin Dictionary of Psychology.* Ed. Arthur S. Reber. London: Penguin, 1985. 238.

Regis, E., Jr., ed. *Extraterrestrials: Science and Alien Intelligence.* Cambridge: Cambridge University Press, 1985.

Reischauer, Edwin O. *The Japanese.* Cambridge, MA: Belknap Press, 1981.

Rice, Paul. "Metaphor as a Way of Saying the Self in Science Fiction." *The Intersection of Science Fiction and Philosophy: Critical Studies.* Ed. Robert E. Myers. Contributions to the Study of Science Fiction and Fantasy 4. Westport, CT: Greenwood Press, 1983. 133–42.

Rieder, John. "Embracing the Alien: SF in Mass Culture." *Science-Fiction Studies* 9.26 (March 1982): 26–38.

Roberts, Robin. *A New Species: Gender and Science in Science Fiction.* Urbana: University of Illinois Press, 1993.

———. "Post Modernism and Feminist Science Fiction." *Science Fiction Studies* 17.2 (July 1990): 136–52.

Robinson, Spider. Blurb for Rebecca Ore, *Becoming Alien.* New York: Tor, 1988. Back cover.

———. Introduction. *Melancholy Elephants.* Toronto: Penguin, 1984. xi–xiv.

Rock, Allan. [The Right Honorable, the Minister of Justice.] "Extradition of Atif Ahmad Rafay and Glen Sebastian Burns to the United States of America." News Release 12 July 1996. Ottawa: Department of Justice, 1996.

Rocklynne, Ross. "Science-Fiction Simplified." *Writer's Digest* 20 (October 1941): 25–30.

Rood, Robert T., and James S. Trefil. *Are We Alone? The Possibility of Extraterrestrial Civilizations.* New York: Scribner, 1981.

Rose, Kenneth Jon. "Making Sense of Extraterrestrial Senses." *Analog* 99.1 (January 1979): 59–67.

Rose, Mark. *Alien Encounters: Anatomy of Science Fiction.* Cambridge, MA: Harvard University Press, 1981.

Rosinsky, Natalie M. *Feminist Futures: Contemporary Women's Speculative Fiction.* Ann Arbor, MI: UMI Researach Press, 1984.

Rupprecht, Carol Schreier. "Archetypal Theory and Criticism." *The Johns Hopkins Guide to Literary Theory and Criticism.* Ed. Michael Groeden and Martin Kreiswirth. Baltimore: Johns Hopkins University Press, 1994. 36–40.

Russ, Joanna. "Alien Monsters." *Turning Points: Essays on the Art of Science Fiction.* Ed. Damon Knight. New York: Harper and Row, 1977. 132–43.

———. "The Subjunctivity of Science Fiction." *Extrapolation* 15.1 (December 1973): 51–59.

———. "Towards an Aesthetic of Science Fiction." *Science Fiction Studies* 6.2 (July 1975): 112–29.

Russell, Dale. *Odyssey in Time*. Toronto: University of Toronto Press, 1989.

Rycroft, Charles."Empathy." *A Critical Dictionary of Psychoanalysis*. Ed. Rycroft. Harmondsworth, UK: Penguin, 1972. 42–43.

Sagan, Carl. *Communication with Extraterrestrial Intelligence (CETI)*. Cambridge, MA: MIT Press, 1973.

———. *Murmurs of Earth: the Voyager Interstellar Record*. 1st ed. New York: Random House, 1978.

Sagan, Carl, and W. I. Newman. "The Solipsist Approach to Extraterrestrial Intelligence." *Quarterly Journal of the Royal Astronomical Society* 24 (1983): 113–21.

Samuelson, David Norman. "From Aliens to Alienation: Gregory Benford's Variations on a Theme." *Foundation* 14 (September 1978): 5–19.

Sanders, Scott. "Invisible Men and Women." *Science Fiction Studies* 4 (March 1977): 14–24.

Sanderson, Ivan T. Introduction. "The Forteans and the Fictioneers." *Ecounters with Aliens: UFOs and Alien Beings in Science Fiction* . Ed. George W. Earley. Los Angeles: Sherbourne Press, 1968. 23–33.

Santesson, Hans Stefan. Introduction. *Gentle Invaders*. Ed. Santesson. New York: Belmont, 1969. 7–8.

Sapir, Edward. *Language: An Introduction to the Study of Speech*. 1921. New York: Harcourt Brace Harvest Book, 1949.

Sargent, Pamela. "Writing, Science Fiction, and Family Values." *Amazing Stories* 69.1 (Spring 1994): 100–11.

Savage-Rumbaugh, Sue, and Roger Lewin. *Kanzi: The Ape at the Brink of the Human Mind*. New York: John Wiley, 1994.

Schmidt, Stanley. *Aliens and Alien Societies: A Writer's Guide to Creating Extraterrestrial Life-Forms*. Science Fiction Writing Series. Cincinnati, OH: Writer's Digest Books, 1995.

———. Editorial Announcement. "In Times to Come." *Analog* 107.9 (September 1987): 122.

———. Editorial. "The Relativity of Emergency." *Analog* 102.9 (September 1982): 6–12.

———. "The Science in Science Fiction." *Many Futures, Many Worlds: Theme and Form .in Science Fiction*. Ed. Thomas Clareson. Kent, OH: Kent State University Press, 1977. 27–49.

Schmitz, James H. Introduction. *A Pride of Monsters*. Schmitz. New York: Collier , 1970. 1–4.

Scholes, Robert. *Fabulation and Metafiction*. Chicago: University of Illinois Press, 1979.

———. *Structural Fabulation: An Essay on the Fiction of the Future*. Notre Dame: University of Notre Dame Press, 1975.

Schweitzer, Darrell. "On the Clunkiness of Science Fiction." *Aboriginal Science Fiction* 51 & 52 (Fall 1996): 59–63.

Scot, Reginald. *The Discoverie of Witchcraft.* 1584. 4th ed. London: Brome, 1589.

Scott, E. C. Letter. *Astounding* 13.6 (August 1934): 154–55.

Scully, Frank. *Behind the Flying Saucers.* London: Victor Gollancz, 1950.

The Search for Extraterrestrial Life: Recent Developments: Proceedings of the 112th Symposium of the International Astronomical Union. Ed. Michael D. Papagiannis. Dordrecht: Reidel/Kluwer Academic Publishers, 1984.

Searles, Baird. On Books. *IASFM* 9.8 (August 1985): 183–90.

Seneca, Lucilius Annaeus. "Epistle XLI—On the God Within Us." *Ad Lucilium epistulae morales.* Tr. Richard Gummere. 3 vols. Loeb Classical Library (Latin Authors) vols. 75–77. London: Heinemann, 1934. 1: 273–79.

Serviss, Garrett Putnam. *Other Worlds: Their Nature, Possibilities and Habitability in the Light of the Latest Discoveries.* 1901. London: Hirschfield Bros, 1902.

"SETI@home: The Search for Extraterrestrial Intelligence." http://setiathome.ssl .berkeley.edu/ (accessed 20 November 2005).

Sexton, Melanie. "Self/Other." *Encyclopedia of Contemporary Literary Theory: Approaches, Scholars, Terms.* Ed. Irena R. Makaryk. Toronto: University of Toronto Press, 1993. 620–21.

Seymour-Smith, Martin. "Empathy." *The Harper Dictionary of Modern Thought.* Ed. Alan Bullock, Oliver Stalleybrass, and Stepen Trombley. New and rev. ed. New York: Harper and Row. 1988. 268.

Shapiro, Robert, and Gerald Feinberg. "Possible Forms of Life in Environments Very Different From the Earth." *Extraterrestrials: Where Are They?* Ed. Michael H. Hart and Ben Zuckerman. 1975. New York: Pergamon, 1982. 113–21.

Shifflett, Francis. "UFO Alien Captured in Russia." *Sun* 8.10 (May 1990): 9.

Shipman, G. R. "How to Talk to a Martian." *Astounding* 52.2 (October 1953): 112–20.

Shippey, Tom. Preface. "Learning to Read Science Fiction." *Fictional Space: Essays on Contemporary Science Fiction* . Ed. Shippey. Essays and Studies 43. Oxford: Blackwell/Humanities Press, 1991.

Shklovskii, Iosef S, and Carl Sagan. *Intelligent Life in the Universe.* San Francisco: Holden-Day, 1966.

Shklovsky, Victor. "Art as Technique." *Debating Texts: Readings in 20th Century Literary Theory and Method.* Ed. R. Rylance. Toronto: University of Toronto Press, 1987. 48–56.

Shostak, G. Seth. G., ed. *Progress in the Search for Extraterrestrial Life: Astronomical Society of the Pacific Conference Series.* Bioastronomy Symposium. San Francisco: Astronomical Society of the Pacific, 1995.

————, ed. *Third Decennial US-USSR Conference on SETI*: Astronomical Society of the Pacific Conference Series. San Francisco: Astronomical Society of the Pacific, 1993.

"Should Mankind Hide?" *New York Times*, 22 November 1976: A24.

Siegel, Mark. "Foreigner as Alien in Japanese Science Fantasy." *Science-Fiction Studies* 12.37 (November 1985): 252–63.

Silverberg, Robert. Blurb for Garrett, "The Best Policy." *Earthmen and Strangers*. Ed. Silverberg. New York: Dell, 1968. 46.

————. Introduction. *Earthmen and Strangers*. Ed. Silverberg. New York: Dell, 1968. 7–9.

Simpson, George G. "Added Comments on 'The Nonprevalence of Humanoids.'" *Communication with Extraterrestrial Intelligence (CETI)*. Ed. Carl Sagan. Cambridge, MA: MIT Press, 1973. 362–64.

————. "The Nonprevalence of Humanoids." *Science* 143.3608 (February 1964): 769–75.

Skeels, Dell R. "Science Fiction as Myth." *Trend in Engineering at the University of Washington* 29 (October 1971): 10–15, 31.

Sloane, William M. Introduction. *Space Space Space: Stories about the Time When Men Will Be Adventuring to the Stars*. Ed. William M. Sloane. New York: Franklin Watts, 1953. 9–12.

Slusser, George E., and Eric S. Rabkin. Introduction. "The Anthropology of the Alien." Ed. Slusser and Rabkin. *Aliens: The Anthropology of Science Fiction* . Carbondale: Southern Illinois University Press, 1987. vii–xxi.

Smith, Beresford. Letter. *Analog* 79.6 (August 1967): 171.

Snider, Clifton. "C. G. Jung's Analytical Psychology and Literary Criticism." *Psychocultural Review* 1.1 (Winter 1977): 96–108.

————. "Jung's Psychology of the Conscious and the Unconscious." *Psychocultural Review* 1.2 (Spring 1977): 216–42.

Snyder, Peter J. "Uncovering the Intellectual and Emotional Lives of Birds: Common Sense, Science and the Problem of Anthropomorphism." *Science Spectra* 19 (2000): 8–14.

"Space Alien Health Manual Found at UFO Landing Site." *Weekly World News*, 19 March 1991: 7.

Söderlind, Sylvia. "Margins and Metaphors: The Politics of Post-***." *Liminal Postmodernisms: The Postmodern, the (Post-)Colonial, and the (Post-)Feminist*. Ed. Theo D'Haen and Hans Bertens. Amsterdam: Rodopi, 1992. 35–54.

Sofia, Zoe. "Exterminating Fetuses: Abortion, Disarnament, and the Sexo-Semiotics of Extraterrestrialism." *Diacritics* 14.2 (Summer 1984): 47–59.

Spector, Judith. "Science Fiction and the Sex War." *Gender Studies: New Directions in Feminist Criticism*. Ed. Spector. Bowling Green, OH: Popular, 1986.

Spek, Inez van der. *A Momentary Taste of Being: Female Subjectivity, the Divine and the Science Fiction of James Tiptree*. Utrecht, Netherlands: Universiteit Utrecht, 1996.

Stableford, Brian. "Aliens." *The Science Fiction Encyclopedia* . Ed. Peter Nicholls. Garden City, NY: Doubleday, 1979. 22–24.

———. "Space Opera." *The Science Fiction Encyclopedia* . Ed. Peter Nicholls. Garden City, NY: Doubleday, 1979. 559–61.

Stevens, Anthony. *Archetype Revisited: An Updated Natural History of the Self*. Toronto: Inner City Books, 2003.

Steveson, P. H. Letter. *Amazing* 13.5 (May 1939): 131.

Stine, G. Harry. "Cultural Differences." *Analog* 107.9 (September 1987): 150–53.

———. "How to Get Along With an Extra-Terrestrial . . . Or Your Neighbor." *Analog* 100.2 (February 1980): 39–47.

———. "Sensory Deprivation." *Analog* 99.11 (November 1979): 155–58.

Stone, David M. "Search for Terrestrial Intelligence." *Analog* 103.7 (July 1983): 50–62.

Strelka, Joseph P. "Comparative Criticism and Literary Symbolism." *Perspectives in Literary Symbolism*. Ed. Joseph P. Strelka. University Park: Pennsylvania State University Press, 1968. 1–28.

Stull, Mark A. "On the Significance of the Apparent Absence of Extraterrestrials on Earth." *Journal of the British Interplanetary Society* 32 (1979): 221–22.

Sturgeon, Theodore. "*Galaxy* Bookshelf." *Galaxy* 4.5 (February 1974): 89–93.

———. "I List in Numbers." *National Review,* 10 March 1970: 266–67.

Sullivan, Walter. "Astronomer Fears Hostile Attack; Would Keep Life on Earth a Secret." *New York Times,* 4 November 1976: 46.

Suvin, Darko, R. *Metamorphoses of Science Fiction*. New Haven, CT: Yale University Press, 1979.

———. "On the Poetics of the Science Fiction Genre." *College English* 34 (1972): 372–82.

———. *Positions and Presuppositions in Science Fiction*. Basingstoke, UK: Macmillan, 1988.

Swanwick, Michael. "A User's Guide to the Postmoderns." *IASFM* 10.8 (August 1986): 20–53.

Takacs, Stephen. Letter. *Astounding* 2.1 (April 1930): 130.

Tang, T. B. "Fermi Paradox and CETI." *Journal of the British Interplanetary Society* 35 (1982): 236–40.

Teeter, Herman. Letter. *Astounding* 9.1 (January 1932): 136.

Tenn, William. "The Fiction in Science Fiction." *Science Fiction Adventures* 2 (March 1954): 66–78.

Thackeray, William. *Vanity Fair*. 1847–48.

Thompson, David. *David Thompson's Narrative of His Explorations in Wester North America [1794–1812]*. Ed. Richard Glover. The Publications of the Champlain Society 12. Toronto: Champlain Society, 1916.

Thompson, William Irwin. *Gaia, A Way of Knowing: The Political Implications of the New Biology*. Great Barrington, MA: Lindisfarne Press, 1987.

Tilton, Lois. Letter. *Analog* 100.7 (July 1980): 174.

Time Magazine. 5 February 1990. cover.

Tipler, Frank J. "Additional Remarks on Extraterrestrial Intelligence." *Quarterly Journal of the Royal Astronomical Society* 22 (1981): 279–92.

———. "Anthropic-Principle Arguments against Steady-State Cosmological Theories." *Observatory* 102 (1982): 36–39.

———. "A Brief History of the Extraterrestrial Intelligence Concept." *Quarterly Journal of the Royal Astronomical Society* 22 (1981): 133–45.

———. "Extraterrestrial Beings Do Not Exist." *Quarterly Journal of the Royal Astronomical Society* 21 (1980): 267–81.

———. "The Most Advanced Civilization in the Galaxy Is Ours." *Mercury* 11 (1981): 5–37.

———. Response to Letters. *Physics Today* 35 (1982): 26–38.

Todorov, Tzvetan. *The Fantastic: A Structural Approach to Literary Genre*. Cleveland, OH: Case Western University Press, 1970.

Toffler, Alvin. *Future Shock*. 1970. New York: Bantam, 1971.

Tomashevsky, Boris. "Thematics." *Debating Texts*. Ed. Rick Rylance. Toronto: University of Toronto Press, 1987. 57–65.

Tremaine, F. Orlin. Editorial Comment. *Astounding* 11.3 (January 1933): 420–21.

———. Editorial Announcement: "Coming Up." *Astounding* 12.6 (February 1934): 9.

———. "Science Discussions." *Astounding* 18.4 (December 1936): 152.

Trenchard, Samuel. Letter. *Analog* 48.1 (September 1951): 164–66.

Trevarthen, Colwyn, and Katerina Logotheti. "Child in Society and Society in Children." *Societies at Peace: Anthropological Perspectives*. Ed. Signe Howell and Roy Willis. London: Routledge, 1989. 165–86.

Trunick, Perry A. "Hal Clement's Aliens: Bridging the Gap." *Foundation* 36 (Summer 1986): 10–21.

Tusa, John. "And Nation Shall Speak unto Nation?" *Times Literary Supplement* (8 May 1992): 13–14.

Tymn, Marshall B., ed. *The Science Fiction Reference Book: A Comprehensive Handbook and Guide to the History, Literature, Scholarship, and Related Activities of the Science Fiction and Fantasy Field*. Mercer Island, WA: Starmont House, 1981.

Vandendorpe, Christian. "Actant." *Encyclopedia of Contemporary Literary Theory: Approaches, Scholars, Terms*. Ed. Irena R. Makaryk. Toronto: University of Toronto Press, 1993

von Franz, Marie-Louise. "Analytical Psychology and Literary Criticism." *New Literary History* 12.1 (1980): 119–26.

von Gesner, Konrad. *Historia Animalium*. 1551–58.

Von Hoerner, Sebastian. "Astronomical Aspects of Interstellar Communication." *Astronautic Acta* 18 (1973): 421–30.

Wallace, Alfred Russel. *Man's Place in the Universe: A Study of the Results of Scientific Research in Relation to the Unity or Plurality of Worlds*. 1903. New York: McClure, Phillips and Co., 1903.

Wallace, Anthony F. C. *Culture and Personality*. 2nd ed. New York: Random House, 1970.

Walrath, Katherine. Letter. *Amazing* 16.12 (December 1942): 228.

Ward, Peter D., and Donald Brownlee. *Rare Earth: Why Complex Life Is Uncommon in the Universe*. New York: Springer-Verlag Copernicus, 2000.

Webb, Janeen. "Monster as Hero." *Contrary Modes: Proceedings of the World Science Fiction Conference*. Ed. Jenny Blackford and Norman Talbot, et al. Melbourne: Ebony Books, 1985. 1–24.

Weedman, Jane B. *Women Worldwalkers: New Dimensions of Science Fiction and Fantasy*. Lubbock: Texas Tech Press, 1985.

Wendland, Albert. *Science, Myth, and the Fictional Creation of Alien Worlds*. Ann Arbor, MI: UMI Resarch Press, 1985.

Westerfield, Jerry K. "The Sky's No Limit." *Writer's Digest* 20 (January 1940): 13–19.

"What Do You Know?" Quiz. *Amazing* 6.2 (May 1931): 186.

"What Should a BEM Look Like?" *Proceedings of the Discon Science Fiction Convention*. Chicago: Advent Publishers, 1964. 87–102.

Whewell, William, ed. *Of the Plurality of Worlds: An Essay; Also, A Dialogue on the Same Subject*. London: John W. Parker, 1854.

White, James. Introduction: "The Secret History of Sector General." *Ambulance Ship*. White. New York: Ballantine Del Rey, 1979. ix–xvii.

White, Michael, and John Gribbin. *Stephen Hawking: A Life in Science*. London: Penguin, 1992.

Whorf, Benjamin L. *Language, Thought, and Reality: Selected Writings of Benjamin Lee Whorf*. Ed. J. B. Carroll. Cambridge, MA: MIT Press, 1956.

Williams, W. T. "Problems of Alien Biology." *Advancement of Science* 22.98 (1965): 198–200.

———. "Science in SF: Alien Biology." *Listener* (December 1964): 1003–4.

Williamson, Jack. "Explorations and Colonies." *The Visual Encyclopedia of Science Fiction.* New York: Harmony Books, 1977. 87–89.

———. "Space Opera." *The New Encyclopedia of Science Fiction.* Ed. James Gunn. New York: Viking, 1988. 433–35.

———. "Will Academe Kill Science Fiction?" *IASFM* 2.2 (April 1978): 61–73.

Wilson, E. O. *On Human Nature.* Cambridge, MA: Harvard University Press, 1978.

———. *Sociobiology: The New Synthesis.* Cambridge, MA: Harvard University Press, 1975.

Winters, Jeffrey. "The Planet at 51 Peg." *Discover* 17.1 (January 1996): 86–87.

Wissler, Clark. *Man and Culture.* New York: Crowell, 1923.

Wolfe, Gary K. *The Known and the Unknown: The Iconography of Science Fiction.* Kent, OH: Kent State University Press, 1979.

Wolheim, Donald A. *The Universe Makers: Science Fiction Today.* New York: Harper and Row, 1971.

Wolmark, Jenny. *Aliens and Others: Science Fiction, Feminism, and Postmodernism.* New York: Harvester/Wheatsheaf, 1993.

———. "The Postmodern Romances of Feminist Science Fiction." *Romance Revisited.* Ed. Jackie Stacey and Lynne Pearce. New York: New York University Press, 1995.

Wood, Margaret M. *The Stranger: A Study in Social Relationships.* New York: Columbia University Press, 1934.

Wood, Susan. "Women and Science Fiction." *Algo/Starship* 16.1 (Winter 1978–1979): 9–18.

Woolf, Virginia. "Character in Fiction." *The Essays of Virginia Woolf, Vol. 3—1919–1924.* Ed. Andrew NcNeillie. 4 vols. London: Hogarth Press, 1988. 3:420–438.

———. "Mr. Bennett and Mrs. Brown." *The Essays of Virginia Woolf, Vol. 3—1919–1924.* Ed. Andrew McNeillie. 4 vols. London: Hogarth Press, 1988. 3:384–89.

———. *Jacob's Room.* London: Hogarth Press, 1922.

Wright, Karen. "The Tarzan Syndrome." *Discover* 17.11 (November 1996): 88–98.

Wright, R. Glenn. "Science Fiction, Archetypes, and the Future." *Clarion III.* Ed. Robin Scott Wilson. New York: Signet, 1973. 174–81.

Zelazny, Roger. "Some Science Fiction Parameters: A Biased View." *Galaxy* 36.6 (July 1975): 6–11.

Zubrin, Roger. "How to Find a Starship." *Analog* 114.10 (August 1994): 68–79.

Index

alien form, 77ff.; analogous 95, 101–10, 113, 114, 117; anatomy of, 13, 79, 85, 118n3; anthropomorphic, 95, 96, 100, 101, 117, 120n15; 152–53, 222–23; as something like a man, 96–97, 99, 226; enigmatically protean form of, 54, 56, 60; exotic, 95, 113–17, 135, 146, 170, 226, 283; heterologous, 95, 110–13, 117, 120n16, 170, 256, 283; homologous, 95–101, 110–12, 117; humanoid, xxx, 13 , 27, 100, 157, 192, 216, 222–28, 231, 261n4, 261n5, 261n6; unclassifiable, 96, 116; undifferentiated, 225, 236

alien function (literary), xxvi, 6, 27, 28, 29, 30, 36, 41, 46, 51, 52, 61, 112, 216, 232–33, 244, 245, 252, 286, 307, 318; as actant, 72n4, 244, 246; as icon, 45–46; as metaphor, xiii, 45; as psychological substrate of literary trope, xxxi; as reference to human life, 45; as heuristic device, xiii, xvi, xxvi, xxxii, 41, 42–53, 49–50, 52, 64–65, 71, 96; as signature trope of science fiction, xiii; special case of trope, 69–70; as structural device, 46

alien psyche, xxx, xxxi, 89, 194–95

alien relation to human, 29, 46, 284, 288–29, 300, 302; companion, 29, 46, 284, 300, 302; monster, xiv, 27, 29, 45, 199, 241; originary form in human psyche, 101

alien society, xv, 6, 13, 48, 71, 148, 163, 169, 208, 263n11, 316

"Alien Sociology" (Manser), 165n4

Alien to Femininity: Speculative Fiction and Feminist Theory (Barr), 61–62, 73n8

alien types: BEM, xxx, 53, 2n7, 80, 216–21; LGM, 216, 228–37; natural, xx, xxi, xxv, 13, 23, 25, 29, 42, 73n11, 91, 218, 261n6, 291, 294, 315, 316; potentiated, xvi, 30, 215, 216, 237, 252, 254–59, 283, 300, 265n19; supernatural, xxvi, 3, 77, 101; unnatural, xx, xxi, xxii

Aliens and Alien Societies (Schmidt), 87, 210n1

"Aliens and Knowability: A Scientist's Perspective" (Benford), 50, 84, 110, 130

Aliens and Others (Wolmark), 66

"The All-Human Galaxy" (Asimov), 202, 203, 222

"Allies" (Landau), 262n8

alterity: and alien form, 78, 154, 170, 237; and alien psyche, 121, 154; and entelechy of human species, 307–8; and knowability, 117, 135; and OtherSelfness, xiv–xvii, 101, 117, 272–73; and potentiated alien, 215, 252, 254; and sapience, xxxi, 18, 117, 308; as archetype, 269, 271, 305, 302; as mythology, 314–15; as trope, 216, 267, 268; extreme otherness and, 125–36, 164; hypothesis of, xxxii, 269, 313; in stories, 110, 133–34, 254–55, 255–58, 258–59, 290, 300–301; insufficient, 116, 219, 224; potential for in alien 220

"Altruism, Evolution, and Society" (Easton), 92

"Ambassador to Verdammt" (Kapp), 117

Ambulance Ship (White), 175

"American SF and the Other" (Le Guin), 47, 177, 287, 312

About the Author

Patricia Monk (BA, Reading, United Kingdom; MA, Carleton University at Ottawa, Ontario; PhD, Queen's University at Kingston, Ontario) taught in the English department at Dalhousie University in Halifax , Nova Scotia, where she specialized in Canadian literature and science fiction, from 1975 to 2003 when she retired. She is the author of three books—*Mud and Magic Shows: Robertson Davies's* Fifth Business (1992), *The Gilded Beaver: An Introduction to the Life and Work of James De Mille* (1991), and *The Smaller Infinity: Jungian Self in the Novels of Robertson Davies* (1982)—and numerous articles on both science fiction and Canadian literature. She is very fond of cats and is also a fan of Manchester United football team.